Towards an Independent Kurdistan: Self-Determination in International Law

Kurdistan is among the world's most notorious cases of self-determination denied, and the reasons why this outcome remains unachieved reveal as much about the biases of international law as they do about the merits of the case for Kurdistan. On the centenary of the Treaty of Lausanne, 24 July 1923, the last of the international instruments establishing the new international order after World War I, this book explores the potential blind spots of international law regarding its differential application in the Middle East. Tracing self-determination over the past century, the work explores how the law applies to Kurdish aspirations and to what extent the Kurds can rely upon the current law of self-determination to achieve internationally recognised statehood.

The book offers an exhaustive historico-legal analysis of changing international legal concepts and geopolitical upheaval, providing a blueprint for Kurdish self-determination in international law. Shedding light on the law's structural biases, it represents a comprehensive historico-legal account of Kurdish aspirations for territorial independence within international law literature, offering a guide to relevant legal problems. It will be of interest to students and academics focused on international law, specifically, peoplehood, statehood, secession, human rights law, political science, and anthropology. Moreover, policymakers, government officials working in peace and conflict, research and advocacy institutes, think tanks, as well as scholars of international relations, historians, political scientists, regional specialists, diplomats, and non-governmental organisation activists will find it a useful reference. The book also illuminates the human rights status of the Kurds in their host states, making it relevant to scholars and activists. Its findings have implications extending beyond Kurdistan to self-determination struggles in Scotland, Catalonia, Ukraine, and elsewhere.

Loqman Radpey is an independent researcher, based in Scotland. He has dedicated the past decade to extensive research and writing on the legal status of the Kurdistan question and the application of international law to the right to self-determination of the Kurdish nation.

Routledge Research in International Law

Peacemaking, Religious Belief and the Rule of Law

Territorial Disputes and State Sovereignty
International Law and Politics
Jorge E. Núñez

Indigenous-Industry Agreements, Natural Resources and the Law
Edited by Ibironke T. Odumosu-Ayanu and Dwight Newman

Secession and Statehood
Lessons from Spain and Catalonia
Edited by Ana G Lopez and Jose Perea Unceta

The International Court of Justice and Municipal Courts: An Inter-Judicial Dialogue
Oktawian Kuc

Global Governance, Human Rights and International Law (2nd Edition)
Combating the Tragic Flaw
Errol P. Mendes

Small Island States and International Law
The Challenge of Rising Seas
Carolin König

Private International Law and Arbitral Jurisdiction
Faidon Varesis

Comparative and Transnational Dispute Resolution
Edited by Shahla Ali

Rural and Remote Communities as Non-State Actors
A Legal and Moral Argument
Ciprian Nicolae Radavoi and David Price

Public Interest Litigation in International Law
Justine Bendel and Yusra Suedi

Law Reforms around the World
An International Economic Law Perspective
Edited by Asif H. Qureshi

Towards an Independent Kurdistan
Self-Determination in International Law
Loqman Radpey

For more information about this series, please visit www.routledge.com/Routledge-Research-in-International-Law/book-series/INTNLLAW

Towards an Independent Kurdistan: Self-Determination in International Law

Loqman Radpey

With a Foreword from Professor Anne Peters

Routledge
Taylor & Francis Group
LONDON AND NEW YORK

First published 2024
by Routledge
4 Park Square, Milton Park, Abingdon, Oxon OX14 4RN

and by Routledge
605 Third Avenue, New York, NY 10158

Routledge is an imprint of the Taylor & Francis Group, an informa business

British Library Cataloguing-in-Publication Data
A catalogue record for this book is available from the British Library

ISBN: 978-1-032-54322-2 (hbk)
ISBN: 978-1-032-54324-6 (pbk)
ISBN: 978-1-003-42431-4 (ebk)

DOI: 10.4324/9781003424314

Typeset in Times New Roman
by Deanta Global Publishing Services, Chennai, India

Dedicated to

Those Kurds and non-Kurds who have advanced the cause of a sovereign Kurdistan

Contents

Maps

Foreword

The author of this fine study does not conceal his preferences: the bold title shows the direction of Loqman Radpey's thinking. His intimate knowledge of the matter is — of course — a situated knowledge, and it is good that he does not pretend otherwise. The book offers rich, detailed, and nuanced insights on the Kurdistan question in its historical, social, political, and, not least, legal dimensions. The Kurds are dispersed across four nation-states and endure varying degrees of discrimination and oppression in each state they reside. In these divergent circumstances, a common thread binds their experience: the struggle for self-determination.

Against this backdrop, the research question is whether and what the international principle of self-determination can offer to help the Kurds. Loqman unfolds the parameters of both the internal and external dimensions of self-determination, examining the conditions that may warrant a remedial secession. With analytical rigour, he applies these parameters to the predicament of the Kurds in each of the four states, scrutinising their complex situation. Loqman's approach is even 'conservative,' assuming that secession remains an internal matter and that international law will basically ratify whatever outcome of political or even military strife. He unveils, not surprisingly, that the entire law of self-determination is inherently beset by internal contradictions and that its application has been governed by inconsistencies and political opportunism.

It is all the more laudable that this book does not offer easy 'solutions.' Rather than presenting a blueprint, it ventures into the case of Kurdistan, problematising and elucidating the core issues. This is not 'schol-activism' but a well thought through and well-crafted study. It shows that rational legal analysis and emotional engagement are not mutually exclusive. And it is a reminder that we international legal scholars need to acknowledge the bounded rationality of our field, and that we accept how the historical accretion of legal layers has led to inconsistencies of the law, which is exacerbated by the politics of interpretation and application to the facts. That said, international legal scholarship might make a very modest contribution to human welfare by explaining and developing principles and procedures for reconciling antagonistic interests with a sense of fairness and in good faith. The study is a shining example of such an undertaking, of scholarship *engagé*. Its findings might resonate beyond Kurdistan and are of interest and relevance for other entities grappling with self-determination struggles — be they Scotland, Catalonia, Ukraine, or many others.

Anne Peters
Max Planck Institute
for Comparative Public Law and International Law
Heidelberg, Germany
June 2023

Abbreviations

AA	Asian Affairs
AANES	Autonomous Administration of North and East Syria
AAU	Abo Akademi University
ACFC	Advisory Committee of the Framework
ACFY	Arbitration Commission for the Former Yugoslavia
ACHPR	African Charter on Human and Peoples' Rights
AFMI	Austrian Federal Ministry of the Interior
AHR	American Historical Review
AIA	Advances in Anthropology
AJIL	American Journal of International Law
AKP	Adalet ve Kalkınma Partisi
ALR	Akron Law Review
AOHR	Age of Human Rights
ARPS	Annual Review of Political Science
Art.	Article
ASEN	Association for the Study of Ethnicity and Nationalism
AUP	Aberdeen University Press
BASLP	Bulletin of the Australian Society of Legal Philosophy
BJMES	British Journal of Middle Eastern Studies
BPS	Berghof Peace Support
BSOAS	Bulletin of the School of Oriental and African Studies
BYBIL	British Yearbook of International Law
CDK	Committee for Decolonization of Kurdistan
CEIP	Carnegie Endowment for International Peace
CERD	Committee on the Elimination of Racial Discrimination
CGP	Carroll and Graf Publishers
Ch	Chapter
CHP	Chelsea House Publishers
CIA	Central Intelligence Agency
CJIL	Connecticut Journal of International Law
CJTL	Columbia Journal of Transnational Law
COHRE	Centre of Housing Evictions and Human Rights

Corr.	Corrigendum
CSCE	Conference on Security and Co-operation in Europe
CSD	Conflict, Security & Development
CUP	Cambridge University Press
DFAT	Department of Foreign Affairs and Trade
DFR	Department of Foreign Relations
DJILP	Denver Journal of International Law and Policy
DLJ	Duke Law Journal
Doc	Document
DWI	Die Welt des Islams
EC	European Community
ECHR	European Convention on Human Rights
ECtHR	European Court of Human Rights
EEP	Edward Elgar Publishing
EGE	Eurasian Geography and Economics
EHRR	European Human Rights Reports
EJIL	European Journal of International Law
ENKS	Encûmena Niştimanî ya Kûrdî li Sûriyê (Kurdish National Council)
EPLF	Eritrean Peoples Liberation Front
EPRDF	Ethiopian People's Revolutionary Democratic Front
EU	European Union
EUI	European University Institute
EUP	Edinburgh University Press
FCPNM	Framework Convention for the Protection of National Minorities
FRY	Federal Republic of Yugoslavia
FSA	Free Syrian Army
GAOR	General Assembly Official Records
GJ	Geographical Journal
GYBIL	German Yearbook of International Law
HDP	People's Democratic Party, Partiya Demokratîk a Gelan (Halkların Demokratik Partisi)
HEDEP	Halkların Eşitlik ve Demokrasi Partisi (Peoples' Equality and Democratic Party)
HJIL	Heidelberg Journal of International Law
HLR	Harvard Law Review
HM	Helsinki Monitor
HMSO	His Majesty's Stationery Office
HO	Home Office
HOHR	Hengaw Organization for Human Rights
HP	Hart Publishing
HRW	Human Rights Watch
HRWWR	Human Rights Watch World Report

HSERC	Hokkaido Slavic-Eurasian Research Center
HUP	Harvard University Press
I&C	Iran and the Caucasus
ICCPR	International Covenant on Civil and Political Rights
ICESCR	International Covenant on Economic, Social, and Cultural Rights
ICFY	International Conference on the Former Yugoslavia
ICJ	International Court of Justice
ICJR	International Commission of Jurists Review
ILC	International Law Commission
ICLQ	International and Comparative Law Quarterly
IJCL	International Journal of Constitutional Law
IJKS	International Journal of Kurdish Studies
IJMES	International Journal of Middle East Studies
IJMGR	International Journal on Minority and Group Rights
IJSL	International Journal of the Sociology of Language
ILR	Israel Law Review
ILSA	International Law Students Association
IO	International Organization
IS	Iranian Studies
ISIS	Islamic State of Iraq and Syria
JCH	Journal of Contemporary History
JICJ	Journal of International Criminal Justice
JICL	Journal of International and Comparative Law
JJPS	Japanese Journal of Political Science
JK	Komala-i Jiyanawi Kurdistan (Society for the Revival of Kurdistan)
JOP	Journal of Politics
JRAS	Journal of the Royal African Society
JRASGBI	Journal of the Royal Asiatic Society of Great Britain and Ireland
JRCAS	Journal of The Royal Central Asian Society
KAA	Kurdish Autonomous Area
KAR	Kurdish Autonomous Region
KDP	Kurdistan Democratic Party
KFOR	NATO-led Kosovo Force
KHRP	Kurdish Human Rights Project
KLI	Kluwer Law International
KNC	Kurdish National Council
KPI	Kurdish Peace Institute
KRG	Kurdistan Regional Government
KRSO	Kurdistan Regional Statistics Office
KS	Kurdish Studies
KSSE	Kurdish Students Society in Europe
KT	Kurdish Times

LJIL	Leiden Journal of International Law
LNOJ	League of Nations Official Journal
LOA	Library of Alexandria
LRB	London Review of Books
LSE MEC	London School of Economics Middle East Centre
LUP	Leicester University Press
MEJ	Middle Eastern Journal
MES	Middle Eastern Studies
MNP	Martinus Nijhoff Publishers
MP	Mazda Publishers
MPEPIL	Max Planck Encyclopedia of Public International Law
MQUP	McGill-Queen's University Press
MRG	Minority Rights Group
MRGI	Minority Rights Group International
MRUP	Mellen Research University Press
MWP	Markus Wiener Publishers
NELR	New Europe Law Review
NJIL	Nordic Journal of International Law
NP	Nationalities Papers
OAU	Organization of African Unity
OCP	Oxford Clarendon Press
ODIHR	Office for Democratic Institutions and Human Rights
OHCHR	Office of the High Commissioner for Human Rights
OJLS	Oxford Journal of Legal Studies
OPC	Operation Provide Comfort
ORIL	Oregon Review of International Law
OSCE	Organization for Security and Co-operation in Europe
OUP	Oxford University Press
PACE	Parliamentary Assembly of the Council of Europe
PAK	Partî Azadî Kurdistan (Kurdistan Freedom Party)
PCA	Permanent Court of Arbitration
PCIJ	Permanent Court of International Justice
PDKI	Democratic Party of Iranian Kurdistan
PHC	Publishing House of the Czechoslovak
PKK	Partiya krêkaren Kurdistanê (Kurdistan Workers' Party)
PPT	Permanent Peoples' Tribunal
PS	Political Studies
PSLR	Penn State Law Review
PSP	Political Science and Politics
PUK	Patriotic Union of Kurdistan
PUP	Princeton University Press
PYD	Partiya Yekîtiya Dêmokrat (Democratic Union Party)
PYIL	Palestine Yearbook of International Law

RAF	Royal Air Force
RIAA	Reports of International Arbitral Awards
RIC	Rojava Information Center
RIS	Review of International Studies
RMES	Review of Middle East Studies
RTFG	Routledge Taylor & Francis Group
S&M	Sweet and Maxwell
S&S	Stevens and Sons
SAP	Sussex Academic Press
SAR	Hong Kong Special Administrative Region
SDF	Syrian Democratic Forces
SFRY	Socialist Federal Republic of Yugoslavia
SJIL	Stanford Journal of International Law
SJILC	Syracuse Journal of International Law and Commerce
SOAS	School of Oriental and African Studies
SOHR	Syrian Observatory for Human Rights
SUP	Syracuse University Press
TG	Thomson Gale
TLCP	Transnational Law and Contemporary Problems
TP	Transvaal Publishing
TPLF	Tigrean People's Liberation Front
TWQ	Third World Quarterly
UAP	University of Alabama Press
UAR	United Arab Republic of Egypt and Syria
UBA	University Book Agency
UNAMET	United Nations Mission in East Timor
UNCHE	United Nations Conference on the Human Environment
UNCIO	United Nations Conference on International Organization
UNESCO	United Nations Educational, Scientific and Cultural Organization
UNGA	United Nations General Assembly
UNHRC	United Nations Human Rights Committee
UNIO	United Nations Information Organisation
UNMIK	United Nations Mission in Kosovo
UNOVER	United Nations Observer Mission to Verify the Referendum in Eritrea
UNSC	United Nations Security Council
UNTS	United Nations Treaty Series
UNWP	United Nations Working Paper
UPA	University Press of America
UPOA	University Publications of America
UPP	University of Pennsylvania Press
USGAO	United States General Accounting Office
USSR	Union of Soviet Socialist Republics

UTP	University of Texas Press
UWP	University of Washington Press
VKW	Verlag fur Kultur und Wissenschaft
VOI	Voice of India
Vol	Volume
WKAP	Western Kurdistan Association Publications
YILC	Yearbook of the International Law Commission
YPG	Yekîneyên Parastina Gel (People's Protection Units)
YPJ	Yekîneyên Parastina Jin (Women's Protection Units)
YUP	Yale University Press
ZB	Zed Books

Acknowledgements

Sustained research on the present book began in 2012 when I began studying Kurdish self-determination. The course of writing elucidated some of the intricacies, but certain delicate aspects of self-determination remained. As time passed, complexities appeared. Then I recognised the need to do a more comprehensive study on the Kurds as a nation and their right to self-determination. I was inspired by the leadership, management, and fortitude of the Kurdish fighters of the *Yekîneyên Parastina Jin* (Women's Protection Units) and the *Yekîneyên Parastina Gel* (People's Protection Units) and their sacrifices in defeating terrorism, barbarism, and darkness across the Middle East. The trauma the Kurds have endured lies at the very core of their quest for self-determination and sovereignty for Kurdistan.

Over the past few years, I had the honour of being led by knowledgeable scholars. Throughout the journey, they assisted me in framing my scattered thoughts and advanced the whole book. I am able to properly recognise their contributions through scrupulous comments and taken-forward insights; however, I truly believe that words cannot express my eternal gratitude. The whole book owes its credit to them as I have immensely profited from their critiques. First and foremost, my deepest thanks to Dr Michelle Burgis-Kasthala and Dr Filippo Fontanelli. This book would not have come to fruition without their constant, unconditional guidance and enthusiastic support for my work over the years. With enthusiasm, diligence, and congeniality, they inspired me to be my own most brutally critical editor, and to ensure that I am not contradicting myself and am accurately conveying all legal and historical facts. I also owe a great deal of appreciation to Professor Nehal Bhuta, the Chair of Public International Law at University of Edinburgh and Co-Director of the Edinburgh Centre for International and Global Law, for a short but meaningful Skype meeting a day before the first national lockdown in Scotland in March 2020. That 30-minute meeting with such an intellect was sufficient to expedite the writing of the project. I owe my biggest intellectual debt — one I cannot repay — to them. Special thanks, with the fullest and gladdest heart imaginable, go to Professor Gregory Rose (University of Wollongong) who proposed the titles of chapters for an earlier version of the study. His contribution will always be remembered and appreciated.

Once I had the plan to do my PhD under the supervision of the late Professor James Crawford, but I ended up being examined by one of his leading students, the late and deeply lamented Professor Karen Knop of Toronto University. The premature loss of Karen Knop was a blow to the international law community. I was fortunate to have been examined by Karen. She was an accomplished legal thinker. I treasure her comments and her groundbreaking book, *Diversity and Self-Determination in International Law*. Her smile and kind voice will stay with me forever. May her spirit soar as high as the mountains of Kurdistan.

Along with Karen, I had Professor James Harrison of Edinburgh Law School whose meticulous doctrinal expertise and questions on theoretical aspects of self-determination made the discussion much clearer. His constructive inputs and suggestions on the book's structure improved the flow of the chapters. I appreciate James for his enlightening insights as a lifeline time and time again. Both, Karen and James, lent their support to the book proposal and the book in ways that went well beyond their original involvement as viva voce examiners of my dissertation.

I also benefited from a group of distinguished scholars versed in international law, philosophy, history, sociology, politics and international relations, and linguistics across the world. They freely imparted knowledge and profound wisdom despite their pressing academic commitments. I would like to express my most sincere appreciation to Professor Michael Gunter (Tennessee Technological University), Professor Marko Milanovic (University of Reading), Dr Kamran Matin (University of Sussex), Dr Miles Jackson (University of Oxford), Professor Erez Manela (Harvard University), Dr Philipp Kastner (The University of Western Australia), Professor Gerry Simpson (London School of Economics and Political Science), Dr Michael Hennessy Picard (The University of Edinburgh), Dr Allan Hassaniyan (University of Exeter), Professor Steve Zipperstein (University of California, Los Angeles), Professor Dr jur. Christian Walter (Ludwig-Maximilians Universität München), Professor Steve Neff (The University of Edinburgh), Professor Sarah Shields (University of North Carolina), and Professor Eyal Benvenisti (University of Cambridge) for their caveats, notes, and feedback on the table of contents and the structure of the manuscript. I am also deeply appreciative of Dr Jawad Mella (Western Kurdistan Association) for selflessly sharing his precious works on Kurdistan. To Professor Bill Bowring (Birkbeck College, University of London), I acknowledge a debt for his opinions on self-determination and for sharing his own works and to Laureate Professor Noam Chomsky (University of Arizona) for reviewing the central conclusion of the book despite his many other commitments.

I owe measure of my gratitude to Professor Frédéric Mégret (a William Dawson Scholar at Université McGill), Professor Yaël Ronen (Hebrew University), Professor Sabri Ateş (Southern Methodist University), Dr Rowan Nicholson (Flinders University), Professor Hamit Bozarslan (Directeur d'études de l'EHESS), Dr Cengiz Gunes (The Open University), Professor Michel Seymour (Université de Montréal), Professor (emeritus) Michael Eppel (University of Haifa), Dr Mehmet Gurses (Florida Atlantic University) Professor Matthew Craven (School of Oriental and African Studies, University of London), and Hemn Seyedi (PhD candidate, University of Exeter) who were unstintingly generous with their time and intellectual input, lending their perceptive advice on an earlier draft of the manuscript.

It is necessary to record and extend my gratitude to Dr James Summers (Lancaster University) and Professor Christian Tams (University of Glasgow) for their insightful comments and corrections on my articles during my PhD studies. I also owe a number of thanks in relation to some invaluable ideas on the Kurdish language to Dr Aran Emînî (Université d'Avignon). I would like to express my sincere gratitude to Professor Anne Peters (Director at the Max Planck Institute for Comparative Public Law and International Law) for the honour and privilege of having her contribute the foreword to the book.

My three-years journey at Edinburgh Law School was made possible by a scholarly fund that supported my doctoral studies. Special appreciation is extended to Professor Martin Hogg, who served as the Dean of the School during my PhD tenure. My studies received further support from a library fund awarded by the University of Edinburgh's College of Arts, Humanities and Social Sciences to purchase *Records of the Kurds: Territory, Revolt and Nationalism, 1831-1979* for my work (comprising facsimile documents on the history of Kurdistan's movements for self-determination). This 13-volume set is now available for researchers at the main library for Arts, Humanities and Social Sciences researchers, especially those specialising in law, politics, and anthropology. I would like to thank the librarians at the Edinburgh University Library, Donna Watson, SarahLouise McDonald (LAW Librarians) and Christine Love-Rodgers, College Lead for Library Academic Support (CAHSS) and Academic Support Librarian as well as the Acquisition Team who processed the purchase and arranged for the set to be available.

Arriving at the point where I stand now was challenging and sometimes tense and intense. Everyone may need a hand sometimes from strangers. This necessitates a mention of my gratitude to those individuals. There have been few occasions in life when someone can produce a quick and totally pleasing moment. Back in 2015, I submitted my second article to such a helper, Michael Gelb, one of the editors of *Holocaust and Genocide Studies*, the scholarly journal of the United States Holocaust Memorial Museum (published by Oxford University Press). Michael played a decisive role in building up a network of friends across the Atlantic over the coronavirus era. Dr Steven F. Sage and the late Dr Jack Frederick Piotrow functioned as surrogate supervisors, copyeditors, and advisors. I am deeply conscious of the debt that I owe them.

Achieving success requires the essential ingredients of unconditional love, inexhaustible tolerance, and steadfast support from family or encouraging friends. I certainly do not stand as an exception to this principle. My appreciation for their unwavering dedication is immeasurable. A profound debt of gratitude is owed, especially to my mother, father, sister, and older brothers, who have played roles extending far beyond that of a typical family.

This book took its final form thanks to the tireless efforts of the Routledge senior editor for law, Alison Kirk, and law editor, Siobhán Poole. I would like to express my gratitude to Sanjeevi Nagarajan who kindly read the whole manuscript to ferret out spelling, grammatical, and other needed changes along the way.

Loqman Radpey
Edinburgh, Scotland
Spring 2023

Two Times Two

I remember being asked at school, 'what does 2 times 2 equal'?
all together wrote four

I got low scores in math and sank in ranks
because two times two equalled one and not four, that was my stance

To me, a human's two hands and two feet would not become four
but rather become useful as one body that they laboured for

To me, a neighbourhood, a house, an alley, a street would not become four
but rather become one city in which there live the rich and the poor

To me, the stem, the root, the branch, the leaf would not become four
but rather become a tree, some short and some tall as the plane tree's core.

To me, love and the heart, beauty and purity would not become four
but rather become a treasure to the loving one that adores

all those examples of two and two equalling one, not four are umpteen
but are those that manifest really seen?

I know only as much if they cut me into a hundred pieces,
shower me in shots, force me to the gallows,
still I will speak from my heart: my

Kurdistan will remain one land

and never become four.

(Nadir Qazî)

Kurdish

Dû Dane Dû

tê bîra min di dibistanê de dihat pirsîn ‘2 + 2 dibe bi çend’?
hemûyan bi hev re dinivîsandin dike çar

tenê min di hesabê de nimreyê kêm dianî û di hatim xwar
ew jî tenê ji berku li ba min wiha bû 2+2 dibe bi yek nabe bi çar

li ba min wiha bû diran û du lêv û ziman nabin bi çar
dibin bi zar bi hev re dikin hawar

li ba min wiha bû du dest û du lingê mirov nabin bi çar
di leşek de wiha têne bikar

li ba min wiha bû tax, xanî, kolan, cade nabin bi çar
dibin bi bajar têde dijîn dewlemend û xelkê hejar

li ba min wiha bû kok, reh, lik, pel nabin bi çar
dibin bi dar hinek kurt û hinek dirêj wekî çinar

li ba min wiha bû evîn û dil, delalî û pakî nabin bi çar
di bin bi yar li ba dildar

ew hemû ye wiha 2+2 dibin bi yek nabin bi çar
yekcar gelekin lê belê li ku têne jimar?

tenê wê dizanim eger laşê min sed parçe bikin
min bidin ber gulle û regbar ez biçim ser dar
gotinê dilê min tên ser zar:

kurdistan her yek welat e

û nabe bi çar.

1 Introduction

As the American novelist William Faulkner observed:

> The past is never dead. It's not even past. All of us labor in webs spun long before we were born, webs of heredity and environment, of desire and consequence, of history and eternity. Haunted by wrong turns and roads not taken.

Wrong turns and roads not taken, indeed. The current geopolitics of the Middle East are still shaped by treaties and agreements signed a century or more ago. These included the Sykes-Picot-Sazonov agreement (16 May 1916), the Treaty of Sèvres (10 August 1920), the Treaty of Lausanne (24 July 1923), and the League of Nations Mandate System. After the First World War and the collapse of the Ottoman Empire, the principle of self-determination facilitated some national peoples with a shared ethnicity, language, culture, and religion to emerge as nation-states. Some, but not all. Borders were largely drawn by states, and this stability facilitated the rapid enrichment of private oil corporations in the region. These borders also excluded the Kurdish people who remained as minorities within the states of Iraq, Iran, Syria, Turkey, and the Soviet Union.

In recent decades, globalisation has depreciated the importance of national and geographical boundaries. Globalisation has eased interaction, trade, and development among nations, and consequently, states have opened their borders and adopted freer markets. However, conflicts in the Middle East have, instead, sharpened due to the great powers' conflicting interests and the area's rich resources of oil, gas, water, and energy. Middle Eastern frontiers have stubbornly regained importance in the wake of national upheavals and the war against the Islamic State of Iraq and Syria (ISIS). In the global village, and especially in this region, the importance of the idea of the state has not withered away.

That past is not dead, not even past. Over the past century, and having been denied their rights by successive governments, the Kurds, at times, mobilised to rebel against the status quo and fashioned an independent territorial state. Their struggle continues. After establishing autonomy in the 1990s, the Kurds in the South of Kurdistan (in Iraq) held a planned independence referendum in September 2017. However, the move was encountered with jointly punitive economic and military measures by the states, retaking the disputed oil-rich Kurdish areas. In 2012, the Kurds in the West of Kurdistan (Rojava in Syria) declared an interim

DOI: 10.4324/9781003424314-1

region of self-rule amidst the unresolved civil war. They are now asserting a *de facto* autonomy, along the same lines of the government of Kurdistan in the South. While being prone to Turkey's intermittent incursion since 2018, the Rojava self-rule has not been recognised by either Damascus or the international community.

In the twenty-first century, *de facto* and even *de jure* international borders have been redrawn, or the borders remained, but their status changed, as has happened in Europe and Africa. The reconfiguration of borders — to achieve a congruence of the borders of states and the boundaries of nations — has played a critical role in the world order and its occasional destabilisation. Self-determination has redefined and restructured international relations, but contentious issues of sovereignty and territoriality affect the debate on self-determination, especially in the Middle East. Self-determination is, thus, one of the most controversial legal rights of the twenty-first century, which is accorded theoretical significance yet haunted by ambiguity and intransigent opposition from existing states. Self-determination has been the driver in the creation of new independent sovereign states, the number of which has tripled since 1945. But unfinished business still remains. The creation of a sovereign Kurdistan remains unfinished, a work in progress and a test for the principle of self-determination.

Self-determination — the mainstream catalyst for a people's journey toward statehood — is traced over the past century. This book demonstrates how it applies to the national aspiration of the Kurdish people and to what extent the Kurds as a whole can rely upon the current law of self-determination to achieve internationally recognised statehood. The legal aspects of their failure to achieve sovereign statehood in the aftermath of World Wars I and II are of importance not only within Middle Eastern geopolitics but globally as well as a case in international law. Thus, the marginalised idea of Kurdistan as a state is both timely and significant.

A dynamic process is underway in the geopolitically critical region of the Middle East. Its map is still contested by regional players and by outsiders (Map 1.1). Meanwhile, the Middle Eastern states of Iran, Iraq, Syria, and Turkey each face internal challenges that could result in further breakup. After eight years of fighting against ISIS and recapturing some disputed areas in Iraq and Syria, the Kurds, who represent the majority populations in their respective regional territories, are preparing themselves for a post-ISIS Middle East. Therefore, Kurdish self-determination and analyses of the legal status of Kurds in international law are again on the radar. In this context, the right to self-determination is the relevant point of international law for allowing the Kurds to plot their own common political status despite their dispersal across four sovereign states.

Kurdistan is among the world's most notorious cases of denied self-determination. On the centenary of the signing of the Treaty of Lausanne in 1923 which officially carved up Kurdistan, the Kurds have entered a new era due to chaotic developments in their host states. They have demanded self-determination by claiming their own national boundaries and by challenging the identities, sovereignty, and boundaries of the host states. Although there has never been a recognised sovereign territorial definition of a Kurdistan comprising all regions with a Kurdish demographic presence, the enduring resilience of Kurdistan as a political,

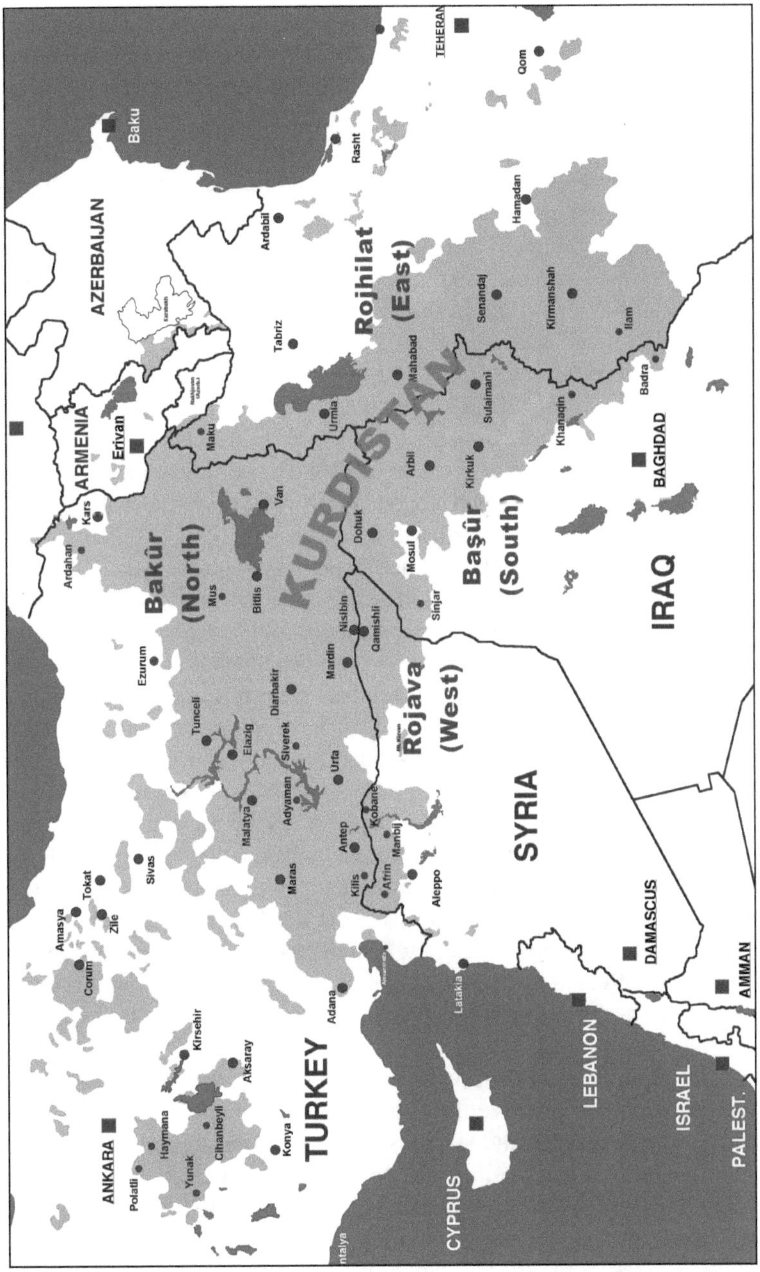

Map 1.1. Kurdistani segments

geographic, and cultural concept has, nonetheless, survived. The crux of Kurdish failure resides in the failure of the international principle of self-determination itself. Self-determination — especially in its external form as secession and the creation of a new state — is arguably the most controversial right of the twenty-first century within international law, plagued by ambiguity even as its tremendous significance is universally recognised. Undaunted by adversity, the Kurds have never abandoned their quest.

Although the case of Kurdistan, like that of many non-state entities around the globe, is geopolitically of current concern, it, nevertheless, remains underrepresented in the discipline of international law. The investigation of the Kurds' international legal potential for a viable Greater Kurdistan, as a distinct national entity transcending existing borders, and the treatment of Kurdish aspirations to statehood within the international law literature on self-determination, over time, builds upon previous scholarship on self-determination and primary sources. Salient problems concern the non-colonial context of the Kurds and their eligibility for self-determination, entitlement to the seal of statehood, qualifications to claim a sovereign independent Kurdistan, and the treatment of the Kurds by their host states. The scope transcends previous approaches limited to the Kurdish population in just one or another of the states among which they are partitioned. It also sets aside the political agendas of defunct and existing Kurdish parties and factions. They have taken various stands and have adopted different tacks for mobilising Kurdish nationalism in their respective states. Kurdistan is considered holistically here as a nation in embryo. The unresolved Kurdistan question and the resistance through a century of oppression are taken as the grounds for the Kurds' quest for independence.

Establishing Kurdistan as an independent state has been a long-held Kurdish aspiration. Throughout the centuries, Kurds have alternately cooperated with and rebelled against empires and central authorities to win control of their land through some degree of self-rule and, at various times, have proactively attempted to set up an independent territorial Kurdish state. But why have they not been able to form their own enduring, internationally recognised nation-state? Kurds have been fighting for independence but have systematically failed. How has international law been applied to their struggle over the decades? Can the Kurds meet the existing criteria for application of the law? How has the international legal status of the Kurds been affected by the evolution of the international legal framework for self-determination from the end of World War I (WWI) through the mid-twentieth century up to today?

The right to self-determination as a multifaceted driving force could be either a radical, progressive, positive thrust or a subversive and threatening concept. Its exercise has led to clashes and tensions between Kurds and ruling governors since 1920. Most secessionist movements in the world have, indeed, been settled by force rather than the rule of law, as violence has often been the engine of self-determination. The alternative is a just and fair application of the principle itself, however long overdue. Present realities as well as the past legal possibility are contemplated for creating Kurdistan as a state of all four existing Kurdish segments. As such, the Kurds, as a totality, are positioned within the contemporary international normative framework of self-determination by addressing to what extent they can leverage the current law of self-determination in their pursuit of statehood.

The problem of using self-determination as an argument requires expansive consideration of the hurdles and problematic flaws in exercising it. From the way self-determination works in practice, it is hard to justify its application, and clear-cut cases have actually been quite rare. A 'people' can enjoy self-determination and have a special definition which differentiates it from a minority. The question then arises as to whether the Kurds qualify as a 'people' under international law. A 'people' is the only unit entitled to self-determination, yet this term has never been defined comprehensively in international law.

The greatest hurdle facing the Kurds is the territoriality of their host states among which they are divided. Any Kurdish entity must be substantially independent and attain a qualified right to statehood consonant with the principle of self-determination. That would be secession, which is a distinct possibility for state creation. When, how, and to what extent can self-determination justify a qualified right to the territorial separation of the Kurds of their host states to establish a new state? Are the Kurds at liberty to secede territorially and to secure legitimate secessions?

By virtue of the law of self-determination, *peoples* freely determine their political status and pursue their economic, social, and cultural development. By plotting political status, people frame their international political status which could be either association with or integration into another state or creation of their own separate state. The reason for the focus on external self-determination is that the Kurds, like other nations longing for their own state, have striven for the formation of a unified Greater Kurdistan comprising all four segments, notwithstanding the current borders drawn among them. Additionally, the Kurdish history of suffering, marginalisation, and discrimination is the very impetus for asserting a claim to external self-determination, empowering the Kurds to be the 'subjects' of their own history, no longer relegated to the status of mere 'objects' at the mercy of others. The Kurds have no recognised right of self-determination but may, nonetheless, qualify as a state according to the criteria for statehood. But under what conditions or qualifications can they then attain their objective of statehood? Would Greater Kurdistan be viable as a territorially independent state?

There are diverse views on self-determination, leading to a number of different interpretations structured by historical issues, e.g., the breakup of empires, decolonisation, and the dissolution of sovereign states. The pre- and post-Cold War period had a critical role to play in shaping self-determination. However, international judgements have not provided an open-and-shut view of self-determination. The interpretation of self-determination has impacted squarely on states and non-state ethnic groups, especially the latter that have been marginalised or excluded from the making of laws.[1] But the various interpretations have rendered the state of the

1 Nathaniel Berman, 'But the Alternative is Despair: European Nationalism and the Modernist Renewal of International Law' (1993) 106(8) HLR 1792.

law unsettled in a post-colonial context which pertains to self-determination as a legal term with a wide 'penumbra of uncertainty.'[2]

Self-determination is described as a broad and all-inclusive principle, but one that has been operationalised into specific rules in a sporadic and fragmented manner, depending on the context and in light of other principles. Indeed, '[t]he notion of a right presupposes identification of the subject of the right.'[3] From a conventional approach toward self-determination, trust and mandated territories and territories treated as non-self-governing under Chapter XI of the UN Charter are the definite subjects of the right of self-determination. The principle applies to cases out of these categories:

> territories forming distinct political-geographical areas, whose inhabitants do not share in the government either of the region or of the State to which the region belongs, with the result that the territory becomes in effect, with respect to the remainder of the State, non-self-governing.[4]

This category is termed *carence de souveraineté*.[5] In this category, the systematic denial of political rights to a distinct collectivity is interpreted as a condition for self-determination through secession. In other words, beyond the peoples of trust and mandated territories and non-self-governing territories, representing a 'controversial' perspective on self-determination,[6] 'interpretation involves a politico-legal choice, and the category of *carence de souveraineté* is offered simply as one possible politico-legal choice.'[7]

The revolutionary force of self-determination has helped non-state groups to formulate their own interpretation of self-determination and to confront hegemony while presenting an alternative. Self-determination is viewed herein as corrective justice to determine future political status through the free and genuine expression of the will of the people of a territory. This broadens the scope of self-determination beyond colonies to other peoples in subordinate positions. Self-determination is, thus, used to restore a people's will or to remove the imposition of an alien will upon a people.[8]

Despite the recurring emphasis on the principle of *uti possidetis*, the intangibility of territorial integrity of states has not remained an absolute bulwark because minority-peoples and ethnic groups have been able to establish self-determination as an alternative qualified right to secession under certain circumstances through a non-unitary formulation. The situation within this approach ought to be a serious

2 Deborah Cass, 'Re-Thinking Self-Determination: A Critical Analysis of Current International Law Theories' (1992) 18(1) SJILC 21.
3 James Crawford, *The Creation of States in International Law* (2nd ed, OUP 2006) 115.
4 ibid 127
5 ibid 126.
6 See Cass (n 2).
7 Karen Knop, *Diversity and Self-Determination in International Law* (CUP 2002) 37–38.
8 ibid 72.

legal matter to be settled by the international community of states, i.e., secession is remedially invoked in cases in which certain human rights abuses have occurred (a rights-based interpretation). However, there is no universally applicable standard of the seriousness of violation of rights as the precondition for a legitimate right to secede.

Nevertheless, under no judicial unit or convention has secessionist self-determination been recognised as a right, although the doctrine has tentatively justified its existence in a few cases. International law has authorised secession in three cases. First, within some terms, the UN has a record of integrating a territory into a state. Thus, the case of Eritrean separation became a legal option because the full requirements for separation were fulfilled. Second, separation may be authorised if it involves the separation of an unlawfully annexed state from an annexing state. It is the re-establishment of a legal situation, and the territorial integrity of the annexing state has no venue here. Examples are the cases of Latvia, Lithuania, and Estonia regaining sovereignty from the Soviet Union. The final instance of authorised separation comes about when a state violates a domestic provision with respect to recognising a right to external self-determination or secession for a people. International law considers the separation of a victimised people to be legal.

When it comes to the Kurds, the issue of self-determination is further complicated by the territorial sovereignty of four host states. According to the Human Rights Covenants, peoples are entitled to exercise the internal aspect of self-determination within the borders of their respective states. The recognition of ethnic differences is the first step in securing internal self-determination or the effective participation of minorities in the public affairs of states. Detailed analysis reveals that a democratic political framework is lacking for the Kurds who inhabit the host states. Also, the states have seriously and persistently violated the prohibition of discrimination and the use of force, but this does not in itself justify unilateral secession.

Although the Kurds may work as public civil servants in the organs of their host states, their participation is not effective. Also, elections (non-territorial arrangements) are held periodically for territorial local public bodies, such as municipal, provincial, local councils or other local public bodies, in which already selected Kurds can stand as candidates and be elected. Although establishing electoral arrangements for any representation is an indication of recognition of an ethnic group, these are not, per se, sufficient and do not guarantee effective participation. These mechanisms do not mean control over their own affairs, as Kurds do not have the ultimate influence on the outcome of decision-making on issues of importance to them. The Kurds are devoid of representation in most governments and governing bodies. They are divested of the right to participate effectively in public affairs and the decision-making process on matters that affect them directly. A perusal of the host states' constitutions reveals that Kurds are not recognised and no special representation mechanisms are provided for Kurds. The 2005 Iraqi constitution provides the Kurds in the South of Kurdistan with their only constitutional recognition, empowering them through self-governance provisions. Other repressive, unitary, and nationalist states follow a non-recognition model. There are no Kurdish parties mainly oriented toward Kurdish concerns in these states, as they are prohibited. Kurds have been able to participate in general elections only through assimilating to the majority. They are then elected on lists of mainstream parties. Although representatives are elected in the scheduled parliamentary elections, representation and access to public office are not based on the principle of proportional ethnic representation. That is, parliamentary seats and public affairs posts are not guaranteed or allocated to the Kurds in proportion to the size of their population. Therefore, they do not have an effective role in the decision-making process. In other words, the states of Iran, Syria, and Turkey have not accommodated the participation of Kurds as minorities.

Although there is evidence of formal discrimination threatening the identity of the Kurds in Iran, Syria, and Turkey, and a degree of discrimination against them in Iraq, the level of oppression or violation criteria is less than the standard that might be recommended based on the cases of Bangladesh, Kosovo, and South Sudan. According to UN reports, evidence of discrimination, for instance, was created by the lack of Kurds' holding any positions in the government. They have become second-class citizens in their host states through the installation of internal colonisation structures. Despite all this, the Kurds do not hold a *fortiori* case or the absolute secession right under the present circumstances. In other words, the Kurdish situation does not yet call for the *ultimum remedium* of secession, although there is still political exclusion, lack of access to the state or meaningful representation of the Kurds in states' governing bodies, and degrees of active discrimination and assimilationist laws aimed against Kurdish identity and language and culture by the states. Despite their legitimate grievances, the Kurds have reached an impasse due to the non-democratic systems of their host states under which their right to self-determination has been uniformly denied.

Speaking of statehood, external self-determination is the focal point. As concerns practice, international law fails to account for the disparity of statehood-related fulfilment. Recent evidence on practice demonstrates that the fulfilment of the conditions of statehood cannot be adequate to render a territorial entity a state. A new state must overcome the conflicting challenge of the territorial status quo of existing sovereign states. Where this process is internationalised, the challenge can be overcome, and state formation consequently is achievable. Therefore, not meeting both checklists of classic and modern criteria cannot debar the emergence of new states. Also meeting the checklists does not result in a factual occurrence.

Since the UN was established, the law of self-determination has become increasingly restrictive, limiting its application to the Kurds. Despite this, there have been instances in which significant changes in the territorial boundaries of the states hosting them have taken place following periods of political turmoil. The Kurds have gained some form of control over their territory by the exercise of power stemming from *de facto* federal and democratic federalism. Through the Kurdish territories in the South and West of Kurdistan, effective sovereignty and administrative control of the states over the Kurdish territories of the Kurdistan Regional Government and Rojava have been suspended. Self-rule has brought legal order to both segments of Kurdistan. Both entities have a demonstrated capacity to enter into relations with other states. However, looking at the facts, they do not meet all traditional legal requirements of statehood in international law, although the Kurdish entities have achieved some degree of international personality (recognition). Nonetheless, they have not achieved statehood, as they need their host states to give up sovereignty over parts of their territory in order to achieve lawful and definite state creation.

While the Kurds have established self-ruled *de facto* entities in the South and West of Kurdistan, the Eastern and Northern segments have not achieved any form of control. Therefore, achieving outright Kurdish sovereign statehood in the name of a Greater Kurdistan comprising all four Kurdish segments is neither imminent nor warranted, although the idea of a greater Kurdistan has been sustained. Their separate chances to achieve statehood are more likely. The most significant challenge lies in altering the territorial status quo and compromising the territorial sovereignty of the host states by lifting or suspending it. Its settlement with the states accelerates the full integration of a new state into the international community, but the failure to settle it does not bar any entity from being qualified as a state or acquiring statehood. In other words, recognition or admission to the UN does not create a state for all purposes, but non-recognition may isolate the state from the world and thwart it from full engagement in foreign relations and from exercising the attributes of legal statehood.

The established facts on the ground can be invoked in favour of accepting their independence. In any scenario, it is crucial for any Kurdish entity to secure a justified right to statehood in alignment with the principle of self-determination, as it can tip the balance in favour of statehood. Although self-determination is a criterion for statehood, its prior possession is not necessary to achieve statehood. In this context, the right to self-determination can serve to create the conditions for recognised Kurdish statehood. Any Kurdish entity should still be legally constructed factually, find some special legal entitlement on the part of the new entities to be independent states, and attain indisputable effectiveness.

Politics or geopolitical and strategic interests play roles in the context of self-determination claims as international law itself cannot determine the outcomes of statehood assertions. Any Kurdish state might be subject to the international political calculus in the application of the measures of recognition. In the politically charged context of the Middle East, the Kurds may rely on external actors to enhance their power for state formation and subsequent recognition. At the practical level, the support of regional state actors and the great powers is critical for the success of an independence movement. Its importance cannot be denied in political and pragmatic terms, but the extralegal or political nature of recognition is not addressed here.

The movement for Kurdish self-determination evolved over three distinct periods: 1) WWI and its aftermath, where self-determination was considered 'a political concept'; 2) the aftermath of World War II (WWII) and the creation of the United Nations which led to a conceptual shift in thought from national self-determination to peoples' self-determination, as well as the movement to end colonisation when self-determination mutated from a decolonisation principle to a post-colonial right;

and 3) modern international law. The study explores how these historical periods influenced the Kurds' quest for self-determination, shedding light on the obstacles they have encountered while navigating the intricate landscape of the international legal framework.

The overall structure is intended first to set out the theoretical basis of the topic, i.e., the literature on the law of self-determination to statehood and second, to apply the extant law on the case of Kurdistan. Chapters 2–3 discuss the current debate in international law literature over the right of self-determination and the definition of peoples in international law; Chapters 4–5 apply the law to the Kurds, examining those cases relied on by most scholars in their interpretation of self-determination and compare them with Kurdish self-determination; and Chapters 6–8 look at the practice of self-determination and the case of Kurdistan within international law. Chapter 4, in particular, and parts of Chapter 5 are focused on historical analysis of how self-determination arguments were treated at key diplomatic moments, with no clear rules ultimately emerging, whereas other chapters, particularly Chapters 7 and 8, are concerned with how international law may currently be applied to implement the principle of self-determination for the Kurds.

Chapter 2 delves into the contexts in which self-determination was established in the system of international law. It discusses how the self-determination doctrine had evolved as well as the application of the current law on self-determination, with different standpoints. The chapter probes how and in what situations self-determination is actually realised together with its consequences. Constraints on that actualisation are also analysed. Additionally, this chapter draws the distinction between internal and external self-determination. The chapter is restricted to *legal* expressions of self-determination; the *political* interpretations of self-determination lie outside the scope. This chapter grounds the central argument about the application of self-determination in different cases.

In studies pertinent to self-determination, the terms 'nation,' 'minority,' 'indigenous people,' and 'people' are seminal concepts. In Chapter 3, these communities are defined and compared to 'people,' as the only bearers of the right of self-determination. The focus of this chapter is on who bears the right to self-determination and what characteristics the right-bearer possesses. It is then followed by defining and characterising *peoples* and the identification of peoples eligible for self-determination to alter a territory's external status. To attain a working definition of a people, various references are investigated for a legal definition of a people. Chapter 3 will concentrate on substantive definitional signifiers (subjective and objective) and the legal principles of territorial integrity, state sovereignty, and *uti possidetis* that characterise and identify communities as peoples. The chapter also investigates whether there are different categories of people who hold the right.

Chapter 4 shows how and to what extent self-determination was applied to the Kurds and how it functions regarding them. It frames Kurdish self-determination through a sustained appraisal of the right, from how the Kurds were treated at the end of WWI through the mid-twentieth century up to today. This chapter discusses how Kurdistan was partitioned. The historico-legal background of Kurds and Kurdistan then provides insight into the Kurds' political and legal status from the twentieth century to the present with regard to self-determination.

In Chapter 5, the Kurds are considered in terms of the substantive or national ties and formal or legal criteria of peoplehood as highlighted in Chapter 3. Chapter 5 focuses on whether the Kurds constitute a people for the purpose of the external aspect of self-determination (independence and state creation), providing background on their historical pedigree. After an analysis of demographic data in the first section, the chapter investigates the emergence of the distinct Kurdish ethno-political identity of the Kurds. Turning to the section on legal texts, documents specifying Kurds for the right of self-determination are examined.

Chapter 6 focuses on internal self-determination in the form of effective participation in public affairs. The first short section clarifies the concepts and the elements of effective participation in public affairs. In the second part of this section, Chapter 6 also elaborates upon the relationship between the effective participation of minorities in public affairs and the internal right to self-determination. This chapter scrutinises political rights in the context of human rights instruments to determine the extent to which these rights guarantee the effective participation of minorities in public affairs. Inasmuch as political rights are not sufficient to ensure minorities an effective role in matters affecting them, the third section of Chapter 6 investigates the content, implementation, and proposed mechanisms of provisions on internal self-determination and effective participation in public affairs in the universal and regional minority rights instruments. The last section of Chapter 6 looks at the mechanisms which could guarantee and implement the right of minorities to internal self-determination or to participate effectively in public affairs and decision-making processes. It gives an overview of some forms or aspects of internal political self-determination with varying degrees and levels. The chapter does not pursue the cultural, social, and economic aspects of internal self-determination, although these facets form part of formulations of internal self-determination; however, they are not legally necessary for a people to realise independent statehood. In this chapter, the focus is on autonomy, federalism, and self-government, examples of which are cited. Their grassroots features and their relevance to and possible implementation of the right to effective participation in public affairs are considered. Due to the regionally dense aggregation of Kurds, Chapter 6 aims only at examining territorial mechanisms of internal self-determination.

Chapter 7 examines the question of secession, that is, whether and under what conditions peoples are at liberty to detach territorially and whether (and under what conditions) international law forbids it. It probes when, how, and to what extent self-determination can justify the separation of component parts of sovereign states to establish new states. To this end, the first section deals with the existing approaches in modern jurisprudential discourse which justify secession based on peoplehood or group purity. Also, by dealing with the existing approaches in modern discourse which justify secession based on peoplehood, the UN Charter, doctrine, judicial decisions, state practice with respect to accomplished and unsuccessful cases, and other legal instruments are considered concerning the cases of secession to clarify the normative position and threshold of secession. Chapter 7 does not address colonial secession, as the Kurds do not fit into the decolonisation framework due to their split condition among decolonised states. The final section concerns the contextual analysis of the Kurds and their eligibility to and entitlement for securing a legitimate secession. The chapter will comprehensively present a contextual analysis of secession concerning Kurdish self-governing territories in Iraq and Syria and the non-self-governing Kurds in Iran and Turkey. It will explore the normative process that should be followed to enable them to establish new boundaries. The chapter will also address whether they are entitled to pursue a legitimate secession from the state in which they find themselves. The final section puts forward a remedial secession argument taking into account different and appropriate considerations bearing directly on the issue of secession.

Following the discussion of a legal definition of the term 'state' in modern international law, Chapter 8 proceeds with discussion and analysis of the requisite criteria for statehood after deliberating the theories of recognition, followed by a demonstration of the intertwining relationships among self-determination, statehood, and recognition. For this purpose, basic or customary characteristics are analysed. Moreover, this chapter also succinctly deals with newly recognised legal attributes of statehood derived from recent state and UN practice. This chapter explores whether the conditions of statehood are in place to assess how a hypothetical external self-determination transition would play out. The following section discusses and illustrates in detail various ways of creating a modern state, of which decolonisation, dissolution of an existing state, union, and re-establishment of an occupied state are examined. The law of statehood is applied to these forms of creating statehood to gauge to what extent statehood criteria (effectiveness and recognition) are qualified in practice. From a legal viewpoint, the final part of Chapter 8 investigates whether the Kurds are entitled to statehood. It scrutinises whether it is possible for a Kurdish state to emerge under the international law of statehood. To this end, the legal framework of statehood is applied to separate Kurdish entities as the status and facts of each territory are analysed.

Having scrutinised, analysed, and studied the documents, facts, charters, conventions, treaties, legal instruments and the practices of states and international organisations, Chapter 9 briefly summarises the key findings and theoretically grounded arguments around the issues of the Kurds and Kurdistan. It concludes by calling for greater critical reflection on the limits of self-determination, with a reflection on avenues for further inquiry.

2 Self-Determination in International Law

Self-determination, whether contemplated as an idea, a theory, a phenomenon, a coveted reward, a guiding canon, an aspirational ideal, a foundational doctrine, a maxim, a constructive axiom, an ordering or operative principle, or a recognised legal right, has proven to be a multifaceted force in reshaping the territorial landscapes of the world. Its influence has been twofold, functioning as both the wellspring from which new nations have emerged and the catalyst fuelling political movements and struggles aimed at securing the rights of various peoples. It is a concept that has inspired countless movements for liberation, human rights, and social justice, transcending borders and ideologies to unite individuals and communities in the pursuit of a more equitable world order.

The concept of self-determination has a rich and dynamic history, marked by its ability to adapt and respond to the evolving demands of a changing world. It has not only shaped the birth of new nations but has also played a pivotal role in redefining the relationships between states and their constituent collectivities. This intricate evolution has been driven by a complex interplay of historical events, international charters, legal doctrines, and the relentless pursuit of justice and equality by marginalized communities.

To comprehend the full scope and significance of self-determination, one must delve into its historical precedents and the myriad ways in which it has been interpreted and applied across diverse cultural, political, and geographical contexts. In essence, self-determination is not merely a static legal principle but a living, breathing idea that continues to evolve in response to the ever-changing dynamics of our global society. To grasp its true essence and potential, it is imperative to appreciate the rich tapestry of historical struggles, legal advancements, and socio-political developments that have contributed to its enduring legacy.

2.1 Historical Metamorphosis

Classical writers claimed that self-determination is the continuation of the principle of *jus resistendi ac secessionis* of Grotius by means of which people unburdened

DOI: 10.4324/9781003424314-2

themselves from the coloniser's yoke and became independent.[1] A variant of self-determination (but not identified as such) was present at the time of the colonisation of the Americas by Europeans (during the fifteenth to eighteenth centuries) in reference to the eligibility of the indigenous peoples of America to the right of sovereignty and autonomy, self-government, liberty, and the right to property under natural law. In the Peace of Westphalia (1648), only 'civilized nations' were imbued with sovereignty, while '*peuples sauvages*' were excluded, since they did not possess a legal persona and were, therefore, not entitled to inviolate sovereignty but, instead, were subject to conquest by civilised nations.[2]

The political origin of a presumed right of self-determination[3] goes back to the American Declaration of Independence (1776), as the conditional right to resistance, the French Revolution (1789), as the right to popular sovereignty,[4] and the Hispanic American decolonisation (or one might say the first decolonisation from 1809 to 1825) as the absolute right to independence (counted as freedom).[5] Substantially, these rights amounted to the same issue.[6]

2.1.1 An Ever-Evolving Standard Prior to the League of Nations

During these eras, rebellions nullified the 'interest of the monarch,' whereas, henceforth, the tenacity of the peoples as the holders of sovereignty became the responsibility of governments deriving their authority from *the governed*. The French enacted it as Article 2 of Title XIII of their constitution (1793) but applied it as a standard for the transfer of territory to France and the annexation of lands belonging to others, including the annexation of Avignon (1791), the Palatinate, and Belgium (1793). In fact, the principle was circumscribed to changing state borders and the distribution of territory; other colonial, ethnic, and religious peoples were not eligible to exercise it. Those to whom the principle applied were not free to choose their sovereigns. The external variant of self-determination originated in this epoch, as states could change their territories though others might object to this or oppose it.[7] Self-determination, as a democratic ideal, was vested in

1 Joshua Castellino, 'International Law and Self-Determination Peoples, Indigenous Peoples, and Minorities' in Christian Walter, Antje V Ungern-Sternberg and Kavus Abushov (eds), *Self-Determination and Secession in International Law* (OUP 2014) 31.

2 Elizabeth Rodríguez-Santiago, 'The Evolution of Self-Determination of Peoples in International Law' in Fernando R. Tesón (ed), *The Theory of Self-Determination* (CUP 2016) 203–204.

3 ibid 129.

4 The Declaration of the Rights of Man and the Citizen. See Jörg Fisch, *The Right of Self-Determination of Peoples: The Domestication of an Illusion* (CUP 2015) 82–90.

5 Hispanic American refers to all of South America including or excluding Brazil. In this process, power was handed over from the colonisers to the European settlers or their descendants on the basis of natural law, though the despotic rule of colonisers, especially Spain, was a factor for independence. See ibid 69–81.

6 ibid 244.

7 Antonio Cassese, *Self-Determination of Peoples: A Legal Reappraisal* (CUP 1995) 11–13.

individuals during the French Revolution[8] but was subsequently transformed into a 'right' of people to independence.[9] Although plebiscites were held between 1789 and 1792, they were exploited not to exercise popular sovereignty but to sanctify a *fait accompli* or existing conditions, that is, to legitimate the territorial questions already decided by the French revolutionaries. No plebiscite for secession from France was ever held inasmuch as power and not a domination-free relation was a deciding criterion.[10] The American Declaration of Independence (4 July 1776), which is a modern remedial secession against an allegedly long train of abuses and usurpations, absolute despotism, and repeated injury on the part of the British Crown,[11] recognised internal (consent of holders) and external types of self-determination. In Latin America, self-determination, as the last recourse, was pressed into service as the driving ideology to decolonise or achieve the independence of territorially entrenched entities suffered from injuries by Spanish and Portuguese colonisers from 1810 to 1825.[12] Nonetheless, their independence led to a strong Westphalian system with a new title, the sovereign state, while other colonies were not granted self-determination. For sovereignty, the right to preserve territory, even to expand it through colonisation of non-civilised peoples, and denial of secession by any group remained main principles in international law until 1960.[13]

Hitherto, the axiom of self-determination has played a critical role in the development of international relations and the world as well. The principle was extended to other states, notably Italy, as the principle of nationality for the consolidation of Italy. However, it was not applied to Italian colonies in Africa. According to this principle, every nation with 'its own ethnical, linguistic, cultural, religious, and historical characteristics' had the natural right of independence by the exercise of *free will*.[14] The axiom was affirmed by France in 1848 and, by virtue of the Treaty of Paris (1856), the Principalities of Moldavia and Wallachia were set upon a path of autonomy and self-determination leading to eventual unity with an independent Romania in consonance with the will of the people.[15]

Self-determination of peoples was considered an ambiguous principle of natural law. Nevertheless, it was the right of conquest and the balance of power by which territories changed hands or were preserved intact. Phrases such as 'self-determination,' the 'right of self-determination,' and 'right of self-determination of peoples' originally date back to the bourgeois nationalism and labour movements of leftist parties after 1849. *Self-determination* was used for the first time, though not in a legal sense, from the outset of the 1860s by various nationalist, radical, and

8 Ove Bring, 'Kurdistan and the Principle of Self-Determination' 35 GYBIL 157, 169.

9 Andrés R. Sureda, *The Evolution of the Right of Self-Determination, A Study of United Nations Practice* (Leiden 1973) 17–19.

10 Fisch (n 4) 85–90.

11 The Declaration of Independence, 4 July 1776.

12 Castellino (n 1) 29.

13 Rodríguez-Santiago in Tesón (n 2) 206, 208, 209.

14 ibid 210.

15 Cassese (n 7) 11.

liberal groupings, along other labour movements. It is not clear in which language it was used first, but it was probably German.[16] The 'right of self-determination of peoples' was first mentioned in 1870 by Eduard Zeller and then in the Austrian Imperial Council (December 1870) by Czech parliamentarians.[17]

The right was recognised by a resolution of International Labour and Trade Union Congress (27 July to 1 August 1896).[18] Pasquale Fiore had bolstered the natural right of nations and people to independence based on the *right of sociability*, but none of these doctrines were inserted into positive international law. Accordingly, and predicated on the *right to conquer*, Africa was partitioned not by the consent of its peoples, but in compliance with the interests of Europeans colonisers with no sovereign rights for indigenous colonised populations.[19] With the ensuing First World War and the Bolsheviks coming into power in Russia, the operative principle of self-determination was promoted separately by Woodrow Wilson and Vladimir Lenin as a means of achieving a post-war international system. The break-up of the Austro-Hungarian and Ottoman empires planted the seeds of the right to self-determination and led to its embodiment it in international treaties and conventions.

2.1.1.1 Lenin's Revolutionary Discourse (Ethno-National Self-Determination)

The Bolshevik revolution contributed to the further evolution of self-determination. The Bolsheviks widely promoted the Russian term *samoopredelenie* (*samo* ('self') with the verb *opredelit* ('to determine' or 'to specify,' 'to decide' or 'to decree'), a principle which had roots in the works of Marx and Engels in the nineteenth century and was adopted by the Russian Mensheviks in the 1903 Programme of the Russian Social Democratic Labour Party (Point or Article 9); it holds: '[t] he right of self-determination for all nations forming part of the State.' To the Bolsheviks, the right was a collective one for an independent state.[20] In *Marxism and the National Question* (1914), Vladimir Lenin referred to the right of self-determination by which 'a nation may arrange its life in the way it wishes' and 'on the basis of autonomy' and, at the same time, the nation 'has the right to complete secession.' The new provisional left-leaning government (Social Democrats)

16 Due to the easy formulation of compound words in German. Fisch (n 4) 117–118.

17 ibid 191–192.

18 In London. Ian Brownlie, 'An Essay in the History of the Principle of Self-Determination' in Charles H. Alexandrowicz (ed), *Grotian Society Papers 1968, Studies in the History of the Law of Nations* (MNP 1970) 93–95.

19 Rodríguez-Santiago in Tesón (n 2) 210–211.

20 '[R]ight of self-determination for all nations included within the bounds of the state.' Fisch (n 4) 119. It was also incorporated in the 1905 programmatic statement of the Socialist Revolutionary Party. Boris Meissner, 'The Soviet Concept of Nation and the Right of National Self-Determination' (1977) 32(1) International Journal 56. On the use of the term by Marx and Engels in 1843, 1863, and 1865, see Bill Bowring, 'Marx, Engels, Lenin, and the right of peoples to self-determination in international law' in Paul O'Connell and Umut Özsu (eds), *Research Handbook on Law and Marxism* (Edward Elgar Publishing 2021) 104–106.

of Russia on 9 April 1917, declared as one of its war aims 'the establishment of permanent peace on the basis of the self-determination of peoples.'[21] The concept had been proposed by Lenin internationally in his *Theses on the Socialist Revolution and the Right of Nations to Self-Determination* (March 1916) followed by the Decree on Peace of 26 October 1917.[22] He defined self-determination as 'the political separation of…nations from alien national bodies, and the formation of an independent national state.'[23]

Lenin's and other Soviet declarations outlined self-determination as a three-component concept: ethnic or national self-determination on choosing status through secession or autonomy, self-determination of occupied territories through a referendum or plebiscite after interstate military conflicts, and self-determination of 'the East,…Asia, Africa, and the colonies,'[24] for gaining independence. This scheme was recognised in the Soviet Constitution of 1918,[25] and it encouraged nationalist aspirations as various ethnic groups pressed for self-determination around the world. The Bolshevik Decree on Peace

> accorded the right to decide the forms of its state existence by a free vote, taken after the complete evacuation of the troops of the incorporating or, generally, of the stronger nation and without the least pressure being brought to bear.[26]

It was a socialist view (not the only one) of self-determination, which could beget full democracy through secession[27] — a radical implication — and as a separate state.[28] This stance was codified in the 1918 constitution of the Russian Soviet Federated Socialist Republic. For Lenin, self-determination was 'complete freedom to agitate for secession and for a referendum on secession by the seceding nation' undertaken peacefully.[29] Lenin, in 1913, had rejected 'the expediency of a given nation's secession.'[30] Nonetheless, before October 1917, he proposed the revision

21 Erez Manela, *The Wilsonian Moment: Self-Determination and the International Origins of Anticolonial Nationalism* (OUP 2007) 37.

22 Fisch (n 4) 131.

23 Vladimir I. Lenin, 'The Right of Nations to Self-Determination' in Julius Katzer (ed), *Collected Works*, vol 20 (PP 1964) 397.

24 Vladimir I. Lenin, 'The Revolutionary Proletariat and the Right of Nations to Self-Determination' in Julius Katzer (trans and ed), *Collected Works*, vol 21 (PP 1964) 407–414.

25 Cassese (n 7) 15–16.

26 Second All Russian Congress of Soviets of Workers' and Soldiers' Deputies, 'Decree on Peace' Adom Getachew, *Worldmaking after Empire: The Rise and Fall of Self-Determination* (PUP 2019) 37.

27 Vladimir I. Lenin, '*Theses on the Socialist Revolution and the Right of Nations to Self-Determination* 1916' in George Hanna (ed), *Selected Works,* vol 22 (PP 1969) 144.

28 Lenin in Katzer (n 23) 397–400. Also see, Vladimir I. Lenin, 'The Tasks of the Revolution 1917' in VI Lenin, *Collected Works,* vol 26 (PP 1964) 59, 62.

29 Lenin in Hanna (n 27) 146.

30 Vladimir I. Lenin, 'Resolution on the National Question (September 1913)' in Robert Daglish (ed), *Selected Works*, vol 19 (PP 1964) 429.

of Article 9 (1903) and the replacement of the misinterpreted *right of self-determination* to the right of 'free secession.'[31] In the peace Treaty of Brest-Litovsk, on 3 March 1918, between Russia (the Bolsheviks) and the Central Powers (Germany, Austria-Hungary, Ottoman Empire, and Bulgaria), the future status of the territories was determined on the underpinning of the axiom of self-determination and 'in agreement with their population.'[32]

The Bolshevik concept of self-determination was 'a general'[33] standard for the disengagement of peoples from 'bourgeois' sovereigns through 'secession,' using force.[34] Lenin harnessed self-determination 'to further his ideological and political objectives' and gain the 'achievement of socialism'[35] but not to secure or realise the peoples' right. He accorded the highest priority to revolution. This became manifest in the Soviet Union's annexation of the Baltic States in 1940, the interventions in Hungary in 1956 and Czechoslovakia (known as the Brezhnev Doctrine) in 1968, and the decade-long Soviet–Afghan War (1979–1989), justified as 'the struggle for socialist-[internationalist] self-determination.'[36] He stated 'the necessity to subordinate' self-determination and demand the establishment of political status while writing his *Theses*. And he proposed federation as well due to the complex realities of separation, but his ultimate goal was the 'integration of nations' through socialism,[37] subversion of the multiethnic capitalist–imperialist system, and 'the liberation of all colonies; the liberation of all dependent, oppressed, and non-sovereign peoples.'[38] In answer to 'which should be put first, the right of nations to self-determination, or socialism?,' his priority was 'Socialism.' The support of the liberation of colonial peoples by the later Union of Soviet Socialist Republics (USSR) was compatible with Lenin's ideological objectives. In fact, the socialist protagonists appealed to exercise self-determination by the working peoples,[39] or

31 Vladimir I. Lenin, 'Revision of the Party Programme (19–21 October 1917)' in George Hanna (ed), *Selected Works*, vol 26 (PP 1964) 175.

32 By virtue of the treaty, the territories of Poland, Lithuania, Latvia, Estonia, and Byelorussia (later Belarus) were transferred to Germany without their peoples' consultation. Peace Treaty of Brest-Litovsk, Art. 3. See Freund Gerald, *Unholy Alliance: Russian-German Relations from the Treaty of Brest-Litovsk to the Treaty of Berlin* (Chatto & Windus 1957).

33 Cassese (n 7) 14.

34 Milena Sterio, *The Right to Self-Determination under International Law: "Selfistans," Secession and the Rule of the Great Powers* (Routledge 2013) 9.

35 Cassese (n 7) 18.

36 The justification was in 1968 *Pravda* article under the title of 'Sovereignty and the International Obligations of Socialist Countries.' Johannes Socher, *Russia and the Right to Self-Determination in the Post-Soviet Space* (OUP 2021) 35–45.

37 Cassese (n 7) 17.

38 Manela (n 21) 37.

39 See Vladimir I. Lenin, 'The Tasks of the Proletariat in our Revolution; The Draft Platform for the Proletarian Party (10 April 1917)' in Bernard Isaacs (trans & ed), *Collected Works*, vol 24 (PP 1964).

proletariats 'of each nationality rather than that of peoples or nations....'[40] Lenin, later and in 1916, extended the right to colonies[41] and colonial peoples.[42]

The Soviet Union was itself a multiethnic state, and the principle might blow back to undermine its unity (as indeed occurred in 1991); however, unlike Wilson's, the Leninist self-determination was meant to be applied — besides the European colonies and the Austro-Hungarian Empire — to the Russian Empire after the 1917 revolution. The independence of Poland, Finland, Lithuania, Latvia, and Estonia achieved after the Bolshevik revolution comprised practical examples of Leninist self-determination implemented (or acquiesced) by the Soviet government. Territorial autonomy as a right was considered for minorities lacking nation status within Russia.[43] Despite the dissolution of the Comintern on 15 May 1943, the endeavours of the Soviet-dominated Third International (Comintern) to incorporate self-determination into international law materialised in the UN Charter of 1945,[44] which paved the way to its becoming a general principle of international law.

2.1.1.2 Wilson's Ideals as Counterrevolution

Western European and American democratic theorists adopted the Wilsonian political conception of the right and 'justice' for 'all peoples and nationalities' by initiating democratic processes.[45] For Woodrow Wilson, the president of a heterogeneous state, the people's free participation 'to choose their government' or representative government, self-government or 'autonomous development' was self-determination, which should be 'an imperative principle of action' by which 'national aspiration must be respected; peoples would henceforth be governed only by their own consent.'[46] By the end of the First World War, Wilson modified his stance. His Fourteen and Four Points addresses (January and February 1918, respectively)[47] on self-determination had four iterations: 1) the people's right to choose their form of government (Point 6 of 14), 2) reconfiguration of Europe's

40 Vladimir I. Lenin, 'The Tasks of the Proletariat in our Revolution; The National Question in our Programme (15 July 1903)' in Clemens Dutt and Julius Katzer (trans & ed), *Collected Works*, vol 6 (PP 1964) 452.

41 See Lenin in Katzer (n 24).

42 Vladimir I. Lenin, 'A Caricature of Marxism and Imperialist Economism (August–October 1916)' in MS Levin (ed), *Collected Works*, vol 23 (PP 1964) 28.

43 Bill Bowring, 'The Soviets and the Right to Self-Determination of the Colonized: Contradictions of Soviet Diplomacy and Foreign Policy in the Era of Decolonization' in Jochen von Bernstorff and Philipp Dann (eds), *The Battle for International Law: South-North Perspectives on the Decolonization_Era* (OUP 2019) 410.

44 Cassese (n 7) 18–19.

45 For more details, see Anthony Whelan, 'Wilsonian Self-Determination and the Versailles Settlement' (1994) 43(1) ICLQ 99.

46 War Aims and Peace Terms, 14-Point Program for World Peace, President Wilson's Message to Congress, January 8, 1918; The Four Points Address of 11 February 1918.

47 ibid. Wilson used the Bolshevik term 'self-determination' for the first time publicly in the latter.

borders based on 'lines of nationality' (external self-determination),[48] 3) territorial adjustment 'for the benefit [not the will] of the populations concerned,'[49] and 4) the settling of colonial claims and 'interests,' granting 'equal weight with the equitable claims of the Government' (Point 5 of 14).[50]

Also, Britain stipulated territorial reconfiguration to be contingent upon 'the right of self-determination or the consent of the governed.'[51] Later Wilson applied this to Europe and to the non-Turkish portions of the Ottoman Empire.[52] To Wilson, the exercise of the right to self-determination was unfettered for 'well-defined national aspirations,' and was contingent on the absence of discord.[53] In his view, the right to ethnic or national self-determination pertained only to the former Russian Empire and to Europeans (Austro-Hungarian and Ottoman empires), not Egyptians, Indians, Chinese, Kurds, or Koreans.[54] This helps explain the Middle Eastern context of Mandates. In his address on 11 February 1918 for the post-war peace, Wilson substituted *the consent of the governed* (in his previous speeches) with the formerly unknown self-determination phrase, thus referencing and countering Bolshevik ideology. To his mind, self-determination (appropriated from the Bolsheviks, then redefined and deemphasised) was equal to 'self-government' or popular legitimacy; 'a right to choose the sovereignty under which they shall live.'[55] Ethnic homogeneity, he believed, would not be considered in the reconfiguration of Poland and Italy, and oppressive regimes and colonial rule could be overthrown through government by consent, self-government, and piecemeal reform rather

48 ibid Points 9, 10, 11, 12, and 13.

49 Four Points, Papers Relating to the Foreign Relations of the United States, 11 February 1918. 'Third, every territorial settlement involved in this war must be made in the interest and for the benefit of the populations concerned, and not as a part of any mere adjustment or compromise of claims amongst rival states.'

50 Point 5 of the Fourteen Points: 'A free, open-minded, and absolutely impartial adjustment of all colonial claims, based upon a strict observance of the principle that in determining all such questions of sovereignty the interests of the populations concerned must have equal weight with the equitable claims of the government whose title is to be determined.' War Aims and Peace Terms (n 46).

51 David L. George, *British War Aims* (George H. Doran Company 1918) 15.

52 Manela (n 21) 39.

53 Four Points Address (n 49).

54 Manela (n 21) 52.

55 Woodrow Wilson, Speech to the League to Enforce Peace, 27 May 1916. At the London International Socialist Congress in 1896, a discussion on Poland featured the first use of the term self-determination. Victor Kattan, 'Self-determination as Ideology: The Cold War, the End of Empire, and the Making of UN General Assembly Resolution 1514 (14 December 1960)' in Klara Polackova Van der Ploeg, León Castellanos-Jankiewicz, and Luca Pasquet (eds), *International Law and Time: Narratives and Techniques* (Springer 2022) 445. Lenin was the first person to publicly declare the notion of self-determination. James Crawford, *The Creation of States in International Law* (2nd ed, OUP 2006) 41; Antony Anghie, *Imperialism, Sovereignty, and the Making of International Law* (CUP 2005) 139; and Cassese (n 7) 14. Lenin's conception of self-determination is distinct from and contrary to Wilson's. Bill Bowring, 'Positivism versus Self-Determination: The Contradiction of Soviet International Law' in Susan Marks (ed), *International Law on the Left: Re-examining Marxist Legacies* (CUP 2011) 141–143 and Cassese (n 7) 14–19.

than by radical transformation.[56] What Wilson had in mind was a variant sort of rule which was later known as internal self-determination.[57] He ultimately shaped the form of self-determination although the essential idea had come from Lenin.

Wilson's foremost Point 5 was his long-lasting 'countermanifesto' to Lenin's stance on imperialism[58] and 'to counter the powerful appeal of Bolshevism.'[59] There are four objections to the Wilsonian solution to national demands.[60] First, it was too general, nebulous, and amorphous in application. Second, Wilson either had no idea about the consequences of his theory concerning the global community, or he underestimated them. Third, his ideas were intended for foreign contexts, i.e., they were not applicable to the United States. He believed that 'America does not consist of groups' (ignoring indigenous people),[61] that is, internal self-determination was not an issue to the US. The US stance regarding secession was manifest in the Civil War (1861–1865), marked by violence and military force.[62] Fourth, Wilson failed to successfully promote these ideas among other nations. Therefore, they were not reflected either in the final draft of the Versailles Peace Treaties or the Covenant of the League of Nations due to obstruction by Republican senators within the US government itself and a mixed reception by prominent British figures.[63] However, Wilson knew that the principle would result in the indefinable reconfiguration of some existing States.[64] Although self-determination as a tenet had been enunciated, its application was 'in the interests of civilisation'[65] and contingent upon peoples capable of reaching a point of *maturity*.[66] For the European powers, civilisation was 'the economic interests of the West' or 'the interests of its oil companies.'[67] Also, international law would apply only to the civilised world, although civilised states were not equal in power and in rights.[68] The Great Powers believed that nations other than whites and Europeans had not reached the capability of self-governing and ruling themselves. Non-white Japan was an exception that had been accepted as self-governing and, indeed, as a peer power worthy of overseeing colonies and

56 Manela (n 21) 42–43.

57 Hurst Hannum, *Autonomy, Sovereignty, and Self-Determination: The Accommodation of Conflicting Rights* (rev, UPP 2011) 30.

58 Manela (n 21) 41.

59 Daniel Yergin, *The Prize: The Epic Quest for Oil, Money and Power* (Free Press 2011) 188.

60 Lord Avebury, 'Self-Determination and International Law: The Kurdish Case' (1994) 7 IJKS 7, 9.

61 Woodrow Wilson: 'Address to Naturalized Citizens at Convention Hall, Philadelphia,' 10 May 1915. Online by Gerhard Peters and John T Woolley, '*The American Presidency Project,*' quoted in Inis L. Claude, *National Minorities: An International Problem* (HUP 1955) 81.

62 Fisch (n 4) 133–135. For the legal arguments of Southern states, see Stephen C. Neff, 'Secession and Breach of Compact: The Law of Nature Meets the United States Constitution' (2012) 45(2) ALR 405.

63 Cassese (n 7) 23.

64 Allen Lynch, 'Woodrow Wilson and the Principle of "National Self-Determination": A Reconsideration' (2002) 28 RIS 419, 425.

65 Timothy Mitchell, *Carbon Democracy: Political Power in the Age of Oil* (Verso 2011) 86.

66 Gerrit W. Gong, *The Standard of 'Civilization' in International Society* (OCP 1984) 21.

67 Mitchell (n 65) 86.

68 Ulrike Barten, *Minorities, Minority Rights and Internal Self-Determination* (Springer 2015) 187.

mandated territories. In practice, supremacy functioned as an excuse to justify their control over the colonies they had seized.

Before WWI, the right of self-determination was reserved in practice as a *racist* right for *some* peoples (civilised or mature, valued capable whites, e.g., in the Australian federation (1901), South Africa (1911), Europeans, and their descendants). To put it another way, it became '*a right to alien determination.*'[69] Under this rubric, the Allied Powers decided the fate of the peoples in the Middle East. The Allies had professed that among their war aims was the achievement of the right of self-determination, although both Germany and Austria objected owing to the status of the minorities in the territories acquired by the Allies' governments. The claim was replaced by the ratification of the Allies' political and ideological interests in the Peace Treaties. Thus, based on the Treaty of Versailles of 28 June 1919, Czechoslovakia and Poland (former German and Habsburg territories) were created through a disintegrative form of self-determination. But the formerly German territory of Kiaochow (now spelt Jiaozhou) in China was transferred to Japan without requesting or exercising self-determination by its Chinese inhabitants. A few plebiscites were conducted under international monitoring, but some territories were ceded without any plebiscite, such as the granting of South Tyrol[70] to Italy despite Point 9 of Wilson's Fourteen Points which stipulated the 'readjustment of the frontiers of Italy…along clearly recognizable lines of nationality.' The Treaty of Neuilly with Bulgaria of 27 November 1919 produced a similar result. A few plebiscites were to be held in Burgenland, Klagenfurt, and Teschen according to the Treaty with Austria.[71] The redrawing of Europe was 'to a great extent on national line[s]' (the external implications of the right of self-determination), although this was difficult to achieve in ethnically mixed areas, and some issues could not be settled by the Allies' Supreme Council. Meanwhile, international agreements by the new Soviet state promoted citizenship predicated on the right to self-determination, including treaties with Afghanistan, Poland, Romania, and Turkey.[72] Depending on circumstances of the 'national line,' a group could be identified as a nation and entitled to statehood or as a minority to be protected by a treaty.[73] In certain instances, the Allies aborted the treaties on the principle of self-determination for nations, particularly in the Middle East. Noteworthy examples include Kurdistan and Armenia, with Chapter 4 dedicated to a comprehensive examination of Kurdistan in particular. Such was the inconsistent post-war application of self-determination.

A provision was embedded in the Treaty of Lausanne (24 July 1923) for a population exchange of Turks and Greeks between Turkey and Greece, carried out without consulting the populations concerned.[74] Even democratic forms of governing

69 Fisch (n 4) 122.
70 Or Alto Adige, which belonged to Austria.
71 Cassese (n 7) 24.
72 Brownlie in Alexandrowicz (n 18) 94–95.
73 Whelan (n 45).
74 Avebury (n 60) 9.

in the newly created states were not successfully imposed by the Allies, though some countries were obliged to support and secure their minority groups' rights as in the peace treaties with Turkey, Yugoslavia, Poland, Hungary, Austria, Romania, Czechoslovakia, and Bulgaria. Self-determination survived but in an attenuated internal form amidst a climate of aggressive nationalism.[75] The system was reserved in practice for defeated parties and was not applied to the victors' territories. It was based on the 1648 pattern of the so-called civilised nations versus *peuples sauvages*. Finally, the principle of self-determination was truncated and not anchored in the provisions of the Covenant of the League. Article 10 of the Covenant emphasised respect for territorial integrity, since many states, especially European imperial powers,[76] were ambivalent about the axiom, although the Mandate System of *advanced nations* or 'the mandate of civilisation'[77] was proclaimed as a sacred trust of civilisation in Article 22 for *peoples not yet able to stand by themselves*.

For the first time, international law recognised colonies (albeit not the colonies of the League's members) as legal entities and accordingly acknowledged their rights.[78] But the system exerted no substantive effect in League practice due to the threat it posed to the colonial powers.[79] The rhetoric of the principle was limited to the 'League of Nations' in which the term 'states' had been rebuffed as the title of the organisation. The legacies of empire, unequal political and economic integration (membership), and racial white hierarchy were preserved.[80] Its rule was recast perpetually in the structure of the league, and self-determination was reforged and redefined as a racially differentiated principle, as Woodrow Wilson had in mind,[81] to justify colonial rule disguising in new terms the mandates system for *adjusting* the capacity of self-government of mandated territories and the 'required tutelage,' i.e., domination, of their peoples.[82] It was a means of delaying or deferring self-determination, whereas the immediate attainment of self-rule was a privilege granted to European territories. Therefore, it was not a universal form or method as Wilson himself maintained.[83] As envisioned by Wilson, *self* meant those who had the capacity of practising self-determination — that is, Europeans.[84] The self-determination of colonies and mandates would take the variant of consent and

75 Brownlie in Alexandrowicz (n 18) 97.
76 Manela (n 21) 60–61.
77 Lugard, quoted in Mitchell (n 65) 101.
78 Rodríguez-Santiago in Tesón (n 2) 214.
79 Brownlie in Alexandrowicz (n 18) 95.
80 White supremacy or exclusion of others. '[A]ny fully self-governing State, Dominion, or Colony may become a Member of the League.' (Art. 1 of the Covenant). However, self-governing territories' dominions were representing by empires — not an independent sovereign state — or some were admitted though as associated status or an observer member, not colony anymore, but without voting rights or some were represented by other states. Getachew (n 26) 41–43.
81 Inspired by Edmund Burke, an Irish parliamentarian.
82 This indirect rule policy was to 'civilise' the peoples of colonies — especially in Africa — through assimilation by the guiding hand of some external authority. Getachew (n 26) 40–45, 47, 49.
83 Woodrow Wilson, 'Democracy and Efficiency.' ibid 46.
84 ibid 45.

consultation through treaties. Therefore, imperial local despotism, not independent statehood for subject populations, was the outgrowth of 'a mechanism of unequal integration.'[85] This was Wilson's conception of equal rights and self-determination attenuated by hierarchy, limited to some territories of Europe. International equality was supposed to be contingent upon 'peaceful and legitimate development of the peoples themselves.'[86] For the colonies of the Ottoman Empire, he supported 'an absolutely unmolested opportunity of autonomous development.'[87] For the whole period of the war, self-determination was generally understood to be internal, whereas its external variation of territorial independence achieved only partial implementation.

Although the League was more inclusive, its process of burdened integration and membership was unequal and fettered by the hierarchical mandates system (A, B, and C), and a racial hierarchy or domination of whites over black Africans.[88] The League, thus, confirmed an aggrandisement of empire, especially those of the British and the French. Wilsonian self-determination came laden with the forms of consent, consultation, opposition to autocracy, and autonomous development, although some territories were integrated without any type of consultation. African nationalists deferred the radical implication of self-determination (independence), although they later revived it, but, meanwhile, scaled back their aspirations to phased self-government under the supervision of the League.[89] The League even undermined the black sovereignty of the African states of Ethiopia and Liberia, charging them with the humanitarian abuse of slavery and imposing special obligations and requirements on them to justify European oversight under the pretext that they lacked a 'government in the European sense.' Their sovereignty was equated with the slave trade.[90] Also, the illegal Italian invasion and occupation of Ethiopia beginning in 1935 encountered ineffectiveness on the part of the League.[91] The international legal ideal was revealed to be a mere 'watchword.'[92] When challenged, the sovereign powers did not unite to enforce the principle.

2.1.2 A Principle of Justice and of Liberty

In July 1920, an International Committee of three jurists was appointed by the Council of the League to investigate the eligibility of the inhabitants of the Åland

85 ibid 50–51.
86 Woodrow Wilson, 'An Address to a Joint Session of Congress,' 8 January 1918, quoted in ibid 50.
87 ibid 51.
88 Burdened or unequal insinuates troublesome obligations and limited rights — that is, responsibilities outweigh entitlements. ibid 54.
89 ibid 52.
90 Lord Noel-Buxton, 'Report on Abyssinia,' 26 April 1932, Lof N Doc, Box R2353, 21243/2053, quoted in ibid 61–62.
91 ibid 63.
92 Fisch (n 4) 9.

Islands to separation from Finland.[93] In the second Åland plebiscite, 95.47% of the Islanders had expressed their desire for union with Sweden in June 1919.[94] The Committee did not recognise the concept of self-determination as an international legal norm and since it was not included in the Covenant, it could not be a part of positive international law but, rather, was part of 'modern political thought' with the goal of *justice* and *liberty*.[95] The principle was restricted in the context of 'definitely constituted' states.[96] The Committee held that 'positive international law does not recognise the rights of national groups, as such, to separate themselves from the State of which they form part by the simple expression of a wish,' although they may be part of a 'certain number of international treaties.'[97] In the view of the Committee, the 'continued abuse of sovereign power, to the detriment of a section of the population of a State'[98] put the status of the suppressed group within the purview of the international community and established the predicate for League involvement. Thus, the axiom would apply only in the context of 'badly misgoverned' territories.[99]

To achieve a final solution, the Council appointed a Commission of Rapporteurs which declared the maintenance of the sovereignty of Finland with 'essential guarantees…[that] ought to complete the Law of Autonomy voted by the Diet on 7 May 1920, in favour of the province of Aaland.'[100] In fact, the Commission considered the Åland Islands *indubitably* one of Finland's provinces. However, it perceived self-determination as 'not, properly speaking a rule of international law' and interpreted it as 'a principle of justice and liberty' established by a 'vague and general formula.'[101] The jurists and rapporteurs balanced self-determination (in the sense of secession) and state sovereignty, by which the latter prevailed over the former. Both bodies concluded that self-determination was not part of positive international law,[102] but the guarantees could be interpreted as an internal variation of self-determination. This case clarified the view that ethnic or national minorities are not necessarily entitled to external self-determination, i.e., sovereign independence.

93 See Philip M. Brown, 'The Aaland Islands Question' (1921) 15 AJIL 268, 268-272; Norman J. Padelford and K. Gösta A. Andersson, 'The Aaland Islands Question' (1939) 33 AJIL 465, 465–487.

94 Sarah Wambaugh, *Plebiscites since the World War: With a Collection of Official Documents*, 2 vols (CEIP 1933) 515–518.

95 Art. 10 of the Covenant recognised external self-determination for members of the League. Rodríguez-Santiago in Tesón (n 2) 213. By citing *the territorial integrity and existing political independence*, it rejects self-determination to minorities or other groups within the League.

96 Report of the International Committee of Jurists Entrusted by the Council of the League of Nations with the Task of Giving an Advisory Opinion upon the Legal Aspects of the Aaland Islands Question. LNOJ (1920–1946), Special Supplement 3, 3–[vi], 5–6.

97 ibid 5. This was just for 'entities definitively established as States.' Crawford, *Creation of States* (n 55) 109.

98 Committee of Jurists (n 96) 14.

99 Crawford, *Creation of States* (n 55) 111.

100 Report Presented to the Council of the League of Nations by the Commission of Rapporteurs (16 April 1921), LN Council Document b7/21/68/106, 10.

101 ibid 27.

102 ibid 3 and Committee of Jurists (n 96) 3.

But they were entitled to maintain their separate ethnic identities through guarantees of certain linguistic, cultural, and religious rights. Therefore, internal self-determination was at least contemplated and raised as the *ultima ratio* and possible solution for the oppressive policy of states toward internal minority groups. It is noteworthy that neither Lenin nor Wilson proposed a means for achieving a corrective justice.

2.1.3 Materialisation under the United Nations

When US President Franklin Delano Roosevelt and British Prime Minister Winston Churchill issued a joint non-binding statement of their war aims (the Atlantic Charter) on 14 August 1941, national self-determination was among its objectives. The declaration including 'certain common principles' rejected any 'territorial changes that do not accord with the freely expressed wishes of the peoples concerned' (Second Point), which expressed subjective criteria of self-determination.[103] The two leaders proclaimed a principle to allow 'all peoples to choose the form of government under which they will live' (Third Point),[104] which, in practice, insinuated internal self-determination rather than external self-determination. Indeed, Churchill, on 9 September 1941, in the House of Commons, clarified the concept by declaring that self-determination was not applicable to the existing far-flung colonies of Europeans outside Europe but only to 'the States and nations of Europe now under the Nazi yoke.'[105] It bears noting, however, that the Charter had no practical function in the victors' eventual attitude toward self-determination.

Resettlements and expulsions became the actual policies, whereas self-determination was rejected in subsequent practice.[106] The Allies subscribed to the principles in the 'Declaration by [the] United Nations' on 1 January 1942 not to make a separate armistice or peace with the Axis enemies. The American Republics bolstered the Atlantic Charter and its principles in their Third Meeting of Ministers of Foreign Affairs in 1942. This could be considered the first broad adherence of nations to the principle of self-determination. In 1944, at the Dumbarton Oaks meeting in Washington DC, the US, the United Kingdom, the Soviet Union, and China set about founding a world organisation, the 'United Nations.' The principles of self-determination and the trusteeship system were not anchored in the draft Charter, although it included many comments relating to self-determination and the status of dependent peoples (propounded by Australia) and the principles of the Atlantic Charter. Ultimately, upon the insistence of the Soviet Union at the United Nations Conference on International Organization (UNCIO) in San Francisco, the four powers identified self-determination and the trusteeship system as the

103 The Atlantic Charter, 14 August 1941, *Declaration of Principles issued by the President of the United States and the Prime Minister of the United Kingdom*.

104 ibid Third Principle.

105 Parliamentary Debates, *House of Commons*, September 9, 1941, 'War Situation,' vol 374, 68–69.

106 Fisch (n 4) 183–185.

purposes of the UN in spite of critiques by other states' delegates, notably Belgium and Egypt, on the ambit, dimensions, and implementation of the principle.[107] What was, in practice, actualised was a body of states like its predecessor, the League. The preamble starts with 'We the peoples of the United Nations…' and Article 1(2) refers to self-determination as one of the purposes of the organisation:

> To develop friendly relations among nations based on respect for the principle of equal rights and self-determination of peoples, and to take other appropriate measures to strengthen universal peace.

To some, the principle of *friendly relations among nations* is superior to equal rights and *self-determination of peoples*; that is, self-determination is relegated to a secondary principle.[108] The opposite view perceives self-determination as 'an end in itself and not a means to some other end.' Friendly relations, thus, lack significance for the interpretation of self-determination because self-determination and its application are instrumental for promoting 'peace and goodwill among nations.'[109] The proposed amendments to Article 1 were offered by the four states jointly on 5 May 1945.[110] The principle of equal rights and self-determination of peoples is also mentioned in Articles 55 and 56 of the Charter.[111] The colonial powers tried to keep Chapters XII and XIII 'voluntary' and 'permissive.'[112] Notable here is that the French version of the article includes both the principle and the right: '*principe de l'égalité des droits des peuples et de leur droit à disposer d'eux-mêmes*' (*principle* of equal rights of peoples and their *right* to self-determination).

Beyond the structure of states, *equality* signifies more than just the equality of states. In this context, self-determination completes the equality. The term *peoples*, to some, might refer to colonial peoples and not the peoples of existing states of the UN who were already sovereign, and self-determination envisions decolonisation.[113] But some were not considered to be peoples, e.g., the indigenous inhabitants in settler states such as Australia, Canada, and the US. Article 1(2) only literally recognised the external self-determination of just the sovereign members of the

107 Cassese (n 7) 38–41.

108 Getachew (n 26) 74 and Bowring (n 55) 158; Cassese (n 7) 38.

109 Karen Knop, *Diversity and Self-Determination in International Law* (CUP 2002) 87.

110 Brownlie in Alexandrowicz (n 18) 98.

111 Art. 55: 'With a view to the creation of conditions of stability and well-being which are necessary for peaceful and friendly relations among nations based on respect for the principle of equal rights and self-determination of peoples, the United Nations shall promote: a. higher standards of living, full employment, and conditions of economic and social progress and development; b. solutions of international economic, social, health, and related problems; and national cultural and educational cooperation; and c. universal respect for, and observance of, human rights and fundamental freedoms for all without distinction as to race, sex, language, or religion.' Article 56: 'All Members pledge themselves to take joint and separate action in cooperation with the Organization for the achievement of the purposes set forth in Article 55.'

112 Brownlie in Alexandrowicz (n 18) 98.

113 Fisch (n 4) 193.

UN, as the Charter aimed to regulate the relations of the members. By referring to the phrase of 'We the peoples of the United Nations,' some equate *peoples* only with the Member States of the UN and not non-members or territories outside of the organisation at the time.[114] They conclude that *peoples* are meant to be states. The French version of the Charter affirms this: '*leur droit à disposer d'eux-mêmes*' is equivalent to 'their right to self-determination.' Therefore, 'their' refers to the same peoples of the Member States.[115] Chapter 3 investigates peoplehood in detail.

According to a report by the Syrian rapporteur, delegates could not define self-determination; consequently, it was reduced to *self-government*. States' interests, including territorial integrity, overrode the principle of self-determination which was considered a means *to develop friendly relations among states* and an instrument of peace. Therefore, self-determination could be ignored if it presented a possibility of conflict between states. Even the varied types and dimensions of self-determination were not distinguished, and the Charter consequently 'did not impose direct and immediate legal obligation' on states on this matter, as Article 56 does not define the *joint* or *separate action* to achieve the purposes enumerated in Article 55. Nevertheless, the UN Charter is a watershed in its albeit 'cryptic' identification of self-determination in a multilateral treaty,[116] which anticipates the maturing of the political principle or postulates into a legal norm.[117]

The Bandung Conference (non-aligned Asian-African Conference, 1955),[118] the Afro-Asian Peoples Solidarity Conference in Cairo in December 1957, and conferences of African States of 1958 and 1960 were turning points in the process toward the independence of colonial peoples. The Socialist Bloc championed anti-colonial self-determination and liberation from racist regimes in accordance with the external self-determination which Lenin proposed and which was followed by the Eastern European countries under Soviet compulsion. To the socialist jurists, internal self-determination was the right of a people to freely elect their rulers, which, in reality, meant the right to opt for a *socialist government*, an ideological conception. Therefore, this notion was applied exclusively to their territories. In the socialist view, external self-determination would lead to independence once the principles of sovereign equality and non-intervention in internal affairs prevailed.[119]

114 Rodríguez-Santiago in Tesón (n 2) 217.

115 ibid 218.

116 Crawford, *Creation of States* (n 55) 112.

117 Cassese (n 7) 42-43.

118 18–21 April 1955, Bandung, Indonesia. It led to the 'declaration on the promotion of world peace and cooperation' in which self-determination, mutual respect, territorial integrity and sovereignty, non-aggression, non-interference in internal affairs, equality and mutual benefit, and peaceful coexistence were adopted. The Soviet Union and the Eastern Bloc were not present at the conference, but they were represented at the Cairo Conference. Kattan in Van der Ploeg, Castellanos-Jankiewicz, and Pasquet (n 55) 462.

119 Cassese (n 7) 45. For self-determination after the WWII, see Frederic L Kirgis, 'The Degrees of Self-Determination in the United Nations Era' 88 AJIL 304; Rupert Emerson, *Self-Determination Revisited in the Era of Decolonization* (Harvard University 1964) and Russell A. Miller, 'Self-Determination in International Law and the Demise of Democracy' (2003) 41 CJTL 601.

For developing states, the legal-political notion of self-determination had three meanings: 1) vying against colonial and racist States, 2) challenging the occupier of a territory (proposed by Arab states against Israel), and 3) eliminating the domination of alien powers over natural resources in developing countries. Unlike the socialist states, they took notice of the internal dimensions of the self-determination principle for their minorities or nationalities within their states. The Western states, at first, opposed weaving the principle into colonies (decolonisation), but upon receiving opposition from their counterparts in the Socialist Bloc and the developing states against colonialism, they objected.[120] For the West, the principle was *internal* and *universal* in application and *democratic self-government* could be its true realisation. In other words, it entailed 'freedom of choice' through 'legitimate, lively dissent and testing at the ballot box with frequent regularity.'[121] A more expansive external self-determination right was, thus, expediently stymied in favour of internal self-determination.

2.1.4 An International Legal Right

The Universal Declaration of Human Rights (UDHR) was the first step in turning the UN Charter provisions into norms through a declaration,[122] which was proposed by the Commission on Human Rights. The UDHR is not binding, but it inspired later binding treaties such as the UN Covenants on Human Rights. However, the declaration made no mention of self-determination, since the framers could not agree on the circumstances (individual or collective right) in which the right of self-determination could be considered a human right.[123] Again, the Soviet Union's tenacity and massive support from developing states led to two treaties, both in 1966, by which self-determination was linked to human rights: one for civil and political rights and the other for social, economic, and cultural rights.[124] These actions were part of the 'International Bill of Human Rights' as a Magna Carta of human rights aimed at fleshing out the general provisions of the UN Charter on human rights into a set of specific rights toward promoting and encouraging respect for human rights and fundamental freedoms for all without distinction,[125] according to the Charter.

The words of Resolution 545(VI) passed in early 1952,[126] '[a]ll peoples shall have the right of self-determination' would be embodied in the identical first articles of twin UN Covenants. The conception of the developing countries and the Socialist Bloc prevailed and, ultimately, the article was adopted in 1955, but with

120 Cassese (n 7) 46.
121 The US delegate to the Third Committee of the General Assembly in 1972 and US Deputy under Secretary of State J.F. Murphy 2 November 1955, quoted in ibid 46–47.
122 UNGA Res 217A(III) (December 1948).
123 Fisch (n 4) 195.
124 ibid 194.
125 Cassese (n 7) 47–48.
126 UNGA Res 545(VI) (5 February 1952).

the broadened scope of the Western States,[127] and with reference to 'peoples and nations,' not just *peoples*. In English, 'nation' signifies the 'state,' and 'people' means the aggregate inhabitants of a territory.[128] The right was incorporated in the International Covenant on Civil and Political Rights (ICCPR) and the International Covenant on Economic, Social and Cultural Rights (ICESCR). It was a transmutation process from slogan to universal right by which:

1. All peoples have the right of self-determination. By virtue of that right, they freely determine their political status and freely pursue their economic, social, and cultural development.
2. All peoples may, for their own ends, freely dispose of their natural wealth and resources without prejudice to any obligations arising out of international economic co-operation, predicated upon the principle of mutual benefit, and international law. In no case may a people be deprived of its own means of subsistence.
3. The States Parties to the present Covenant, including those having responsibility for the administration of Non-Self-Governing and Trust Territories, shall promote the realization of the right of self-determination, and shall reverence that right, in conformity with the provisions of the Charter of the United Nations.[129]

The right to self-determination is now formulated as a broad and all-inclusive right, which hitherto was not conditional on the treatment or mistreatment by the superior authority. Peoples are endowed with this right independent of the conduct of another. The right to an independent state for a people is still conditional, but contingent on their meeting the criteria of peoplehood. On the basis of natural law and human rights, every people, merely because of its status as a people, has a right to independence. The right is only trammelled by other peoples having equal rights. The only prerequisite for becoming a domination-free political unit is popular sovereignty.[130]

The word *freely* in Article 1(1) has two meanings: first, peoples would choose their sovereigns 'free from any manipulation' and free from the undue influence of local authorities. This is guaranteed through exercising the rights and provisions of the ICCPR including freedom of expression (Article 9); peaceful assembly (Article 21); freedom of association (Article 22); the right to take part in the conduct of public affairs, directly or through freely chosen representatives (Article 25a); and the right to vote (Article 25b). These rights could be abrogated in times of public emergency by virtue of Article 4 of the Covenant. Based on Article 4(3), the state concerned could derogate from these rights directly (via an explicit declaration)

127 Cassese (n 7) 52.
128 Fisch (n 4) 196.
129 ICESCR and ICCPR, 16 December 1966.
130 Fisch (n 4) 235, 244.

or indirectly (when a state avails itself of the right of derogation), i.e., Article 1 is hedged by the other provisions in the Covenant.[131] States, especially single-party regimes, easily restrict the exercise of self-determination in a way that agrees with their own respective needs,[132] since the phrasing of the Covenant has been termed generic such as 'genuine periodic elections,' 'peaceful assembly,' and 'freedom of association.' Despite these defects, Article 1 turned self-determination into a legal norm. A people's participation in *internal* periodic elections (internal self-determination) in a *democratic society* would be a continuing process for democratic self-governance.[133]

Determining political status; pursuing economic, social, and cultural development; and the realising of self-determination all need preparation, and this is another indication of a continuing right. Second, the word 'freely' intimates the principles of non-intervention 'without foreign direction'[134] or 'the absence of constraint'[135] and territorial integrity of states. In other words, the provision of Article 1(1) bans states from doing anything against exercising the right. Also, it prohibits the parties from occupying other states' territory, as this could foreclose the implementation of self-determination in that land. Therefore, military occupation and annexation of a territory could be evidence of a transgression of Article 1(1).

The terms *status* and *development*, respectively, connote being permanent and being subject to change.[136] The former refers to external self-determination, while the latter refers to internal self-determination. By determining political status, *people* determine their international political status or state affiliation — the political community of their own choice — which could be association with another state or the creation of their own state through a clean referendum, a necessary though not sufficient requirement. It does not include the right to elect rulers democratically or to found a democratic government.[137] The most fundamental right bestowed upon a people through the principle of self-determination is the right of a people to independently decide the fate of its territory.[138]

2.2 General Principle and Customary Law

A general and incipient standard for self-determination is found in the UN Charter (Article 1(2)) concerning the destiny of peoples in the world community, namely the free expression of will. Thus, peoples themselves choose their fate without any hindrance. However, as this principle was the result of conflicting attitudes on the matter, the unit of the principle, its scope, variants, objective, and the means to

131 Cassese (n 7) 53–56.
132 Fisch (n 4) 9.
133 Sterio (n 34) 11.
134 Rodríguez-Santiago in Tesón (n 2) 6.
135 James Summers, *Peoples and International Law* (2nd rev edn, BRILL 2014) 43.
136 Barten (n 68) 201–202.
137 Rodríguez-Santiago in Tesón (n 2) 6.
138 Catriona Drew, 'The East Timor Story: International Law on Trial' (2001) 12(4) EJIL 651.

exercise it were not specified. In other words, it entails only general guidelines on self-determination, although as a dynamic force, certain rules could be identified which have been used by states, and these rules have been rendered customary. For example, the province, units (colonial people), its forms (independent state, association or integration with another sovereign state), and methods (plebiscite or referendum) of implementing external self-determination of colonial occupied territories have been crystallised. For peoples under foreign occupation, only the unit and objective (withdrawing from the occupied territory) of self-determination were specified. In the cases of Kampuchea (1979)[139] and Afghanistan (1980),[140] the international community decided on the application of the general principle of self-determination through free elections in the area involved. Therefore, the existing legal rules are not adequate. This is what happens in disputes about granting internal self-determination to racial groups. The unit (racial group) and objective (limited to access to government) of the right have been defined, but the means and procedures to achieve it are not specified. Concentration on deconstructing racist frameworks might be a method for achieving that goal.[141] In any case, the will of the people is of the greatest import, and it must be identified through a freely implemented process of referenda, elections, consultation, rights of petition, and recall of public officials.[142]

2.3 As *Erga Omnes* and *Jus Cogens*

The obligation and norms emanating from the principle of self-determination, as well as the link between the national and the international,[143] are considered *erga omnes*, pertinent to all members of the international community. Several reasons could countenance such a claim. First, all states (members and non-members of the UN) have imbibed and maintained a persistent reverence for self-determination, and any State and international body can demand respect for it. Deference to the right is not a reciprocal obligation, that is, a failing by one State is not an excuse for non-compliance.[144]

A rule to be contemplated *jus cogens*, or the highest hierarchical standing of all norms, based on Article 53 of the Vienna Convention on the Law of Treaties must be 'accepted and recognized by the international community of States as a whole as a norm from which no derogation is permitted and which can be modified only by a subsequent norm of general international law having the same character.' On occasion, there is no need for States to vindicate the existence of a norm. States' attitudes are expressed in general meetings and international forums through their pronouncements. Regarding self-determination, Western states have always

139 UNGA Res 34/22 (14 November 1979).
140 UNGA Res ES-6/2 (14 January 1980).
141 Cassese (n 7) 130.
142 Summers (n 135) 47.
143 ibid 3.
144 Cassese (n 7) 134.

confirmed the existence of the principle as one of the fundamentals of international law and have endorsed the *universality* of self-determination in international multilateral treaties, such as the 1970 Declaration on Principles of International Law concerning Friendly Relations and Co-operation among States in accordance with the Charter of the United Nations (hereinafter Friendly Relations Declaration, General Assembly Resolution 2625(XXV)) and the 1975 Helsinki Final Act.[145] The Helsinki Act refers to (internal and external) self-determination applicable to all peoples, including peoples without a state and sub-people of a state. Unlike the developing and socialist states, these states, except France, have intended to extend the spectrum of the right from sovereign to stateless peoples. They insisted on the principle of self-determination as *jus cogens* and non-derogable.[146] The right also was replicated in Article 20 of the 1981 African Charter of Human and Peoples' Rights (ACHPR) as *unquestionable and inalienable*, while adding 'colonized or oppressed peoples shall have the right to untether themselves from the bonds of sway by recoursing to any means recognized by the international community.' Additionally, Article 2(1) of the Arab Charter on Human Rights (2004) stipulates the right of self-determination for all peoples.[147] The International Law Commission (ILC) also mentions *the principle of self-determination* as a 'possible' case of *jus cogens*[148] or the core element with the incomparably highest status in international law,[149] while the illegality of secession and the preservation of territorial integrity dispute and oppose the principle.

However, its long relationship to other principles refutes the recent deduction. Self-determination has been subordinate to *uti possidetis* and territorial integrity, although *uti possidetis* is 'a pragmatic rather than a fundamental principle.'[150] It could not, therefore, be considered as a *jus cogens* principle since many borders have been modified thus far. Also, there are entities that have successfully seceded from their mother states and, thus, have challenged the immutability of territorial integrity. The existing practice vindicates the non-*jus cogens* status of these principles; however, they have often overridden, or been interconnected with, the exercise of self-determination. It is worth noting that the former concerns the internationalisation of former administrative boundaries, while the latter safeguards the boundary and framework of existing sovereign states.[151]

145 CSCE: Final Act, Helsinki, 1 August 1975, *Equal Rights and Self-Determination of Peoples:* 'all peoples always have the right, in full freedom, to determine, when and as they wish, their internal and external political status, without external interference, and to pursue as they wish their political, economic, social and cultural development.'

146 Cassese (n 7) 136–140.

147 The Arab Charter, in Art. 2(1), refers to the *political structure* rather than political status as in the Covenants; that is, all peoples have the right to choose the form of their governments, not forming new states.

148 Art. 37: Commentary, Report of the Commission to the GA (A/5509) YILC (1963) II, 199, [3].

149 Fisch (n 4) 10.

150 Summers (n 135) 82.

151 See Anne Peters, 'The Principle of *Uti Possidetis Juris*: How Relevant Is It for Issues of Secession?' in Christian Walter, Antje von Ungern-Sternberg and Kavus Abushov (eds), *Self-Determination and Secession in International Law* (OUP 2014) 95–137.

It is commonly acknowledged that although all peremptory norms entail obligations *erga omnes*, not all *erga omnes* obligations stem from peremptory norms. These two may be linked to the same interests, and there may be substantial overlap between them, which is the safeguarding of essential communal concerns, but they are functionally separate. Because of their inherent character, *jus cogens* norms may inevitably lead to *erga omnes* obligations. Nonetheless, this does not imply the reverse relationship.[152] The International Court of Justice (ICJ), in the *East Timor* (1995) and the *Chagos Archipelago* (2019) cases, referred to self-determination as *erga omnes* that is 'irreproachable' and 'one of the essential principles of contemporary international law.'[153] It also, in the advisory opinion of *Wall Case* of 2004,[154] reaffirmed the existence of the right to self-determination in the UN Charter, the Human Right Covenants of 1966, and the resolutions of the General Assembly (GA), especially Resolution 2625(XXV) of 1970, and approached self-determination's scope as *erga omnes* and even 'a further level' or may be *jus cogens*,[155] but with a weaker normative strength in comparison with the competitive territorial integrity of states, the prohibition on the use of force, and 'preserving peace and security.' When an obligation is characterised as *erga omnes*, it generates a procedural right of standing for all states to hold a state accountable for breaching such an obligation. The consequence of such characterisation is the generation of a right of standing on all states.

And in Paragraph 156, the Court binds states as:

> Every State has the duty to promote, through joint and separate action, realization of the principle of equal rights and self-determination of peoples, in accordance with the provisions of the Charter, and to render assistance to the United Nations in carrying out the responsibilities entrusted to it by the Charter regarding the implementation of the principle...

The duty to cooperate here emanates from 'a self-standing rule of customary international law,'[156] as manifested in the GA Resolution 2625(XXV).

A few factors are involved in denoting the right as an *erga omnes* obligation: 1) having an underlying role in the foundation of international law (Articles 1(2) and 55 of the UN Charter, the Friendly Relations Declaration, the Human Rights

152 Craig Eggett and Sarah Thin, 'Clarification and Conflation: Obligations Erga Omnes in the Chagos Opinion' (2019) EJIL:Talk.

153 *Case Concerning East Timor (Portugal v. Australia) (Judgement)* [1995] ICJ Rep 16, [29] and *The Chagos Archipelago (Advisory Opinion)* [2019] ICJ Rep 48, [180].

154 Upon the request by UNGA Res ES/10–14 (12 December 2003).

155 *Legal Consequences of the Construction of a Wall in the Occupied Palestinian Territory (Advisory Opinion)* [2004] ICJ Rep [86], [89]. To Rodríguez-Santiago, the Court in the Palestinian wall case 'was under the understanding that it was dealing with a jus cogens norm.' Rodríguez-Santiago in Tesón (n 2) 229–230; Michla Pomerance, *Self-Determination in Law and Practice: The New Doctrine in the United Nations* (MNP 1982) 63–72.

156 Eggett and Thin (n 152).

Covenants), universally directed at *all peoples* and compelling all states to realise it, associating with a number of state-biased principles (equal sovereignty, non-intervention, and the prohibition of the threat or use of force); and 2) having a central role in the treaties that many states are parties to and are considered customary law (the UN Charter, the ICCPR, and the ICESCR).[157] Although the amalgamation of *usus* and *opinio juris* could beget the crystallisation of customary rules, this is not the case with self-determination. Regarding the matter, *usus* is expressed through the political will of the majority of Member States of the UN, which is usually consolidated by the adoption of resolutions in the United Nations General Assembly (UNGA). However, these resolutions are not considered *opinio juris* or *usus* but show the legal stand and attitudes of the states toward the standards articulated by the resolutions.[158]

2.4 Modalities of Implementing Self-Determination

The Friendly Relations Declaration specified the customary variations of exercising the right to self-determination, including the establishment of a sovereign and independent state, the free association or integration with an independent state, or the emergence into any other political status freely determined by a people,[159] which could be applied to colonial relationships. In the case of alien military occupation, four alternatives are available: first, withdrawal of the foreign power from the occupied territory with a democratic system could be the realisation of self-determination. Second, the liberation of a country — in which the government has no authority while strife exists between political factions — from the aggressive power is not sufficient for implementing self-determination. In this situation, democratic realisation of internal expression of the right is a prerequisite for the external form of self-determination, i.e., implementing internal self-determination by free will could lead to realising the external type of the concept. Afghanistan and Kampuchea are instances of state practice in this case. The third situation could be envisaged in the case of Namibia, in which there was neither civil war nor alien occupation, but South Africa was exercising its authority illegally after the UN decision on South Africa's illegitimate presence in that country. As in the second situation, withdrawal of foreign troops would not lead to realisation of the principle. Before that, the people should be able to determine their internal arrangement — choosing the government system and organisations — and international status. Palestine could be the final situation in which there is an occupying power. Palestinians have not been able to vent their will freely and determine their internal and international status since self-determination is not realised through the mere withdrawal of an alien power. It should be accompanied by initiating the implementation of internal self-determination and determining the international status

157 Summers (n 135) 84–86.
158 Cassese (n 7) 69–70.
159 UNGA Res 2625(XXV) (24 October 1970), para. 5.

of the respective territory.[160] This could take varying forms, such as creating a sovereign state, integrating with other states, and so forth, although many political challenges would remain.

Neither customary law nor treaty law on self-determination constrains the right to circumstances of colonialism, conquest, and foreign domination. Article 1(2) of the UN Charter and Article 1 of each of the Covenants have had a decisive impact on highlighting the significance of the right. The latter achieved the realisation of one of the UN-assigned goals and paved the way for the development of standards concerning self-determination. The implementation of the right through the UN has broadened its spectrum and necessity. Customary law, generally, gives wider support to self-determination, since it portrays this general principle as an overarching standard. In terms of scope and content, both take a similar stand on the external variant of self-determination, meaning that external self-determination is granted to colonial people and divested peoples under alien power, although 'people' have the vested right in general international law to resort to force in active situations involving the denial of self-determination.[161]

In the area of internal self-determination, the right is a special obligation that is endowed by customary law to racial groups provided that the ruling government blocks their equal access to government. Here, there is 'no general obligation to afford all citizens a right to participate in the government of the state and thereby to determine its future.'[162] However, the Covenants confer the right to whole peoples of the Contracting States except racial groups, although they have licence to use force according to customary law if self-determination is not achieved peacefully.[163] The covenants do not authorise the recourse to violence or specify the means of implementing the right. The difference was engendered by the various perspectives of putting the developing and Eastern Bloc countries on one flank and the West on the other side while the former implicitly granted the right of self-determination to dependent, non-self-governing, and colonial territories, with the latter emphasising the universality of self-determination applicable to all states. The provisions of the Covenants echo the respective ideologies of the two categories of states during that era. In problematic situations, both have jurisdiction, e.g., if a State Party to the Covenants faces a situation which is regulated by both bodies, it must comply with both since it does not beget dissonance if it gives priority to one of them, i.e., two bodies of treaty law and customary law have cumulative effects, and neither is paramount over the other.[164]

160 Cassese (n 7) 147–150.
161 ibid 159-160.
162 James Crawford, 'Book Review: Self-Determination of Peoples: A Legal Reappraisal' (1996) 90(2) AJIL 331.
163 Cassese (n 7) 159.
164 ibid 159-160.

2.5 Self-Determination and Other Rights and Principles

The right, nevertheless, has now been bound up with popular sovereignty and the nationality principle,[165] and its obscure language and Janus-like nature is capable of various interpretations.[166] Its status has changed dramatically from a colonial to a post-colonial right as well. Self-determination should be contemplated with other principles of international law, which complicates its application. The question here is, if these principles limit the right to self-determination, how can *all peoples* enjoy it? The balance is 'more a political than a legal one' since self-determination applies to 'peoples,' but other principles, including sovereign equality and non-intervention, focus on states.[167] The right to self-determination is not absolute and unconstrained but tempered and conditional on the concurring implementation of other principles.

Among principles, some coincide with self-determination, but others collide with it. The principles of sovereignty and non-interference as the heritage of Westphalia are at odds with self-determination as a reverberation of the UN era. Self-determination acts as a hallmark for measuring the legitimisation of states, and it alters the status quo. Other principles such as prohibition of the use of force, the peaceful settlement of disputes, and the respect for human rights, international cooperation, and good faith harmonise with self-determination and are indicative of a non-statist world community.[168]

The principle of state sovereignty restricts self-determination since 1) national and ethnic groups and minorities may not secede from a mother state; 2) the right to choose their own kind of ruling government is not granted to the people of a sovereign state, as it is a domestic issue; 3) only peoples of colonial territories and people under foreign domination may exercise self-determination, even though they retain their territorial integrity; 4) ethnic groups are not considered in the process of decolonisation of peoples ruled by colonial powers; and 5) colonial boundaries are not manipulated by virtue of *uti possidetis*. State sovereignty has been tied to granting the right of equal access to government to ethnic groups and determining popular will by means of a referendum or plebiscite in the case of any actual or prospective border change by states. In the case of a third state's bilateral or international involvement, encroachment on self-determination by an oppressive state has narrowed the sphere of the principle of non-interference.[169] Third states can offer various assistance short of sending troops to liberation movements. In a similar vein, territorial integrity and *uti possidetis juris* are deemed obstacles to the exercise of self-determination.[170] In other words, they are contradictory approaches: one aims at preserving the external boundaries, and the other

165 Summers (n 135) 30.
166 Cassese (n 7) 5.
167 Summers (n 135) 142.
168 Cassese (n 7) 333.
169 ibid 334–335.
170 Summers (n 135) 63–66.

may result in secession or dissolution. Territorial integrity protects the territorial framework of existing independent states. The *uti possidetis* principle operates the same as territorial integrity. It guarantees the inviolability of borders. *Uti possidetis* transforms formerly established boundaries into international borders for a constituent part of a state from which another part seeks to secede.[171] Sovereignty and territorial integrity make self-determination a declaratory right or less of a right.[172] Non-interference makes self-determination a normative right, as it honours other states' self-determination[173] by disregarding or challenging their internal affairs.

2.6 The Expression of Self-Determination

There are varied stratifications of self-determination as the first and the clearest right of peoples,[174] but the dichotomy between expressions of self-determination, as internal and external, has been noted by academics, the Canadian Supreme Court,[175] the General Recommendation XXI on secession by the Committee on the Elimination of Racial Discrimination (CERD),[176] the 1975 Helsinki Final Act (Principle VIII(2)), the 2007 Declaration on the Rights of Indigenous Peoples (Article 4), the separate opinions of Judges Simma and Cançado Trindade in the ICJ *Kosovo Advisory Opinion* (2010), and the United Kingdom Supreme Court in its 2022 ruling on the independence of Scotland. The distinction was first employed by the Netherlands in its negotiations on the independence of Indonesia in 1949. This has broadened self-determination, which was fettered to independence at the time of decolonisation. It also offers an alternative for secession entities, and it strengthens state sovereignty and territorial integrity, thus restraining self-determination in practice.[177]

2.6.1 Internal Manifestation

In both forms of self-determination, whether the variation is internal or domestic,[178] the implementation of self-determination is safeguarded through guaranteeing and adhering to the freedoms enshrined in ICCPR Articles 18, 9, 21, 25, and 26, aiming at groups or *self*. As an ongoing right, internal self-determination is the

171 Edward McWhinney, *Self-Determination of Peoples and Plural-Ethnic States: Secession and State Succession and the Alternative, Federal Option* (MNP 2007) 54–59.

172 Barten (n 68) 204.

173 Martti Koskenniemi, 'National Self-Determination Today: Problems of Legal Theory and Practice' (1994) 43(2) ICLQ 241, 219.

174 James Crawford (ed), *The Rights of Peoples* (CPO 1988) 164.

175 *Reference re Secession of Quebec* [1998] 2 SCR 217, [126].

176 General Recommendation XXI (48), (CERD/C/365/Rev.1 (2000), 16, [4].

177 Summers (n 135) 63–66.

178 Domestic and international aspects of self-determination were proposed by Syrian delegates in 1952. Syria, 6 GAOR (1951) 3rd Committee, 397th mtg., (A/C.3/SR.397) [5]. And external and internal were expressed by the Netherlands while the debate on UNGA Res 637(VII). Netherlands, 7 GAOR (1952) 3rd Committee, 447th mtg., (A/C.3/SR.447), [4].

right to self-government in matters relating to local affairs and, to the Canadian Supreme Court, 'a people's pursuit of its political, economic, social and cultural development within the framework of an existing state.'[179] In other words, it is a people's right to participate in the decision-making process and subsumes the right 'to exercise cultural, linguistic, religious or (territorial) political autonomy within the boundaries of the existing state.'[180] It is a non-territorial approach to self-determination.[181] Unlike its external form, the internal conception of self-determination is 'neither destroyed nor diminished' once implemented;[182] it is a continuous right using an ongoing procedure over a period of time.

Enjoying external self-determination is concurrent with enjoying the internal logic of self-determination, but the converse does not have this implication; they are not inversely related. Internal self-determination is, in fact, partial or limited self-determination[183] or a delegation of state functions or power sharing to peoples or minorities within a state. In this matter, there should be a distinction between the rights of a whole people of a state, the right to a representative government, the right of minority groups including racial and religious groups within the state, and the right of ethnic, linguistic groups, and indigenous people within a federal state. The right of *all peoples* to internal self-determination has been recognised in Article 1 of the twin Covenants. However, there is a dearth of literature regarding states' actions on the matter, since they contemplate it as undue influence according to the general comment of the Committee on Human Rights No 12 (1984), in which States are asked to 'refrain from interfering in the internal affairs of other States and thereby adversely affecting the exercise of the right to self-determination.' They are, nonetheless, asked, at the beginning of the paragraph, to 'take positive action to facilitate realization of and respect for the right' under the UN Charter.[184]

The states' predilection for the principle of state sovereignty has led to a prudent and conservative view toward bestowing internal self-determination to their people to ward off the peril of disruption. Also, the UN itself has not treated the matter in support of ethnic groups such as Kurds (within their host states) and the Basques, linguistic minorities such as the Québécois, and religious groups such as the Catholics in Northern Ireland, although it supported internal self-determination for the indigenous peoples of Australia, New Zealand, Canada, the US, and the Inuit majority in Greenland in the UN Declaration on the Rights of Indigenous Peoples. However, the right has been invoked by the UN to a minority group as in

179 *Quebec* (n 175) [126].

180 International Conference of Experts on the 'Implementation of Right to Self-Determination as a Contribution to Conflict Prevention,' Barcelona, 21–27 November 1998.

181 Barten (n 68) 193.

182 Cassese (n 7) 101.

183 Fisch (n 4) 47–51.

184 UNHRC, General Comment No 12, Art. 1, 'The Right to Self-Determination of Peoples,' 13 March 1984, UN DOC HRI /GEN/1/Rev.7.

South Tyrol on which two resolutions were passed by the UNGA.[185] Nonetheless, it has not been efficient in provoking internal self-determination of ethnic groups within the boundaries of sovereign states.[186]

The variants of internal self-determination have not been detailed in the existing rules and treaties pertinent to self-determination. However, regional self-government and autonomy may be perceived from state practice in the cases of Southern Rhodesia (later Zimbabwe) and South Africa,[187] in which the UN did not recognise the quasi-independent Transkei and the so-called independence of other South African Homelands or Bantustans (Bophuthatswana, Venda, and Ciskei), as these regions were designed 'to destroy the territorial integrity' of South Africa and would lead to 'white minority domination.'[188]

2.6.2 External Manifestation

2.6.2.1 Customary Self-Determination

The process of seceding from a state or adopting a territorial approach of self-determination is an exercise of external self-determination, by which the existing boundaries of states are reconfigured. Here, self-determination is perceived as a result, determining a status and rights by the *self* once and for all — a one-time right.[189] The treaty provisions of the UN Charter (Article 1(2)) and two Covenants (Article 1) moulded customary rules on self-determination, since Member States of the UN took various positions while negotiating its provisions. Also, the growing number of states that adhered to the course led to the piecemeal formation of general norms on self-determination.[190] The UN practice has played a critical role in the development of self-determination through actions and the adoption of resolutions on the matter. The gradual formation and adjustable content of these general rules compelled the West to approve them since they were not rigid.[191]

2.6.2.2 Elaboration through UN Resolutions

The UNGA linked the right of self-determination and human rights by adopting several resolutions, including 545(VI) of 1952 incorporating the right to self-determination in the texts of the Human Rights Covenants, 637(VII) of 1952 as the Right of Peoples and Nations to Self-Determination,[192] 738(VIII) of 1953, 837(IX) of 1954 and 1188(XII) of 1957. The UN Declaration on the Granting of Independence

185 UNGA 1497(XV) (31 October 1960) and UNGA 1661(XVI) (28 November 1961). See Antony E. Alcock, *The History of the South Tyrol Question* (En vente Chez M. Joseph 1970).

186 Cassese (n 7) 101–108.

187 ibid 124–125.

188 UNGA Res 31/6A (26 October 1976) and UNGA Res 32/105N (14 December 1977).

189 Barten (n 68) 201.

190 Cassese (n 7) 68.

191 ibid 68–69.

192 It recognised the right for the non-self-governing and trust territories.

to Colonial Countries and Peoples (hereinafter Colonial Independence Declaration, UNGA Resolution 1514(XV), 1960)[193] and the Friendly Relations Declaration[194] are considered part of the customary international law of self-determination,[195] a significant move forward to a new 'just' rearrangement of the world as well as a unique human right that is a prerequisite for all other human rights.[196]

The outset of the second decade of the establishment of the UN coincided with a request from socialist and developing countries to terminate the colonial epoch — that is, to bring about a second round of decolonisation,[197] which led to the adoption of two significant UNGA resolutions on 14 and 15 December 1960: 1514(XV), Colonial Independence Declaration[198] and 1541(XV), the three options for self-determination resolution,[199] respectively. Resolution 1514(XV) paved the way to turning the principle into a legal right for *colonial* peoples. Anti-colonial nationalists reconstituted and elevated self-determination as a secondary principle into an essential requisite right for other human rights, reforming its meaning as well as a rejoinder to the *problem of empire* (enslavement) by disputing imperialism and its outgrowth, racial hierarchy and domination in demands for self-determination,[200] and reconstituting a new international order. Resolution 2625(XXV) — although it made no reference to Resolution 1514(XV) and colonial situations while reiterating the rights in it — extended the outline of self-determination beyond the colonial realm by recognising it for *all* peoples by 'virtue of the principle of equal rights and self-determination of peoples enshrined in the Charter of the United Nations.' The states' declarations and practice and their stand expressed in other meetings and international bodies' decisions constitute the *opinion juris* and *usus* of self-determination.[201] There are also many resolutions that have reiterated Resolution 1514(XV) as the Magna Carta of decolonisation or non-domination (anti-imperial project) during the last decades,[202] such as UNGA Resolutions 1810(XVII), 1956(XVIII), 2105(XX), 2189(XXI), 2326(XXII), 2465(XXIII), 2548(XXIV), 2708(XXV), 2878(XXVI), 2908(XXVII), 3163(XXVIII), 3328(XXIX), 3481(XXX), and many

193 Although Guinea proposed an amended draft of the Soviet Union debated in the UNGA, the Afro-Asian draft was approved as an outcome of a coalition among 'the Soviet Union, the Eastern Bloc, the PRC, and the Third World.' Kattan in Van der Ploeg, Castellanos-Jankiewicz and Pasquet (n 55) 463.

194 For the resolution, see Vaughan Lowe and Colin Warbrick (eds), *The United Nations and the Principles of International Law: Essays in Memory of Michael Akehurst* (Routledge 2002).

195 Cassese (n 7) 69–70.

196 Fisch (n 4) 9–10.

197 For Second Decolonisation, see ibid 190–217.

198 It was referred to by the UNSC in UNSC Res 301 (20 October 1971) (*Namibia*); UNSC Res 377 (22 October 1975) (*Western Sahara*); UNSC Res 384 (22 December 1975) (*Portuguese Timor*); UNSC Res 1598 (28 April 2005) (*Western Sahara*).

199 Principles which should guide Members in determining whether an obligation exists to transmit the information called for under Article 73e of the Charter under Chapter XI.

200 Getachew (n 26) 74.

201 Cassese (n 7) 69–70.

202 Hector G. Espiell, *The Right to Self-Determination: Implementation of United Nations Resolutions* (UN 1980) 8.

others. A committee of decolonisation was even created to guarantee the establishment of the resolution by the Resolutions 1654(XVI) (27 November 1961) and 1810(XVII) (17 December 1962) in the UNGA.[203]

There are two discrepancies between the Charter and Resolution 1514(XV): while the Charter refers to gradual and progressive development of colonies to achieve self-government (Articles 73 and 76) under the tutelage and determination of a coloniser, 1514(XV) asks for the speedy and unconditional end of colonialism through independence. Also, the Charter envisioned independence only for trust territories but not for non-self-governing territories for which self-government was supposed to be the outcome. The Charter does not protect the territorial integrity of colonies, but colonies with self-determination must maintain territorial integrity according to Resolution 1514(XV). The resolutions of the UNGA are not simply interpretations of the Charter. The Colonial Declaration and the Friendly Relations Declaration of the UNGA regarding self-determination — as a general and immediate right — are also interpreted as going 'beyond the terms of the Charter.'[204] The reference to self-determination 'can refer to the sovereign equality of existing States, and in particular, the right of the people of a State to choose its own form of government without external intervention.' Thus, self-determination, in this context, is exercised virtually by states as self-determination units vis-à-vis other states' intervention in internal affairs.[205] Also, it can be interpreted as 'the right of a specific territory (or more correctly its 'people') to choose their own variant of government irrespective of the wishes of the rest of the State of which that territory is a part.'[206] Before the UN was established, international law only acknowledged the former interpretation. Articles 1(2) and 55 of the Charter refer to this interpretation by citing 'equal rights and self-determination.' However, the latter was articulated implicitly in Articles 73(b) and 76(b). Although the UNGA resolutions are only recommendations, the practice of states in law-assenting resolutions can have quasi-legislative effect;[207] 'elements of law are mixed with declarations of intention[,] or recommendations.' Therefore, they could be normative.[208]

2.7 Summary

Through nationalism, linguistic, religious, and cultural identity are expressed where there is congruence between ethnicity and state boundaries. Earlier versions of self-determination envisioned the creation of ethno-culturally

203 UNGA Res 1810(XVII) (17 December 1962).

204 Crawford, *Creation of States* (n 55) 114.

205 Rowan Nicholson, 'The Meaning Self-Determination' in Ryan D. Griffiths, Aleksandar Pavković, and Peter Radan (eds), *The Routledge Handbook of Self-Determination and Secession* (Routledge 2023) 11.

206 Crawford, *Creation of States* (n 55).

207 ibid.

208 Ian Sinclair, 'The Significance of the Friendly Relations Declaration' in Lowe and Warbrick (n 193) 21.

homogeneous nation-states. The principle of self-determination was proclaimed by the French Revolution and its philosophical tenets of liberalism, nationalism, and independence,[209] although in practice, it stood for territorial annexations by ignoring the peoples and inhabitants of the territories. Subsequently, two progenitors, Lenin and Wilson, introduced self-determination to the international community respectively as an anti-colonialist concept and as a standard for liberating peoples under the sovereignty of vanquished empires. In the post-WWI peace treaties, peoples had no opportunity to express themselves, and neither Russia nor the US insisted on representative governments. Still, state sovereignty and territorial integrity overrode the principle and were consecrated. After WWI, the powers had scant interest in demands for self-determination due to the economic and strategic importance of their colonies; it degenerated into a slogan which was perverted and exploited as an instrument for achieving the goal of expansionism. It was a point in which the power principle, in fact, supervened and determined the fate of peoples and territories.[210] In the post-war era, the departure of imperial powers and the League of Nations from self-determination aimed at creating fully sovereign states through political independence was critical in the failure of self-determination claims. During that era, self-determination was reformulated for the purpose of 'the reordering of political influence.' The military and ideological drama of the conflict and imperialist world policies hindered self-determination and the satisfaction of national claims in the aftermath of WWI.[211] Consent of the powers was critical for any border change.

Uti possidetis (preserving the status quo ante of the colonial borders without considering the will of those affected), in two forms of *uti possidetis juris* for Hispanic American States and *uti possidetis facto* for Portugal and Brazil, was pressed into service to settle the external boundaries.[212] The right to self-determination was referred to indirectly in the principle of non-intervention by the Final Acts of Inter-American conferences (1925–1939). Its decolonisation variant was reflected locally in the Final Act of the Second Meeting of Ministers of Foreign Affairs of the American Republics (signed in Havana, July 1940) as 'the desires of the inhabitants of the said islands or regions' to determine their own destinies, which was mentioned in the Act of Habana concerning the Provisional Administration of European Colonies and Possessions in the Americas.[213] The principle acted as an estoppel in the Peace Treaties of Europe, although it inspired nationalist movements in the Arab world and colonial territories of Asia. Nevertheless, it did not become a legal norm. In fact, the principle acted as a bar to denying nationalist groups' claims for expanding their political status.

209 McWhinney (n 171) 1–2.
210 Fisch (n 4) 181, 190.
211 Deborah Whitehall, 'A Rival History of Self-Determination' (2016) 27(3) EJIL 719, 728, 730.
212 The legal or *de jure* and existing or *de facto* status of possession. Fisch (n 4) 79.
213 Brownlie in Alexandrowicz (n 18) 95–96.

The Nazi regime justified its military aggression as an application of self-determination to reunite the German nation through irredentism. The aftermath of WWII saw a switch in UN ideals from national self-determination to peoples' self-determination understood as self-government. Initially, as a goal of the UN without forcing its members to adopt exhortatory provisions legally,[214] it took the form of *self-government*. For the Western European and US versions of self-determination, ethnicity did not have a role owing to the emphasis on representative government and individual liberty. But for the Central and Eastern European (socialist) version of it, ethnicity was a valid issue.[215]

After WWII, self-determination was attained by the peoples of colonial territories and meant *de facto* decolonisation or self-determination from European metropolitan control and exploitation, i.e., Resolution 1514(XV), as stated by Judge Robinson in his 2023 separate opinion in the case of Guyana vs. Venezuela, 'wrested the attainment of independence from the grasp of the colonizers and placed it firmly in the hands of colonized peoples themselves.'[216] In 1966, and with the adoption of common Article 1 of the Human Rights Covenants, it was approved as a legal norm but with a broader contour — an expanded right. The Covenants endowed the right to *all peoples* of the Member States, although as loosely understood, it thwarted states from intervening in the internal affairs of other states. It crystallised the UN Charter provisions germane to dependent peoples and adopted a new variant of self-determination as asserting control over natural resources, i.e., economic self-determination. Now, Article 1 has become part of customary international law, as it is invoked by all states, even non-contracting parties. In other words, the principle of self-determination of peoples is now 'a paramount principle of Contemporary International Law.'[217]

Self-determination has, thus, made the transition from a principle or political concept into a legal right. Five iterations of it have been recognised in international law: 1) as a criterion, it was exploited by people to choose their state through referendum or plebiscite; 2) as a democratic principle, it was the right to choose the rulers; 3) as a decolonising principle or standard, it was utilised to secure the independence of colonies from the colonial powers; 4) as a principle of freedom, it was used to determine internal and international statuses by means of secession, integration, and association; and 5) as a ban and bulwark against aggression and foreign occupation.

By virtue of self-determination, *peoples* freely determine their political status and freely pursue their economic, social, and cultural development. Therefore, the conceptualisation of the term *people* as the bearer of the right to self-determination is a pivotal issue. But who are 'peoples'? What kind of group, sub-state, or collectivity constitutes a *people* or *self*? How do they differentiate themselves from a 'minority'? Who can qualify as a 'people' under international law?

214 Ian Brownlie, *Principles of Public International Law* (OCP 1990) 596.
215 Thomas D. Musgrave, *Self-Determination and National Minorities* (OUP 2000) 2, 5–14.
216 *Guyana v. Venezuela (Separate Opinion of Judge Patrick Robinson)* [2023] ICJ Rep, [3].
217 McWhinney (n 171) 6.

3 What Is a 'People' in International Law?

'Now what belongs together, grows together.'
Willy Brandt (1989)

While, collectively, there is widespread concurrence that peoples enjoy the right to self-determination, the right to exercise it still begs the cardinal question of who is the addressee and beneficiary of the right to yearn for forming an independent, self-determined sovereign state. Peoples? What kinds of population collectivities or sub-state groups constitute or could identify as a single homogeneous *people* or legal '*self*' in order to be recognised as a self-determination unit?

Although an accepted definition of a *people* would resolve many issues in the application of the right to self-determination, what defines *peoples* has been debated. To achieve a conclusive definition of a *people* is difficult, as it has been defined differently for various purposes. However, a definition for a particular object cannot be employed in other conditions and cases. Thus, it is essential to determine for what purpose the term *people* has been used and to what group or groups the right to self-determination has been applied.

Self-determination is linked to a multitude of selves: people, nation, minority, and indigenous people. These categories have some degrees of overlap and some differences as well. It is necessary to briefly examine the terms *minority* (and their rights) and *nation* to elucidate their difference from the concept of a people. A few minorities assert themselves as the rightful holders of the right. How are peoples differentiated from minorities?

3.1 Minorities

The Treaty of Westphalia (1648) was probably the first attempt to protect certain (not all) religious minorities within the treaty parties' jurisdiction.[1] The *millet* system of the Ottoman Empire conceded a relatively 'acceptable' cultural and religious autonomy to non-Muslim communities. The Congress of Vienna (1815)

1 Mahmood Mamdani, *Neither Settler nor Native: The Making and Unmaking of Permanent Minorities* (HUP 2020) 1–8.

DOI: 10.4324/9781003424314-3

also debated the rights of national minorities, including the Polish minority within Russia. The Treaty of Berlin (1878) is another example which provided protections for Mount Athos as a religious community in Greece. With the end of WWI, minority treaties granted comprehensive protection to ethnic, national, and other minorities. The system adopted by the League of Nations was later called 'self-determination' in the United Nations Charter.[2] The case of the Åland Islands was the first case to which the regime on minorities applied.[3]

Minority rights were also recognised in some treaties and international agreements, including the Treaty of Trianon (1920), the Treaty of Lausanne (1923), the German-Polish convention relating to Upper Silesia (the Geneva Convention, 15 May 1922), and the International Convention on the Prevention and Punishment of the Crime of Genocide (9 December 1948).[4] Furthermore, the United Nations Educational, Scientific and Cultural Organization (UNESCO) adopted the Convention Against Discrimination in Education by the General Conference at its eleventh session in Paris (14 December 1960), which generally aims to recognise the right of members of national minorities to carry on their own educational activities.[5] But what defines minorities?

3.1.1 Definition

There has never been a universally accepted definition of a minority. Even minority rights conventions lack a definition. Domestic legislation may have various definitions of the term. Many definitions or descriptions take the same characteristics into account; this may be an indication of some measure of agreement on the main elements of a definition. Aside from the subjective (wishing to be a group or a sense of unity) and objective (being distinct) factors, the circumstances of citizenship, historic and lasting ties to the territory, and the criteria of numbers and time all contribute to the designation of a community as a minority.

There are cultural, ethnic, racial, religious, linguistic, and national minorities. A national minority, having a kindred state across the border, may serve as an umbrella of all kinds of minorities that can include some or all of the distinct elements of other minorities plus a political desire to achieve autonomy or independence.[6] In the 1930 *Greco-Bulgarian Communities* case, the Permanent Court of International Justice (PCIJ) defined the category of a minority as

2 Hurst Hannum, *Autonomy, Sovereignty and Self-Determination: The Accommodation of Conflicting Rights* (UPP 1996) 50–51.

3 Thomas D. Musgrave, *Self-Determination and National Minorities* (OUP 2000) 6.

4 UNGA Res 260 A(III) (9 December 1948).

5 Art. 5(c), 14 December 1960 (entered into force on 22 May 1962).

6 Ulrike Barten, *Minorities, Minority Rights and Internal Self-Determination* (Springer 2015) 165; Annelies Verstichel, *Participation, Representation and Identity. The Right of Persons Belonging to Minorities to Effective Participation in Public Affairs: Content, Justification and Limits* (Intersentia 2009) 13.

> [a] group of persons living in a given country or locality, having a race, religion, language and traditions of their own and united by this identity of race, religion, language and traditions in a sentiment of solidarity, with a view to preserving their traditions, maintaining their form of worship, ensuring the instruction and upbringing of their children in accordance with the spirit and traditions of their race and rendering mutual assistance to each other.[7]

Also, the UN Sub-Commission on Prevention of Discrimination and Protection of Minorities proposed a definition for minority in 1985 as

> [a] group of citizens of a State, constituting a numerical minority and in [a] non-dominant position in that State, endowed with ethnic, religious or linguistic characteristics which differ from those of the majority of the population, having a sense of solidarity with one another, motivated, if only tacitly, by a collective will to survive and whose aim is to achieve equality with the majority in fact.[8]

This definition was not approved by the Sub-Commission. Francesco Capotorti, Special Rapporteur of the Sub-Commission, had defined a minority in 1979, for the purpose of Article 27 of the IICCPR, as

> [a] group numerically inferior to the rest of the population of a State, in a non-dominant position, whose members — being nationals of the State — possess ethnic, religious or linguistic characteristics differing from those of the rest of the population and evince, if only implicitly, a sense of solidarity, directed towards preserving their culture, traditions, religion or language.[9]

Numerical inferiority to majority groups of a region, a province or a state, and having a non-dominant position are uncontested issues for defining a minority.[10] Their number is less than one half of the population of a state. Regarding the time element, a minority should have been living with the inhabitants of a state for 'at least one or two generations';[11] that is, some time less than a century is sufficient to qualify. They may be marked also as separate or different from the majority or may

7 *Interpretation of the Convention between Greece and Bulgaria Respecting Reciprocal Emigration (Greco-Bulgarian Communities) (Advisory Opinion)* PCIJ Rep 1930, Series B No 17, [31].

8 Jules Deschenes, United Nations Sub-Commission on Prevention of Discrimination and Protection of Minorities, *Proposal Concerning a Definition of the Term "Minority"*, UN Doc. E1CN.41Sub.211985131 and Corr. 1 (1985) 30.

9 Francesco Capotorti, UN Study on the Rights of Persons Belonging to Ethnic, Religious and Linguistic Minorities, Symbol E/CN.4/Sub.2/384/Rev., UN Sales No E.78.XIV.1 (1979), [568].

10 Barten (n 6) 163.

11 Gudmundur Alfredsson, 'The Right of Self-Determination in International Law' in Olgun Akbulut and Elçin Aktoprak (eds), *Minority Self-Government in Europe and the Middle East: From Theory to Practice Studies in International Minority and Group Rights* (BRILL 2019) 21.

perceive themselves, the minority and its individuals, as different, but they remain as a non-dominant collectivity with shared ethnic, linguistic, racial, and religious characteristics.[12] There is also a threat element or a *latent fear of dissolution*. This feeling raises the issue implicitly or expressly of preserving the culture, traditions, religion or language of the minority[13] and its struggle 'to achieve equality with the majority in fact and law.'[14] There are a few legal instruments that refer to the rights conferred upon minorities.

3.1.2 Legal Instruments

The rights of ethnic, religious, or linguistic minorities are mentioned in Article 27 of the ICCPR: '[i]n those States in which ethnic, religious or linguistic minorities exist, persons belonging to such minorities shall not be denied the right, in community with the other members of their unit, to enjoy their own culture, to profess and practise their own religion, or to use their own language.' The rights granted to persons belonging to such minorities include cultural, religious, and linguistic rights. The term *person* here implies the individualistic rather than group inclination of the Covenant.[15] Paragraph 4 of Principle VII of the Helsinki Final Act (1975) refers to 'national minorities.' Nonetheless, it does not protect their national attributes, but it does guarantee their 'equality before the law,' actual enjoyment of human rights, and fundamental freedoms.[16] The Act does not refer to ethnic, religious or linguistic minorities.

After the Cold War, the Declaration on the Rights of Persons Belonging to National or Ethnic, Religious and Linguistic Minorities (1992) was adopted by the UNGA.[17] The Declaration protects 'the existence' and 'identity' of these minorities 'within their respective territories' (Articles 1 and 4(2)),[18] in order that they may 'enjoy their own culture,...profess and practise their own religion, and...use their own language, in private and in public, freely and without interference or any form of discrimination.'[19] It further allows them to participate in 'social, economic and public life.'[20] Articles 2 and 3 prohibit discrimination against minorities on various grounds. These provisions oblige states to promote the identity and welfare of minorities, which is a significant change in the approach of the international community. Also, the Council of Europe passed the Framework Convention for the Protection of National Minorities (FCPNM) in 1995. Article 1 of the Framework

12 Hannum (n 2) 50. Capotorti refers to the weak position of minorities, which need protection. Capotorti (n 9) [55].
13 Barten (n 6) 171.
14 Capotorti (n 9) [96].
15 Hannum (n 2) 60.
16 CSCE, Helsinki Final Act 1975.
17 UNGA Res 47/135 (18 December 1992).
18 Art. 1(1), UNGA Res 47/135 (18 December 1992).
19 ibid.
20 ibid Art. 2(2).

agreed that '[t]he protection of national minorities and of the rights and freedoms of persons belonging to those minorities forms an integral part of the international protection of human rights, and as such falls within the scope of international co-operation.'[21]

The rights conferred to minorities in the relevant treaties are for groupings that are distinct from and numerically inferior to the majority of a state, although they are determined to keep their distinct culture, religion, or language alive.[22] But do the rights enumerated in Article 1 of ICCPR involve minorities under the rule of sovereign states? On ethnic, religious, or linguistic minorities, Article 27 of the Covenant holds that they have the right 'to enjoy their own culture, to profess and practise their own religion, or to use their own language.' Two points are deduced here. First, these rights are conferred on *persons* and *members* of these groups, i.e., on individuals, not on groups. Second, the rights encompass guarantees related to culture, religion, and language, which are not commensurate with political or social rights. Preparatory works vindicate this deduction. Fearful of the future consequences of granting the right to self-determination to minorities, most of the states in the debates of the Third Committee and the Commission of Human Rights agreed that the term *peoples* does not refer to minorities.[23] Consequently, the Covenant denies self-determination to those minorities claiming it.

Given the above discussion, minorities are primarily defined based on certain characteristics, with common ethnic, linguistic, or religious elements and their longing to build up and maintain their status as collectivities. But peoples are primarily defined based on the territory they inhabit. Minorities are numerically inferior to the rest of the inhabitants of a state, remaining in a non-dominant position. In addition, a group is designated as a minority by its relation to its host state. The rights of minorities differ from those of peoples in the sense that they are held by individuals rather than by a collectivity. Also, minorities, in principle, are not entitled to self-determination as per international instruments. However, this matter is debatable. If they are eligible to practise self-determination, and if self-determination is not confined to its external form, it could be exercised within the boundaries of a state through autonomy or other forms of participation in public affairs. Chapter 6 returns to the issue. Peoplehood can be granted to a minority if the minority is never represented in the state's government. Failure to grant representation systematically, or by seriously violating its human rights, provides the grounds for granting a minority the status of a people. This is another significant distinction between peoples and minorities. It is an exception because, in minority rights, the sovereignty and territorial integrity of states are preserved in any setting. The term is also distinguishable from a nation.

21 FCPNM, drawn up within the Council of Europe by Ad Hoc Committee for the Protection of National Minorities (CAHMIN) (1 February 1995).

22 Capotorti (n 9).

23 Antonio Cassese, *Self-Determination of Peoples: A Legal Reappraisal* (CUP 1995) 61–62.

3.2 Nation

The idea of nation (*natio*, the Roman goddess of birth in Latin) means 'origin or membership of a community, a relationship with a community one was born into.' It was brought into use in politics and public law in the late fifteenth century, when it implied 'the embodiment of political organs' led by the king in a state or 'a community of culture and descent' not affiliated with the state. In the middle of the eighteenth century, the notion was redefined and perceived as the nation-state. In the French and American revolutions, it was perceived as 'free and voluntary association' (the *civitas* of the inhabitants of a territory).[24] No ethnic or historical backgrounds were taken into account.[25] In the nineteenth century, Mazzini defined the nation as humans with culturally homogeneous commonality and national consciousness that are naturally eligible for recognition and having a political rule or a nation-state to protect their existence.[26] In Germany, which was not a state until later in the second half of the nineteenth century, the nation referred to 'a person and likened its cultural traditions to individual traits of human beings' or a collective with a 'coherent and specific set of hopes, emotions, and actions.' That is the cultural nation. In American constitutional law, the notion is now synonymous with the use of *the federal state*.[27] In a nutshell, nations comprised cultural societies in a region and with a majority to claim an independent homeland. By the end of the nineteenth century, and concurrent with the nationality principle of self-determination, the term nation as a natural unit of humans with shared features of history, language, and culture on a given territory became entitled and legitimate for nationhood and the consequent building of a new national state by exerting the right of self-determination.

The rhetoric of the principle of self-determination was retained in the 'League of *Nations*' (emphasis added), as part of the title of the organisation. The principle was introduced for some *nations*, i.e., European nations, in the Wilsonian era. It was subsequently granted to peoples in the decolonisation era. In this era, the concept of nation, which was associated with ethnicity and a uniform nation-state, was replaced by peoples; national self-determination was replaced by peoples' self-determination in the UN epoch.[28] The concepts of *nation* and *people* were used in both eras. Both terms, *nation* and *people*, encompass and describe the same assemblage of individuals.[29] Peoples is a term less loaded with nationalistic sensitivity and political aspirations, while the term nation is political.

24 Armin von Bogdandy and Stefan Häußler, *Nations* (MPEPIL updated 2019), [5]–[10].

25 Jane A. Hofbauer, *Sovereignty in the Exercise of the Right to Self-Determination* (BRILL 2016) 25.

26 Joseph Mazzini, *An Essay on the Duties of Man Addressed to Workingmen* (Funk & Wagnalls 1898) 61.

27 Bogdandy and Häußler (n 24).

28 Gudmundur Alfredsson, 'Minorities, Indigenous and Tribal Peoples: Definitions of Terms as a Matter of International Law' in Nazila Ghanea-Hercock and Alexandra Xanthaki (eds) *Minorities, Peoples and Self-Determination* – Essays in Honour of Patrick Thornberry (MNP 2005) 163–172.

29 Barten (n 6) 178.

However, their likeness is not so simple. The similarities between a people and a nation are reflected in many languages, e.g., *Volk* and *folk* mean nation and people in German and Danish, respectively.[30] Folk has a similar sense in English. Also, developing friendly relations 'among nations' on the basis of honouring 'the principle of equal rights and self-determination of peoples' is one of the founding purposes of the UN. On the one hand, the nation encompasses all political entities, states and non-states, including colonies, mandates, protectorates, and states, according to the UN Secretariat. On the other hand, *peoples*, as a broader term, are 'groups of human beings who may or may not comprise States or nations.'[31] A nation can also be a minority. Inhabitants of a state, as a people, are eligible to exercise self-determination. That is, the term nation links and overlaps all concepts.[32] This term currently has three permutations: state, people, and national minority.[33]

People and nation, as the bedrock for statehood, are equivalent with regard to the right of self-determination; they are not separated in legal texts, although the nation is broader and includes political institutions.[34] The UN Charter utilises the term *peoples* to refer to the states because *nation* and *state* had been used largely interchangeably until then in international law.[35] The term *people* has been a prevailing word choice for bearers of the right of self-determination since 1850. It was formally instituted in 1966 with the adoption of the Human Right Covenants. However, *nation* could also attain that degree of prevalence. In the *travaux préparatoires* of the 1950s, that understanding prompted the drafting of the Covenants of 1966, wherein both self-determination of peoples and peoples and nations were employed. This was due to variations in languages.[36]

3.3 Peoples

As of the nineteenth century, the right of self-determination was associated with the term *peoples*, applied to 'the whole of humanity' and not to specific sub-divisions such as whites or blacks, Asians or Europeans, primitive or civilised. However, the outcome of WWI made it clear that the right would only be applied to Europeans and to residents of the Americas (albeit expediently omitting the indigenous American tribes). Otherwise, the European powers would be obliged to withdraw from their colonies.[37] This was the case also regarding former imperial holdings of the Austro-Hungarian and Ottoman empires. President Wilson reaffirmed the right

30 ibid 179.
31 Documents of the UNCIO, UNIO, vol 18, 1945 (vol xviii) 657–658.
32 Barten (n 6) 180–181.
33 Bogdandy and Häußler (n 24).
34 James Summers, *Peoples and International Law* (2nd rev edn, BRILL 2014) 7–8, 15–16.
35 Elizabeth Rodríguez-Santiago, 'The Evolution of Self-Determination of Peoples in International Law' in Fernando R. Tesón (ed), *The Theory of Self-Determination* (CUP 2016) 217.
36 Jörg Fisch, *The Right of Self-Determination of Peoples: The Domestication of an Illusion* (CUP 2015) 30.
37 ibid 172.

at the First Annual Assemblage of the League to Enforce Peace, declaring that 'every people has a right to choose the sovereignty under which they shall live.'[38] It is something 'inherent' in peoples.[39] But of course, Wilson did not mean all peoples. The term *people*, nonetheless, has remained mired in controversy. It has never been defined and specified comprehensively in international law. Lacking a universally accepted definition has given rise to a semantic obstruction, which would render the application of the right of self-determination complicated and induce contradiction between the rights of peoples, individuals, and minority groups.[40] The usage of peoples in legal instruments with territorial and ethnic signifiers, both generically and legally, has caused this difficulty. However, lacking a definition does not mean that the term *people* is an indefinable object. Otherwise, we should avoid claiming a right of self-determination for peoples. At the same time, not just any collective laying claim to the right is necessarily a people. Nonetheless, peoples, as such, do exist and have successfully exercised their right to self-determination.

Common Article 1 in the UN Human Rights Covenants stipulates that: '[a]ll peoples have the right of self-determination.' The article identifies peoples as the beneficiary of the right. Nevertheless, the phrase 'all peoples,' as the central idea of the right of self-determination, has made the application of the right difficult. Who are these peoples? Are they a group? The ICJ clarified, in 1975 in its *Western Sahara* Opinion, that 'a certain population did not constitute a people.'[41] That is, a particular grouping constitutes a people although tribes, populations, minorities, religious groups, clans, and parties do not always constitute a people. So, what classifies a population as a people or as a legal self? Here, *all* refers to those entities that can qualify as peoples — colonial and non-colonial peoples.[42] Also, in submitting his memo on 18 June 1945 to the Co-ordination Committee, the UN Secretariat defined peoples as 'groups of human beings who may, or may not, comprise states or nations.'[43] The word *all* intimates that there are other groups that are not peoples per se and are, therefore, not entitled to enjoy the right. This means that the law of self-determination does not automatically confer self-determination on various groups seeking it, but only to peoples. But this situation is not in harmony with the demands of any collective seeking recognition as a people.

In a historical sense, which was developed during the Cold War, peoples have been defined as the colonised indigenous populations of Africa and Asia, such as Eritreans, Papuans, Malayans, and Timorese, by Europeans. It is also used by

38 Presidential Address, Woodrow Wilson, address delivered at the First Annual Assemblage of the League to Enforce Peace: "American Principles" (27 May 1916).

39 Frédéric Mégret, 'The Right to Self-Determination Earned, Not Inherent' in Tesón (n 35) 46.

40 David Makinson, 'Rights of Peoples: A Logician's Point of View' in James Crawford (ed), *The Rights of Peoples* (OUP 1988) 73–76, 86.

41 *Western Sahara (Advisory Opinion)* [1975] ICJ Rep, [59].

42 Milena Sterio, *The Right to Self-Determination under International Law: "Selfistans," Secession and the Rule of the Great Powers* (Routledge 2013) 11.

43 The Secretary, Memorandum, List of Certain Repetitive Words and Phrases in the Charter, 18 June 1945. Doc. WD 381, CO/156, UNCIO, vol XVIII, 658.

Europeans about Westerners, e.g., 'the Scottish people,' 'the British people,' etc. The colonised populations were decolonised since they had a collective right to self-determination, which often led to independence — that is to say, they fit within the colonisation perspective. Despite this, the Soviet Union did not recognise this right for Estonia, Lithuania, and Latvia (known collectively as the Baltic States) because they were not colonies in the historical sense of peoples. The collapse of the Berlin Wall in 1989 put an end to the unjust view that the right of self-determination applied only to colonial peoples. There is also a nationalist-ethnic view on peoples. From this perspective, peoples are constituted based on ethnicity, such as the Inuits in Greenland, the separatists in Ukraine who emphasise language (Russian), and the natives of South Ossetia and South Abkhazia who emphasise their ethnic status. Another defining trait is religion. For example, Kosovars relied upon religious difference (Muslim) and their Albanian ethnicity to justify their secession from the Serbs. For some scholars, the nationalist view requires a comprehensive culture.[44] However, the ethno-nationalist view is not definitive, as its justification requires a range of political arguments.[45] Also, no nation has all the elements of peoplehood. Currently, this standard is not in harmony with the democratic exigencies of self-determination.[46]

What about those who do not share the ethnic traits of race, religion, language, and culture? If a state is created out of shared ethnicity, then people who do not exhibit the same traits could not be considered as citizens of the state. Postulating a continuous correspondence between ethnicity and citizenship is absurd. For instance, the Kurds and Armenians in Turkey could not be recognised as nationals of that state, as they do not possess the Turks' ethnic status. Even colonies with the most proven category of people,[47] which became independent 'artificially,' were of different ethnic and national groups.[48] Were they qualified as people, the grassroots unit for the right? If so, then how? Within a state, there might be a group of different traits.

Self-determination is mostly predicated on the concept of people, that is to say, wedded to it, but international law has indulged in romanticising the concept.[49] Also, international law fails to identify which peoples are potentially self-determination units. In other words, enjoying self-determination has been as ambiguous as non-identification of the units aspiring to the right has been obscure. When there is no superior authority to designate a group as a people or a legal self, the one that regards itself as a people (self-definition) contingent on its own shared concerns or interests (actual or imagined) would be eligible to create its state as a political unit

44 Fernando R. Tesón, 'Introduction: The Conundrum of Self-Determination' in Tesón (n 35) 3.

45 Mégret in ibid 58.

46 Rodríguez-Santiago in ibid 202.

47 Summers (n 34) 5.

48 Anna Michalska, 'Rights of Peoples to Self-Determination in International Law' in William L. Twining (ed), *Issues of Self-Determination* (AUP 1991) 82.

49 Mégret in Tesón (n 35) 45.

through self-determination. This is not illegal under international law.[50] The onus is on the collective to prove that it belongs to a certain category before it can assert the right to self-determination.[51] As per common Article 1 to the UN Human Rights Covenants, a group that can freely decide its political status decides for itself; nobody has the right to direct it to do anything else. This is further strengthened by the accentuation of the pursuit of economic, social, and cultural development. In other words, these peoples are sovereign polities that reject superior authority. This is the case for the next two paragraphs of Article 1. Paragraph 2 notes that 'all peoples may, for their own ends, freely dispose of their natural wealth and resources,' and that is, 'without prejudice to any obligations arising out of international economic co-operation.' Here, too, is a restatement of the principle that no higher power is above a people.[52]

Still, many sub-state collectivities designate themselves as the holders of the right to external self-determination in order to fashion a self-determined sovereign state. How do these units define or describe themselves so as to entitle themselves to the right? What does the term *people* mean to them? To be sure, the term *people* has a particular legal meaning different from its conventional usage, although legal instruments do not provide a clear reference to its legal sense.

3.3.1 Legal Instruments

No legal instrument has clarified what group counts as a legal self to whom the right is attributed; nevertheless, the colonial powers considered the European colonies or their non-European inhabitants as peoples eligible for self-determination within their existing boundaries.[53] Decolonisation led to the dispersal of single peoples among different states and also to the gathering of distinct peoples within a state.[54] It was territory that determined their status, and their only shared characteristic was anti-colonialism.[55]

The many attempts to define the term have given rise to flexible descriptions. On further study of the concept of the rights of peoples in its forum in Paris (1989), the UNESCO's International Meeting of Experts, while playing up the universal acceptance and the existence of the right to self-determination and conferring ownership of the right to peoples themselves, not states, regarded the definition of peoples as uncertain. However, the forum described a people as 'a group of individual human beings' and mentioned inherent specific characteristics of the concept as 1) a common historical tradition, 2) racial or ethnic identity, 3) cultural homogeneity, 4) linguistic unity, 5) religious or ideological affinity, 6) territorial connection, and

50 Fisch (n 36) 12.
51 Barten (n 6) 162.
52 Fisch (n 36) 29–30.
53 Hannum (n 2) 36.
54 Makinson, quoted in Crawford (n 40) 74.
55 Hannum (n 2) 36.

7) [a] common economic life.[56] According to the experts, their number does not have to be large; however, they 'must be more than a mere association of individuals within a State,' that is, they must be conscious of their distinctiveness ('to be identified as a people or the consciousness of being a people') and have institutions or other means for expressing their common characteristics and their desire to consolidate their identity.[57] This description, which was presented by an authoritative source, could encompass a broad range of groupings.

The Indigenous and Tribal Peoples Convention (1989) recognises self-consciousness as the 'fundamental criterion' of the definition of peoples.[58] In this regard, 'a nationality exists when its members believe that it does.'[59] In other words, nationalism or self-consciousness is sufficient to constitute a nation or a people.

Different collectivities could be identified as peoples, albeit for different objectives of international law. To UNESCO's international experts, if the function of rights is clarified and desirable objectives and rights are distinguished, the meaning of a people is understandable. The experts proposed further study on the subject by legal experts, anthropologists, sociologists, and psychologists. The 1991 UNESCO forum also regarded the concept as controversial and sensitive, which could present the menace of secession by both peoples and indigenous peoples. For the peaceful procedure of secession, the meeting suggested holding a referendum under the aegis of the UN for Kurds, Palestinians, and Cambodians.[60] Achieving the accurate identification of peoples also specifies the territories entitled to self-determination.

3.3.2 Self-Determined Territories

The identification of a territory to which self-determination applies has a direct relationship with the definition of a *people*. This right applies to separate political territories: first, to mandated, trust, and non-self-governing territories whose right to self-determination is recognised and predicated on an agreement. The second category is established states in which self-determination is a continuous right and is exercised to determine the form of government without external intervention. The third possible category is non-self-governing territories (the phrase also includes the quasi-non-self-governing territories) over which metropolitan states have very little sovereignty;[61] that is, these territories have no access or insufficient access to the government, despite being part of the respective states. East Pakistan (later Bangladesh), Eritrea, and Kosovo were three examples, among others.

56 International Meeting of Experts on Further Study of the Concept of the Rights of Peoples, UNESCO, Paris, 27–30 November 1989. Final Report and Recommendations, SHS-89/CONF.602/7, 7.

57 ibid 7–8.

58 Art. 1(2), Indigenous and Tribal Peoples Convention, 27 June 1989.

59 Mégret in Tesón (n 35) 56.

60 Peoples' Rights and Self-Determination, UNESCO International Meeting of Expert, Budapest, Hungary, 25–29 September 1991, 11–12.

61 James Crawford, *The Creation of States in International Law* (2nd ed, OUP 2006) 126–127.

The International Commission of Jurists (1972), on the events at that time in East Pakistan, designated 'the population of' Bangladesh as a people in terms of common 'historical, racial or ethnic, cultural and linguistic, religious or ideological, geographical or territorial, economic, quantitative' features.[62] To the jurists, however, none of these attributes are essential or sufficiently exhaustive, as a group inhabiting a given territory may not constitute a people despite sharing these signifiers, while a less homogeneous community with fewer commonalities can be designated as a people. To remove this paradox, the Commission added the element of being conscious of identity and the will to exist, which is an ideological, historical, and, of course, political phenomenon. Indeed, a people exists when it asserts its existence. Instead of formulating a definition, the Commission applied the above characteristics to Bengalis to contemplate whether they constitute a people. The term *people* also lies at the core of self-determination cases brought before courts. Despite the lack of a legally accepted definition of the term, courts have enumerated relatively similar objective and subjective characteristics for a definition or description of peoples.

The ICJ in the *Western Sahara Case* refrained from identifying the Sahrawis as a people, although the peoples of the territory had a right to self-determination. Instead, it used terms such as 'the tribal groups'[63] and 'the peoples of Western Sahara,'[64] and 'nomadic tribes'[65] to refer to them. The Canadian Supreme Court in *Re Secession of Quebec* (1998) judged the precise meaning of people 'uncertain'; however, it held that '"a people" may include only a portion of the population of an existing state.' To the Court, the juxtaposition of 'nation' and 'state' indicates that a people 'does not necessarily mean the entirety of a state's population.'[66] The Court concluded that the characteristics of a common language and culture were determinative in defining a specific assemblage as a people.[67]

Kevin Mgwanga Gunme vs Cameroon (2009) is not the only case in which the Southern Cameroonians were recognised as a people and, consequently, were entitled to the collective right of self-determination. According to the ACHPR, a people is bound 'together by their historical, traditional, racial, ethnic, cultural, linguistic, religious, ideological, geographical, economic identities and affinities, or other bonds.' The commission contemplated numerous characteristics and affinities, including 'common history, linguistic tradition, territorial connection and political outlook' as the objective features that qualified the Southern Cameroonians as people 'with a separate and distinct identity.' It considered identity as 'an innate characteristic within a people.'[68] The commission referred to the same stance in *Sudan*

62 The Events in East Pakistan, 1971: A Legal Study by the Secretariat of The International Commission of Jurists (1972) 70.
63 *Western Sahara* (n 41) 50, [133].
64 ibid [152].
65 ibid [159].
66 *Reference re Secession of Quebec* [1998] 2 SCR 217, [124]–[125].
67 ibid [125].
68 *Kevin Mgwanga Gunme et al. v. Cameroon*, Communication No 266/2003 (2009) 171, 179.

Human Rights Organisation and Centre of Housing Evictions and Human Rights (COHRE) versus Sudan (2009). It enumerates the 'language, religion, culture, the territory,' within a state with 'common history, [and] ethno-anthropological factors' for defining 'a people' that 'might be a majority or a minority in a particular State.' In the context of states with mixed racial composition, to the commission, race turns out to be 'a determinant of groups of "peoples", just as ethnic identity can also be a factor.'[69] The commission finds that the people of Darfur in their collective are a people as described under Article 19 of the African Charter.[70] Also, in the *Endorois Case* (2009), the commission concluded that the Endorois in Kenya are a people based on the subjective criteria of self-identified distinctiveness and the objective criteria of 'a common history, culture and religion.'[71] Therefore, they can benefit from collective rights according to the African Charter.

The ICJ, in its *advisory opinion* on Kosovo (2010), did not define the term *people*. It simply addresses the population of Kosovo as *Kosovars* or *Kosovo*. Judge Cançado Trindade's separate opinion, however, enumerated certain signifiers for defining peoples, such as 'traditions and culture, ethnicity, historical ties and heritage, language, religion, sense of identity or kinship, the will to constitute a people,' and proposed that the 'common suffering' of these people 'creates a strong sense of identity.'[72] He confirmed this definition by referring to a phrase from the 2001 Constitutional Framework of UN Mission in Kosovo (UNMIK)that alluded to the Kosovars as a people with 'unique historical, legal, cultural and linguistic attributes.'[73] But, it is worth noting that the phrase 'people of Kosovo' was only mentioned in the constituent instruments of both the UNMIK and the NATO-led Kosovo Force (KFOR).

According to the ICJ in the *Western Sahara* case and the Supreme Court of Canada in the case of Quebec, the considering[74] and the 'characterizing'[75] of a community or an ethnic group as a people are central to self-determination. Therefore, the meaning of the concept is critical to understanding and exercising self-determination, as a people is the only entity entitled to that right as well as nations; nonetheless, there is no generally accepted legal definition for a people or features thereof. It is, however, present in legal texts, and any unit or population can stake out its claim as a people. The term still needs clarification, and its characterisation will be helpful.

69 *Sudan Human Rights Organisation and Centre of Housing Evictions and Human Rights v. Sudan*, African Commission on Human and Peoples' Rights, Communication No 279/03-296/05, Recommendations (27 May 2009) 220.

70 ibid 223.

71 *Centre for Minority Rights Development (Kenya) and Minority Rights Group International on behalf of Endorois Welfare Council v. Kenya*, Communication No 276/2003 (2009) 162.

72 *Kosovo (Advisory Opinion) (Separate Opinion of Judge Cançado Trindade)* [2010] ICJ Rep, [228]–[229].

73 ibid [229].

74 *Western Sahara* (n 41) [59].

75 *Quebec* (n 66) 437, [123].

3.3.3 The Characterisation of Candidates for Self-Determination

There is no universally accepted formula for constructing a people; however, national ties and the legal axioms of territorial integrity, state sovereignty, and *uti possidetis* — the formal characteristics of defining a people — could be useful in identifying a group as a people.[76] Various national ties encompass government of the past,[77] history, identity, language, race, religion, politics, and territory. The reading of the legal tenets referred to could be used to profess and frame self-determination as legitimate, as there is a close association between the principles as mentioned earlier and national ties, i.e., territorial integrity with the territory, state sovereignty with politics.[78]

There are four levels of identifying a people. First, national ties have a functional role in uniting a community, such as the same language and religion. Second, substantive definitional characteristics (subjective and objective)[79] should be national, not symbolic, because religion cannot be an issue in peoplehood, or a people can select different languages to communicate with one another, or different peoples can utilise the same language. For example, Kurds can utilise Kurdish, Farsi, or Arabic, or both Kurds and Arabs can speak Arabic. Kurds speak Arabic, Farsi, or Turkish depending on where they live. In addition, the population of a state may not have a sentiment of peoplehood. Third, a people does have a legitimate right to determine its political status, which makes the identification of people a political topic. Individual members of a people would have different interpretations of nation and self-determination. Therefore, defining a people based on a specific factor specifies the establishment of self-determination. Finally, legal principles can realise national ties, as they are intricately connected; however, a different hierarchy of national ties could beget a clash of principles such as self-determination against territorial integrity.[80]

Specifying characteristics of a people is possible but vague and would be hardly adequate. Through the integration of normative elements into the term, a people is a cohesive and distinct community in terms of 'descent, language, religion, culture, history, and others.' This unit's cohesiveness and distinctness should be sufficiently significant to attain the right of self-determination.[81]

Brownlie (1985) considered a people as having a distinct character that is mirrored in their governmental institutions. He also enumerates a conflation of relevant criteria for being distinct: race or nationality is one of the criteria tested in scientific studies in which 'culture, language, religion and group psychology' can be determined. Also, the physical appearance of any race can indicate cultural distinctiveness, although this is not necessarily valid. However, the purely ethnic criterion would rule out other established national identities, such as those of the United States.[82]

76 Fisch (n 36) 35.
77 Lord Avebury, 'Self-Determination and International Law: The Kurdish Case' (1994) 7 IJKS 7, 16.
78 Summers (n 34) 89–90.
79 Fisch (n 36) 35.
80 Summers (n 34) 91–93.
81 Makinson, quoted in Crawford (n 41) 75.
82 Ian Brownlie, 'The Rights of Peoples in Modern International Law' (1985) 9 BASLP 104, 108.

There are three approaches to understanding the term: ethnic, territorial, and political.[83] The ethnic approach, referring to ties, is found in reference dictionaries: the word *people* denotes 'human beings making up a group or assembly or linked by a common interest and the mass of a community as distinguished from a special class.' Also, the term *people* means 'a body of persons that are united by a common culture, tradition, or sense of kinship, that typically have common language, institutions, and beliefs, and that often constitute a politically organized group' (*Merriam-Webster Dictionary*). *Oxford Advanced Learner's Dictionary* presents 'all the persons who live in a particular place or belong to a particular country, race, etc.' as a meaning for a people. Geographical dimensions are considered in the territorial approach, which makes it less inclusive when compared with the ethnic conception of the term. The political approach refers to '[t]he whole body of citizens of a country, regarded as the source of political power or as the basis of society.'[84] Legally, people are humans with national characteristics that are not limited. However, this is, 'significantly narrower' than its common use.[85] Defining *people* legally would simplify the difference between its legal and common usages.

3.3.4 Definition

The conceptualisation of the concept of a people, with many different aspects to the task, is difficult and complex. It is also problematic for many independent states where it may lead to raising the clamour for self-determination by specific groups, their outright secession, and the subsequent spectre of territorial impairment. Despite various proposals, including 'large compact national groups,' 'ethnic, religious or linguistic minorities,' and 'racial units inhabiting well-defined territories,'[86] the definition of people for the purposes of the ICCPR and the ICESCR remained unnecessary. It was also off the table advisedly in drafting the ACHPR.[87] There is, nonetheless, some consensus on recognising some groups as peoples, while some have not been supported for potential peoplehood such as the Basques and Catalonians in Spain, Kashmiris between Pakistan and India, Chechens in the Russian Federation, communities of Transnistria, Nagorno-Karabakh, South Ossetia, and Abkhazia. Recent cases have politicised the conceptual interpretation of peoples.[88] These communities are understood as 'minorities' ineligible for self-determination.

83 Hofbauer (n 25) 2.
84 Oxford English Dictionary Online.
85 Summers (n 34) 7.
86 Marc J. Bossuyt, *Guide to the Travaux Préparatoires of the International Covenant on Civil and Political Rights* (MNP 1987) 32.
87 Crawford (n 61) 125.
88 Joshua Castellino, 'International Law and Self-Determination Peoples, Indigenous Peoples, and Minorities' in Christian Walter, Antje von Ungern-Sternberg, and Kavus Abushov (eds), *Self-Determination and Secession in International Law* (OUP 2014) 33.

To achieve a conclusive definition for international law is not an easy task, due to the varying purposes, as well as the interests, of those claiming to constitute a people. The difficulty is also due to the historical development and application of peoples in legal instruments and documents, both as a generic term and as a legal term. For example, it was used in both the Preamble of the Covenant of the League of Nations[89] and its Mandate System (Article 22).[90] The territorial approach was used in the Mandate System for colonies and territories. Additionally, an ethnic element is involved in the utility of the term *peoples* in the UN Charter and the 1966 International Human Rights Covenants.[91] The Charter also refers to peoples in its Preamble (the populations of the Member States as political fictions) and its discussion of the purposes (Article 1(2)).

Having a definition is crucial in implementing the right to self-determination. Regarding the definition of the term, two issues should be considered. First, those groupings claiming to qualify as people should have an absolute majority connected to an acceptable extent throughout their territory. Second, if there are two collectives in a particular territory, the one wishing to form a people has priority over the other, even if the latter is in the majority. Then it would be *ipso facto* a people dominating the state — i.e., a self-determined nation. Therefore, the destiny of territories is decided by the wishes of those affected.[92] The common article of the Covenants confirms this because it does not designate the self-determining peoples,[93] and some collectives may consider or form themselves as a people at some other time.

The lack of an authoritative definition of a people is an issue; however, it is feasible to provide an outline of the common significance of a people and of potential definitional criteria and steps. The definition of peoples has been decided on a case-by-case basis, as there is no general definition of the term. This allows different cases to be classified and measured differently. There are, however, certain commonly used definitions in some cases where self-determination was exercised, with various examples of criteria and procedures. In most cases, a people is constituted or formed on the underpinning of a common language, territory, economic life, and a common culture. With a mélange of ethnicity and culture, these features refer to a whole series of substantive definitional characteristics shared by individual members of a people. These elements are part of the criteria for identifying groupings as peoples. Since the twentieth century, these criteria have been applied for designating inhabitants of territories as peoples in self-determination settings. The criteria are formal or legal, remedial and substantive.

89 '[B]y the maintenance of justice and a scrupulous respect for all treaty obligations in the dealings of organised peoples with one another.'

90 'The character of the mandate must differ according to the stage of the development of the *people*, the geographical situation of the territory, its economic conditions and other similar circumstances.'

91 Hofbauer (n 25) 21.

92 Fisch (n 36) 12–13.

93 ibid 33–34.

3.3.5 Criteria for Definition of a People

3.3.5.1 Formal or Legal Criteria (Uti Possidetis)

The formal or legal element of any definition of people is *uti possidetis*. This principle stipulates that the frontiers remain the same but, in practice, define a people geographically; groups are designated as peoples by administrative boundaries set by the imperial powers during the colonisation era or before the separate disintegrating crises of the Soviet Union and Yugoslavia. A majoritarian and territorial or whole people formula was applied in these contexts, i.e., entire populations within these borders as a whole were designated as peoples, but individual sub-groups were not granted that status. Subsequently, the borders became the international boundaries of their independent states.[94] In other words, the self-determination units (colonies) were coterminous with the established imperial administrative boundaries but not necessarily with ethnically defined national units. Thus, *uti possidetis* serves as a definitional feature of a people.

Colonies are 'a legal artefact.'[95] A people, in the colonial realm, is not defined and predicated on ethnic or national signifiers because colonial inhabitants were of different tribes that did not necessarily have a common ethnicity, religion, or language. Thus, they were 'neither *demos* nor *ethnos* in origin.'[96] Rather, it is 'a collective awareness' of domination or subjugation, 'the wrong' by the colonial power itself, 'resistance to colonialism,' and the collective will of inhabitants to determine the status of the territory[97] that make them a self-determination unit in order to alter the territory's external status. The wrongs perpetrated against them are the violation of human rights; racial, linguistic, and religious discrimination; oppression, and exploitation.[98] Plebiscites showing a tendency to legitimise the break-up of a territory have not generally been allowed, except when the majority of the territory's inhabitants desired it.[99] In the case of the Western Sahara, the ICJ accepted that in some situations the UNGA had waived the obligation to consult the inhabitants of a particular territory, either because they did not constitute a people entitled to self-determination or because the requirement was 'totally unnecessary' in the light of specific conditions. The formal criteria, thus, disadvantage ethnic or national groups within the sovereign states.

3.3.5.2 Remedial Criteria

Categorising some groups as minorities deterred distinct ethnic units within nation-states from claiming a right to self-determination in the form of secession. Despite this, many ethnic groups do categorise themselves as a people and invoke the right

94 Fisch (n 36) 34–35.
95 Karen Knop, *Diversity and Self-Determination in International Law* (CUP 2002) 62.
96 ibid 55.
97 Charles Chaumont, quoted in ibid 55–57.
98 Karl Doehring, quoted in ibid 57.
99 Crawford (n 61) 620.

of self-determination. Insofar as the various definitions of a minority are similar, to a large extent, to nation or nationality, ethnic groups may claim to be peoples by means of the theory of the 'right of reversion.' This deals with the affinity of a minority to a people. Through this relationship, the status of people is granted to a minority to allow them to exercise a right to external self-determination — if the minority is not treated well or oppressed by its host state.[100] This right is stipulated in Paragraph 7 of UNGA Resolution 2625(XXV).

In remedial secession, peoplehood is not essential, but it is the injustice that is the bedrock by which a people is defined politically, not organically.[101] This can be called *injustice* or *remedial* peoplehood. Although this criterion is related to non-colonial contexts, it is similar to the formal criteria if injustice is considered as the wrong mentioned above. The ACHPR follows the remedial approach of peoplehood, which has identified a distinct community as a people when it is a victim of the violation of human rights. In other non-colonial contexts, a people might be defined by substantive criteria.

3.3.5.3 Substantive Criteria (National Ties)

In the context of external (non-colonial) self-determination, the positive concept of the people as an aggregate of humans who are linked by specific factors is emphasised.[102] As a natural unit, a people is tied by a particular language, culture, race, religion, and history.[103] It is alluded to as a *demos* and *ethnos* approach.[104] These are ethno-anthropological attributes or substantive definitional signifiers (substantive criteria), which refer to a whole series of subjective and objective characteristics, strengthening the ties binding the individuals of a people.[105] These components are part of the social construction of a people. However, these factual attributes are not sufficient when determining the existence of a people to accord them the enjoyment of the right to self-determination.

3.3.5.3.1 SUBJECTIVE ELEMENTS

The subjective criterion of a people is self-identified distinctiveness, being the will of individuals wishing to belong to a distinct people. To be consonant with self-determination, the wish should be primarily expressed through informed and democratic processes or in a free plebiscite based on full awareness of the choices available.[106] It should not be based on arbitrary desires, and it is not to be imposed by an external force.

100 Musgrave (n 3) 167–171.
101 Mégret in Tesón (n 35) 52.
102 Fisch (n 36) 34.
103 Carlile A. Macartney, *National States and National Minorities* (OUP 1934) 97.
104 Knop (n 95) 57.
105 Fisch (n 36) 34–35.
106 ibid 35–37.

A people perceives itself through a conscious feeling of unity that can be envisaged in diverse identities of ethnicity, language, and religion. It may sometimes coalesce into a national identity or sentiment, but it does not necessarily lead to a wish for self-determination. Other national institutional ties are politically and legally shared, such as the administration, the army, the legal system, parliament, schools, citizenship, traditions, and constitutional rights. These ties have a determinative role in enhancing the national consciousness of peoples or a sense of nationality. The United Kingdom, Canada, and the United States are a few political nations in which a common language, religion, or race unites them, although the population consists of different groups. These states were not defined ethnically, linguistically or on the basis of a shared religion or race as in Croatia and now North Macedonia. This is problematic for North Macedonia as a large Albanian-speaking Muslim population is left out of this formula. Therefore, politicians exert a decisive role in appealing to self-determination, as they could show themselves as representatives of all the whole people of a unit. Politicians of national liberation movements, holding positions in the colonial states, played a prominent role in the self-determination of colonies. Also, this is the case in aspiring to self-determination by politicians of Eastern Europe and the Soviet Union's constituent republics, in which newly created states had their own parliaments, administrations, and flags.[107] Therefore, political ties are incipient in promoting nationality, and the subsequent identification of people as members of political units is decisive in the ultimate status of a people.[108] Strictly national ties or expressions of nationality can take various forms.

3.3.5.3.2 OBJECTIVE ELEMENTS

The various communities claiming their status of peoplehood in the context of self-determination evince common objective elements of history, ethnicity, culture, or language, which give them a distinct character, along with a subjective element of self-identification. They also seek to achieve a common objective of independence or autonomy.[109]

3.3.5.3.2.1 Language

Linguistic homogeneity among group members is one of the mechanisms that contribute to nation-building, that is, language is one of the most *sine qua non* national ties in ethnic-national self-determination. It is more easily recognisable than other characteristics of peoplehood, as this characteristic can be patently established. Language is pressed into service to identify a people appealing for self-determination and in seeking to determine its political boundaries. That is, it has had a pivotal

107 Summers (n 34) 94–100.
108 ibid 104.
109 Hofbauer (n 25) 31.

role in those positing national identity while pursuing their political status.[110] After WWI, a number of states in Central and Eastern Europe were created based on nationality and language. Linguistic ties not only were used to identify peoples or to define a people claiming the right of self-determination, but also to devise political boundaries on the basis of nationality. But defining peoplehood based solely on language does not offer a clear understanding of complicated situations. This is the case with other substantive signifiers. Language, later on and at the time of new state creation in Eastern Europe, was in second place of importance because it was the republics themselves that actualised self-determination. Nevertheless, it was a primary consideration for some, e.g., Estonians and Slovaks. Linguistic ties played a less appreciable role for the peoples of Asian and African colonies; their self-determination was predominantly racial. However, seceding entities in Africa and Asia have enlisted language as a primary feature of their new claims to independent status.[111]

If self-determination is exercised against the background of other principles, such as territorial integrity or the unassailability of frontiers, language would be an issue. However, in cases where a language defines a distinct people, and a country is subsequently identified or created based on that language, there would be no dissonance between self-determination and territorial integrity. In Eastern Europe of the 1990s, on the other hand, self-determination was, nonetheless, implemented within or in the light of the principle of *uti possidetis*, although some linguistic groups straddled new borderlines or were already living within entrenched borders.[112]

A common language can be spoken by different nations, as is the case in Belgium, Benin, Burkina Faso, Cameroon, Switzerland, etc. Conversely, different languages can flourish in a single nation, as do English and French in Canada. Nonetheless, language as a national tie can unite or divide peoples and can be employed as a political tool to enhance nationalism, as in Turkey. Linguistic minorities within states can also endanger political unity, which is why some states impose a single language or a neutral language, but this can create a situation conducive to ethnic conflicts and consequent breakaway attempts, as in the secession of Bangladesh (1971) from Pakistan and Eritrea from Ethiopia (1993).[113] Religion is another recognisable signifier of peoplehood.

3.3.5.3.2.2 Religion

Self-determination may be staked out by religious minorities who use religion as an identifier of their ethnicity. Also, religion is used by a people or a country to justify their self-determination or to define their political borders. Religious ties have been

110 Sarah D. Shields, *Fezzes in the River: Identity Politics and European Diplomacy in the Middle East on the Eve of World War II* (OUP 2011) 8.

111 Summers (n 34) 106.

112 ibid 107.

113 ibid 106–109.

utilised to create states, such as India, Pakistan, Bosnia Herzegovina, Serbia, and Croatia, or to define political borders, such as Israel. Religion can establish political institutions, the pantheon, mosques, or churches, to consolidate national identities and promote shared values, language, and the aspiration to promote national ties or identities. South Sudan is a good example in which the Christian church defined a Sudanese people, feeling drawn to Christianity, as a national unit. Despite being a key element in nationalism, few religious groups have achieved their objective of creating their own state, as Israel and Pakistan have done. On the contrary, as in Flanders, religion has on occasion countered the development of a nationalist movement.[114] Ethnicity can play a decisive role in such situations.

3.3.5.3.2.3 Ethnicity

Historically, ethnicity has been a decisive factor in defining peoples and ethnic minorities with a shared past and legacy. They may be eligible for self-determination, but their actions may be discriminatory. French nationals with Latin origins and Bulgarian citizens with Turkic origins are a few examples. Anybody can change their language or religion, but ancestry is everlasting. It constantly displays its 'exclusionary nature' and is the most exclusive of national ties. Descent and ethnicity played decisive roles in establishing anti-colonial self-determination (nationalism) of colonial populations in Asia and Africa, and non-white individuals or nationalists (e.g., a black identity). Yet self-determination had not been hedged to 'race' in the Colonial Independence and Friendly Relations declarations. The inhabitants of colonies that have implemented colonial self-determination have usually been politically defined as peoples, but they have a racial component as well: the freeing of non-white populations from arbitrary white rule and racist regimes. In international law, their right of self-determination (independence and freedom) has been practised without 'any distinction as to race, creed or colour' (the principle of non-discrimination).[115] Racial and ethnic discrimination has certainly been a key factor in the secessionist movements of South Sudan and Bangladesh.[116] As such, ethnicity can be instrumental in identifying peoples in multiracial states, strengthened by their territory.

3.3.5.3.2.4 Motherland

Every people or nation is naturally connected to a specific territory and, thus, claims historical ownership over it. This possession is rooted in the values, real or abstract in any form, that a nation appends to the territory.[117] Thus, a people and

114 ibid 110–111.

115 UNGA Res 1514(XV) (14 December 1960).

116 Summers (n 34) 112–115. For ethnicity and nationhood, see Rogers Brubaker, *Ethnicity without Groups* (HUP 2004) and Siniša Malešević, *Identity as Ideology: Understanding Ethnicity and Nationalism* (Palgrave MacMillan 2006).

117 David Miller, 'Territorial Rights: Concept and Justification' (2012) 60(2) PS 252, 262.

territory are interdependent and embody each other.[118] A territory or motherland, with its history, inhabitants, culture, resources, fauna and flora, environment, and geographical features, defines a nation. Territory acts as a concrete manifestation of history and race. Although the territory is a national symbol for a nation — attributing a national value to a non-human element — its natural configuration or boundaries, including rivers and mountains, can connect peoples on both sides rather than separate them. Also, a river can connect peoples of two states. However, states are geographically insulated to apply their sovereignty. Some states have also been delimited by geographical features, such as rocks, rivers, and seas. For both the political (statehood) and economic exercise of self-determination, the land and its 'natural wealth and resources' (Article 1(2) of the Human Rights Covenants) are striking characteristics that frequently have national implications.[119]

Territory is a key component in the ideas of state and country. All three together make up the fabric of the principle of territorial integrity. It has, likewise, been critical in self-determination, as established territorial units of colonies, sovereign states, or federal bodies have typically exercised the right. The territorial dimension is further strengthened by the fact that self-determination is usually balanced by territorial integrity and *uti possidetis*. Thus, the nation-territory link constitutes a reality, with a shared history.

3.3.5.3.2.5 History

Although the past is objectively unchangeable, history, as an account of the past, is subject to change. It is, however, quite capable of being a changing criterion and may comprise different groups, contingent upon changing circumstances. Some states base their claim on a long connection to a territory that is called a historical title. Azerbaijan and Armenia had a claim to control Nagorno-Karabakh in order to restore their territoriality. Their competing claims to Nagorno-Karabakh, submitted to the UN Human Rights Committee (UNHRC), were constituted on foundations of history.[120] Azerbaijan, with an agreement brokered by Russia excluding European and UN involvement, gained control of a substantial part of the region through a full-fledged 44-day war in 2020, supported by Turkey. On 19 September 2023, Azerbaijan regained control over the entire self-proclaimed Nagorno-Karabakh Republic, following a prolonged blockade and a one-day shelling by Azerbaijani forces, as observed by Russian peacekeepers. This event triggered a mass exodus, with 90% of the ethnic Armenians leaving the region and fleeing to Armenia, marking a significant episode of ethnic cleansing. It is possible that there will be no Armenians left in Nagorno-Karabakh. On 21 September, the government of the

118 Margaret Moore, 'Which People and What Land? Territorial Rights-Holders and Attachment to Territory' (2014) 6(1) International Theory 121, 124.

119 Summers (n 34) 116–120.

120 *Armenia* (1998) CCPR/C/92/Add.2, 6 [21] and the Fifty-fifth Session of the Commission on Human Rights (E/CN.4/1999/123) 2.

'Republic of Artsakh' signed a decree dissolving its rule by 1 January 2024, effectively ending its independence project.[121] Morocco and Mauritania both claimed Western Sahara based on a historical connection. Even nations in the process of creating states rely on the past and cite historical ties to legitimise their distinctive character, add depth to nationalism, and bolster their argument for self-determination. African states, as entities of colonialism, changed the name of their countries and peoples after independence to their past names or to the names of medieval empires. Ghana, previously known as the Gold Coast, is an example. History also added its weight to the burgeoning contributions of language and culture.[122]

The relationship between historical title and self-determination is not well defined, although Paragraph 6 of Resolution 1514(XV) is the legal basis for claims based on historical title: '[a]ny attempt aimed at the partial or total disruption of the national unity and the territorial integrity of a country is incompatible with the purposes and principles of the Charter of the United Nations.' It is not clear whether historical title takes precedence over self-determination or vice versa. The inconsistency in the UNGA's practice underlines this uncertainty. Paragraph 6 applies to situations in the territorial integrity of a state, which has been disrupted by colonisation, so that a return of the territory in question simply restores the state to its original condition. However, territorial claims based on historical ties favour the principle of territorial integrity over self-determination. The issue of historical title arises whenever a state claims territory that belonged to it in the past. In that case, it should be returned to the *status quo ante* to restore the territorial integrity of the claimant state. The territory claimed in such cases must revert to the claimant state without the inhabitants of that territory being permitted to determine their political status.[123] History is also a key component in the rights of indigenous peoples, e.g., the Inuit in Greenland, to self-determination due to their longer link with a territory compared to that of the rest of the inhabitants.[124]

Historical relations play a complicated function and are significant in deepening national ideas. They are, however, understood according to the needs of a claim to self-determination rather than according to their functional role in forming nations. The right to self-determination is not an especially ancient concept. A considerable proportion of its key thoughts originated in the eighteenth century. During the First World War, the term was invented; the legal principle only originated after the Second World War. In this way, genuine consideration should be practised when deciphering and evaluating history with regard to a modern right.[125] Based on the above national ties, there are different sorts of peoples which makes the definition of the people difficult.

121 For an exhaustive overview of the Nagorno-Karabakh conflict, the historical development of the dispute, and the political and social aspects of it, see M. Hakan Yavuz and Michael Gunter (eds), *The Nagorno-Karabakh Conflict: Historical and Political Perspectives* (Routledge 2022).

122 Summers (n 34) 128.

123 Musgrave (n 3) 151–152.

124 Summers (n 34) 123.

125 ibid 129.

3.3.6 Different Sorts of Peoples

Taking into account national elements, there are seven kinds of peoples based on different national self-determination: ethnic, cultural, socio-political, civic, multisocietal, multiterritorial, and diasporic. Ethnic peoples, e.g., Rohingyas in Myanmar, possess a common sense of ancestry, language, culture, and history, yet they may lack self-governance within states that consist of multiple nationalities, much like some indigenous peoples. Cultural peoples are multiethnic populations with varying ancestral backgrounds that share a similar language, culture, and history, and have no governmental or administrative institutions, such as multiethnic Metis, Western Saharans, Acadians (in Canada), and Rom peoples. Socio-political peoples are characterised by a single language, public institutions, and history, while simultaneously being recognised as multicultural, -national and -ethnic. The Quebecois, Catalonian, and Scottish peoples are a few examples of peoples that reside on non-sovereign administrative territory yet possess their own governmental institutions. A civic people may encompass a diverse population with multiple ethnicities and cultures, *composita*, under a single sovereign state — that is, a community that embodies the concept of 'one people, one language, and one sovereign State': France, Iceland, Portugal, and Korea (the latter albeit divided now) are categorised within this class.[126] More than one language might be spoken in these countries, e.g., indigenous linguistic minorities of Bretons, Basques, and speakers of German (in Alsace) as well as Roma-speaking Romani and the Arabic-speaking minority in France, but minority languages are given no legal recognition.

Multisocietal peoples are those who reside within a sovereign state that comprises different peoples, similar to the United Kingdom, Belgium, Canada, and Spain. A multiterritorial or territorially fragmented people refers to a population that resides in a geographic area that comprises a contiguous territory albeit divided among different sovereign states. These people share the same culture, language, and history. Kurds as well as Mohawks in Akwasasne occupying an area overlapping parts of Ontario, Quebec, and New York state are the best examples of a fragmented people. Finally, a diasporic people is a dispersed population with a shared language, culture, and history that inhabits non-contiguous territories.[127] They are treated as a minority in each of these territories. Roms and the Jewish people would be an example before the creation of Israel in 1948.

There are also minority segments of peoples, commonly referred to as national or ethnic minorities, who may not actively participate in nationalist movements and do not constitute peoples all by themselves. However, they are national groups that share certain cultural and historical characteristics. These groups can be either contiguous diasporas (or kin minorities), such as extensions of adjacent nations

126 The above typology stems from a talk represented in the UK Lectures by Professor Michel Seymour, under the title of 'Peoples, Self-Determination and Secession' (ASEN Seminars, London, 23 February 2012). Professor Seymour presented an extensive version of the talk, 'Secession as a Remedial Right,' at the Universitat Girona in June 2019.

127 ibid. Also see Michel Seymour, *A Liberal Theory of Collective Rights* (MQUP 2017) 15, 228.

such as the Russian minorities in the Baltic States, Palestinian minority in Israel, Basque and Catalan minorities in France, the South Tyrolian minority in Italy, or the Croatians and Serbs in Bosnia and Herzegovina; or non-contiguous diasporas, such as immigrant populations who identify with home states. Although these groups may not identify themselves as a distinct people, they may still have entitlement to certain rights. It is obvious that two versions of peoples, territorial and ethnic, are endowed with the right to self-determination.

The various types of peoples (and minority fragments of peoples) are considered ideal types in Max Weber's sense or as Anthony D. Smith refers to them. This means that any real nation may fall halfway between these different ideal types. This is so because these different sorts of peoples may share similar objective criteria such as language, culture, institutions, history, and territory (sometimes also religion). The other reason is that the concept of people also has subjective features such as self-representation (directed toward the past), the collective will to survive as a group and the actual determination of what they want to be (a formal or informal constitution directed toward the future). Within the population, there may be different ways of representing themselves in the past and different ways of asserting what they want to be in the future. Therefore, the category to which a group belongs largely depends on the presence of a majority that shares the same self-representation and assertive characteristics.

3.4 Peoples as Self-Determination Units

Three distinct groups stake out a claim to the right of self-determination because of the self-determination entitlement: peoples or nations, indigenous peoples, and minorities. The third group was the ethnic minorities that created new states after WWI.[128] This unit was adapted from the *Greco-Bulgarian Communities* judgement mentioned above. The Contracting States to the UN Covenants, according to Article 1, are obliged to vest self-determination in peoples. Acknowledging the right of self-determination does not depend upon the political status of a territory. Who then are the beneficiaries of this right? Perusing the preparatory works and dwelling on the provisions of the Covenants, one may conclude that the right is applied to the following categories of peoples.

3.4.1 Peoples of Colonies and Dependent Territories

Inhabitants of non-self-governing and trust territories under Chapters XI and XII of the Charter of the UN, and mandate territories under Article 22 of the Compact of Nations 1919 of the League of Nations, fall into this category. Article 1(3) of both Human Rights Covenants conceded the right of self-determination to non-self-governing and trust territories; this entails the right to create a state or to associate with an independent sovereign state. This outdated provision makes administrating state

128 Karl Doehring, 'Self-Determination,' quoted in Knop (n 95) 63–64.

parties responsible for the realisation of the right of self-determination. Chapters XI and XII of the UN Charter do not make use of self-determination, although Article 76 refers to 'independence' as one of the objectives of the trusteeship system. Article 1(3) of the Covenants gives teeth to the Charter regarding dependent territories.[129]

The underlying principle has been successfully applied to the colonial peoples of the sacred trust and to non-self-governing and mandate territories.[130] Aside from Article 73 of the Charter, the ICJ recognised the right of colonial self-determination in the *Namibia Opinion* (1971),[131] Kosovo (*Advisory Opinion*),[132] and in the East Timor (*Portugal v. Australia*) judgement as a right corresponding to an obligation *erga omnes*.[133] Currently, there is no colonial or trusted territory, as all of them have achieved self-determination; however, 17 non-self-governing territories expect to attain it.[134]

In the phase of colonial collective self-determination, inhabitants of non-self-governing, trust, or mandate territories are tantamount to a people, even if there are different ethnic groups within a given territory.[135] This territorial or *uti possidetis* approach to defining a people (one colony, one people) contradicts 'a territory and its peoples' in Resolution 1541(XV), Principle II. In this context, the inhabitants were regarded as a territorial appurtenance.[136] This has not been the case with some groupings that have been considered a people, or those *ab initio* of decolonisation, which have been partitioned, such as Palestine and the trust territory of British Togoland, British Cameroons,[137] and the Belgian trust territory of Ruanda-Urundi,[138] or have been joined together while exercising self-determination.[139] However, the ICJ rendered self-determination applicable to all non-self-governing territories in Namibia. Nonetheless, Principle 6 of the Colonial Independence Declaration undergirds the territorial integrity of a country. This means that each

129 Cassese (n 23) 58.

130 Summers (n 34) 435.

131 *Namibia (Advisory Opinion)* [1971] ICJ Rep 31, [52]–[53].

132 The ICJ expanded self-determination to the independence of non-self-governing territories. *Kosovo (Advisory Opinion)* [2010] ICJ Rep, [79].

133 *East Timor* (*Portugal v. Australia*) *(Judgement)* [1995] ICJ Rep 102, [29]. Also, see Catriona Drew, 'The East Timor Story: International Law on Trial' (2001) 12(4) EJIL 651 and Iain Scobbie and Catriona Drew, 'Self-Determination Undetermined: The Case of East Timor' (1996) 9(1) LJIL 185.

134 The UN and Decolonization, available at https://www.un.org/dppa/decolonization/en. Non-Self-Governing Territories, available at https://www.un.org/dppa/decolonization/en/nsgt.

135 Margaret Moore, 'Introduction: The Self-Determination Principle and the Ethics of Secession' in Margaret Moore (ed), *National Self-Determination and Secession* (OUP 1998) 3.

136 Christian Tomuschat, 'Secession and Self-Determination' in Marcelo G. Kohen (ed), *Secession: International Law Perspectives* (CUP 2006) 25.

137 See UNGA Res 1352(XIV) (16 October 1959); UNGA Res 1471(XIV) (12 December 1959); UNGA Res 1608(XV) (21 April 1960).

138 UNGA Res 1746(XVI) (27 June 1962).

139 Summers (n 34) 438–439.

colony is 'both a people and a country' and for self-determination, their *status quo* should be preserved.[140]

Consequently, the UN strongly condemned the detachment of the port of Walvis Bay from Namibia in 1977 and its annexation by South Africa.[141] Also, the separation of Mayotte from the Comoros archipelago by France was denounced, and the subsequent referendum was considered null and void.[142] It was the same with Britain's violation of international law in separation of the Chagos Archipelago from Mauritius in 1965.[143] There are some cases in which territorial integrity did not prevail, such as the British non-self-governing territory of the Gilbert and Ellice Islands, in which the Polynesian Ellice islanders (then Tuvalu) separated from the Micronesian Gilbert Islands (then Kiribati) in 1974.[144] The division of Micronesia into the Mariana Islands, the Federated States of Micronesia, the Marshall Islands, and Palau is another instance.[145] The non-self-governing territories of the Falkland Islands (*Islas Malvinas*) and Gibraltar have not been found eligible for the right of self-determination because their inhabitants have been identified as 'population[s]' by the UNGA.[146] Residents of those territories are perceived to be settlers, as reflected in the related resolutions.[147]

Other non-self-governing territories whose inhabitants were identified as peoples, despite being subject to a territorial claim and having acquired independence, are Belize (British Honduras)[148] and Djibouti (French Somaliland).[149] Also, some territories that were designated non-self-governing in the UNGA were forcibly annexed such as Benin (erstwhile Dahomey),[150] Goa, Daman and Diu on India's west coast,[151] and Sikkim. Despite upholding the right of self-determination of East Timor in 1976,[152] it took 25 years for the country to become independent in 2002.[153] The UN recognised the independence of Western Sahara and its peoples' strongly

140 ibid.
141 UNGA Res 32/9D (16 December 1977); UNSC Res 432 (27 July 1978).
142 UNGA Res 31/4 (21 October 1976).
143 UNGA Res 2066(XX) (16 December 1965).
144 UNGA Res 3288(XXIX) (13 December 1974); UNGA Res 3426(XXX) (8 December 1975).
145 See UNSC Res 683 (22 December 1990) and UNSC Res 956 (10 November 1994).
146 See UNGA Res 2065(XX) (16 December 1965); UNGA Res 2353(XXII) (19 December 1967); UNGA Res 31/49 (1 December 1976); UNGA Res 37/9 (4 November 1982); UNGA Res 39/6 (6 November 1984); UNGA Res 2231(XXI) (20 December 1966).
147 Summers (n 34) 441.
148 See UNGA Res 3432(XXX) (8 December 1975); 30 GAOR (5 December 1975) 4th Committee, 2173rd mtg., (A/C.3/SR.2173), [57]. UNGA Res 31/50 (1 December 1976); UNGA Res 32/32 (28 November 1977); UNGA Res 33/36 (13 December 1978); UNGA Res 34/38 (21 November 1979); UNGA Res 35/20 (11 November 1980).
149 See UNGA Res 3480(XXX) (11 December 1975).
150 UNGA Res 1542(XV) (15 December 1960).
151 UNGA Res 1542(XV) (15 December 1960).
152 UNSC Res 384 (22 December 1975) and UNSC Res 389 (22 April 1976).
153 UNSC Res 1272 (25 October 1999).

advocated self-determination;[154] however, the right has not been exercised thus far due to the dispute between Morocco and the Polisario Front of the Sahrawis.[155]

As regards external self-determination, the meaning of the term *peoples* has become quite clear in the decolonisation process. Generally, the notion of peoples is associated with territory in UN instruments and resolutions. The titles assigned to them suggest this, e.g., trust- and non-self-governing *territories*. Even in the title of the Declaration on the Granting of Independence to Colonial Countries and Peoples, the term *countries* precedes *peoples*. Also, the notion of territory is overemphasised in the principles adopted by the UNGA, to guide Members in determining whether an obligation exists to transmit the information called for under Article 73-e of the Charter (Transmission of Information Principles). Despite alluding to peoples and their right to self-determination, the ICJ based its verdicts on the historical existence of colonial territories. Geographical distinctness is an objective element in this context. Ethnical or cultural distinctness from the country administering the colonial territories (Principle IV, Transmission of Information Principles) has played a marginal role. Other factors have also not been duly heeded.[156] The *uti possidetis* principle has played a decisive role in drawing decolonised borders and in defining colonial peoples. In the decolonisation process, peoples were identified with territories. Despite this, the inhabitants of tiny enclaves were not commonly recognised as peoples, and their territories have been governed as enclave entities, as in the cases of Hong Kong and Macau (China), Goa (India), and Ifni (Morocco). Peoples within sovereign states stand in a different situation.

3.4.2 Peoples of Independent Sovereign States

As per the preparatory works on drafting Article 1, self-determination for peoples in sovereign states means liberation from an 'authoritarian regime' and the adoption of 'representative institutions' through holding elections and plebiscites; this was proposed by the Western States such as Denmark, Greece, New Zealand, the United Kingdom, and the United States, and buttressed by some developing countries, such as India, Pakistan, Lebanon, Syria, and Egypt.[157] The term *peoples* has not been limited to colonial situations, as the UNGA recognised many non-colonial peoples and their right to self-determination, including South Africans.

The term *people* in this context amounts to the aggregate of the different peoples or all persons within the boundaries of a state. A legal right to democratic government for peoples within sovereign states has been stipulated in the Friendly Relations Declaration (Paragraph 7), Article 21(3) of the UDHR (1948),

154 UNGA Res 3458(XXX) A and B (10 December 1975); UNGA Res 34/37 (21 November 1979) and UNSC Res 621 (20 September 1988).

155 See Report of the Secretary-General on the Situation Concerning Western Sahara, S/2007/202 (19 October 2007) and Report of the Secretary-General on the Situation Concerning Western Sahara, S/2012/197 (5 April 2012).

156 Gudmundur Alfredsson, *Peoples*, (MPEPIL updated 2007) [7].

157 Cassese (n 23) 59–60.

the Organization of American States in its Santiago Commitment to Democracy and the Renewal of the Inter-American System (June 1991), and the European Convention on Human Rights (ECHR, Article 3, Protocol I 1952). In this setting, self-determination and representative democracy are connected, and the expression of the right is guaranteed through free elections at specified intervals and by affirmation of the right to take part in public affairs and to vote and to be elected, as referred to in the ICCPR (Article 1 alongside Article 25). In a representative government, 'the people' means the entire population of political entity. This definition is applied to both sovereign states and non-self-governing territories,[158] which is reflected in the Helsinki Declaration 1975 (Principle VIII). The right to a democratic government was bolstered in the comments of states made during the preparatory works and before the UNHRC. However, this is not a universal right. Although Article 25 ICCPR is about individual rights, its enforcement is via self-determination of peoples under Article 1;[159] Article 1(1) ICCPR links with Article 25 ICCPR. Any form of self-determination practised by this category of peoples is restricted to the external borders of their state; that is, the existing boundaries of the respective state remain unaffected. Self-determination is also asserted by minorities and indigenous peoples.

3.4.3 Indigenous Peoples, Minorities, and Other Communities of a State

International law has not vindicated the existence of distinct peoples within states; there is, however, an exception: the ACHPR, which refers to 'colonized or oppressed' peoples, peoples under 'foreign domination' (Article 20(2)), and peoples under 'foreign exploitation' (Article 21(5)). Also, it refers to peoples of states in Article 23(1). Some African states grant a right of self-determination to peoples, minorities, ethnic groups, and indigenous peoples within their territory, i.e., internal self-determination, in their periodic reports. These states include South Africa, composed of multiple cultural and linguistic communities; Nigeria, for the various peoples of the Federation; and Kenya and the Democratic Republic of Congo, for their indigenous populations.[160]

State practice indicates, though not conclusively, that certain groups have been recognised as peoples, such as Palestinians and Tibetans. Some of these peoples have been identified by colour, such as the blacks in South Africa.[161] A few constitutions of sovereign states followed the practice of identifying their constituent distinct peoples, nations, and communities within their territories and their right to self-determination. Among these states were the former Czechoslovak Federation (Article 1(2), 1968), which led to its break-up, Yugoslavia (1974), the Soviet Union (Article 70, 1977), Uzbekistan (Article 74, 1992), Russia (preamble and

158 Musgrave (n 3) 151–152.
159 Summers (n 34) 469–470.
160 ibid 371–372.
161 Robert McCorquodale, 'Self-Determination: a Human Rights Approach' (1994) 43(4) ICLQ 857.

Article 5(3) 1993), Bosnia and Herzegovina (Preamble, 1995), Ethiopia (Article 39(5), 1995), South Africa (Article 235, 1996), and the State Union of Serbia and Montenegro (2003). Also, some state agreements have allowed distinct peoples of sovereign parties to agree to activate their right to self-determination, such as the 'Good Friday' Agreement (1998) between Britain and Ireland, the Machakos Protocol (2002) between the Sudanese government and the Sudan People's Liberation Movement, and the Memorandum of Understanding (2005) between the Indonesian government and the Free Aceh Movement.[162] Nonetheless, the characterisation of communities within states, through legislation or in constitutions, does not entitle them to exercise the rights stipulated in international law, although they are entitled to cultural and linguistic rights, minority rights, and rights to self-government and autonomy (Articles 3 and 4 of the Declaration on the Rights of Indigenous Peoples 2007). Article 39(5) of the Ethiopian Constitution presents a definition of 'Nation, Nationality or People' for the purpose of self-determination: 'a group of people who have or share a considerable measure of a common culture or similar customs, mutual intelligibility of language, belief in a shared or related identities, a common psychological make-up, and who inhabit an identifiable, predominantly contiguous territory.' But the war in Tigray (since November 2020) reveals that the government in Addis Ababa is opposed in practice to self-determination for that part of the country. In November 2022, a truce agreement was reached between the Ethiopian government and the Tigray People's Liberation Front. However, hostilities continued.

The UNGA referred to some ethnic minorities as peoples, such as the Ewe tribe of West Africa[163] in its series of resolutions regarding the Chinese invasion of Tibet.[164] It also sanctioned partitions of the non-self-governing territories of British Cameroon and Ruanda-Urundi based on ethnic disparities.[165] This implicitly recognised the entitlement of some ethnic collectives, as peoples, to self-determination,[166] such as the peoples of Palestine[167] and Bangladesh.[168]

Minorities and indigenous populations have been provided with grounds to be designated as peoples and concurrent eligibility to practise the right to external self-determination in the Friendly Relations Declaration (1970) and the Vienna Declaration and Programme of Action adopted by the Vienna World Conference on Human Rights of 25 June 1993. In these instruments, territorial integrity is conditional on certain guarantees; the groups, conditioned to being exposed to severe, systematic, and widespread oppression of human rights and the denial of

162 Summers (n 34) 496–497.
163 UNGA Res 441(V) (2 December 1950).
164 UNGA Res 1353(XIV) (21 October 1959); UNGA Res 1723(XVI) (20 December 1961). It demanded self-determination for the Tibetan people.
165 UNGA Res 1746(XVI) (27 June 1962).
166 Musgrave (n 3) 158.
167 UNGA Res 2672(XXV) (8 December 1970).
168 UNGA Res 3203(XXIX) (17 September 1974).

participation in government or public affairs, are eligible to implement external self-determination. This is not the case with peoples under alien subjugation.

3.4.4 Peoples under Alien Subjugation and Foreign Occupation

It has been recognised that external self-determination applies to inhabitants of colonial territories and collectivities subject to alien subjugation and foreign occupation. These terms, which were spelt out in the UNGA Resolution 2625(XXV), could be ambiguous; however, they have been appropriated by the world community. Also, the ILC, in its 1998 Report to the UNGA, agreed on the applicability of self-determination to people under 'colonialism and alien subjugation' and 'other cases' widely.[169] The UNGA has adopted resolutions on military occupation in cases of the Soviet invasion of Hungary,[170] the Chinese occupation of Tibet,[171] the Israeli occupation of Palestinian territories,[172] the Turkish occupation of northern Cyprus,[173] the Indonesian occupation of East Timor,[174] the Vietnamese invasion of Kampuchea,[175] the Soviet invasion of Afghanistan,[176] and the Iraqi invasion of Kuwait.[177] In most of these cases, the UN demanded that its members neither recognise nor legitimatise the situations, such as Israel's control of Jerusalem, the invasion of Kampuchea, and the proclamation of the Turkish Republic of Northern Cyprus. In some cases, the UN could not apply self-determination due to the intricacy of a situation or a veto by one of the permanent members of the Security Council . Moreover, in some situations, the absence of conflicting interests of powers made the application possible, as was the case with Iraq's invasion of Kuwait. Briefly put, alien subjugation and foreign occupation involve the use of force by a dominant power against the people of an occupied territory. Therefore, military occupation is evidence of a violation of self-determination, unless the attack corresponds with the exercise of this right of self-defence under Article 51 of the UN Charter.[178] In this situation, exercising self-determination is to undo the illegal wrongful action inside the previously established boundaries. In other words, no geographical or territorial limit is implied.

169 Report of the ILC on the Work of its Fortieth Session (9 May–29 July 1988), YILC, 1988, vol II (pt Two), [265]–[267].

170 UNGA Res 1127(XI) (21 November 1956) and UNGA Res 1128 (21 November 1956).

171 UNGA Res 2079(XX) (18 December 1965).

172 UNGA Res 2252 (4 July 1967); UNGA Res 2253(ES-V) (4 July 1967); UNGA Res 2254 (14 July 1967); UNGA Res 2256 (21 July 1967); UNGA Res 2257 (18 September 1967) and UNGA Res 2304 (13 December 1967).

173 UNSC Res 353 (20 July 1974).

174 UNGA Res 3485(XXX) (12 December 1975).

175 UNGA Res 34/22 (14 November 1979).

176 UNGA Res ES-6/2 (14 January 1980).

177 UNGA Res 687 (3 April 1991).

178 Cassese (n 23) 98–99.

Both the ICJ in the Kosovo case[179] and the Canadian Supreme Court in *Re Secession of Quebec*[180] recognised the right of peoples under foreign domination or alien subjugation to external self-determination. However, there are no criteria to identify this setting, and such peoples have not been defined. The Friendly Relations and Colonial Independence declarations also reject this form of sovereignty. People of this kind are different from the people of non-self-governing territories. Thus, if a people is not categorised under non-self-governing territories, it can be classified under alien domination.[181] States may also fall into this category if they are occupied. Palestinians are included in this category. Also, in the Definition of Aggression, there is a reference to 'peoples under colonial and racist regimes or other forms of alien domination.' Article 1 of the UN Stockholm Declaration on the Human Environment (1972) unfolded the scope to include 'apartheid, racial segregation, discrimination, colonial and other forms of oppression and foreign domination.'[182] Southern Rhodesia and South Africa are examples of such instances. Other instruments, such as the Additional Protocol I (1977) to the 1949 Geneva Conventions (Article 1(4)), the Vienna Declaration (1993), the UN Fiftieth Anniversary Declaration (1995), and the UN Millennium Declaration (2000)[183] alluded to alien domination or foreign occupation. None of these instruments specifies who those peoples are.

3.5 Summary

The law of self-determination allots all peoples the right to decide their political status. Nonetheless, the practice of the law has been stranded in the designation of collectivities as peoples, rather than how and in what way peoples could settle or decide their political fate by choice of alternatives or possibilities. Indeed, self-determination creates precisely the very problem that it seeks to resolve, e.g., the challenges involved in constituting a collectivity as a people for the purpose of self-determination. The foregoing discussion made some points clear. First, there is no permanent or standard definition for the term *people*. However, it is a definable object. Groups have been designated as peoples differently, depending on the circumstances territorially (spatial delimitation) or ethnically. For example, the inhabitants of a colony were designated as a people due to their shared wish to jettison the colonial power. The cases of the peoples considered indicate that they have not conformed to one single standard or a precise definition but, instead, that they were founded on different definitions contingent on diverse situations. It is national ties and the legal principles of territorial integrity, state sovereignty, and the intangibility of frontiers or *uti possidetis* which define peoples that influence

179 *Kosovo* (n 132).
180 *Quebec* (n 66) [133].
181 Summers (n 34) 469–470.
182 UNCHE (5–16 June 1972).
183 UNGA Res 55/2 (18 September 2000).

statehood. There is also injustice peoplehood; a group subject to a grave violation of human rights is designated as a people. Its exercise of self-determination through remedial secession may then lead to the creation of their state. That is, in the case of remedial secession, there is an alternative way to construct peoplehood that is different from the classical approach (ties, language, religion, culture, etc.).

Second, outsiders have decided who a people are, not the peoples themselves. Third, the common features of definitions are the particular objective and subjective criteria or ethno-anthropological roots applicable to the case under review. The substantive elements of a case have a varying degree of objectivity, with language and religion requiring little effort to distinguish them from other characteristics, especially history. Defining a people using a sole objective criterion is possible, although it may not be valid for all situations. On a fundamental level, a people could be defined utilising any combination of at least two objective criteria. This makes a nearly infinite range of definitions feasible, even within the scope of objective standards. A correct and pervasive definition is unlikely without additional supportive criteria. Even recognised peoples, such as Germans and Swiss, are based on multifarious definitions and standards. The accomplishment of the pertinent endeavour depends on their feasibility, the consideration of all signifiers, and, of course, their harmony with self-determination; that is, the definition should take into account objective characteristics, and the wish to belong to the people (subjective element) should be expressed in a free plebiscite. For the object of self-determination, subjective and objective characteristics have different values; that is, the objective considerations are decisive, and subjective leanings are sufficient.[184] No element should be forced on groups by aliens. Otherwise, this definition is not genuine self-determination. Considering substantive definitional elements is a method resorted to by an entity seeking self-determination whose population is dispersed among two or more different states.

Fourth, no definition for a specific purpose is valid for other cases. Therefore, the decision of which gathering will comprise itself as a people must be made according to the particular circumstances of each case. Fifth, not all peoples are necessarily self-determination units entitled to the external right to self-determination, as there are different sorts of peoples, such as ethnic, cultural, socio-political, civic, multisocietal, territorially fragmented, and diasporic peoples. In the absence of any specific definition, and as far as external self-determination is concerned, trust- and non-self-governing and topographically isolated territories, entities under alien subjugation and foreign occupation, and gravely oppressed minorities and groups are designated as peoples who could benefit from the right of self-determination. The fourth category of peoples is the populations of states. Despite these difficulties, as stated above, no one has refrained from speaking of a right of self-determination of peoples or naming many collectivities as peoples. In conclusion, a people is a social entity or a group of persons having common objective ties with supportive institutions, distinctiveness, and a territorial connection (a geographical link)

184 Fisch (n 36) 35–37.

that generally has a political desire or commonality of interest to achieve autonomy or independence (majority rule) or is 'concerned about its political status.'[185]

Ethno-anthropological affinities may be added to the attributes of a people, but the primary foundation for the definition of peoples is 'territory'; the actualisation of self-determination must not disrupt the political unity, and the territorial framework of existing independent states remains unchallengeable, except where the states or the parties concerned concur in some other way. That is to minimise the impact of the right of self-determination in order to not impair or disrupt the independence of other states and 'stability' of international frontiers.[186] In other words, territory is the foundation of self-determination and a core principle of international law, inasmuch as the UN and regional instruments emphasise it. Thus, many groups, particularly territorially dispersed national groups claiming self-determination, are ignored by the current law of peoples.

Do the Kurds constitute a people or identify themselves as such in the sense of asserting and vindicating a right of self-determination? To which categories of peoples (decolonisation, the territorial conception of peoples, or injustice peoplehood) do they belong? Chapter 5 will deal with these questions. Before that, Chapter 4 looks at the legal history of Kurds and Kurdistan and Kurdish self-determination.

185 Deborah Cass, 'Re-Thinking Self-Determination: A Critical Analysis of Current International Law Theories' (1992) 18(1) SJILC 21.

186 *Frontier Dispute (Burkina Faso v. Republic of Mali)* [1986] ICJ Rep, 567, [25].

4 Kurdistan

The Historical Background of Kurdish Self-Determination

Kurdistan, the land of the Kurds, was partitioned in the twentieth century. Could the Kurds not advance their political status through self-determination? Participation is one of the three ways in which groups are affected by the right of self-determination. It refers to different ways of constructing that take into account groups' views, aside from real engagement in the determination of meaning. The other two are identity and interpretation.[1] To what extent did the Kurds participate in the interpretation and development of the right and the determination of its meaning?

Developments through history as an ethnic community or a coherent nation address the question of why they were unable to build a modern nation-state. Kurdistan is not a recognised sovereign state according to the modern Western nation-state model, although it existed under that name as a provincial division within the Ottoman Empire and now also in Iran. The term *Kurdistan* is used here to refer to Greater Kurdistan, that is, those areas of four sovereign states where Kurds constitute the dominant population. Within Greater Kurdistan, the following terms are used: *Eastern Kurdistan* (in Iran), *Western Kurdistan* (in Syria), *Northern Kurdistan* (in Turkey), *Southern Kurdistan* (in Iraq) (Map 4.1), and *Central Kurdistan* (referring to the connection of the Kurdistani segments, Map 4.2). These terms commonly appeared up to 1926 in British government documents. There is no certainty on whether the intention behind using these terms by the British government officials was arbitrary, deliberate, or just a matter of convenience. However, the vocabulary was established, and it affected the British policy on Kurdistan. The terms along with East, West, North and South of Kurdistan, are re-utilised here to serve as geographic directions referring to the segments of the Greater Kurdistan. The West of Kurdistan is not fully coterminous with Rojava's *de facto* boundaries as these oscillate due to developments in Syria.

Prior to the nineteenth century, Kurdistan was initially partitioned among the Mamelukes and Mongols. It was later occupied and integrated into the Persian and Ottoman empires and mostly enjoyed administrative recognition by way of autonomy and independence under Persian and Ottoman suzerainty. The Kurdish autonomous entities were aborted in the following century as centralised states,

1 See Karen Knop, *Diversity and Self-Determination in International Law* (CUP 2002) 4, 50.

DOI: 10.4324/9781003424314-4

Map 4.1. Kurdistan

Source: Kurdistan, French map. Appears with *Bulletin Mensuel du Centre d'Etudes Kurdes*, issue No. 8, August 1949 (FO 371/75123). Anita Burdett, *Records of the Kurds: Territory, Revolt and Nationalism, 1831-1979: British Documentary Sources*, vol 13 (CUP 2015).

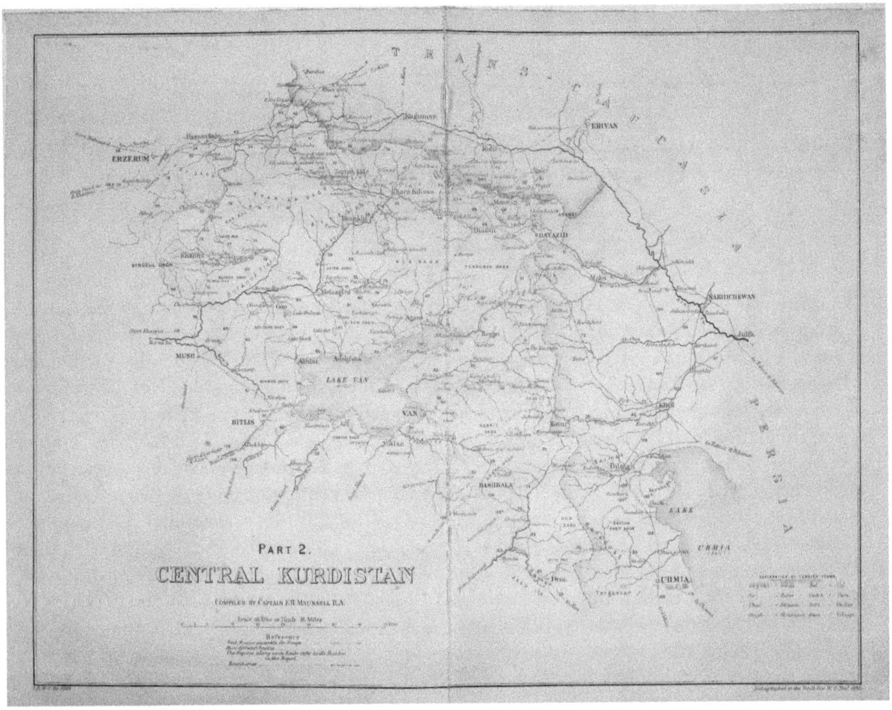

Map 4.2. Central Kurdistan

Source: Central Kurdistan, compiled by Captain F.R. Maunsell, R.A., Intelligence Division War Office, 1894 [FO 925/2829]. Anita Burdett, *Records of the Kurds: Territory, Revolt and Nationalism, 1831-1979: British Documentary Sources*, vol 13 (CUP 2015).

imposed by European powers, revoking earlier long-standing Kurdish regional autonomy arrangements.

4.1 Pre-Twentieth-Century Kurdistan

Kurdistan achieved relative stability in the sixteenth century as religious conflicts between the Sunni Ottomans and the Shi'a Safavids ran their course. The Kurds were geographically situated at the peripheries of these two empires. The centralised Ottoman Empire established Sunni networks in western Anatolia and Thrace. Nonetheless, the Safavids (established in 1501) took over the Kurdish regions of Amed in 1507, Mosul in 1508, and central Anatolia in 1511. The Ottoman Sultan Salim Yavuz clashed with the Safavids at Chaldiran (northeastern Kurdistan) on 23 August 1514 and defeated them. In 1514, the Sunni Kurds signed an agreement with the Sultan which bound the Ottoman Empire to preserve 'the independence and freedom of the Kurdish princedoms' and 'support[ing] the Kurds against foreign aggression.'[2] The new boundaries were drawn indistinctly in the Treaty of Zehaw (1639).[3]

Following sporadic warfare, the Treaty of Amasya was signed on 21 May 1555. The Ottomans recognised the Safavids as a new religio-political sovereign entity. The Treaty of Zehaw (Qasr-e Shirin)[4] endorsed the Amasya Treaty and determined the respective Ottoman–Persian geographic spheres on 17 May

2 The treaty was violated by the Ottomans 15 years later. Jawad Mella, *Kurdistan and the Kurds: A Divided Homeland and a Nation without State* (WKAP 2005) 65. For Chaldiran, see Sabri Ateş, *Ottoman-Iranian Borderlands: Making a Boundary, 1843–1914* (CUP 2013). After the Ottoman withdrawal from the East of Kurdistan in the middle of the sixteenth century, direct administration of the newly acquired territories was complicated. Therefore, Sultan Salim, upon the advice of his Kurdish diplomat Idris Bitlisi, ordered a return to the *status quo*, acknowledged 'nominal' Ottoman rule, and accorded 'semi- or virtual' independent status to the Kurdish chiefs by recognising a form of emirate, which led to a new configuration of the Kurds. By confirming this structure, the Ottomans established a 'quasi-feudal system' in which 18 *Kurd hukumats* (government units). Michael Eppel, *A People Without a State: The Kurds from the Rise of Islam to the Dawn of Nationalism* (UTP 2016) 30. Along with the 'quasi-feudal system,' there were 20 hereditary Kurdish emirs of the *sanjaqs* (subdivision of *Vilayet*) enjoying 'total sovereignty.' Wadie Jwaideh, 'The Kurdish Nationalist Movement: Its Origins and Development' (PhD Thesis, Syracuse University 1960) 39. Additionally, there were *sanjaqs* under administrators whom Istanbul appointed centrally. They lasted to the nineteenth century and were then replaced by Turkish governors. Martin van Bruinessen, *Agha, Shaikh, and State: The Social and Political Structures of Kurdistan* (ZB 1992) 159–173. Administrative units existed in the Ottoman Empire: 1) the *vilayah* or *Vilayet* (province) governed by a governor-general or *vali,* appointed by the Sultan; 2) the *sanjaq* (or sanjak, subdivision of *Vilayet*), the (approximately the same as sanjak), the *Qaza* (*Kaza* or *Qadi* (judge), the territorial jurisdiction of a judge; township or subdivision of *Liwa),* and the *nahiya* (a subdistrict of Qaza governed by a 'Mudir'). Kurdistan, thus, consisted of six *Vilayets*. Eppel cites 'seven' Kurdish emirates which were called *eyelet*, implying their autonomous status. They were *Mamurat-ul-Aziz, Diarbekr, Erzerum, Van, Bitlis* (in the North of Kurdistan), and *Mosul* (in the South of Kurdistan). Qatar National Library, 'Kurdistan and the Kurds 1919 (CE, Gregorian)' (British Library: India Office Records and Private Papers 1919) 4, IOR/L/MIL/17/15/22, available at https://www.qdl.qa/en/archive/81055/vdc_100036703908.0x000001. Northern Kurdistan was given autonomous Kurdish government status as *eyelet* of Kurdistan, lasting to the nineteenth century, in the *vilayah* of Amed (Diarbekr). In the South of Kurdistan, two semi-independent emirates of Soran (later Rawanduz) and Baban had conventional institutions with the Empire; these were abolished in the first half of the nineteenth century, and the emirs were replaced by Turkish governors. Mukrian and Ardalan also were in the eastern part of Kurdistan. Botan (Bohtan), Hakkari, and Badinan (or Amêdî) had their fiefdoms as well. Cecil J. Edmonds, 'Kurdish Nationalism' (1971) 6(1) JCH 87. Soran, Botan, Ardalan, and Baban were the most prominent emirates. Soran, with its *Diwan* (advisory council) and an established army, controlled an extensive area bigger than any other land ruled by the Kurdish emirs. With its own currency, Botan, as the last strong Kurdish emirate, preserved its autonomy up to the end of the conflict between the Ottoman Empire and Egypt. Eppel (n 2) 51–66 and Michael Gunter, *The Kurds: A Modern History* (MWP 2016) 13–14. For the demise of Kurdish autonomies and emirates and their replacement with central appointees, see Sabri Ateş, 'The End of Kurdish Autonomy: The Destruction of the Kurdish Emirates in the Ottoman Empire' and Boris James, 'The Rise and Fall of the Kurdish Emirates (Fifteenth to Nineteenth Centuries)' in Hamit Bozarslan, Cengiz Gunes and Veli Yadirgi (eds), *The Cambridge History of the Kurds* (CUP 2021).

3 David McDowall, *Modern History of the Kurds* (IB Tauris 2021) 26–28.

4 Zahaw or Zohab.

1639.[5] This border was not definitive until it was recognised in 1914 as an international boundary following intermittent negotiations through several international and bilateral commissions on demarcation.[6] Although a regional order demarcated boundaries, European states confirmed them later through recognition. The Zehaw Treaty divided the contiguous Kurdish territory vertically into two halves; 70% of Kurdistan came under the suzerainty of the Ottoman sultan.[7] However, the agreement became unstable as both Turks and Persians were tempted to extend their territory and their fluid sovereignty,[8] encouraged by the veering allegiance of communities, including Kurds with their anti-centralist uprisings. The Treaty remained effective until the Safavid demise in 1722. Confrontations continued, but later the disputants concluded the Treaty of Kurdan (4 September 1746), reinstating the boundaries of the 1639 treaty. Subsequently, the first Treaty of Erzirom (Erzerum; 28 July 1823), in which Kurdistan is mentioned, ended the wars and set the future economic and diplomatic relationships between Ottomans and Persians, excluding religious disparities.[9] The second Treaty of Erzirom was concluded in 1847 with the intervention of Russia and Britain to demarcate the final boundary and to end intermittent warfare. The final protocols were signed by the Qajar and Ottoman empires on 27 October 1914 to fully set the territorial extents of both empires.[10]

However, Kurdistan, consequently, underwent great political, social, and religious changes in the nineteenth century as national consciousness grew among the Kurds, nationalism arose among other groups in the region, and the Ottoman and Persian empires each became more centralised in the next century. Both empires sought to subjugate Kurdistan, to curb the Kurds, exert influence over them, to cement their own sovereignty, and partly to try and stave off European encroachment.

Despite such policies, the Kurds found themselves capable of governing their territory.[11] Relinquishing his totalitarian power, Ottoman Sultan Salim III recognised and ratified the authority of local potentates and the Kurdish chiefs in 1807. But his successor, Mahmud II, restructured the Sublime Porte's institutions, suppressed and expunged the local hereditary Kurdish emirates (Map 4.3), installed his own government officials, and brought the tribal chiefs under his direct administration. The removal of emirs caused cleavages among the Kurds themselves and vis-à-vis the

5 Thomas J. Barfield, 'Turk, Persian and Arab: Changing Relationships between Tribes and State in Iran and along Its Frontiers' in Rudi Matthee and Nikki R. Keddie (eds), *Iran and the Surrounding World: Interactions in Culture and Cultural Politics* (UWP 2011) 74.

6 Sabri Ateş, 'Treaty of Zohab, 1639: Foundational Myth or Foundational Document?' (2019) 52(3–4) IS 397.

7 Mehrdad Izady, *The Kurds: A Concise Handbook* (Routledge 1992) 51; van Bruinessen (n 2) 144.

8 Edgar O'Ballance, *The Kurdish Struggle* (Palgrave Macmillan 1996) 3.

9 Maria Th. O'Shea, *Trapped between the Map and Reality: Geography and Perceptions of Kurdistan* (Routledge 2004) 73.

10 Ateş, 'Zohab' (n 6) 411–420.

11 McDowall (n 3) 40–42.

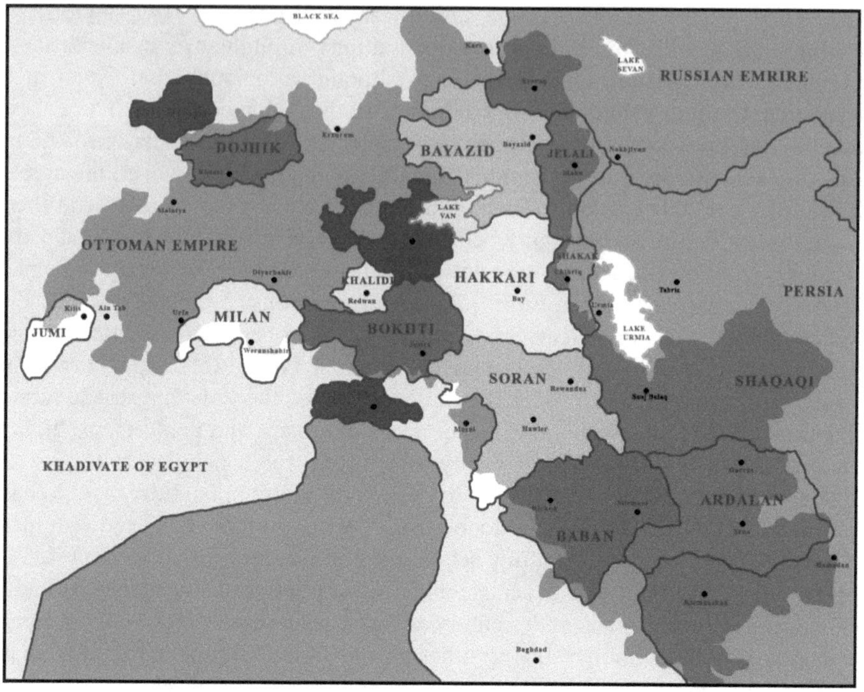

Map 4.3. Kurdistan's Houses, principalities, and emirates

Ottomans.[12] In the 1830s, the Kurds perceived their independence as a right when the Ottomans resolved to subordinate them. Although the Porte had enough power to suppress the semi-independent emirates, the Kurds still resisted. The autonomous emirates on both sides of Kurdistan existed until the late nineteenth century, when the system vanished with the appointment of Turkish officers as governors in the wake of centralisation reforms. Also, the Qajars dethroned Kurdish chiefs by the end of the century, although this operation aroused considerable resentment on the part of the Kurds. Kurds still retained close contact with their co-ethnics in the Ottoman Empire while relishing relative freedom under the Qajar.[13]

4.2 Twentieth-Century Kurdistan

Before the nineteenth century, ethnic self-determination as a democratic ideal played at best a trivial role in the configuration of borders and in international

12 Michael A. Reynolds, 'The Ends of Empire Imperial Collapse and the Trajectory of Kurdish Nationalism' in So Yamane and Norihiro Naganawa (eds), *Regional Routes, Regional Roots? Cross-Border. Patterns of Human Mobility in Eurasia* (HSERC 2017) 34. For a list of Kurdish emirates, see Mella (n 2).

13 McDowall (n 3) 45–50; O'Ballance (n 8) 6–7. Also see, Ateş, *Borderlands* (n 2) 31–85.

relations. Prior to WWI, alien determination reconfigured the geopolitics of the Middle East. However, it was also employed as a principle of nationality for reorganising certain selected territories in Europe. That is, the operative principle of self-determination was instrumentalised as a way of making peace during and after WWI, albeit too general, vague, uneven, and unclear in application. This was reflected both in the final drafts of the Peace Treaties and the Covenant of the League of Nations (hereinafter the League).[14]

The aftermath of WWI was conceived, by some, as an ideally opportune moment to realise the right of peoples to self-determination. It, nevertheless, was supplanted by the political and cultural interests revealed in the peace treaties; territories were created and transferred without any affirmation of self-determination by their peoples. Adjustments in the map of Europe took place largely along national lines. The result was incoherence and inconsistency in the exercise of self-determination.[15] Kurdistan was not an exception in this regard. Concurrently with the Arabs, Turks, Jews, and Armenians, the Kurds were then fostering ethno-national aspirations to build their own state.

4.2.1 A New Era of Political Life without Consultation

Although it could not be denied that Britain had entered into secret deals with local Arab leaders, plans during the war were drawn up to divide Ottoman territories without taking much notice of the peoples affected. Before WWI ended, the peoples of the Middle East had already been expected to accept the new boundaries bargained in the Sykes-Picot-Sazonov collusive deal (15 and 16 May 1916),[16] officially known as the Asia Minor Agreement. Britain, France, and Tsarist Russia were to split up the Ottoman territories: Cilicia, Lebanon, and Syria for France; Iraq and Palestine for Britain; and Istanbul and the Straits for Russia.[17] Upon Russia's retreat and forfeiture of all its claims, and pursuant to the deal of 23 December 1917 between France and Britain, Kurdistan was assigned to the 'English zone' of influence.[18] The C Zone (Southern Anatolia) was belatedly assigned to Italy when the government in Rome learned of the deal (Map 4.4).

Based on the Sykes-Picot-Sazonov deal — for which secret negotiations had begun in December 1915 — Kurdistan would have been partitioned among the

14 See Chapter 2.1.

15 See Chapter 2.1.1 and 2.1.2.

16 See David Fromkin, *A Peace to End All Peace: The Fall of the Ottoman Empire and the Creation of the Modern Middle East* (Owl Books 2001). Although commonly referred to as the 'Sykes-Picot' agreement, this overlooks the Russian involvement in this deal, despite the fact that it emerged as the outcome of several letters exchanged among Edward Grey (British Foreign Secretary), Paul Cambon (French ambassador in London), and Sergey Sazonov (Russian Minister of Foreign Affairs). For secret letters during WWI, see Hussein-McMahon Correspondence.

17 Alan Palmer, *The Decline and Fall of the Ottoman Empire* (Barnes and Noble 1994) 239–240.

18 Convention between France and England on the subject of activity in southern Russia. E. L. Woodward and Rohan Butler (eds), *Documents on British Foreign Policy, 1919–1939*, Series I, vol III, 1919 (HMSO 1949) 369–370.

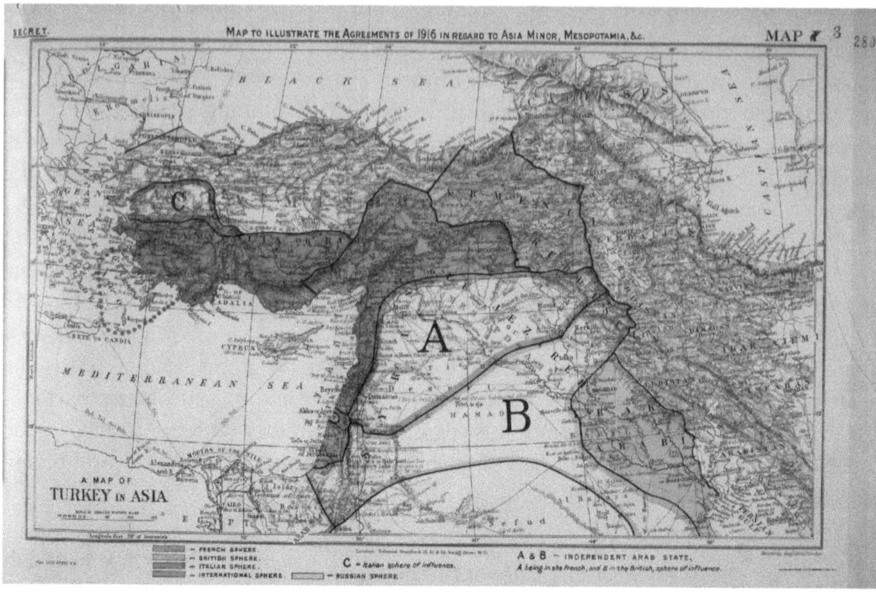

Map 4.4. New borders as per the Sykes-Picot-Sazonov Collusion of 1916

Source: Map to illustrate the Agreement of 1916 in regard to Asia Minor, Mesopotamia, etc. upon 'A Map of Turkey in Asia,' Edward Stanford, London. Appears with 'Mesopotamia,' Memorandum by Sir Erle Richards to Lord Curzon, c. January 1919, [FO 608/96]. Anita Burdett, *Records of the Kurds: Territory, Revolt and Nationalism, 1831–1979: British Documentary Sources*, vol 13 (CUP 2015).

French-administered area (Region A under influence or protectorate and the blue (more green than blue on the map) areas under direct control); the British-administered area (Region B under influence or protectorate and the red areas under direct control); and the majority Russian-administered area (today's Armenia and Azerbaijan). The Persian sphere was to remain intact. Any adjustments to boundaries were undertaken without addressing the affected populations, as self-determination remained an empty slogan. Notwithstanding their rhetoric, the Allies failed to put force proposals for democratic forms of government or countenance minority rights in practice. All of this was provisional, and nothing was really finalised until the League of Nations Mandate System.

Because the Kurds were not a primary concern for Britain, the demands of the people of Kurdistan remained unheeded. Although Mosul came under the French protectorate, the political and economic interests of Britain shifted the focus toward Mosul, making it a focal point. Arnold Toynbee proposed 'an autonomous Kurdistan' to Sykes.[19] But the plan did not entail all of Kurdistan.[20] Toynbee even

19 Arnold Toynbee was then a member of the Political Intelligence Department of the British Foreign Office.

20 Foreign Office 371/3407, Toynbee to Sykes, Memorandum, 12 October 1918.

raised the cession of the North of Kurdistan to Persia conditionally by establishing 'an autonomous province with foreign, presumably British, assistance.'[21] Sykes refused these proposals since he had other ideas to create 'an independent Kurdish Emirate' in Southern Kurdistan including Mosul. In a report presented to the British Prime Minister, Sykes stated that

> [a] consolidated Kurdistan is [an] impossibility. There is no reason why the distribution of the Kurds should dictate frontiers or why Kurds should be regarded as people who require consolidation. And so, it is the powerful, the arrogant and the more developed nations with a modern army and technology that win.[22]

Britain ultimately hesitated to alter the Persian border and rejected the proposal of a 'United Kurdistan.'[23]

4.2.2 The Allied Powers and Kurdistan

Woodrow Wilson assessed the political life of the non-Turkish peoples and reconfigured the borders of Ottoman territories in his Fourteen Points for World Peace in January 1918: '[t]he Turkish portions of the present Ottoman Empire should be assured a secure sovereignty, but other nationalities which are now under Turkish administration should be assured an undoubted security of life and an unmolested opportunity of autonomous development.'[24] In July 1916, Turkish troops seized parts of southeastern Kurdistan, but the Russians recovered it in March 1917 only to withdraw after the Bolshevik Revolution in October of the same year. It ended with a truce between the Bolsheviks and the Turks in December and the subsequent Russian support of Turkish nationalists against Britain.

Sheikh Mahmud Barzinji, who was elected democratically by all notables of Kurdistan, established a government in Silêmanî (Sulaymaniyah), Southern Kurdistan, aiming to lay the foundation for the creation of the Greater Kurdistan.

21 McDowall (n 3) 133–141.

22 Lieutenant Colonel Sir Mark Sykes, 'Proceedings and Appendices of a Committee Appointed by the Prime Minister,' March 15, 1915/British Public Record Office, Kew. Sykes's idea was declined by Picot as being 'contrary to French interests.' Report on the Situation in Kurdistan from the Secretary's note for the Inter-Departmental Conference on Middle Eastern Affairs, 15 September 1919 [FO 608/95]. Anita Burdett, *Records of the Kurds: Territory, Revolt and Nationalism, 1831–1979: British Documentary Sources*, vol 5 (CUP 2015) 519.

23 Telegram, Chief Political Officer, Baghdad, to India Office, 12 May 1919, No. 5354 [FO 608/95]; Foreign Office Minutes, 26 May 1919 on the Future of Kurdistan [FO 608/95]; Letter, Sir Louis Mallet for Mr Balfour, London, to Lord Curzon [Acting Foreign Secretary], 27 May 1919, No. 821 [FO 608/95]; and Brief by Political Department, India Office, on 'Mesopotamia: British Relations with Kurdistan,' 27 August 1919, [FO 608/95]. ibid 333, 354, 357, 508.

24 The Twelfth Point. War Aims and Peace Terms, 14-point Program for World Peace, President Wilson's Message to Congress, 8 January 1918. Also, see Woodrow Wilson, *The Papers of Woodrow Wilson* (PUP 1966).

This Kurdish *de facto* state boasted its own military force and displayed its unique flag and national emblem. In October 1918, Barzinji's government received recognition from Britain.[25] Britain occupied Kirkuk on 25 October 1918, Xaniqîn and Silêmanî in December, and Mosul on 3 November — four days after concluding an armistice with the Ottoman Turks.[26] The timing was likely due to the late arrival to the warring forces of the news and the full terms of the Armistice. In addition, Article 7 of the Armistice had authorised the Allies to occupy strategic points for their security.[27] Britain already had a plan to separate the South of Kurdistan due to its economic prominence — e.g., oil — as well as links to India, from the rest of Kurdistan. Within the British government, personal views and bureaucratic wrangling among the Secretary of State for India, the War Office, the India Office, and the Foreign Office entangled the formation of policy. But Kurdish self-determination never figured high on the Britain agenda. Policy regarding the Kurds and the territory of Kurdistan remained inconsistent and marginal as was the case, too, with other local populations.

The Mudros Armistice on 30 October 1918 ended WWI for a capitulated Ottoman Empire expecting partition by the victorious powers.[28] On 7 November 1918, a joint Anglo-French declaration called for 'the complete and final emancipation [or liberation] of all those peoples so long oppressed by the Turks, and to establish national governments and administrations which shall derive their authority from the initiative and free [or choice] will of the [native] people themselves.'[29] These arrangements were to be established by the 'free will' of the oppressed and determined 'on the principles of self-determination.' Britain and France agreed 'to encourage and help the establishment' of these arrangements.[30] Their role would be encouragement and assistance in establishing new states, yet no mention of self-determination for the Kurds was made. It was a call made by Britain and France that was never implemented regarding the Kurds. The Armenians faced the same fate at this point.

25 Saad Eskander, 'Britain's Policy in Southern Kurdistan: The Formation and the Termination of the First Kurdish Government, 1918–1919' (2000) 27(2) BJMES 139. Also, see Eppel (n 2) 119.

26 Habibollah Atarodi, *Great Powers, Oil and the Kurds in Mosul: (Southern Kurdistan/Northern Iraq) 1910–1925* (UPA 2003) 52–55.

27 Conference on Eastern Affairs, The Territorial and Military Commission on Mosul, 23 January 1923. Anita Burdett, *Records of the Kurds: Territory, Revolt and Nationalism, 1831–1979: British Documentary Sources*, vol 6 (CUP 2015) 287–288.

28 Veli Yadirgi, *The Political Economy of the Kurds of Turkey: From the Ottoman Empire to the Turkish Republic* (CUP 2017) 161.

29 Anglo-French Joint Statement of Aims in Syria and Mesopotamia (8 November 1918). The text in the official report of House of Commons is: 'the complete and definite emancipation of the peoples so long oppressed by the Turks and the establishment of national administrations deriving their authority from the initiative and free choice of the indigenous populations.' House of Commons, 'Anglo-French Joint Statement of Aims in Syria and Mesopotamia 8 November 1918,' Official Report, 5 CXLV, 1920, Col 36. Also, Mesopotamia, Memorandum by Sir Erle Richards to Lord Curzon, January 1919. Burdett, vol 5 (n 22) 672.

30 Mesopotamia, Memorandum by Sir Erle Richards to Lord Curzon, January 1919. ibid 672.

Britain, while rejecting annexation of the liberated areas, sanctioned 'an Arab government or Governments,' based on its earlier promises.[31] In May 1919, it laid bare its first withdrawal from the goal of creating a single Southern Kurdistan state by presenting the idea of creating the Arab province of Mosul with autonomous Kurdish states on its frontier,[32] with 'no special regime to be stipulated.'[33] However, new economic considerations and the oilfields of Kirkuk and Mosul, under the principle of self-determination, changed British policy toward Kurdistan and Iraq.[34] Oil was relatively unimportant for Britain, as it was not highlighted in the Churchill-Cox correspondence, but other economic and commercial issues prevailed.[35] The oil issue was also rejected by Curzon in his arguments against the rendition of Mosul to the Turks in the Territorial and Military Commission on Mosul, 23 January 1923.[36] But the subsequent reality provides a counterpoint.

There were differing opinions on the Kurds. On 13 June 1919, J.E. Shuckburgh, a Civil Commissioner of the British government, had proposed that Britain should accept responsibility for the predominantly Kurdish area[37] to enable the Kurds to 'progress peacefully on civilised lines.'[38] In a telegram from the Political Officer in Baghdad to the Foreign Office in London on 29 August 1919, the policy of creating 'autonomous Kurdish States' under British supervision was reiterated. This had already been approved by His Majesty's government on 9 May 1919.[39] Despite major nationalist movements such as Simko Şikak's, the Kurds of Eastern Kurdistan (in Persia) were not considered candidates for self-determination. By virtue of the Anglo-Persian Treaty (9 August 1919), Britain was obliged to be firm with respect to the territorial integrity of Persia, subverting any chance of a 'United Kurdistan' and thereby retaining significant British authority over the territory under Persian rule, customs, and oil resources.[40] Thus, Britain created a dilemma for the Kurds

31 ibid.

32 Arnold T. Wilson, *Mesopotamia, 1917–20: A Clash of Loyalties: A Personal and Historical Record* (OUP 1931) 143.

33 FO 371/5067 Civil Commissioner to India Office, Baghdad, 4 February 1920.

34 Timothy Mitchell, *Carbon Democracy: Political Power in the Age of Oil* (Verso 2011) 98–99. Also, see Sevtap Demirci, 'The Lausanne Conference: The Evolution of Turkish and British Diplomatic Strategies, 1922–1923' (PhD Thesis, LSE 1997).

35 O'Shea also adds the lack of a reliable Kurdish leadership, to other reasons. O'Shea, *Map and Reality* (n 9) 125–126. But what was obvious is that Kurdish leadership was not an issue for the Allies, especially the British government.

36 Burdett, vol 6 (n 27) 288–289. Also, see George E. Gruen, 'The Oil Resources of Iraq: Their Role in the Policies of the Great Powers' in Reeva S. Simon and Eleanor H. Tejirian (eds), *The Creation of Iraq, 1914–1921* (Columbia University Press 2004).

37 Despatch, J.E. Shuckburgh, India Office, to the Under-Secretary of State, Foreign Office, 1 August 1919, No P.1284, [FO 808/95]. Burdett, vol 5 (n 22) 494.

38 Brief by Political Department, India Office, on 'Mesopotamia: British Relations with Kurdistan,' 27 August 1919, [FO 608/95]. ibid 507.

39 Telegram from the Political Officer, Baghdad, to the Foreign Office, London, 29 August 1919, No 10081, [L/PS/10/833]. ibid 515.

40 Heather L. Wagner, *Iran; Creation of the Modern Middle East* (2n ed, CHP 2009) 18. Also, see Fromkin (n 16) 455–456 and Maria Th. O'Shea (ed), *Kurdistan, Economic and Political Potential*

due to the contradictions of its policies in the region. When the United States lost interest in Kurdistan, it became even more of a British strategic concern.

4.2.3 The Paris Peace Conference

To formulate the conditions for peace following the culmination of WWI, the Paris Peace Conference convened at Versailles from 18 January 1919 to 20 January 1920. In Paris, the principle of self-determination was mainly advanced as some forms of autonomy for internal application within states, while downplaying the external form of sovereign statehood. Wilsonian self-determination was, therefore, practically limited to consent, consultation, and advancing self-governing arrangements,[41] but certain territories such as Kurdistan were partitioned without consulting the inhabitants.

It was within this context that Britain tried to promote Kurdistan at the Paris Peace Conference. Britain induced the Kurds and Armenians to combine their forces to resist Turkish sovereignty, although the British also took steps to thwart Russian Bolshevik expansion. Boghos Nubar Pasha, as the Armenian representative, signed a declaration with General Sharif Pasha, representing the Kurds, on 20 November 1919. In their accord, they agreed on territorial concessions and a united and independent Armenia and an independent Kurdistan with great power assistance; Sharif Pasha argued for the whole of Kurdistan in his map submitted to the British High Commissioner in Istanbul on 1 March 1920. The short-lived accord caused a schism among the Kurds in Northern Kurdistan. Sharif Pasha resigned, and Paris was left without a Kurdish delegation. However, the Kurds still carried on their lobbying efforts with France and Britain.[42] Refusing a federal mechanism between the North (French) and the South (British) of Kurdistan, Lord Earl Curzon of Kedleston, for the first time, urged the Kurds to give up on any self-determination of the political status of Kurdistan. An Inter-Departmental Conference on

(SOAS 1992). The British Delegation in Paris on British Policy in the Middle East declared: '[i]t is impossible to include all Kurdish tribes and settlements in a Kurdish State without violating the integrity of Persia; nor would the Kurds, if united, be capable of governing themselves.' Michael Dockrill (ed). Doc 34 11435 Memorandum British Delegation, Paris 18 February 1919, British Policy in the Middle East, British Documents on Foreign Affairs: Reports and Papers from the Foreign Office Confidential Print, vol 11: The Turkish Settlement and the Middle East; the Far East, pt II: From the First to the Second World War Series I: The Paris Peace Conference of 1919 (UPOA 1991) 148.

41 See Chapter 2.1.1.2.

42 FO 371/4193 File 44/156272 of 28 November 1919. Britain had not given any assurance of British mandate to Pasha. Letter, Sir Louis Mallet for Mr Balfour, London, to Lord Curzon [Acting Foreign Secretary], 27 May 1919, No. 821 [FO 608/95]. Burdett, vol 5 (n 22) 357. Also see, Sherif Pasha, 'Memorandum on the Claims of the Kurd People' (2001) 15(1/2) IJKS 131. For the activities of Kurdish nationalists after WWI to secure a Kurdish state through lobbying France and Britain, see Othman Ali, 'The Kurds and the Lausanne Peace Negotiations, 1922–23' (1997) 33(3) MES 521 and Djene R. Bajalan, 'The First World War, the End of the Ottoman Empire, and Question of Kurdish Statehood: A "Missed" Opportunity?' (2018) 18(1) Ethnopolitics 13.

Middle Eastern Affairs was held at the Foreign Office in London on 17 November 1919 to discuss the future of Kurdistan and British policy toward the Kurdistan question as its main concern. France made clear that it would not 'undertake the responsibility of administering or in any way mixing themselves up with the political future' of Kurdistan.[43] Major Edward W.C. Noel (British military officer and diplomat) believed that Kurdish nationality was 'inchoate,' though national consciousness 'certainly existed' but was not 'organised'; that is, the '*western sense of*' (emphasis added) nationality was 'almost non-existent.' Therefore, making any promise to the Kurds was 'impossible'; however, the Allied Powers in the Peace Conference would not lose sight of Kurdish national aspirations. Curzon as the Chairman of the Conference declared that Britain 'should evacuate Kurdistan altogether,' and 'must look to the future.'[44]

On 22 November 1919, the Secretary of State in London apprised the Civil Commissioner in Baghdad that 'His Majesty['s] Government will in no circumstances take a mandate for Kurdistan.' However, he stated that 'the restoration of Turkish sovereignty over Kurdistan cannot be allowed.' In this telegram, Major Noel recommended that '(1) Turkish authority should be excluded from Kurdistan; (2) Kurdistan should not be partitioned; and (3) that the frontier should follow as nearly as possible the ethnological line between Kurds and Arabs.'[45] Sir Erle Richards, in a memorandum to Lord Curzon on January 1919, had rejected under any circumstances putting the people of Mesopotamia (today Iraq) back under the sovereignty of Turkey, for they have suffered too much from 'the bloody tyranny of the Turks.'[46] Meanwhile, the Kurds had rejected 'French tutelage in any shape or form,'[47] as France was only a 'protector of Christian communities,' according to Kurdish leaders who tended to be Sunni Muslims.[48] The Kurds' concerns in this regard were valid.

At President Wilson's request (in his capacity as the president of the Conference), the King-Crane Commission was formed to investigate the preferences of the residents of the Levant. The investigation was carried out through what Lord Milner, British Secretary of State for the Colonies after the war, called 'rule [of] subject races through their chiefs.'[49] After interviewing the religious leaders and local chiefs (1,863 representative petitions), the Commission recommended the administration of Syria by a single Mandatory power — not as a colonising power with a monopolistic power — under the League for a given limited time to 'train the Syrian people to independent self-government as rapidly as conditions allow, by

43 Inter-Departmental Conference on Middle Eastern Affairs, Foreign Office, 17 November 1919, [L/PS/10807]. Burdett, vol 5 (n 22) 680–682.

44 ibid 685.

45 Telegram, Secretary of State, London to Civil Commissioner, Baghdad, 22 November 1919, No P.7495, [FO 608/95]. ibid 550.

46 Mesopotamia, Memorandum by Sir Erle Richards to Lord Curzon, January 1919. ibid 699–670.

47 'Kurdistan,' no author, 15 October 1918, [FO 608/95]. ibid 559.

48 ibid 558.

49 Quoted in Frederick J.D. Lugard, *Dual Mandate in British Tropical Africa* (Routledge 1965) 194.

setting up all the institutions of a democratic state.' It should be granted 'as soon as it can safely be done.' The Commission also argued in favour of the unity of Syria on decentralised principles, where its boundaries should be determined by a special commission.[50] The King-Crane Commission proposed the would-be Turkish state to be under a Mandatory, American Mandate as desired by a 'great majority' of Turkish leaders, as the way out of imperialistic conditions to a democratic state. To the Commission, the Turkish people themselves generally recognised and desired this, although the Peace Conference might assign a power to mandate Turkey to secure genuinely good government, without oppression, bribery, or corruption, to guarantee the rights of all minorities, racial or religious, and to have a state of a high order on a modern underpinning of equal rights to all before the law and of full religious liberty.[51] The Commission also proposed that Syria and Armenia come under an American mandate.

About 'Kurdistan,' due to the presence of Armenians, Turks, and others, and division among themselves into Shi'a and Sunni, the Commission recommended that it be limited:

> to the natural geographical area which lies between the proposed Armenia on the north and Mesopotamia on the south, with the divide between the Euphrates and the Tigris as the western boundary, and the Persian frontier as the eastern boundary. A measure of autonomy can be allowed them under [the] close mandatory rule, with the object of preparing them for ultimate independence or for federation with neighboring areas in a larger self-governing union. It is possible to shift most of the comparatively small numbers of both Turks and Armenians out of this area by voluntary exchange of population and thus obtain a province containing about a million and a half people, nearly all Kurds.[52]

The Inter-Departmental Conference on 23 February 1920 declared that British forces would withdraw from Kurdistan to give the new entity the opportunity 'to form itself into an autonomous State,' which could be attained by the evacuation of Turks from all Kurdish areas. Notwithstanding such arguments, the Conference deferred that 'the final decision on the future of Kurdistan' to the conclusion of the Peace Conference.[53] However, a series of significant developments unfolded prior to any agreement being reached, shaping the destiny of Kurdistan.

50 King-Crane Commission, 28 August 1919, Section One, Report upon Syria, Submitted by Charles R. Crane and Henry Churchill King, 41, available at http://dcollections.oberlin.edu/digital/collection/kingcrane/id/578.

51 ibid Section Three, Report upon non-Arabic Speaking Portions of Former Ottoman Empire, 35–37.

52 ibid 38–39.

53 Minutes of an Inter-Departmental Conference on Middle Eastern Affairs, Foreign Office, 23 February 1920, [L/PS/10/807]. Burdett, vol 5 (n 22) 687–692.

An Arab government was established in Damascus, and its parliament declared the independence of Syria on 7 March 1920.[54] Britain and France, however, did not extend immediate recognition. But in a separate agreement, France did recognise the independence of Syria. In return, Syria recognised the French mandate over itself (Syria), which was assigned by the Allies' Supreme Council on 20 April 1920. The Mandate System was imposed once again in the San Remo Resolution of 25 April 1920[55] as a continuation of the Sykes-Picot-Sazonov agreement.[56] Although Syria and its people, including Kurds, had not been consulted at all, the League later confirmed and defined the French Mandate for Syria and the Lebanon on 24 July 1922.[57] Nonetheless, part of Kurdistan was still on the line at the Peace Conference.

4.2.4 The Treaty of Sèvres (1920): National Self-Determination within Reach

The Ottoman Sultan signed and endorsed the Treaty of Peace with the Allies known as the Treaty of Sèvres on 10 August 1920 in the French town of Sèvres.[58] It is worth noting that the United States and Russia were excluded from dealing with the Kurdistan issue in any active sense.[59] The Treaty had 13 parts referring to 433 articles starting with 26 Articles of the Covenant of the League. It was signed between the Ottomans on one side and the principal Allied Powers (the British Empire, France, Italy, and Japan) and the lesser Allied Powers (Armenia, Belgium, the Hedjaz, Poland, Portugal, Romania, the Serb-Croat-Slovene state, and Czecho-Slovakia) on the other.

Article 62 (Section III, Kurdistan) postulates:

> [a] Commission…shall draft within six months…a scheme of local autonomy for the predominantly Kurdish areas lying east of the Euphrates, south of the southern boundary of Armenia…,and north of the frontier of Turkey with Syria and Mesopotamia…,and with this object a Commission composed of British, French, Italian, Persian and Kurdish representatives shall…decide what rectifications, if any, should be made in the Turkish frontier.

54 Jordi Tejel, *Syria's Kurds: History, Politics and Society* (Routledge 2009) 14.

55 Philip Sh. Khoury, *Syria and the French Mandate: The Politics of Arab Nationalism, 1920–1945* (PUP 1987) 122–123.

56 Tejel, *Syria's Kurds* (n 54) 14.

57 LNOJ 3(8 pt II), 1922, 1013.

58 Sarah D. Shields, *Fezzes in the River: Identity Politics and European Diplomacy in the Middle East on the Eve of World War II* (OUP 2011) 20. It was mostly drafted without consultation with the British Foreign Office. PRO FO 371/4231, No 121884. Andrew Mango, *Ataturk: The Biography of the Founder of Modern Turkey* (1st ed, John Murray 1999) 182.

59 John Bulloch and Harvey Morris, *No Friends but the Mountains: The Tragic History of the Kurds* (OUP 1992) 90.

According to Article 63, Turkey would agree 'to accept and execute the decisions' of both mentioned commissions 'within three months from their communication to the said Government.'

Article 64 follows with the required political process:

> [i]f within one year from the coming into force of the present Treaty the Kurdish peoples...shall address themselves to the Council of the League of Nations in such a manner as to show that a majority of the population of these areas desires independence from Turkey, and if the Council then considers that these peoples are capable of such independence and recommends that it should be granted to them, Turkey hereby agrees to execute such a recommendation, and to renounce all rights and title over these areas.

Within one year, Kurds would be granted independence provided that the desire for independence was expressed by a majority of their people. Upon the renunciation by Turkey of these areas, the Kurds in the Mosul *vilayet* (of Southern Kurdistan) could adhere to the future independent Kurdistan.[60] Also based on Article 139, Turkey was bound to abandon 'all rights of suzerainty or jurisdiction of any kind over Moslems [sic] who are subject to the sovereignty or protectorate of any other State.'

Kurds expected full-fledged independence, but the Treaty did not affect the Kurdish territory of the West and East of Kurdistan, and its boundaries with Armenia had not been set. Indeed, it did not cover what previously was put under the French and British administrations. Thus, most Kurds in Eastern Anatolia rejected it.[61] Still, a flimsy government in Istanbul could not guarantee the execution of its terms. Attempts to convince the Kemalists to be bound to the Sèvres provisions failed, as Mustafa Kemal (later Ataturk) was intent on holding on to the Ottoman Muslim majority.[62] Mustafa Kemal had organised resistance to preserve the territorial dominance of the Ottoman state against any Kurdish movement to create 'an independent Kurdistan.'[63]

Following the end of WWI, the Kurdish Independence Committee in Cairo and the Society for the Advancement of Kurdistan (SAK) in Istanbul both emerged as significant players in post-war lobbying efforts and publicising nationalist demands. Even if it is asserted that the Kurds were devoid of unified objectives, it was attributed to the 'uncertainty' of the British intentions toward Kurdistan

60 Treaty of Peace with Turkey 1920, Treaty Series 11. HMSO.

61 Reynolds in Yamane and Naganawa (n 12) 43.

62 Metin Heper, *The State and Kurds in Turkey: The Question of Assimilation* (Palgrave Macmillan 2007) 124.

63 Note, Commenting on Britforce Telegrams up to 24 July 1919, General Headquarters, Mesopotamian Expeditionary Force, 25 July 1919. Views of Mustafa Kamal in Paris regarding the future of Kurdistan [AIR 20/512]. Burdett, vol 5 (n 22) 470.

confirmed by their own correspondence,[64] stirring factionalism among the Kurds to serve Britain's own objectives; whereas 'the hesitation of British policy in the face of Kurdish nationalist programme,'[65] their non-representation to Europeans,[66] and the hazy boundaries of Kurdistan due to demographic changes by Arabs, Turks, and Persians were factors hindering the international ratification of Kurdish independence.

The Kurds were in a precarious situation, facing significant disadvantages that would have further fragmented their homeland if the Treaty of Sèvres had been enforced. The implementation of the Treaty would have resulted in the division of Kurdistan into multiple smaller segments, with the portion designated as an independent state being the least prosperous (as depicted in Map 4.5). However, the details regarding the implementation of the Treaty were inadequately defined, leaving room for ambiguity and potential complications.[67] Under the provisions of the Treaty, the region west of the Euphrates, constituting approximately one-third of Kurdistan's territory, would have fallen within the French zone of interest. Another third of Kurdistan, the northeastern part, was to be placed under the control of Soviet Armenia. This division would have further fragmented the Kurdish people,

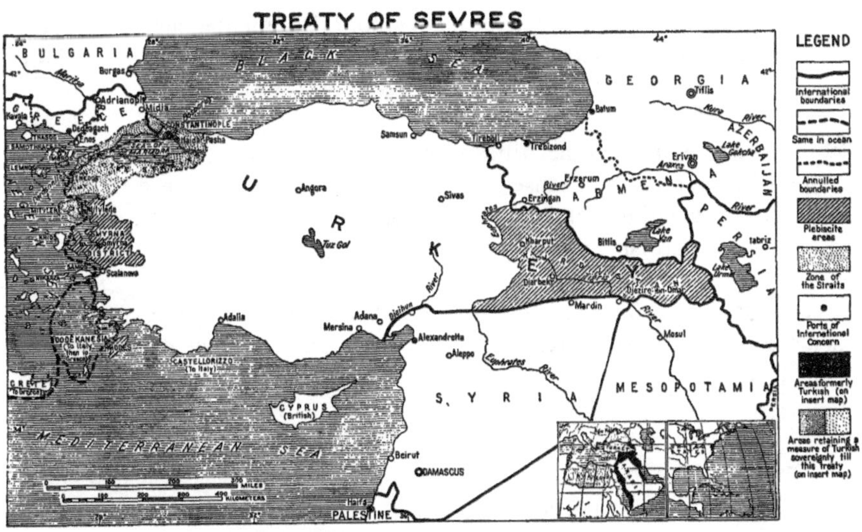

Map 4.5. Map of the Treaty of Sèvres (1920)

Source: Compiled by Lawrence Martin (ed), *The Treaties of Peace 1919–1923 vol. II* (CEIP 1924).

64 Telegram from the High Commissioner of Iraq (Cox) to the Secretary of State for the Colonies, 16 November 1922, No. 804. Burdett, vol 6 (n 27) 195.

65 The Situation in Iraq, Memorandum by the Secretary of State for the Colonies, 7 February 1924. ibid 340.

66 For their representation, see O'Shea, *Map and Reality* (n 9) ch 10.

67 Nezan Kendal, 'The Kurds under the Ottoman Empire' in Gerard Chaliand (ed), *A People without a Country: The Kurds and Kurdistan* (1st 1980, rev and updt, ZB 1993) 35.

subjecting them to varying political influences and potentially undermining their cohesive identity and collective goals. The fertile territories within Kurdistan were detached, resulting in Persia (modern-day Iran) acquiring Eastern Kurdistan, thereby nullifying self-determination. The Foreign Office's Political Intelligence Department had studied the Ottoman Empire before the Peace Conference in which they stated — while highlighting the strategic value of Kurdistan — '[w]e are thus committed to the partition of Kurdistan into three sections, in the two largest of which certain rights are secured to ourselves, the French, and the Arabs, but none to the Kurds.'[68] These divisions were imposed through the assertion of the right of conquest, rather than through self-determination.[69]

In the post-war period, self-determination was perceived and interpreted as an ambiguous, hazily defined principle of justice and liberty.[70] By October 1920, Britain had disavowed its interest in creating Kurdistan, heralding the creation of an Arab government in Iraq. At the end of the year, the Colonial Office, led by Winston Churchill who had previously served as Secretary of War, assumed Britain's responsibility through the mandates for Mesopotamia and Palestine, with Iraq being under the India Office. In November 1920, the Provisional National Government of Iraq was established with Silêmanî under British control and with Kirkuk and Hewlêr (Erbil) under a local governor.[71] Britain, thereupon, backed out of its commitment to an independent Kurdistan[72] in its correspondence with the Turks on 12 March 1921:[73]

> [i]n regard to Kurdistan the Allies would be prepared to consider a modification of the Treaty in a sense in conformity with the existing facts of the situation, on condition of facilities for local autonomies and the adequate protection of Kurdish...interests.[74]

At a conference in Cairo (March 1921), Kurdish autonomy was replaced by the Mandate System of 'Anglo-Kurdish' administration, in which Kurds would be

68 Michael Dockrill (ed). Doc. 18 11908 Memorandum Political Intelligence Department 21 November 1918 Settlement of Turkey and the Arabian Peninsula, British Documents on Foreign Affairs: Reports and Papers from the Foreign Office Confidential Print. vol 11: The Turkish Settlement and the Middle East; the Far East, pt II: From the First to the Second World War Series I: The Paris Peace Conference of 1919 (UPOA 1991) 57.

69 Jörg Fisch, *The Right of Self-Determination of Peoples: The Domestication of an Illusion* (CUP 2015) 155.

70 See Chapter 2.1.2.

71 Cecil J. Edmonds, 'The Kurds of Iraq' (1957) 11(1) MEJ 52.

72 Robert Olson, 'Battle for Kurdistan: The Churchill-Cox Correspondence Regarding the Creation of the State of Iraq, 1921–1923' (1992) 5(1–2) KS 29, 40.

73 Brief by Political Department, India Office, on 'Mesopotamia: British Relations with Kurdistan,' 27 August 1919, [FO 608/95]. Burdett, vol 5 (n 22) 508.

74 FO 371/6467 E 3357.

considered a minority in the new Iraq[75] until they espoused integration into a new state.[76] This occurred against the backdrop of Churchill and Major Edward Noel vigorously arguing for a sovereign Kurdistan.[77] Noel had expressed the view that the 'goal of an independent Kurdistan...can now be easily attained.' The Kurds had also considered federation under British protection, until a representative body of Kurdish opinion opted for inclusion in the new state.[78] However, self-determination in practice meant nothing more than autonomy, i.e., what was supposed to be encouraged albeit not established.

In an attempt to take into account the genuine aspirations of both Kurds and Arabs, a purported referendum was conducted in 1921 across Iraq, encompassing Southern Kurdistan. Percy Cox, serving as the High Commissioner of Iraq, deemed the consultation to be essential. The so-called referendum (Cox's consultation) aimed to gauge the sentiments of prominent figures, elected local councillors, recognised *aghas* (landlords), and community representatives under the banner of 'self-determination' or the governance of subject races through their chiefs.[79] The majority of respondents renounced separation from Mosul, while a minority expressed their desire for detachment and the establishment of a new Kurdish administrative division. According to the British government,[80] Silêmanî (Sulejmanie [sic] on the accompanying map) should have been excluded from the referendum due to the provisions of Article 64 of the Treaty of Sèvres, which called for the establishment of an independent sovereign Kurdistan (Map 4.6). As a result, Silêmanî did not participate in the referendum.

While Churchill was emphasising a policy of limiting Iraq[81] to purely Arab areas, Percy Cox[82] and Gertrude Margaret Bell[83] referred him to 'a non-separatist

75 FO 371/6346 High Commissioner Mesopotamia to Secretary of State for the Colonies (12 June 1921).

76 Lord Avebury, 'Self-Determination and International Law: The Kurdish Case' (1994) 7(1–2) IJKS 7, 10.

77 Saad Eskander, 'Southern Kurdistan under Britain's Mesopotamian Mandate: From Separation to Incorporation, 1920–23' (2001) 37(2) MES 153, 155, 156.

78 Note by the Political Department, India Office, 'Kurdistan,' 14 December 1918, by Sir J.E. Shuckburgh. Burdett, vol 5 (n 22) 220. Noel also had proposed 'one mandatory Power for the whole of Kurdistan and Armenia.' Report on the Situation in Kurdistan from the Secretary's note for the Inter-Departmental Conference on Middle Eastern Affairs, 15 September 1919 [FO 608/95]. Burdett, vol 5 (n 22) 524.

79 Quoted in Lugard (n 49) 194. For detail on the consultation, see McDowall (n 3) 176.

80 This position referred to in the Report (of 20 August 1925) of the Commission instituted by the Council of the League with regard the Mosul *vilayet*.

81 Churchill was persuaded not to create an independent Kurdistan despite having earlier been in favour of the idea. At the same time, the British Middle East Department was supportive of creating independent or autonomous Kurdistan. Christopher Catherwood, *Churchill's Folly: How Winston Churchill Created Modern Iraq* (CGP 2004) 113.

82 The British High Commissioner in Iraq who then strove for the inclusion of Southern Kurdistan in Iraq. Eskander, 'Southern Kurdistan' (n 77) 157–160; Olson, 'Battle for Kurdistan' (n 72) 33.

83 English administrator, traveller, political officer, and archaeologist.

policy' (or integration with Iraq) expressed by the subjects covered in the consultation.[84] Cox regarded the fulfilment of Section III of the Sèvres Treaty 'highly problematical' owing to the considerable changes in circumstances. Concerning 'safeguards for the Christian communities,' he asked for the essential remodelling of the ethnographical frontier to include Assyrians, 'the Nestorian country,' and the Kurds within the emerging Iraq due to their economic dependence on Mosul. He believed that the British government had 'moral obligations' to protect the Assyrians, otherwise, they would 'turn again to their old friends, Russians,' by this time propagating the Bolshevik enterprise.[85] He also militarily justified his considerations.

To Cox, the rectification of Mosul — even in the event of surrendering territory to the Turks — without any referendum should be based on 'natural features and on the existing facts of the local situation' and 'tribal divisions,' which were advantageous to 'the Ottoman and Iraqi Governments.'[86] Cox went even further in the following year and was of the opinion that a procedure should be devised that was helpful in the 'excision of Kurdish clauses of Treaty' and 'nullifying concluding sentence of Article 64' which led to fulfilling the wishes of the British government.[87] Churchill was convinced and declared his concurrence.[88] Later, however, he would call his acquiescence on attaching the South of Kurdistan to Iraq as one of his 'worst mistakes.'[89]

In a formalised election in 1921, from which Silêmanî abstained, Kirkuk voted against it.[90] Later, the Commission of the Council of the League with the agenda of the Mosul *vilayet* did not consider this method of expression as a plebiscite, as no individual or secret vote was taken, and there was no guarantee of the freedom and independence of the voting. Also, referenda were not held across the whole territory. Thus, these expressions are not incontestable evidence of the wishes of the population in the unstable political conditions of military occupation.[91] Britain anchored the Kurds in Iraq to utilise them as a card to balance the power dynamic between the Arabs and to bolster Sunnis against a Shi'a preponderance within the Iraqi government.[92] The idea of creating a sovereign Kurdistan or even Kurdish autonomy was, thus, crushed. This rationale for maintaining ethnic balance in Iraq remained in effect up to today.

84 Olson, 'Battle for Kurdistan' (n 72).

85 Telegram, Cox to Churchill, 9 December 1921, No. C.O./120. Burdett, vol 6 (n 27) 63, 66.

86 ibid 65–66.

87 Telegram from the High Commissioner of Iraq (Cox) to the Secretary of State for the Colonies, 5 January 1922, No. 7. ibid 73.

88 Telegram from the Under Secretary of State, Foreign Office, 64129/1921, 5 January 1922. ibid 65–66.

89 Olson, 'Battle for Kurdistan' (n 72) 29–34.

90 Edmonds (n 71).

91 Question of the Frontier between Turkey and Iraq, Report submitted to the Council by the Commission instituted by the Council Resolution, 20 August 1925, 17–18.

92 McDowall (n 3) 178.

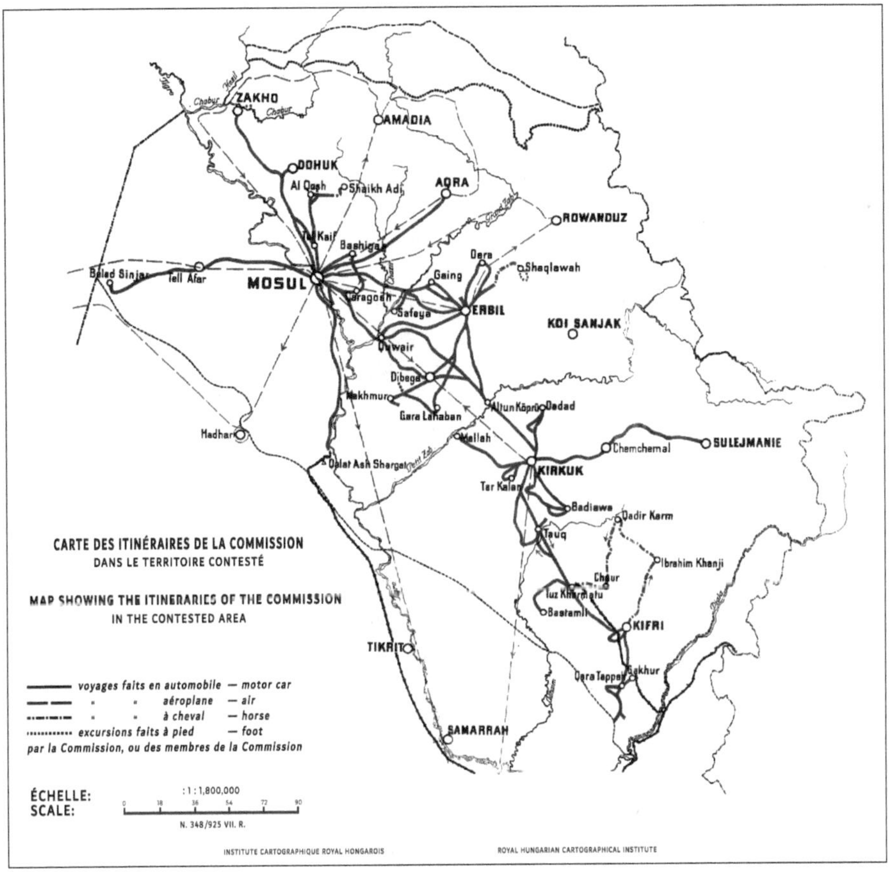

Map 4.6. The itineraries of the Commission in the Contested Area

Source: United Nations Archives at Geneva. Royal Hungarian Geographical Institute, attached to Question of the Frontier between Turkey and Iraq, Report submitted to the Council by the Commission instituted by the Council Resolution, 20 August 1925.

In March 1919, Britain occupied Istanbul. Following the abolition of the Sultan's position and the dismantling of the monarchical system in October 1920 by the Grand National Assembly established in April 1919, the Kemalists assumed control of the government in Ankara. The Kemalists prevailed upon defeating the Allies vis-à-vis the situation on several fronts.[93] France signed the Treaty of Ankara with the Turks and, in the process of doing so, ceded Cilicia.[94] The new boundaries, favouring Turkey, were set by France and Mustafa Kemal on 20 October 1921

93 Peter J. Beck, '"A Tedious and Perilous Controversy': Britain and the Settlement of the Mosul Dispute, 1918–1926' (1981) 17(2) MES 256.
94 Fromkin (n 16) 536–537.

(the Franco-Turkish Agreement signed at Angora).[95] According to this agreement, which contradicted the Treaty of Sèvres, the West of Kurdistan was placed under the French mandate of Syria.

The Mesopotamian Mandate was superseded by the Anglo-Iraqi Treaty of Alliance of 10 October 1922 (the Treaty with King Amir Faysal from the Hedjaz). In the Treaty, which was supposed to remain in force for 20 years (Article 18), Britain recognised Faysal as the King of Iraq and was committed to assisting the Iraqi army (Article 7). Also, Faysal was obliged to act so that 'no discrimination of any kind shall be made between the inhabitants of Iraq on the ground of race, religion or language and shall secure…the right of each community to maintain its own schools for the education of its own members in its own language' (Article 3).[96] However, the Kurds became the very target of discrimination by the Iraqi government. Britain undertook 'to secure the admission of Iraq to membership of the League of Nations as soon as possible' (Article 6) and to provide support and assistance to the Iraqi armed forces (Article 7). Both parties, in Article 8, pledged themselves not to cede or lease territory in Iraq 'in any way placed under the control of any Foreign Power.'

Despite being aware of the potential for Kurdish unrest, in December 1922, Curzon's proposals were submitted to the British government for consideration as a concession in its negotiations with the Turks, despite lacking a solid ethnographic underpinning for the cession of the whole or a portion of Kurdistan.[97] His proposals were rejected because Britain had 'already promised the Kurds an Independent State within the boundaries of IRAK.'[sic][98] To hand over 'their country to Turkey without consulting them would be regarded as a signal breach of faith,' according to Secretary of State for the Colonies.[99] Despite these objections, Britain made a compromise with the Turks, although it was sure the Turkish government would not contemplate 'any more liberal régime for the Kurdish population.'[100]

4.2.5 The Treaty of Lausanne (1923): Alien Determination

The Allies, especially the British government, were reluctant to use force to implement the Sèvres Treaty. According to the Armistice of Mudanya between Britain and Turkish nationalists on 11 October 1922, the terms of the abortive Treaty of

95 This treaty is also known as the Accord of Ankara and Franklin-Bouillon Agreement (20 October 1921).

96 Treaty with King Feisal (The Treaty of Alliance (with protocol), 10 October 1922). Burdett, vol 6 (n 27) 167–172.

97 Curzon's Tentative Proposals Regarding Cession of Portion of Kurdistan (Lausanne Telegram No. 80), 6 December 1922, ibid 210–211.

98 Tel. No. 676, 28 November 1922 from Secretary of State for the Colonies to High Commissioner Irak [sic]. ibid 215.

99 Telegram from the High Commissioner for Iraq (from Basrah) to Secretary of State for the Colonies, 10 December 1922. ibid 216–217.

100 The Marquess Curzon of Kedleston to Ismat Pasha, 26 December 1922. ibid 230.

Sèvres were to be renegotiated. The formal treaty of alliance between the Angora (Ankara) government and the Russian Soviet government on October 13, along with the subsequent conclusion of the Franco-Turkish Agreement on October 20, were the primary factors leading to the renegotiation of the Sevres Treaty.[101] The Allies and the Kemalists — now as the sole representatives of Turkey — assembled accordingly in Lausanne on 20 November to hold a peace conference.[102] Alongside Britain, France, Japan, Italy, Greece, Romania, Yugoslavia, Bulgaria, Belgium, Russian representatives, and American observers were present at the negotiations. Mustafa Kemal had overturned the Treaty of Sèvres and declined it in its entirety. The Kurds received a blow at the end of October 1922 when Churchill, a leading proponent of setting up Kurdistan as a sovereign buffer state between Iraq and Turkey, was replaced by William Cavendish, who opposed that view.[103] Sheikh Mahmud was ousted by Britain, and his government buildings were bombed by the British Royal Air Force (RAF) in March 1923. After his reinstatement in July 1923, he refused the restricted powers proposed by Britain, and his government was bombed again by the RAF using gas bombs in August and December 1923.[104]

During the negotiations in Lausanne, the Turks still considered the Kurds as a distinct ethnicity but then did a complete *volt-face* from this policy,[105] i.e., they presented the Kurds as part of the Turkish nation. The divergence of views among Britain, France, and Italy in Lausanne weakened the Allies and prevented them from adopting a unified stance. After negotiations in which each side tried to wear down the other, the Treaty of Lausanne and other instruments were concluded on 24 July 1923 between Turkey on one side and the governments of the British Empire, France, and Italy in agreement with the governments of Japan, Greece, Romania, the Serb-Croat-Slovene state, and Czecho-Slovakia on the other.[106] The Lausanne Treaty has five parts with 143 articles. 'Turkey' by that name was recognised as an independent state. However, the status of Mosul remained in dispute

101 Turkey: Treaty of Lausanne: Confidential Prints, February 1924 — the Synopsis of and Memorandum on the Main Events in Turkey since June 1921, PRO 30/69/107, UK National Archives, Copyright material from the Ramsay MacDonald papers is reproduced by permission of his granddaughter. This document exposes Turkey's historical utilisation of the 'Russian card' to extract additional concessions from the Allies. And now, as then, Turkey again plays the Russia card. See Loqman Radpey, 'Unhappy Anniversary: 100 Years After the Lausanne Treaty, Turkey is Still Using the Russian Alliance to its Advantage' (*ABC News*, 24 July 2023).

102 Heather L. Wagner, *The Division of the Middle East: The Treaty of Sèvres* (CHP 2004) 90.

103 Eppel (n 2) 128–129.

104 Gorgas J. Tejel, 'Urban Mobilization in Iraqi Kurdistan during the British Mandate: Sulaimaniya 1918–30' (2008) 44(4) MES 537.

105 McDowall (n 3) 194. Mustafa İsmet İnönü referred to the equality of Kurds and Turks at Lausanne. However, he later reconsidered it as the 'Turkish nation is above all other nations. Those who do not admit this superiority are in a state of battle with us.' Martin Strohmeier, *Crucial Images in the Presentation of a Kurdish National Identity: Heroes and Patriots, Traitors and Foes* (BRILL 2003) 106.

106 Treaty of Peace with Turkey 1923, Treaty Series 16. HMSO. Other instruments are Straits Conventions, Commercial Convention, Declaration relating to the Amnesty, etc.

and was shelved.[107] Article 2(1) of the Lausanne Treaty recognised the frontier between Turkey and Syria, as agreed in Article 8 of the Franco-Turkish Agreement of 20 October 1921. According to Article 3(2) of the Treaty:

> [t]he frontier between Turkey and Iraq shall be laid down in friendly arrangement to be concluded between Turkey and Great Britain within nine months. In the event of no agreement being reached…, the dispute shall be referred to the Council of the League of Nations.[108]

Turkey and the British government undertook not to utilise military force or other means to modify the state of the territories.

While certain parts of the Sèvres Treaty unrelated to Kurdistan were confirmed, the Lausanne Treaty made no allusion to the terms 'Kurdistan' and 'Kurd' or any safeguard about their rights.[109] This was not a priority concern for Britain. Article 39 was an exception:

> no restrictions shall be imposed on the free use…of any language in private intercourse, in commerce, religion, in the press, or in publications of any kind or at public meetings. Notwithstanding the existence of the official language, adequate facilities shall be furnished to Turkish nationals of non-Turkish speech for the oral use of their own language before the courts.

Nonetheless, the articles germane to minority rights (Articles 37 to 44) and other undertakings under the 'Protection of Minorities' were limited to non-Muslims (i.e., principally Armenians). The Lausanne Treaty purported to grant no rights to ethnic, linguistic, and other religious minorities.[110] Thus, the Treaty effectively annulled the proposed Kurdish state. As per Article 38, the nascent Turkish state was supposed to 'assure full and complete protection of life and liberty to all inhabitants of Turkey without distinction of birth, nationality, language, race or religion.' The provisions of this section would constitute obligations of international concerns and were parts of the guarantees of the League as per Article 44. Any modification in these provisions had to be approved by a majority of the Council of the League of Nations.

The Kurdish question in the South of Kurdistan was conditional on the settlement of the Mosul *viyalet*.[111] The case of Mosul had been submitted to the League of Nations Council on 25 January 1923 but suspended on 4 February for further negotiations. The negotiations had no outcome, as Britain rejected Article 1 of the

107 For Mosul, see Major H. I. Lloyd, 'The Geography of the Mosul Boundary' (1926) 68(2) GJ 104.

108 Art. 3(2), Treaty of Peace with Turkey 1923 (n 106).

109 See Carl Dahlman, 'The Political Geography of Kurdistan' (2002) 43(4) EGE 271 and Michael M. Gunter, *The Kurds and the Future of Turkey* (St. Martin's Press 1997) 4.

110 McDowall (n 3) 152–157.

111 The High Commission of Iraq to the Secretary of State for Colonies, 8 February 1923. Burdett, vol 6 (n 27) 293.

National Pact (Misak-i Milli) of the new Turkish government[112] concerning Mosul and its restoration as raised by the Turks.[113] Britain was determined to retain Mosul, as it perceived the return of the Turks to Iraq as 'the inevitable prelude to an agitation' that would extend to Syria and Palestine. And this 'would plant an aggressive Islamic State' that could control the Middle East.[114] A Commission of Inquiry was established on 30 September 1923 to advise on and investigate the views of the people.[115] In October 1923, the British High Commissioner in Baghdad abandoned the idea of Kurdish autonomy and independence included in the Sèvres Treaty 'in the view of changed circumstances.' The alternative was the incorporation of all Kurdish areas of Mosul *vilayet* into Iraq.[116]

A new constitution was promulgated on 29 October 1923 in Turkey, and on 13 August 1924, a new republican system was established,[117] defining the people under the republic's rule as 'Turkish.'[118] However, the boundaries of the new republic were yet to be set. Modern Iraq had been created in 1920,[119] and its survival was contingent on annexing Southern Kurdistan.

In May 1924, the RAF once again targeted the government buildings of Sheikh Mahmud's administration with bombings,[120] further exacerbating its involvement in the incorporation of the South of Kurdistan into Iraq. Britain had the obligation of safeguarding the rights of Iraqis by virtue of the Treaty of Alliance (1924). The League initially drew the temporary Brussels Line (or Brantling Line) on 29 October 1924 after Britain referred the case to the League on 6 August 1924. On the advice of cartographers, a sub-committee advised the League on demarcation on 27 October based on the Brussels Line.[121] Ultimately, the report and its attachments (maps, statistics, and charts) were due by the Commission instituted by the Council of the League with regard to the Mosul *vilayet* in August 1925 after a long delay in considering the 'geographical, ethnic, historical, economic and strategic factors' and the 'wishes' of the people residing there as determined in a plebiscite.[122] But the League's International Commission of Inquiry refrained from adhering to the

112 Article 1 of the Pact rejects the secession of territories with the Muslim majority.

113 Counter Reply to the Memorandum of the Turkish Delegation Concerning the Question of the Vilayet of Mosul, 26 December 1922. Burdett, vol 6 (n 27) 230–234. Conference on Eastern Affairs, The Territorial and Military Commission on Mosul, 23 January 1923. Burdett, vol 6 (n 27) 248–292.

114 Committee on Iraq, Draft Report for the British Cabinet for Consideration (Prepared by Lord Curzon), 19 March 1923. ibid 294–295.

115 LNOJ, iv, 1923, 201–2. For Britain's stand on referring the Mosul case to the League. See Beck (n 93).

116 Telegram from the High Commissioner (Baghdad) to the Secretary of State for the Colonies, 1 October 1923. Burdett, vol 6 (n 27) 317.

117 Mango (n 58) 235.

118 Shields (n 58) 24.

119 See Simon and Tejirian (n 36).

120 Tejel, 'Mobilization' (n 104).

121 Lloyd (n 107) 104–113.

122 Beck (n 93).

ethnic line, due to the economic interdependence of Kurds and Arabs in Mosul itself[123] and the strategic interests of Britain; 'the frontier proposed by the British Government is an excellent strategic frontier,' the Commission concluded.[124] Hence, its denouement 'would be that a sovereign Kurdish state should be created, since the Kurds form five-eighths of the population' of the *vilayet*. In another calculation, Kurds comprised seven-tenths of the whole population of the *vilayet* with an ethnic composition of Kurds including Arabs, Christians, Turks, and Jews.[125] But an independent sovereign Kurdistan did not happen.

The Kurds' national consciousness was growing 'reasonable [sic] enough' especially in Silêmanî with 189,900 Kurds (out of 191,525 inhabitants), who supremely desired their 'complete independence' while there was 'a strong movement for local autonomy, allowing of the use of the Kurdish language in education, administration and the courts of law.' Kurds in this province 'did not evince any special attachment to the Arab Government. Union with Turkey was rejected, and a desire was expressed for economic union within Iraq.' The Kurds 'recognised the advantages of an enlightened and intelligent trusteeship.' In Kirkuk, with a population of 111,650, Kurds (47,500) were less unanimous; the majority of Kurdish declarations, without analysis, were 'strong pro-Turkish.' But, the declarations of the great Kurdish chiefs suggested they were 'more in sympathy with Iraq,' according to the Inquiry Commission.[126]

In the city of Hewlêr with 191,780 inhabitants, the majority of Kurds of Koi Sanjak were for independence as in Silêmanî. A considerable number of Kurds in Hewlêr were pro-Turkey as were most of the Torkmans and Arabs in this region. Certain chiefs were in favour of 'a Kurdish Free State under European — preferably British — protection,' and some pro-Iraq Kurds preferred 'a prolongation of the British mandate.' Hewlêr had, as a whole, 'a pro-Turkish majority,' with Arabs (11,700), Kurds (170,650), Turks (2,780), Christians (3,900), and Jews (2,750). Kurdish national feeling was 'much less developed' and, in some parts, 'non-existent' among the Kurds in the city of Mosul, with 88,000 Kurds out of 306,000 inhabitants. A majority of the Kurds favoured Turkey with some favourable to Iraq. The Kurdish Êzdî (Yazidi) were 'mainly in favour of Iraq provided it is under a European mandate.'[127] Britain could not stand by the allocation of sovereignty to the Kurds in any external or internal form of self-determination due to the priority of its interests in creating Iraq. Thus, the Kurds' role was for nothing more than balancing between Sunni and Shi'a Arabs. Cox perceived them as 'a most valuable

123 For a detailed account, see Fadhil Hussain, *The Mosul Problem: A Study in Anglo-Iraqi-Turkish Diplomacy and Public Opinion* (Privately Printed 1955).

124 Frontier between Turkey and Iraq (n 91) 87.

125 ibid 43, 57.

126 ibid 76.

127 ibid 76, 77, 78.

weapon for countering Turkish activities' or 'any serious attack' within Iraq, i.e., threats which were causing trouble for Britain.[128]

The Commission of Inquiry added: '[o]pinion among the Kurds is divided; the group in Sulaymaniya and the neighbouring districts which ask [sic] for autonomy within the Iraq State includes almost half the total Kurdish population.'[129] The people in the Mosul *vilayet* had backed up their pro-Turkish proclivities by suppressing and deporting Kurds, thus ending the rule of the caliphate that was sacred for Kurdistan[130] and had codified the apparent secularist and Kemalist features of a new Turkey. Therefore, the Commission rejected, though not completely, the Turkish argument on the separation of the *vilayet* of Mosul from Iraq in the Sykes-Picot-Sazonov deal and its placement in the French zone as parts of Anatolia.[131]

With a majority of Arabs, the Kurdish Êzdîs, Jews, and Christians in the city of Mosul in favour of Iraq rather than Turkey, and under an effective European tutelage, the Commission wrapped up its work by proposing the conditional cession of the *vilayet* to Iraq:

> (1) The territory must remain under the effective mandate of the League of Nations for a period which may be put at twenty-five years; (2) Regard must be paid to the desires expressed by the Kurds that officials of Kurdish race should be appointed for the administration of their country, the dispensation of justice, and teaching in the schools, and that Kurdish should be the official language of all these services.

Before reaching its conclusion, the Commission would perceive the attachment of the *vilayet* to Iraq as 'the most advantageous settlement,'[132] based on the purely economic aspects of the dispute,[133] despite the fact that partitioning the area might have been desirable for non-economic reasons. Also, it suggested that

> (1) The country will remain under [the] League of Nations for a period of about 25 years. (2) The desire of the Kurds that the administrators, magistrates and teachers in their country be drawn from their own ranks, and adopt Kurdish as the official language in all their activities, will be taken into account.[134]

128 Telegram from the High Commissioner of Iraq (Cox) to the Secretary of State for the Colonies, 16 November 1922, No. 804. Burdett, vol 6 (n 27) 195.

129 Frontier between Turkey and Iraq (n 91) 87.

130 Mustafa Kemal toppled the caliphate on 4 March 1924, ending the ideological connection between Kurds and Turks. Robert W. Olson and William F. Tucker, 'The Sheikh Sait Rebellion in Turkey (1925): A Study in the Consolidation of a Developed Uninstitutionalized Nationalism and the Rise of Incipient (Kurdish) Nationalism' (1978) 18(3/4) DWI 195.

131 The Commission considered the Turkish argument 'only partly accurate.' Frontier between Turkey and Iraq (n 91) 24.

132 ibid 72.

133 Mitchell (n 34) 98.

134 Frontier between Turkey and Iraq (n 91) 88–89.

The Commission underscored the maintenance of the status quo or the historical unity of Baghdad and Mosul as well as the British mandate over Iraq for maintaining the existence of Iraq, despite its unstable internal situation and for settling the tension between Sunnis and Shi'a Arabs. This was contrary to the claim of the Commission itself where it confirmed that '[a]mong the Kurds we find a growing national consciousness, which is definitely Kurdish and not for Iraq,' there is no 'national Iraqi feeling' or solidarity with the Arab Kingdom in the territory, except among those with some degree of education, and 'pro-Iraq sentiments are somewhat tepid.' Even nationalist Arabs mostly 'would prefer Turkey to an Iraq under foreign control.'[135] Furthermore, economic considerations plus having foreign tutelage for a long time were significant for those in favour of Iraq. To the Commission, the British and Iraqi authorities still had no legal sovereignty over the territory occupied, as Turkey did not renounce its rights, although it was occasionally willing to 'give up the purely Arab territories.'[136] Iraq had already been established, and to the Commission, it was deemed 'morally' entitled to have defined borders in order to ensure its political and economic survival and development.[137]

The Commission achieved a vague conclusion. It also refuted the Turkish argument of the peoples' indisputable aspiration to return to Turkey and the British argument as well to take districts and ethnicities separately. As this analysis shows, the varying sentiments of ethnic groups were not taken as the foundation for the future political status of Iraq. Self-determination was being realised only internally within states, whereby minorities were entitled to maintain their separate identities through guaranteed rights. External self-determination was reduced to this fall-back, which was included in the Covenant of the League in the form of minorities' rights.

According to the Commission, 'it would be more advantageous for the territory [Mosul *vilayet*] to remain under the sovereignty of Turkey' should the mandate expire before Iraq could be regarded 'as ripe for self-government without League support.' People of the Mosul *vilayet* preferred Turkey to Iraq if the aforementioned conditions were not fulfilled,[138] although the Commission intended to ignore the first condition that postulated Iraqi membership in the League for 25 years. Nevertheless, no political or cultural rights were granted to the Kurds despite the Commission's pledges. Turkey's attempts to retake the *vilayet*'s *quid pro quo* oil concessions were in vain.[139] Despite some British authorities advocating for the Kurds' rights pursuant to the Commission's decision, Turkey followed the policy of impugning the Kurds' rights: it rejected both the report and the Council's jurisdiction and their binding decisions, while Britain disavowed direct negotiation. The Council's judgement was referred to the PCIJ, whereas Turkey did not admit

135 ibid 78.

136 ibid 84.

137 ibid 85.

138 See Robert Olson, *The Emergence of Kurdish Nationalism and the Sheikh Said Rebellion, 1880–1925* (UTP 1989).

139 O'Shea, *Map and Reality* (n 9) 125–126.

the Court's jurisdiction.[140] At the League's request, the Advisory Opinion of the Court closed the dispute on 16 December 1925,[141] declaring the Commission's decision and Article 3 (Paragraph 2) of the Treaty of Lausanne binding for both parties. As the Turkish independence war repudiated the Sèvres Treaty, and once the Mosul dispute was resolved in favour of Britain, Britain weighed the costs and benefits of an alliance with the Kurds versus an alliance with the Sunni Arab elite, organised around the Hashemite family in Iraq. The Kurds increasingly lost out in this diplomatic struggle. Britain prioritised other interests and scaled back its commitments to the Kurds. Kurdish self-determination took a back seat to other superpower concerns.

No state committed to a Kurdish mandate, although some politicians in the British government were, for a limited time, enthusiastic about establishing a sovereign Kurdistan or protectorate.[142] But that disposition was secondary, and it disappeared as time passed. On 22 and 23 December 1922, the Anglo-French Conference on Turkey had declared that 'no mandate, whether English or French or Anglo-French, was possible or desirable for Kurdistan as a whole, except perhaps for the more settled areas in the South of Kurdistan.'[143] Britain, in its Protocol (23 April 1923) with Iraq had disavowed its former policy and,[144] less than four months after the Treaty of Lausanne (declaration of December 1923), wittingly bypassed the Kurdistan issue once and for all. A combination of factors compelled the British to establish direct rule in the South of Kurdistan. The escalating threat posed by the Bolsheviks in the neighbouring regions of Kurdistan, particularly in the East, necessitated Britain's complete control over events in this area. Furthermore, the existence of an independent Kurdistan posed a risk to the unity of Persia, as any connection between Kurds in the East of Kurdistan and this new state could expose Persia to similar threats, which contradicted Britain's policy of maintaining a strong barrier against Russia through Persia. Moreover, British officials, including Arnold Wilson, believed that the prosperous regions of Southern Kurdistan should not be governed by an independent state but, rather, by a weak and dependent entity like Iraq. The promise of a sovereign Kurdistan was ignored because it did not align with British imperial interests, i.e., 'it did not serve British

140 Beck (n 93).

141 *Article 3, Paragraph 2, the Treaty of Lausanne (Frontier between Turkey and Iraq) (Advisory Opinion)*, PCIJ Rep 1925.

142 See Eleanor H. Tejirian, 'The United States, the Ottoman Empire, and the Postwar Settlement' in Simon and Tejirian (n 36) 159.

143 Michael Dockrill (ed), Doc. 50 11760(i) Minutes [Earl Curzon] 23 December 1919 Anglo-French Conference on Turkish Settlement: Third Meeting, 11.30 a.m. British Documents on Foreign Affairs: Reports and Papers from the Foreign Office Confidential Print. vol 11: The Turkish Settlement and the Middle East; the Far East, pt II: From the First to the Second World War Series I: The Paris Peace Conference of 1919 (UPOA 1991) 267.

144 McDowall (n 3) 180.

interests to fragment the Iraqi mandate, especially if it threatened the disputed oil-rich area of Mosul.'[145]

Territorial changes over Kurdistani lands became unlikely after 1923. Kurdish petitions remained unanswered by Britain, which had imposed its mandate over Iraq in the Treaty of January 1926. Military cooperation among Britain, France, and Italy regarding sanctions on Turkey proved decisive. Having acquiesced in the League's decision and the conditions attached to it, Britain, Turkey, and Iraq concluded the tripartite Treaty of Angora on 5 June 1926,[146] demarcating the 'definite and inviolable' frontiers between Iraq and Turkey, ceding Mosul to Iraq (Map 4.7), and assigning a 10% share of the oil resources to Turkey for 25 years.[147] The land of the Kurds was shattered on 5 June 1926 in practice, in total opposition to 'the interests of the populations' and their 'defined national aspirations,'[148] and Kurdistan was erased from world maps. With the dissolution of the Soviet Union in 1991, the regional Kurdish minorities in Soviet territories were split between the separate newly independent Republics of Armenia and Azerbaijan (Diagram 2.1). Many Kurds had earlier been deported to other Soviet republics.[149] Thus, Kurdistan came to be a contiguous ethnic region divided across only four states.

The Anglo-Iraqi Treaty of Alliance (30 June 1930),[150] which replaced the 1922 and 1926 treaties,[151] declared Iraq to be an independent state, although its emancipation from the Mandate was not welcomed by either the League Council or the Permanent Mandates Commission.[152] Ultimately — upon Britain's falsified report on the fulfilment of the conditions[153] and meeting political development for

145 Antony Best, Jussi Hanhimaki, Joseph A. Maiolo, and Kirsten E. Schulze, *International History of Twentieth Century* (Routledge 2015) 94.

146 The Treaty between the United Kingdom and Iraq and Turkey, UK Treaties Online, available at https://treaties.fcdo.gov.uk/awweb/awarchive?item=59159.

147 McDowall (n 3) 160.

148 Four Points, Woodrow Wilson, 'An Address to a Joint Session of Congress [4 Points],' quoted in Arthur S. Link (ed), *The Papers of Woodrow Wilson, Volume 45, November 11, 1917–January 15, 1918* (PUP 1984) 322–333.

149 See Daniel Müller, 'The Kurds of Soviet Azerbaijan, 1920–91' (2000) 19(1) Central Asian Survey 41; Manuel Hasratian, 'The Kurds in the USSR and in The CIS (A Brief Account)' (1998) 2(a) I&C 39; А. Н. Бижан, 'Курдский Вопрос» И Изучение Истории Курдов в Советской России / СССР (1920–1980-е Годы)' Вестник Вгу. Серия: История. Политология. Социология. (2020) 3 and Г. ШАХБАЗЯН, 'РОССИЯ И ПРОБЛЕМА КУРДОВ' Обозреватель – Observer (in Russian).

150 The 1930 Treaty was replaced by the special agreement of 4 April 1955 to rein in the Iraqi Army and its military airbases by Britain, which later led to the continual quell of the Kurds in their rebellions, available at https://treaties.fco.gov.uk/awweb/pdfopener?md=1&did=65637. For the impact of the Anglo-Iraqi Treaty on the Kurdish position, see Anita Burdett, *Records of the Kurds: Territory, Revolt and Nationalism, 1831–1979: British Documentary Sources*, vol 7 (CUP 2015) 715.

151 The Anglo-Iraqi Treaty of 13 January 1926, regarding ceding the Mosul region to Iraq, did not allude to the Kurds' rights.

152 For Iraq's road to statehood, see Susan Pedersen, 'Getting out of Iraq—in 1932: The League of Nations and the Road to Normative Statehood' (2010) 115(4) AHR 975. For Britain's withdrawal from Iraq, see Peter Sluglett, *Britain in Iraq: Contriving King and Country* (IB Tauris 2007).

153 Mitchell (n 34) 98.

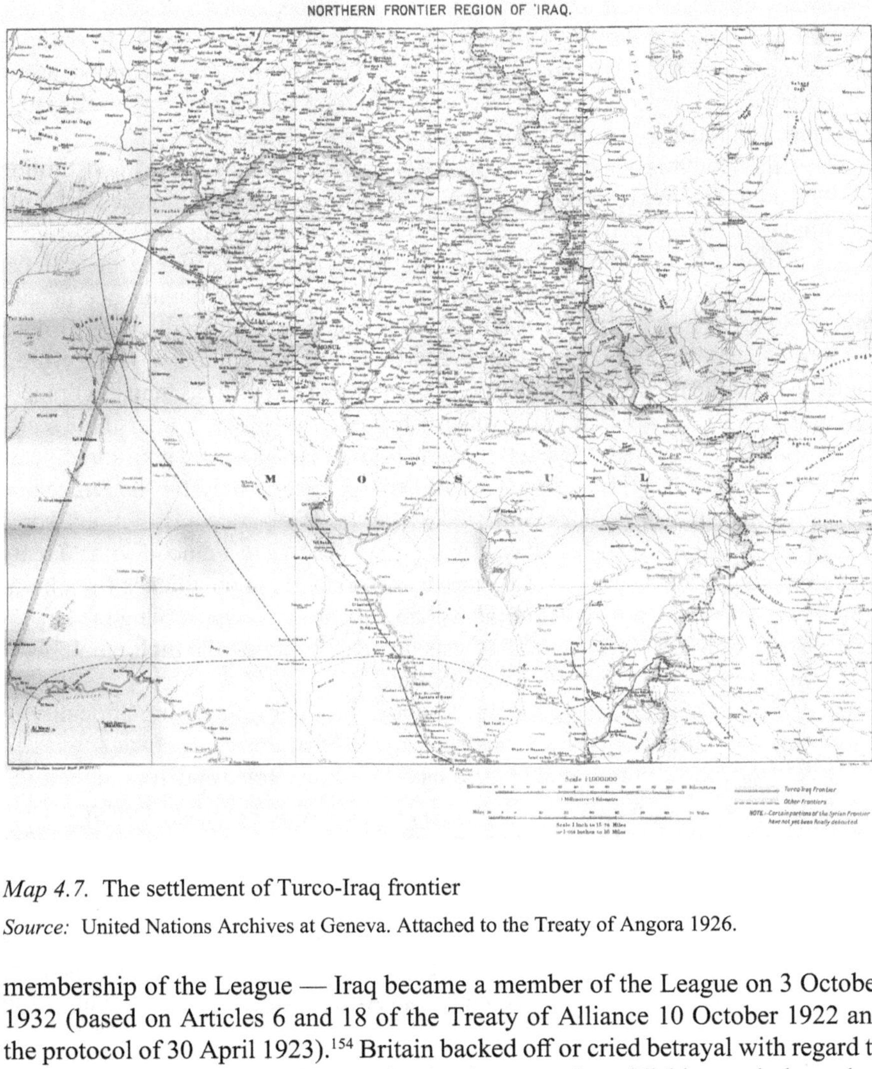

Map 4.7. The settlement of Turco-Iraq frontier

Source: United Nations Archives at Geneva. Attached to the Treaty of Angora 1926.

membership of the League — Iraq became a member of the League on 3 October 1932 (based on Articles 6 and 18 of the Treaty of Alliance 10 October 1922 and the protocol of 30 April 1923).[154] Britain backed off or cried betrayal with regard to its promise for Kurdish self-determination by way of establishing an independent state. But in fact, the British government was 'contemptuous' of Kurdish independence.[155] Therefore, it imposed a preponderance of Arab influence on the Kurds. 'Owing to the underdeveloped state of the country, the lack of communications, and the dissension of the tribes,' Britain found the creation of an independent

154 David McDowall, 'The Kurdish Question: A Historical Review' in Philip G. Kreyenbroek and Stefan Sperl (eds), *The Kurds: A Contemporary Overview* (Routledge 1992) 20; The Treaty of Alliance, available at https://treaties.fcdo.gov.uk/awweb/awarchive?item=64124.

155 Bulloch and Morris (n 59) 99.

Kurdistan 'impossible' at least for *that time* (emphasis added), despite 'a strong national movement towards self-determination and independence.' However, a Kurdish administration or a 'very large measure of autonomy,' with Kurdish as the official language, was deemed merely 'possible.'[156] Kurdish sovereign self-determination was, thus, not a priority in British policy implementation.

The High Commissioner of the Mandatory Power, in its declared constitution of 1930, adopted a regressive policy toward the autonomy of minorities in Syria, contemplating the integrity of the country through underscoring individual rights. Kurds petitioned three times for administrative autonomy to evince their 'local support for the French administration [rather] than a desire to obtain specific cultural or political rights' for Kurdistan along the border, disentangling the Turkish and Syrian territories. France was not prepared to concede autonomy to the Kurds. Under the League Mandate, France rebuffed the Kurdish petitions, and the Franco-Syrian Treaty (1936) put an end to Kurdish-French relations. Under the Treaty, which should have lasted 25 years, Syria had to be recognised within three years to join the League,[157] with a special administrative regime only for the Druze and Alawite territories. The country consisted of a series of separate jurisdictions, some of them ethnically defined for Alawis and Druze. The 1936 Franco-Syrian Treaty triggered the 'Kurdo–Christian bloc' movement in 1936, as an alliance for administrative autonomy in lieu of becoming Syrian citizens while conserving the territorial integrity of Syria. A common flag was created, implying the multiethnic facet of the community. Their demands were not met.

In 1935, Persia was renamed 'Iran' to apparently mark the multinationality of the modern Iranian nation-state. It has been alleged that this change was suggested by Hitler, to imply 'pure-blooded Aryans.'[158] Turkey, Iraq, and Iran signed the Treaty of Sa'adabad (8 July 1937), which recognised the existing borders. They felt themselves obliged to cooperate in suppressing the Kurds' demands.[159] The need for maintaining entrenched sovereign state borders cancelled any move to set up a new state.

The defeat of France in 1940 provided a rationale for ending the French mandate in the Levant. With the victory of Syrian nationalists in the parliamentary elections of July 1943 and the launching of an Arab revolt, the new government in

156 Circular Memo, No. 43, 8 December 1918 from Major E.W.C. Noel, C.I.E. P.O. Sulaimaniyah to A.P.O's Kifri, Kirkuk and Altun Keupri. Burdett, vol 5 (n 22) 189–192. Also, a Aecret Memo to The Secretary to the High Commissioner, Baghdad, Burdett, vol 6 (n 27) 204. 1 November 1922. Britain had relinquished his support of the Kurds by December 1921. See Olson, 'Battle for Kurdistan' (n 72).

157 Tejel, *Syria's Kurds* (n 54) 29–37.

158 The government in Tehran was sympathetic to Nazi Germany during the early stage of the WWII, prior to the occupation of Iran by the Soviet Union and Britain in August 1941. See Howard Blum, *Night of the Assassins: The Untold Story of Hitler's Plot to Kill FDR, Churchill, and Stalin* (HarperCollins 2020). Also, see Mohammed Alsulami, 'A French Writer Triggers Debate about Iranian History' (trans by Watan SA, 2018) Rasanah. For the 'Theory of Aryan,' see David Frawley, *Myth of the Aryan Invasion of India* (VOI 2005).

159 McDowall (n 3) 224–232.

France recognised the independence of Syria and Lebanon. In 1946, Syria declared its independence from the French mandate and the Fourth Republic of France pulled its troops out of Syria with no concessions to the Kurds.[160] The ending of the French mandate in the Levant and Syria's independence in the 1940s again occurred without any change to the Kurds' rights. Thus, self-determination or even democratic governance remained a chimera.

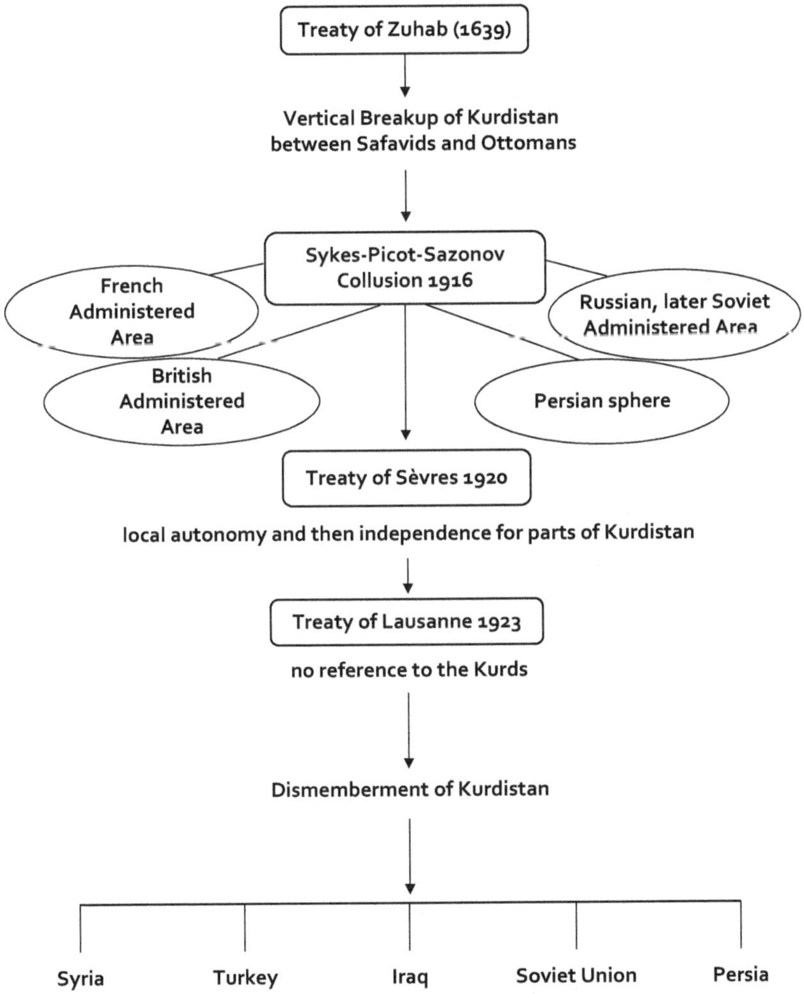

Diagram 4.1 Kurdistan breakup

160 See David Romano and Mehmet Gurses, *Conflict, Democratization, and the Kurds in the Middle East: Turkey, Iran, Iraq, and Syria* (Palgrave Macmillan 2014) 90.

4.3 Modern Nation-States' Rejection of Sovereign Kurdistan

Self-determination was, at best, unevenly applied during the period between the two World Wars. Coercive removal in one form or another often became the *de facto* policy, which did not accord with the freely expressed wishes of the peoples concerned. This was also extensive after WWII, for example in the case of ethnic Germans across Central and Eastern Europe. Many died being forced to relocate.[161] Ultimately, after WWII, self-determination was identified as one of the purposes of the UN. National groups hoped to achieve their objective through the exercise of external self-determination. Nevertheless, in practice, this meant internal self-determination rather than external self-determination; peoples were theoretically permitted to opt for their preferred governmental form. But for national groups in developing states, implementing the legal-political concept of self-determination necessarily entailed confronting the imperial overlords in their territories.[162] The Kurds were not an anomaly to this.

4.3.1 The Republic of Kurdistan

In 1945, the presence of Russia and a power vacuum in the East of Kurdistan provided a great opportunity for the Kurds to make progress toward achieving the first Kurdish state. Qazi Muhammad, a Kurdish leader in Mahabad, sought support from the Soviet Union. Kurds in the other three territorial fragments of Kurdistan approved the project. Qazi was elected the president of *Komala-i Jiyanawi Kurdistan* (the Committee for the Revival of Kurdistan, Known as JK) in April 1945. Mustafa Barzani of the South of Kurdistan joined in October 1945. The Iranian government had lost its sway over Kurdistan. With 15 members, a Kurdish national parliament was established on 15 December. Qazi promulgated a genuine Kurdish Republic of Kurdistan[163] on 22 January 1946 on a small scale,[164] referring to the right to self-determination.[165]

161 Mahmood Mamdani, *Neither Settler nor Native: The Making and Unmaking of Permanent Minorities* (HUP 2020) 22.

162 See Chapter 2.1.3 and 2.1.4.

163 AKA the Democratic Republic of Kurdistan. Extract from Intelligence Summary by Military Attaché, Iran, for the period 15–21 July 1946, No. 28, [FO 406/84]. Anita Burdett, *Records of the Kurds: Territory, Revolt and Nationalism, 1831–1979: British Documentary Sources*, vol 10 (CUP 2015) 304.

164 Ghassemlou believes that Qazi strived for autonomy, not independence, although he was charged with having a map of Greater Kurdistan at the martial court which was designed by the Kurdish Society in Beirut. Abdul Rahman Ghassemlou, (Secretary-General) Report of the Central Committee to the Fifth Congress of the Kurdistan Democratic Party of Iran (PDKI Publications, Paris 1981) 96. On the other hand, declaring the Azeri republic in the vicinity made the Kurds declare their sovereignty the 'Republic of Kurdistan.' David Romano, *The Kurdish Nationalist Movement: Opportunity, Mobilization and Identity* (CUP 2006) 226 and William Eagleton, *The Kurdish Republic of 1946* (OUP 1963) 107. However, a telegram from Acting Vice-Consul, Tabriz, to Tehran, 27 April 1946, No. 163, refers to Kurdish demands for autonomy within the Persian State as defined by Qazi Muhammad [FO 248/1463]. Burdett, vol 10 (n 163) 287. Also, see McDowall (n 3) 246–250.

165 Bulloch and Morris (n 59) 106.

Having no protection against the government in Tehran due to an agreement reached between the Soviets and Iran on oil supplies,[166] all Kurdish regions were to revert to Iranian sovereignty. By virtue of the Anglo-Soviet-Iranian Treaty of Alliance (January 1942), the powers were bound to withdraw from Iranian territory six months after the end of WWII.[167] The Republic of Kurdistan was left isolated.[168] Mahabad was retaken on 15 December 1946 by the Iranian army. Qazi Muhammad, along with his brother Sadr Qazi, cousin Saif Qazi, and other members of the Republic submitted in order to save people but, under the reign of Muhammad Reza, were executed in March and April 1947. Mustafa Barzani sought refuge in the Soviet Union.[169] The San Francisco Conference turned a deaf ear in 1945 to the Kurdish goal of attaining independence.[170] Self-determination then and to the present day has been subordinated to *uti possidetis* and existing territorial integrity.[171]

The early second decade of the United Nations organisation corresponded with a call for an end to colonisation, which prompted the adoption of the UNGA Resolution of Colonial Independence Declaration. Many of the current UN Member States are former colonies and have, following WWII, realised their claim to self-determination and, therefore, to statehood. The most important factor in the process is that colonial boundaries were not altered by virtue of *uti possidetis*. The internal self-determination of colonies was completely overlooked, i.e., the mode of their governance could not be decided. Moreover, ethnic and national minorities were not considered in the process of decolonising specific countries and regions. The ideal of self-determination was, thus, actually thwarted in the implementation. The Kurds, whose territorial units were decolonised separately, were denied the opportunity to exercise self-determination because the principles of state sovereignty and territoriality restricted self-determination. Now the Kurds are fragmented within decolonised units whose self-determination has already been implemented ostensibly on their behalf. But moves to set up an autonomous or truly independent Kurdistan were actually suppressed through genocide, discrimination, and repression. On February 24, 1955, Iran, Iraq, and Turkey made a tacit commitment to cooperate on the Kurdistan cause through the Baghdad Pact (also known as the Central Treaty Organization or the Middle East Treaty Organization). In August 1944, as a mutual support gesture, Kurdish delegates representing the North, South, East, and West of Kurdistan had signed the *Peymana Sê Sinor* (the Treaty of the Three Boundaries) on the connecting point of the four

166 ibid 107.

167 McDowall (n 3) 249.

168 Romano (n 164) 228.

169 McDowall (n 3) 250–253. For the Mahabad Republic, see Archie Roosevelt, 'The Kurdish Republic of Mahabad' (1947) 1(3) MEJ 247.

170 Tejel, *Syria's Kurds* (n 54) 43.

171 See Chapter 2.5.

Kurdistani segments (Dalanper Mount) emphasising transnational Kurdish aspirations.[172] Although it did not yield any practical outcome, the Kurds in the South of Kurdistan persevered.

4.3.2 The March Manifesto (1970)

The Iraqi Ba'ath party government which seized power in February 1963 was disposed to a centralisation agenda and, accordingly, refused to grant territorial independence to the Kurds. For the Ba'athists, the South of Kurdistan was an integral part of the Arab world. Subsequently, however, the Ba'athists officially recognised *Newroz* (the Kurdish New Year) and the Kurds' nationality in 1970, as explicated in the June 1966 Bazzaz Declaration. The Iraqi government countenanced these alterations of policy not for the sake of the Kurds but to thwart the influence of Iran. The negotiations between the Kurds and the Iraqi government culminated in the March Manifesto (a Peace Accord) on 11 March 1970 with the assistance of Saddam Hussain.[173] However, the agreement collapsed due to mutual suspicion and the political conduct of Saddam and his Ba'ath regime.[174] Despite reaching an accord on many issues, the goal of an autonomous Kurdish region did not come to fruition since the boundaries of the region could not be set.[175] Eventually, the Interim Constitution of 1971 recognised the national rights of the Kurds and acknowledged that Iraq comprised Arabs and Kurds (Article 5b).[176]

An attempt on the life of Mustafa Barzani's son, Idris, [177] on 6 December 1970 and the assassination of Barzani on 29 September 1971 put an end to any hope of trust between the Kurds and Arabs.[178] Oil was nationalised on 1 June 1972, and Baghdad controlled the Kirkuk oilfields. The Autonomy Law, published on 11 March 1974, denied the Kurds any form of self-control as this was not consonant with Arab nationalist ideology or Arab readiness to act on it. Article 1 of Act. No. 33 declared that the region of Kurdistan 'shall be deemed as one administrative unit which has a body corporate enjoying Autonomy within the framework of the legal, political and economic unity of the Republic of Iraq.' But Barzani and the Kurdistan Democratic Party (KDP), erstwhile 'Kurdish Democratic Party' headed by Ibrahim Ahmad, rejected the Law since it did not refer to all Kurdish areas,

172 Michael M. Gunter, *Out of Nowhere: The Kurds of Syria in Peace and War* (C. Hurst & Co. 2014) 36.

173 He was then appointed vice president and later president on 16 July 1979.

174 Izady (n 7) ch 4.

175 van Bruinessen (n 2) 29.

176 Human and Constitutional Rights, 'The Interim Constitution, Republic of Iraq' (26 August 1971).

177 Despatch, M.K. Jenner, British Embassy, Baghdad, to P.R.M. Hinchcliffe, Near Eastern Department, Foreign and Commonwealth Office, 14 December 1970, No. 1. [FCO 17/1238]. Anita Burdett, *Records of the Kurds: Territory, Revolt and Nationalism, 1831–1979: British Documentary Sources*, vol 12 (CUP 2015) 333.

178 Izady (n 7) ch 4.

especially the strategic city of Kirkuk.[179] Saddam's aim was to destroy Kurdish national leadership and to thwart the Kurdish national movement. The March Manifesto was a tool to strengthen the isolated regime and pave the way of Saddam to absolute rule in Iraq.

The war resumed in April 1974. Iraqi forces captured the Kurdish regions by taking advantage of their military and logistical reserves, 'thanks to the close guidance of Soviet military advisors.' Muhammad Reza of Iran signalled a new policy harmful to the Kurds when he signed the Algiers Agreement (6 March 1975 at the OPEC Conference)[180] with Saddam on gaining partial sovereignty over the Shatt al-Arab waterway, resulting in the suffocation of the Kurds' aspirations for autonomy. The revocation of Iranian, US, and Israeli support for the Kurds gave rise to the Iraqi regime's application of drastic security measures to wield its authority over the South of Kurdistan, razing 1,400 villages,[181] executing Kurds regardless of age and sex, expelling them from disputed areas, and resettling them with Arabs, especially in Kirkuk. Many Kurds had to seek refuge in the North and East of Kurdistan. Saddam upheld the policy of Arabisation, steadfast in its implementation.[182] The Kurds in the east of Kurdistan, undeterred by arrests and various obstacles, tenaciously pursued their activities to further their cause.

4.3.3 The 'Islamic Revolution' in Iran (1979)

Reza Palani (MirPanj, who later adopted the surname 'Pahlavi') abdicated, and his son (Muhammad Reza) was enthroned in September 1941. After the collapse of the Republic of Kurdistan, several unsuccessful intermittent rebellions transpired up to 1979. Muhammad Reza was overthrown in February 1979, and the Kurds seized on this moment as an opportunity to advance their position. The autocratic rule of both the father and son, coupled with their monolithic nation-building project through assimilationist policies and the oppressive treatment of non-Persian nationalities via a racially biased depiction of Aria and Aryanism,[183] ultimately contributed to the emergence of religious fascism. The new 'Islamic' (Shi'a) regime — contrary to the Kurds' expectations — did not countenance any possibility of autonomy or attempts at secession. Nevertheless, in December 1979, the government finally reached an agreement with the Kurds on recognising the East of

179 Hurst Hannum, *Autonomy, Sovereignty and Self-Determination: The Accommodation of Conflicting Rights* (UPP 2006) 193. Ibrahim Ahmad later founded the Patriotic Union of Kurdistan in 1975.

180 UNTS, 'The Demarcation of the Water Border (of Shatt Al-Arab)' (26 December 1975, 22 July 1976), available at https://treaties.un.org/doc/Publication/UNTS/Volume%201017/volume-1017-I-14903-English.pdf.

181 Bryan R. Gibson, 'The Secret Origins of the U.S.-Kurdish Relationship Explain Today's Disaster' (*Foreign Policy*, 14 October 2019).

182 McDowall (n 3) 334–339.

183 See Ailreza Asgharzadeh, *Iran and the Challenge of Diversity: Islamic Fundamentalism, Aryanist Racism, and Democratic Struggles* (Springer 2007).

Kurdistan's autonomy, but it was later practically nullified by the hardline religious regime that was in power.[184]

The new constitution of Iran made no reference to the Kurds or their demand for autonomy, which was perceived as being tantamount to secession. The theocratic regime, like the states of Iraq, Turkey, and Syria, perpetuated the ideology of its predecessor, championing 'one nation, one religion, one state.' Nonetheless, Kurds have persistently defied the respective central governments across the different Kurdistani segments.

4.4 Summary

The primary sources for the historical account of Kurdish self-determination demonstrate how the interpretation of self-determination has actually marginalised the Kurds. The historico-legal survey of the Kurdish striving for self-determination also encompasses international law's construction of the identity or image of the Kurds.

Self-determination was internationalised, and the Kurds were acknowledged or treated as an undeniable political-social nation from a political perspective in the Wilsonian sense after WWI. The Kurdish union against the Turkish state played a critical role in this respect. At the time, however, the desire for and the notion of self-determination had not solidified into a legal right, and there were no practical implications compelling great power support for the Kurds' political standing as a nation. The Allied Powers' political and economic interests, especially those of Britain, France, and the Soviet successor state to Russia, could not then be overlooked in the Kurds' failure to achieve territorial independence (statehood). In this era, as was elaborated in Chapter 2, self-determination was reformulated as a result of imperialist world policies to reorder political influence.

During the interwar decades, the Kurds endured the denial of their rights. They were emboldened toward resistance against the central governments. But the host states denied their aspirations and failed to accommodate the Kurds democratically within existing boundaries. Embattled and subjected to the vicissitudes of politics, the Kurds were numerically gerrymandered as minorities among five sovereign states. Since the division of Kurdistan among the states of Iran, Iraq, Syria, Turkey, and the Soviet Union, the Kurds have at times cooperated with or rebelled against these hegemonic powers in attempting to gain self-governance. At times, they have seized the initiative to carve out a *de facto* self-ruled territorial entity or an independent Kurdistan. However, Kurdish independence negatively affected the political and economic interests of the Allied powers, and the cause was also dropped as a rational political consideration at the League of Nations. The right of alien determination, i.e., the right of outsiders, was implemented by the powers to

184 The Iranians were supposed to answer the 'Islamic Republic–Yes or No?' Abdul Rahman Ghassemlou, 'Kurdistan in Iran' in Chaliand (n 67) 212.

determine the political destiny of the nations or peoples concerned and to redraw the borders of states.

Despite the adoption of self-determination as one of the purposes of the United Nations in 1945, a conceptual change from national self-determination to peoples' self-determination, and the crystallisation of self-determination as a legal right in 1966 and the consequent campaign of decolonisation, the Kurds' status was not revised, and they remained invisible to the principle of self-determination, as applied. The concept of self-determination was now to be invoked by the whole people of a state, not by an ethno-culturally homogeneous minority. The Kurds had already been fragmented into separate decolonised units, i.e., they were not decolonised as a unified territorial entity. They have, therefore, been unable to implement self-determination externally in order to create their own nation-state. Several questions arise here: is there a way of thinking about self-determination that can elevate the status of the Kurds so as to fulfil some of the underlined purposes of what self-determination is about? Does the attainment of self-determination require actual self-determination over the entire territory of Kurdistan? These points are thoroughly explored in Chapter 6.

Do the Kurds, as an ethnolinguistic nation, meet the substantive (subjective-objective) and territorial elements of peoplehood, thereby identifying them as a people claiming the right to self-determination? Has the Kurdish collectivity ever been regarded as or referred to as a people in any legal text?

5 Are the Kurds a 'People'?

'I am the torch of the knights of Kurdistan.'
Melayê Cezîrî (circa 1600)

'All peoples have the right of self-determination.' Obviously, peoples existed before the ICCPR was drafted, otherwise, how could they have been identified in 1966 as eligible to exercise the right to self-determination? Do the Kurds constitute elements of peoplehood for the purpose of the external aspect of self-determination (independence and state creation)?

The Kurds are generally recognised as the largest nation in the world without a state of their own. However, there are no official and reliable population statistics that document this because government censuses do not count them as a separate ethnic group; no headcount or demographic survey focusing on Kurds has been conducted. In the dearth of an exhaustive survey of Kurdish demography, reliance on national estimates is inevitable. On the basis of the newest demographic estimates in their individual states, the Kurdish population approximates between 43 and 53 million; this includes 25–30 million in Turkey (17%–25% of the total), 10–12 million in Iran (10%–12.5% of the total), 6–8 million in Iraq (17%–20.5% of the total), and 3–3.5 million in Syria (10%–15% of the total).[1] This is an esti-

1 For Kurds in Rojhilat, see OHCHR, Human Rights Situations and Reports of Special Rapporteurs and Representatives, Iran (the Islamic Republic of) 20, available at https://www.ohchr.org/EN/Countries/MENARegion/Pages/IRIndex.aspx. MRG, *Kurds*, available at https://minorityrights.org/minorities/kurds-4/. For Kurds in Başûr, see US Department of State, Report on International Religious Freedom 2018 – Iraq, Section 1. Religious Demography, December 2018, available at https://www.state.gov/reports/2018-report-on-international-religious-freedom/iraq/. For Kurds in Rojava, see CIA World Factbook, Syria, People and Society (Updated 30 January 2020). For Kurds in Bakûr, see CIA World Factbook, Turkey, People and Society (Updated 30 January 2020). US Department of State, Country Reports on Human Rights Practices: Turkey (2018), available at https://www.state.gov/reports/2018-country-reports-on-human-rights-practices/turkey/. Australian Department for Foreign Affairs and Trade, DFAT Country Information Report Turkey (10 September 2020), available at https://www.dfat.gov.au/sites/default/files/country-information-report-turkey.pdf. Sarah Leduc, 'The Kurdish Population' (Fondation-Institut kurde de Paris, 12 January 2017). Professor Mehrdad Izady (1992) conducted the first demographic study of the Kurds. There have been some religious and linguistic (mother tongue) censuses conducted in the Ottoman Empire of 1850s (1 m), 1880s (1.5 m) and

DOI: 10.4324/9781003424314-5

mate, and the real number might be much more than that. There is no doubt that the Kurds are the Middle East's largest stateless collectivity. To some authors, and to the Kurds themselves, the Lak (Lur and Kurdish) and Lur in the East of Kurdistan are also Kurdish, while some might be ambivalent about their Kurdish *ethnie*, although they were often classified as Kurds. Kurdish language and culture constitute their daily life and their areas were historically an integral part of the ancient Kurdish dynasties, principalities, city-states, and empires prior to the integration of Kurdistan into the Persian and Ottoman empires in the sixteenth century, e.g., the Median Empire,[2] and of what was referred to as Kurdistan on old maps. This is so with the Bakhtiari as well. Obviously, the coercive assimilation and hegemonic-suppressive practices of the Iranian state have influenced them to the extent that they might not identify themselves as Kurdish. In any case, the Kurds are more than numerous enough to constitute a separate nation-state.

Kurds have also lived in Egypt, Sudan, and the Caucasus region for thousands of years. They currently make up portions of the population in Azerbaijan,[3] Armenia, Georgia, Turkmenistan, Kazakhstan, Kirghizia, Uzbekistan, Tajikistan, Siberia, and the Russian city of Krasnodar. With the formal recognition of the Kurds in the 1920s, the predominantly Kurdish part of Azerbaijan between the Soviet Republic of Armenia and Nagorno-Karabakh was called the *Krasnyi Kurdistan* (*Kurdistanskii uezd* aka 'Red Kurdistan'), with Laçîn ('falcon,' later Shusha or Shushi) as its capital (Map 5.1). In 1930, Stalin reincorporated it into Azerbaijan[4] and forcibly deported most of the Kurds in Red Kurdistan to other Soviet republics.

Due to the hardships and periodic instances of oppression experienced in their host states, Kurds were forced or voluntarily decided to leave for other safe havens as asylum seekers or students.[5] Kurdish emigration has led to a far-flung diaspora,

in 1879 (848 thousand) by British Consul of 'Kurdistan,' Henry Trotter; and the Republic of Turkey in 1935 (1.4 m), 1945 (1.4 m), 1950 (1.8 m), 1955 (1.6), 1960 (1.8 m), and in 1965 (2.3 m). Mutlu Servet, 'Ethnic Kurds in Turkey: A Demographic Study' (1996) 28(4) IJMES 520 in Metin Heper, *The State and Kurds in Turkey: The Question of Assimilation* (Palgrave Macmillan 2007) 35–36.

2 For Kurdish empires, principalities, dynasties, autonomies, and city-states and and their replacement with central appointees, see Sabri Ateş, 'The End of Kurdish Autonomy: The Destruction of the Kurdish Emirates in the Ottoman Empire' and Boris James, 'The Rise and Fall of the Kurdish Emirates (Fifteenth to Nineteenth Centuries)' in Hamit Bozarslan, Cengiz Gunes and Veli Yadirgi (eds), *The Cambridge History of the Kurds* (CUP 2021).

3 World Directory of Minorities and Indigenous Peoples, MRGI, Azerbaijan: Kurds.

4 David McDowall, *Modern History of the Kurds* (IB Tauris 2021) 674. For minorities in Kurdistan, see Mehrdad Izady, *The Kurds: A Concise Handbook* (Taylor & Francis Inc 1992) Ch 4.

5 For Kurdish diaspora and the key issues that caused Kurdish migration, see Jowan Mahmod, *Kurdish Diaspora Online: From Imagined Community to Managing Communities* (Palgrave Macmillan 2016); Lord Russell-Johnston, The Cultural Situation of the Kurds (Report to the Committee on Culture, Science and Education, Council of Europe Parliamentary Assembly 2006) Doc 11006, available at http://assembly.coe.int/nw/xml/xref/x2h-xref-viewhtml.asp?fileid=11316&lang=en. Bahar Baser, Kurdish Diaspora Political Activism in Europe with a Particular Focus on Great Britain (BPS 2011); Amir Hassanpour and Shahrzad Mojab, 'Kurdish Diaspora,' *Encyclopedia of Diasporas* (Springer 2005); Östen Wahlbeck, *Kurdish Diasporas: A Comparative Study of Kurdish Refugee Communities* (Palgrave Macmillan 1999).

Map 5.1. Red Kurdistan

developed as a transnational community,[6] in the United States, the USSR and the states of the former Soviet Union,[7] Lebanon,[8] Europe,[9] the United Kingdom, and the northeast province of Xorasan (Khorasan) as an enclave in Iran,[10] and areas

6 Barzoo Eliassi, 'Kurdish Diaspora: A Transnational Imagined Community' in Bozarslan, Gunes and Yadirgi (n 2).

7 For the Kurds in the Soviet Union and the USSR, see Ismet Ch. Vanly, 'The Kurds in the Soviet Union' in Philip G. Kreyenbroek and Stefan Sperl (eds), *The Kurds: A Contemporary Overview* (Routledge 1992) and Derk Kinnane, *The Kurds and Kurdistan* (OUP 1964).

8 For the Kurds in Lebanon, see Vanly in Kreyenbroek and Sperl (n 7).

9 Izady, *Concise Handbook* (n 4) ch 4.

10 Some Kurds were deported to Khorasan to defend Safavid territory from the Uzbeks in 1600. They have been ensconced there ever since. Edgar O'Ballance, *The Kurdish Struggle* (Palgrave Macmillan 1996) 2. For the Kurds in Xorasan, see Kalimola Tawahodi, *Harekate Tarikhiye Kurd be Khurasan [The historical Move of Kurds to Khurasan]* (Iranian Publication 1991); 'Abbas-'Ali

south of the Caspian Sea e.g., Mazandaran, Golestan, Gilan, Qazvin and the Adrabil and Zanjan provinces.[11] Nevertheless, the highest numbers reside in Turkey, many reduced numbers of them dispersed in large cities beyond the sphere of historic Kurdistan, especially in Istanbul,[12] Ankara, and Izmir, as well as in Tehran, the Iranian capital. Considerable numbers have also been assimilated by Turks, Arabs, and Persians,[13] whether via the state educational system or through intermarriage. Despite that, national ties have sustained a Kurdish self-portrayal and have bonded Kurds across four Kurdistani segments.

5.1 Substantive Criteria (National Ties)

Self-determination is mostly wedded to peoplehood. As discussed in Chapter 3, the various efforts to define the concept have resulted in diverse descriptions by specific characteristics binding individuals to a group. The factual signifiers comprising national ties are historical tradition, race, culture, linguistic and religious unity, territorial connection and a shared consciousness of being distinct. These characteristics strengthen the ties among individuals and are the constitutive elements of a people.[14] Studying these characteristics requires a non-legal or an ethno-anthropological survey toward constructing a persuasive image of a collectivity to transcend it to a people. The objective here, however, is not to present random historical and cultural aspects of the Kurds but to investigate whether they constitute a distinct people. For that reason, this survey is relevant.

Madih, 'The Kurds of Khorasan' (2007) 1 I&C 11, 31; Wilfried Stanzer, 'Kordi: Lives, Rugs, Flatweaves of the Kurds in Khorasan' (Kollektion Adil Besim Ohg im Eigenverlag 1988).

11 Izady, *Concise Handbook* (n 4) Ch 1.

12 For the Kurds in Istanbul, see Heidi Wedel, 'Migration and Displacement: Kurdish Migrants in Istanbul in the 1990s' in Ferhad Ibrahim, *The Kurdish Conflict in Turkey: Obstacles and Chances for Peace and Democracy* (LIT Verlag Münster 2000) 181–193. For deportations of the Kurds from the North of Kurdistan to western Turkey, see Ugur Ümit Üngör, *The Making of Modern Turkey: Nation and State in Eastern Anatolia, 1913–1950* (OUP 2012). For Turkish planned mass deportation of the Kurds, see Anita Burdett, *Records of the Kurds: Territory, Revolt and Nationalism, 1831–1979: British Documentary Sources*, vol 7 (CUP 2015) 3.

13 Michael Gunter, *The Kurds: A Modern History* (MWP 2016) xix.

14 See Chapter 3.3.5.3. It is crucial to differentiate between the structure and character of culture. Differences in terms of interests, beliefs, values, and goals are related to the character of a people's culture. Meanwhile, the structure of culture composed of a common public language (compatible with minority public languages), public institutions (where the common public language is mainly spoken and compatible with minority public institutions), and public history (the history of the common public institutions, compatible with a common public history of public minority institutions). These aspects, along with a shared self-representation, daily plebiscite, and constitution, comprise the structure of culture. While the character of culture is in a constant state of flux and subject to disagreements among the populace, the structure of culture changes at a much slower pace and tends to generate a more solid consensus among a people. See Will Kymlicka, *Liberalism, Community and Culture* (OXP 1989) 165–168.

5.1.1 Self-Identified Distinctiveness

The Kurds' competition with the Chaldeans in their antiquity indicates that their distinctiveness dates back prior to the ninth century. *Ansab al-Akrad* ('Ancestry of the Kurds'), written in the ninth century by the Kurdish scholar Abu Hanifa al-Dinwari, serves as evidence that highlights the ethnicity and self-awareness of the Kurds.[15] Kurdish pride was in vogue among the Kurdish leaders, kings, and poets of the medieval age. *Al-Kurdi* ('the Kurd') as a title was a common component of their names. The ethno-political identity or ethnic awareness as a distinctive group[16] and their desire for an independent homeland later re-appeared in Kurdish poetry of the seventeenth century: 'I am the torch of the knights of Kurdistan.'[17] The Kurds had been an identifiable collectivity for 'more than two thousand years.'[18] An undeniable ethnic-linguistic Kurdish identity existed in the tribes and emirates of Kurdistan prior to Islam and throughout the Islamic era. This cultural and ancient ethnical distinction, though not conforming to modern political conceptions, was always suppressed by other, hostile cultures of the region.[19] The falsification of records pertaining to the Kurds, the omission of manuscript allusions related to them, especially in Turkish and Persian translations, and systematic misrepresentation are all anti-Kurdish policies adopted by the Kurds' host states.

The Kurds' self-view gained momentum in the nineteenth century, with their revolts and uprisings starting in the 1830s. Partly opposed to the centralisation arrangements (*Tanzimat*) by Ottomans and partly to retain their territorial control, large Kurdish revolts were initiated by the Mir Muhammad Pasha of Soran emirate and Bedirxan Pasha of the Botan emirate in the 1830s and 1840s, respectively. In 1826, Muhammad Pasha of Rewandiz, a prominent Kurdish figure, proclaimed the independence of Kurdish regions including Mosul, Mêrdîn, and Jazira-ibn-Omar, breaking away from Ottoman rule. An extensive Kurdish nationalist movement of Sheikh Ubeydullah of Nehri (of the House of Şemzînan), known as Sayyid Ubeydullah, with a religious persuasion entangled with ethno-nationalism called for an independent state of 'Kurdistan' for '[t]he Kurdish nation' after the 1877–1878 Russo-Ottoman War.[20] His movement, self-referring to distinct ethnic-

15 Ludwig W. Adamec, *The A to Z of Islam* (Scarecrow Press 2009) 84.

16 For Kurdish identity, see Amir Hassanpour, 'The Making of Kurdish Identity: Pre-20th Century Historical and Literary Discourses' in Abbas Vali (ed), *Essays on the Origins of Kurdish Nationalism* (MP 2003); Hakan Özoğlu, 'Politics of Memory: Kurdish Ethnic Identity and the Role of Collective Forgetting' in Gareth Stansfield and Mohammed Shareef (eds), *The Kurdish Question Revisited* (OUP 2017) 47–59 and also Christopher Houston, *Kurdistan: The Crafting of National Selves* (Berg Publishers 2008).

17 By Melayê Cezîrî of the Principality of Bohtan.

18 McDowall (n 4) 1–2.

19 Michael Eppel, *A People without a State: The Kurds from the Rise of Islam to the Dawn of Nationalism* (UTP 2016) 1, 6, 19.

20 A letter from Sheikh to Cochran, the American missionary, on 5 October 1880, quoted in Hakan Özoğlu, '"Nationalism" and Kurdish Notables in the Late Ottoman–Early Republican Era' (2001) 33(3) IJMES 383, 384. In October 1880, Ubeydullah exhorted his followers on both sides of Kurdistan to join him in invading the East of Kurdistan to establish the 'Kurdish Autonomous State.'

ity, language, and religion, is denominated in Kurdo-Islamic nationality, ethno-nationalistic self-consciousness.[21] In other words, he implemented 'the idea of modern nationalism'[22] with the political demand of detachment from the Ottoman Empire imbued with the aura of religion that was rendered a breeding ground for later ethno-nationalist movements up to the mid-twentieth century. Put differently, in this era, religion and nationalism were co-constitutive of the Kurdish identity. There is no doubt that Ubeydullah's exclusionary religio-political movement had great influence that transcended the Kurds of both sides of Kurdistan.

In 1866, the Mukri tribe in the East of Kurdistan had embarked upon a short-lived autonomy movement which ended with the unintended death of the local governor. Later, Sheikh Qazi Fattah instigated a new insurrection in 1900, but he was arrested. Kurds subsequently claimed distinctiveness through their submissions to British missions in the region and to central government officials. The Kurds had conceived themselves in the twentieth century as a protonational community concurrently with Arabs, Turks, and Persians. It is important to distinguish between subjective definitional identity criteria and epistemic identification criteria when determining whether a particular group qualifies as a people. Self-ascription as a nation does not serve as a defining feature of a nation's identity. Instead, it functions as an epistemic identification tool for identifying a nation from the outside.

Prior to WWI, the Turks were enticed into supporting extreme Turkic ethno-nationalism as a means of ensuring the integrity of the empire. This was developed in the post-1913 years. With the Young Turk Revolution in July 1908, ethnic and national titles were prohibited by the Law of Associations of August 1909. The Law

McDowall (n 4) 70. He was motivated by the Treaty of Berlin (13 July 1878) which settled the Russo-Turkish Wars referring to an Armenian state (in Article 61) granted by the Porte in parts of Kurdistan to protect Armenians, although he had the military backing of the Nestorian Christians for a limited time against the Persian and Ottoman states. To Ubeydullah, these states were unable to stop aggression and restore peace and order in the region. He was later exiled to and died in Hijaz in 1883. For the Kurdish revolts before Ubeydullah, see Saad Eskander, 'Britain's Policy towards the Kurdish Question, 1915–1923' (PhD Thesis, LSE 1999) 24. The existence of the power vacuum resulting from eliminating the Kurdish emirates and tribal chiefs in the first half of the nineteenth century left disputes unsettled; therefore, new religious characters rose, the Sheikh was the leader of most of the Kurdish tribes who settled the disputes based on Islam, tribal law, and Kurdish conventions. Sheikh belonged to the *Sofî* (*derwêş*) order or *tariqa* and the Naqshbandi order dated back to twelfth–thirteenth centuries and fourteenth century, respectively. Soon, three Sheikh of the Barzanis, the Qadiri Barzinjis, and Sayyids of Nehrî with *sayyid* status ('descent' from the prophet Muhammed) played a central factor in Kurdistan politically through mediation skills, religious eagerness, and marriage to chief Kurdish tribes. McDowall (n 4) 69–70. Before that, these spritual figures acted as advisors to tribal leaders and emirs. The donations from their followers made them prominent landowners. Also, see Metin Atmaca, 'Fragile Frontiers: Sayyid Taha II and the Role of Kurdish Religio-Political Leadership in the Ottoman East during the First World War' (2018) 54(3) MES 361.

21 Kamal Soleimani, 'The Kurds and "Crafting of the National Selves"' in Michael M. Gunter (ed), *Kurdish Issues: Essays in Honor of Robert W. Olson* (MP 2016) 236–257.

22 Kamal Soleimani, *Islam and Competing Nationalisms in the Middle East, 1876–1926* (Palgrave Macmillan 2014) 158.

also forbade nationality-based clubs from engaging in politics to create a country based on national lines. As a result of the Committee of Union and Progress's 1916 decree, many Kurds were forced to settle in central and western Anatolia. The continuous sense of Kurds' distinctness stimulated resistance or opposition to two institutions: Ottoman citizenship and membership in the *millet*, or the Islamic identity. The Kurdish self or political identity was a re-definition confronting the new and modern inimical Perso-Iranian, Turkish, and Arabic identities and their denial of a Kurdish identity.[23] The modern Turkish identity was predicated on social conditioning, not ethnicity, by means of which all other ethnical and religious groups were denied.[24] The Turkish ethno-statism was intensified by the Kemalists. In Iran, the existence of the Kurdish minority was not denied officially but was subordinated to the ideology of Iranian Shi'a Persians. In Iraq, the Kurds have been considered residents under an Arab hegemony. In Syria, they were considered a menace and illegal migrants or foreigners from Turkey. These, along with oppressive and homogenisation policies by the host states, begat a stronger Kurdish nationalism. A commitment to the legitimacy of this nationalist cause has survived throughout the twentieth and twenty-first centuries. Denial by sovereign rulers of Kurdish particularity, in turn, served to positively enhance the development and definition of a Kurdish national identity and a Kurdish drive for liberation from subjection under other, hostile nationalistic creeds. But Kurdish sentiment has not succeeded in achieving an internationally recognised Kurdish sovereign state.

Through clashes, trade, and contacts with invaders and other foreigners over time, the Kurds' distinctiveness became more explicit. *Kûrdayetî* (Kurdishness), ethno-political distinctiveness compared with the 'others,' and the early Kurdish nationalism aspiration for territorial independence (Kurdistani) are conspicuous in the verses of the epic chronicles of *Sharafnâma* (1597)[25] and the *Mem û Zîn* (1695):[26]

23 McDowall (n 4) 2, 105–118. Martin van Bruinessen, 'Kurdish Identities and Kurdish Nationalisms in the Early Twenty-First Century (2020). Published in Turkish as: 'Erken 21. Yüzyılda Kürt Kimlikleri ve Kürt Milliyetçilikleri' in Elçin Aktoprak and A. Celil Kaya (eds), *21. Yüzyılda Milliyetçilik: Teori ve Siyaset* (Iletisim 2016) 349–373.

24 McDowall (n 4) 3. For Turkic ethno-nationalism, see Üngör (n 12).

25 Sharaf al-Din Bitlisi, *Sharafnama: History of the Kurdish Nation* (trans from Farsi by Mehrdad R. Izady, Mazda Pub 2005). Mîr Sharaf Xân Bitlîsî (Prince Sharaf al-Dîn Bitlisi, 1543-1603-04) as the emir of the Emirate of Bitlis. See Sacha Alsancakli, 'Historiography and Language in 17th-Century Ottoman Kurdistan: A Study of Two Turkish Translations of the Sharafnāma' (2018) 6(2) KS 171 and Martin van Bruinessen, 'Ehmedê Xanî's Mem û Zîn and its Role in the Emergence of Kurdish Nationalism' in Vali (n 16).

26 The patriotic poem or the popular romance as the Kurdish Romeo and Juliet was written by Ehmedê Xanî (1650–1706). Reference to Kurdistan and Kurdish identity is also seen in other works, such as *Seyahatname* (Ottoman traveller Evliya Çelebi, 1611–1685), *Kamus-ul Alem* (Haji Qadir Koyi, 1817–1897), and the Ottoman intellectual Semseddin Sami (1850–1904). Zeynep N. Kaya, *Mapping Kurdistan; Territory, Self-Determination and Nationalism* (CUP 2020) 27–29.

Look, from the Arabs to the Georgians,
The Kurds have become like towers.
The Turks and Persians are surrounded by them.
The Kurds are on all four corners.
...
Each tribe forming a formidable bulwark.
Whenever the Ottoman Sea [Ottomans] and Tajik Sea [Persians]
Flow out and agitate,
The Kurds get soaked in blood
Separating them [the Turks and Persians] like an isthmus.
...
We would perfect our religion, our state,
and would educate ourselves in learning and wisdom.[27]

In the twentieth century, self-consciousness has helped many groups to build nation-states, such as the Armenians, Arabs, and Jews. But the Kurds, while able to self-identify, failed to secure political recognition of modern nationhood. Diplomatic and military reports as well as the Kurdish applications to British and French missions for recognition marked them out as a distinct group.

The Kurdish sheikhs of Mosul, including Abul Salam Barzani, presented a petition in 1909 for the second time to the Kurdish nationalists in Istanbul,[28] proposing regional autonomy for Kurdistan and urging 'the adoption of Kurdish for official and educational purposes; the appointment of Kurdish-speaking officials; [and] the adoption of the Shafi'i school of law.'[29] In 1911, with the idea of creating a Kurdish nation with national consciousness,[30] Abdulrezzaq Bedirxan, Mulla Salim, Simko Şikak (Simîtko or Smail Agha) in Urmîye (Urmia) led a movement with the intention of declaring 'the independence of Kurdistan.' Sheikh Taha spearheaded another independence movement. They asked for Kurdish self-determination modelled on 'other Nations'[31] to establish an autonomous entity under Russian protection. Nevertheless, their proposal was not supported by many Kurds because Russia sought to retain eastern Anatolia for itself. In a report on his mission to investigate Kurdish attitudes in 1918, British Captain C.L. Woolley referred to 'a strong national sense over a far wider area' of Kurdistan and the impetus to 'be

27 Part of '*Derde me*' ('our ills'). Ehmedê Xanî (n 26).

28 The first one had been presented in 1907 following a conference of Kurdish leaders. Abul Salam Barzani was executed in December 1914 by the governor of Mosul.

29 McDowall (n 4) 114.

30 Michael A. Reynolds, 'The Ends of Empire Imperial Collapse and the Trajectory of Kurdish Nationalism' in So Yamane and Norihiro Naganawa (eds), *Regional Routes, Regional Roots? Cross-Border. Patterns of Human Mobility in Eurasia* (HSERC 2017) 39–41.

31 O 608/95, Telegram, Political Officer, Baghdad, to [Foreign Office?], April 15, 1919, No. 4380; Note entitled 'Kurdistan,' 10 February 1919, Referencing Summary Intelligence, No. 291 of 15 January 1919 [AIR 20/512]. Anita Burdett, *Records of the Kurds: Territory, Revolt and Nationalism, 1831–1979: British Documentary Sources*, vol 5 (CUP 2015) 264, 307. For Simko, see Kamal Soleimani, 'The Kurdish Image in Statist Historiography: The Case of Simko' (2017) 53(6) MES 949.

recognized as a nation' with 'a government of their own.' Woolley also referred to the 'national consciousness' of Kurds, demanding 'an independent Kurdistan' or 'a united Kurdistan' at the time.[32] Their demand for a Kurdish state was sometimes expressed through their leaders. In December 1918, Sureya Bedirxan, Secretary-General for the Committee of Kurdish Independence, explained the rationale for 'Kurdish Statehood.'[33] In another appeal to 'all Governments of Europe' on 16 December 1918 and to Britain on 21 December 1918, the Kurds declared their desire to free Kurdistan as a 'country' from 'servitude.'[34] Sharif Pasha, in his letter in June 1919 to the British Secretary of State, referred to the 'Kurdish nation.'[35] In another report by the British Military Intelligence on the Kurdish situation in July 1919, Major Noel, after enumerating some movements between the 1830s and 1914, mentioned the 'nationality' of Kurds as 'distinct,' adding that it 'has never been submerged.' He alluded to their 'national aspiration' for 'independence.' He also referred to the Kurdish claim of 'self-determination and autonomy.'[36] In January 1919, the Committee of Kurdish Independence in Cairo appealed to the British government for the establishment of a 'Kurdish State.'[37] Kurdish national movements demanded independence or autonomy, including notably the Society for the Advancement of Kurdistan (SAK) established on 17 December 1918. Their activity exerted great influence on the Kurds' self-portrayal, strengthening the sentiment of belonging to a shared fate even though political suppression had retarded Kurdish nationalism. The SAK was the first modern national Kurdish organisation.[38] It represented the Kurds at the Paris Peace Conference with the objective of independence.[39]

The Committee of National Kurdish Democratic Party (KDP), headquartered in Constantinople (later Istanbul), submitted a petition to His Majesty's High Commissioner on 31 August 1919. It requested the application of 'the accepted principles of President Wilson…in favour of the Kurdish Nation,' that deserves 'liberty' and the right to revolt 'to recover their independence.' The memorandum asked the British government to recognise the Kurds' 'national right of existence'

32 Report by Capitan C. L. Woolley on his mission to Viranshehir from 11–18 May 1918, [WO 106/64]. Burdett, vol 5 (n 31) 76–78.

33 Appeal from Sureya Bédir Khan, Secretary-General of the Committee for Kurdish Independence, Cairo, 7 December 1918. ibid 197–209.

34 Translation of a letter from Sureya Bédir Khan, Secretary-General of the Committee for Kurdish Independence, to the High Commissioner, Cairo 16 December 1918 [FO 141/810]. ibid 369.

35 Telegram from Secretary of State to Civil Commissioner, Baghdad, 6 June 1919, No P3052, [FO 608/96].

36 'Note on the Kurdish Situation': a report on the aspects of the Kurdish situation, by Military Intelligence, High Commissioner Office, Constantinople, [name obscured, probably Major Noel], 18 July 1919. Burdett, vol 5 (n 31) 429–461.

37 Report on the Situation in Kurdistan from the Secretary's note for the Inter-Departmental Conference on Middle Eastern Affairs, 15 September 1919 [FO 608/95]. ibid 519.

38 Özoğlu (n 20) 386–387.

39 Eppel (n 19) 123–126.

and 'independence' against 'external and internal enemies.'[40] In the second memorandum on 7 October, the Secretary-General of the KDP urged 'the independence of a United Kurdistan within its natural and national boundaries.'[41] In 1920, with the breakup of the SAK, Amin Ali Bedirxan established the Society for the Kurdish Social Organization openly promoting full independence.[42] The disgruntled Kurdish dynasties of Bedirxan and the Sayyids of Nehri inaugurated the autonomist and breakaway tendencies of Kurdistan; the former with a secular and the latter with a religious persuasion to pursue the Kurdistan question within Ottoman boundaries. Under the leadership of Celadet and Kamuran Bedirxan (Amin Ali's sons), the *Xoybûn* League ('be yourself' or 'be oneself')[43] as a 'national pact'[44] for all classes of Kurds had a critical role in promoting a common Kurdish culture and creating a school of Kurdish nationalism to liberate 'Kurdish national soil' in the Levant from under Kemalism. It was established in October 1927, which later led to the Mount Ararat rebellion under the command of Ihsan Nuri Pasha in the 1930s.[45] Other independence movements by Ibrahim Pasha of the Milli, Sheikh Sa'id Barzinji, Hussain Bedirxan, Abdulrezzaq Bedirxan, Mahmud Hafid, Sheikh

40 Despatch from J.M. de Robeck, High Commissioner, Constantinople, to Lord Curzon, 18 September 1919, No. 1702/M2201, [FO 608/95]. Burdett, vol 5 (n 31) 526–528.

41 Letter from the Secretary-General of the Kurdish Democratic Party to the High Commission, Constantinople, 7 October 1919, No 21, [FO 608/95]. ibid 536–537.

42 Sheikh Abdulqadir (Sheikh Ubeydullah's son) publicly declared the Kurds' demand for autonomy, due to his own religious considerations and proclivities, in 1918 under British auspices with the support of Britain. He along with Amin Ali Bedirxan had established the first political organisation of Kurdish Society of Mutual Cooperation and Progress on 2 October 1908 in Istanbul. This demand caused a split between the secessionists (Bedirxan family) and autonomists (Şemzînan) members of the SAK. In the years to come, however, both families opposed the Kemalist movement against the Caliphate in Istanbul because of Kemalist hostility to any future Kurdish state or the autonomy of Kurdistan. Özoğlu (n 20).

43 In October 1927, the self-exiled Kurds of various strata formed the party of '*Xoybûn* League' in Bhamdoun, Lebanon. Some sources refer to its establishment in 1924. Disappointed in Britain and France, they cast about for patronage of Italians and Americans. Its headquarters were based in Aleppo with missions in London, Paris, and Detroit and clandestine branches in Iraq, Syria, and Turkey. Nelida Fuccaro, 'Kurds and Kurdish Nationalism in Mandatory Syria: Politics, Culture and Identity' in Vali (n 16) 197. The *Xoybûn* had commenced a 'pen' (cultural and linguistic) movement to bolster the national identity of the Kurds through teaching the Kurdish language (Kurmanji), literature, and the history and geography of Kurdistan in schools. The periodic journal of *Hawar* ('The Calling') was published in Kurdish and French from 1932 to 1943. After that, *Roja Nû* (New Day) was produced up to 1946. The Kurds had also used radio from March 1941. Concurrently, other Kurdish societies such as *Ciwanên Kurd* ('Young Kurds') and the Sharaf al-Din Bitlisi Club, the Salah al-Din Club established in Cizîr and Damascus. Also, the French Kurdologists and orientalists aided them in providing materials and nation-building as well. The Kurdish cultural movement had a creative aspect, the Kurdish women that Bedirxan referred to as 'one of the elements of the eastern renaissance.' It could be considered the basis of founding the special armed force for women, YPJ in Rojava. Jordi Tejel, *Syria's Kurds: History, Politics and Society* (Routledge 2009) 23–28.

44 Martin Strohmeier, *Crucial Images in the Presentation of a Kurdish National Identity: Heroes and Patriots, Traitors and Foes* (BRILL 2003) 109. See Benedict Anderson, *Imagined Communities: Reflections on the Origin and Spread of Nationalism* (Verso books 2006).

45 Cecil J. Edmonds, 'Kurdish Nationalism' (1971) 6(1) JCH 87.

Abdulqadir, and Sheikh Sa'id of Piran, induced by the nationalist organisation of *Azadî* ('liberty') to liberate Kurdistan and 'the Kurdish nation' from 'the despotism of the Turks,' were brutally oppressed and the leaders were either executed or murdered by the Turks.[46] Simko was likewise assassinated at the hands of the Persians during the rule of Reza Pahlavi. After enduring repeated bombings of his government's premises by the RAF, Sheikh Mahmud Barzinji ('the king of Kurdistan') was arrested in September 1930. As a result of his arrest, a riot ensued, prompting a brutal response by the Iraqi Army which led to his deportation from Kurdistan, never to return.[47]

As part of the resistance against the oppressive rules including the 1935 Law of Resettlement, the people of Dêrsim in the North of Kurdistan submitted a letter to the League of Nations in 1937, seeking help against the policy of banning the Kurdish language even on the street, using 'barbarous methods' of forcing Kurds to work on military projects, manipulating the internal borders of Dêrsim region, and deporting Kurds selected by Ankara. In another memorandum to the UN, the Kurds referred to their desire to have 'their own national state,' conducting a protracted revolt against 'occupiers' across Kurdistan, and 'their total refusal to submit to slavery.'[48] In the spring of 1938, the Turks demolished the whole of Dêrsim, home to a fierce rebellion against the Kemalist state. Thousands of Kurds were killed by poison gas — purchased from Germany — ordered by Mustafa Kemal and his prime minister İsmet İnönü.[49] The Dêrsim resistance was subdued in 1938 with the execution of its leaders, including Seyid Riza, leading to the Dêrsim massacre.[50]

The popular *Rizgarî* ('liberation') party based in Lebanon, with backing of the Allied powers, the UN, and other international groups, made an appeal to the UN and the American Legation in Baghdad regarding self-determination and sovereignty of all four Kurdistani segments in January 1946, but Britain's priority was to retain the integrity of the existing states at any cost. Dozens of Rizgarî members were arrested leading to the party's disbandment.[51] In several other letters to the Secretary of the League of Nations, the UN, Britain and their host states, Kurds demanded fulfilment of their national rights and formation of a Kurdish

46 Strohmeier (n 44) 89.

47 Eskander (n 20). His epitomised rule is an exponent of Kurdish nationalism. Eppel (n 19) 119. Also, see Gunter, *The Kurds* (n 13) 65 and Gorgas J. Tejel, 'Urban Mobilization in Iraqi Kurdistan during the British Mandate: Sulaimaniya 1918–30' (2008) 44(4) MES 537.

48 John Bulloch and Harvey Morris, *No Friends but the Mountains: The Tragic History of the Kurds* (OUP 1992) 180. Dêrsim has been Turkified to 'Tunceli' along with many other Kurdish toponyms.

49 See Robert Olson, 'The Kurdish Rebellions of Sheikh Said (1925), Mount Ararat (1930), and Dersim (1937–38): Their Impact on the Development of the Turkish Air Force and on Kurdish and Turkish Nationalism' (2000) 40(1) DWI 67–94; Izady, *Concise Handbook* (n 4) 62; Andrew Mango, *Ataturk: The Biography of the Founder of Modern Turkey* (1st ed, John Murray 1999) 288–297. For evidence confirming the use of gas in Dêrsim, see Taner Akcam, 'Dersim Katliamı'nda zehirli Gaz Kullanma Emri Mustafa Kemal ve İsmet İnönü'den' (Agos, 31 March 2023).

50 Dilek Kurban, *Limits of Supranational Justice: The European Court of Human Rights and Turkey's Kurdish Conflict* (CUP 2020) 89; Strohmeier (n 44) 128.

51 McDowall (n 4) 297–300.

state in the name of Kurdistan.[52] All these grievances, statements, and appeals for self-determination, in which Kurds communicated their identity and referred to their distinctiveness, fell on deaf ears from the Wilsonian era until the present day. It should be noted that the United States played a decisive role in facilitating the establishment of an autonomous Kurdish zone in the South of Kurdistan starting in 1991. Indeed, the Kurds' demands were illustrative of a distinct collectivity that defined their national identity. But that self-perceived distinctiveness proved insufficient to the Allied powers or their host states for creating a new Middle Eastern nation-state. The will of Kurds as a distinct people, 'with varying degrees,'[53] was never expressed through an informed and democratic process or in a free plebiscite throughout the Kurdish lands although the Kurds have re-emphasised a shared consciousness of themselves as a people apart up to this date, demonstrating the continuity of being Kurdistani.

5.1.2 Objective Elements

The Kurds reify the subjective element of separateness by means of diverse objective characteristics. The ethno-anthropological characteristics of origin, ethnicity, history, land, language, religion, and calendar link the Kurds across the four states and have given them a distinct character with an understood purpose of achieving eventual independence.[54] Substantive or national ties, plus a common interest in being independent or autonomous, further entrench the Kurds' self-definition and shape their claim to self-determination as a people.

5.1.2.1 Origin

There are various myths concerning the Kurdish lineage. The first one considers them the descendants of children harboured in the mountains to be protected against the ravages of Zuhak (*Astyages/Azhdahak* meaning 'dragon') — the Median ruler who ate youngsters of various ancestries and was ousted by *Kawey Asinger* (Kawa the Blacksmith) in 603 BCE. This myth was especially referred to by Kurds in the Wilsonian era and was used in the period between the two world wars as well as the 1970s during efforts to form a secular Kurdish identity.[55] The second myth alludes to the Kurds as descendants of the children of 'slave girls of King Solomon, sired

52 See Appendix 1.

53 van Bruinessen, 'Kurdish Identities' (n 23) 3.

54 It should be noted that rejecting independence or autonomy by a particular group of Kurds in a hypothetical referendum does not negate their Kurdish identity. The disputes among the Kurdish population regarding their historical myths and future aspirations are regarded as the character of their culture, rather than its structure. Being a member of the Kurdish community is an element of the unified structure of culture that endures over time, despite variations in the historical narratives, shifting beliefs, values, interests, and potential political directions that the populace may choose to pursue. The existence of national ties is the fount of Kurdish hopes for self-determination.

55 Kutbettin Kılıç, 'Negotiating the Meaning of Kurdishness: The Construction of a Secular Kurdish Identity Perception by Kurdish Political and Intellectual Elites in Turkey' (2020) 56(6) MES 811.

by a demon named Jasad, and driven by the angry king into the mountains.'[56] The last one links Kurds to Sarah, the Prophet Abraham's wife (a Kurd of Harran);[57] it confirms that the Kurds were monotheistic.[58] These stories, as subjective components, have been invaluable in instilling a sense of nation-building,[59] since they refer to the collective identity of Kurds.

Having alluded to a few documented linguistic similarities between Kurdish and Persian, the Kurds were labelled a 'half Aramaeic and half Median-Persian people' by the linguist Barthold Georg Niebuhr. This theory is called the 'out-of-Medes hypothesis,' which considers Kurds rooted in the northwest, northeast, and southeast of Iran, based on linguistic assumptions by the Russian orientalist Vladimir Fedorovich Minorsky, the Swiss orientalist Albert Socin, and the Armenian Garnik Asatrian. Other linguists dwell on the Kurds' as offspring of the Guti (and Lulubi)[60] who were 'indigenous, autochthonous (Zagros) people (Speiser, Mesopotamian Origins, 1930, 110-119),' It posits a 'pre- and non-Indo-European (pre-non-Iranian)' lineage as was also claimed by Ephraim Avigdor Speiser and Nikolaĭ Yakovlevich Marr.[61] Kurds also could be regarded as the descendants of the Hurri, Kurti, Mard, Carduchi (Qardu), Gordyene, Adianbene, Zila, and Khaldi (Khaldeans). These peoples had their empire, kingdom or city-state in Kurdistan from 4300 BCE onward.[62] However, the most common hypothesis is that Kurds are descendants of the *Medes* — a group of indigenous, ancient Indo-European peoples who moved into the Middle East around 4,000 years ago to establish their empire (728–550 BCE).[63] They are mentioned in the Old Testament of the Bible (Isaiah 13:17). The Mede Kingdom ('Carduchians' or 'Gordions' referred to in

56 Bitlisi (n 25).

57 An ancient city in the Upper Mesopotamia.

58 '[W]ith the Garden of Eden, with Noah and with Abraham.' William A. Wigram and Edgar T.A. Wigram, *The Cradle of Mankind: Life in Eastern Kurdistan* (LOA 1922) vii.

59 McDowall (n 4) 5.

60 Sheikh A. Waheed, *The Kurds and Their Country: A History of the Kurdish People from Earliest Times to the Present* (2nd ed., UBA 1958) 42–57.

61 *Vorträge über alte Geschichte* Berlin 1847, quoted in Ferdinand Hennerbichler, 'The Origin of Kurds' (2012) 2(2) AIA 64–79.

62 Mehrdad Izady, *Origin of The Kurds*, The Encyclopaedia of Kurdistan (1988, 1992). For Kurdish governments from ancient times, see Jawad Mella, *Kurdistan and the Kurds: A Divided Homeland and a Nation without State* (WKAO 2005) pt 2, Ch 1.

63 Taufiq Wahby, *The Origins of the Kurds and their Language* (KSSE, No. IX and X, 1966) 23–28; Nezan Kendal, 'The Kurds: Current Position and Historical Background' in Philip Kreyenbroek and Christine Allison (eds), *Kurdish Culture and Identity* (ZB 1996) 7–19; Gerard Chaliand (ed), *A People without a Country: The Kurds and Kurdistan* (1st pub 1980, rev and updt, Zed Books Ltd 1993); Arshak Safrastian, *Kurds and Kurdistan* (Harvill Press 1948) 16–31; Momammad Amin Zaki, *A Summary of the History of Kurdistan and the Kurds from Earliest Times to the Present Day* (Dar-al-Salam 1931) 61; Wadie Jwaideh, *The Kurdish National Movement: Its Origins and Development* (SUP 2006) iii. This view has been challenged on the lingual footings by David N. MacKenzie, *Kurdish Dialect Studies* (OUP 1961b, 1962); Hennerbichler (n 61) 68–70 and Eppel (n 19) 5.

Xenophon)[64] was a powerful empire that ruled modern-day East and North of Kurdistan, from 612 BCE after overthrowing the Assyrians.[65]

The International Commission of Inquiry of the League on the Question of the Frontier between Turkey and Iraq or the *vilayet* of Mosul (1925), by referring to the 'compound' origin of the Kurds, introduced 'the autochthonous inhabitants who lived at the dawn of history in the mountains overlooking Assyria, Babylon and the Iranian Plateau' as some of the ancestors of the Kurds. Despite the obscurity of their origin, the Commission concluded that '[t]he Kurds are neither Arabs, Turks nor Persians, though they are most nearly related to the Persians. They are different and clearly distinguishable from the Turks, and still more different and remote from the Arabs.'[66] Ethnicity is another way that may identify a people.

5.1.2.2 Ethnicity

Genetics, a matter of biological anthropology or population genetics, can also throw light on the lineage of Kurds. In an interdisciplinary study published in 1994, 'The History and Geography of Human Genes,'[67] Kurds are categorised genetically into 'Kurdish and Caspian in the West,' in Iran, while having overall similarities with other peoples in the Middle East. The findings are based on the DNA data of 18 different people in the West of Asia, encompassing the Kurdish Complex (Kurdish inhabited areas). According to the DNA research data: 1) the Kurds matrilineally 'co-founded the Near East (Eurasia/West Asia) and Europe'; 2) they are descendants of the '(first) Neolithic Northern Fertile Crescent farmers and shepherds'; 3) there is 'the closest genetic' bond between Kurds, Jews, and Armenians; 4) their forefathers 'have obviously existed from very beginnings simultaneously at the same time in the far North (E-Anatolia, N-Mesopotamia) and the far North-East' (Zagros and eastern plains of the East of Kurdistan).[68] To sum up, the ethnic and linguistic ancestors of modern Kurds have inhabited their land, 'a wider Eurasian Northwest, largely outside and northwest of Iran of today.'[69]

A new study in 2019, *Distinct Genetic Variation and Heterogeneity of the Iranian Population*,[70] corroborates that the Kurds in the East of Kurdistan present hetero-

64 Kardouchoi, Carduchin, Carduchian or Kardokhoy has been referred to in Xenophon, *Anabasis* (composed in 370 BC, 430–354 BC) 287–325. Also, Marco Polo refers to the Kurds in Teresa Waugh, *The Travels of Marco Polo* (Sidgwick & Jackson 1984) 25. Strabo and Pliny referred to the Kurds as well. Carl Dahlman, 'The Political Geography of Kurdistan' (2002) 43(4) EGE 271.

65 Stephen Mansfield, *The Miracle of the Kurds: A Remarkable Story of Hope Reborn in Northern Iraq* (Worthy Publishing 2014) 24–25; Hassan Arfa, *The Kurds* (OUP 1966) 2.

66 Question of the Frontier between Turkey and Iraq, Report of the League of Nations' Commission of Inquiry, 20 August 1925, 44, 46.

67 Luca Cavalli-Sforza, Paolo Menozzi and Alberto Piazza, *The History and Geography of Human Genes* (PUP 1994).

68 Hennerbichler (n 61) 64–69.

69 ibid 69–79.

70 Zohreh Mehrjoo and others, 'Distinct Genetic Variation and Heterogeneity of the Iranian Population' (2019) 15(9) PLoS Genet e1008385.

geneity and different levels of consanguinity with other ethnicities within Iran, including Persian, Lur, Azeri, Arab, Baluch, Torkman, Qashqai, and Armenian. It is based on genome-wide data from a stratified ethnic-group sampling (1,021 samples from 11 ethnic groups) and reveals the distinct genetic diversity of the population in Iran. Kurds have spread across the two Arab states of Iraq and Syria; however, the recent results cannot scientifically be overgeneralised or extended to the Kurds and Arabs in these states. To prove the genetic difference between the Kurds and other nations or ethnic groups in Iraq, Syria, and Turkey requires further study. However, regarding the eligibility to exercise external self-determination, international organisations have not considered origin as such. Other affinities have been deemed of greater importance.

Some researchers believe that the Kurds do not have common ancestry, which is also true of many nations, such as the British.[71] Still, the majority are descendants of Indo-European tribes arriving in the Middle East in the middle of the second millennium BCE. While one could argue that the Kurds may possess one of the 'longest' genealogies in the world,[72] there is no concrete scientific evidence to support this claim. Genealogies and ethnic histories are intricate and multifaceted, making it difficult to establish definitive comparisons regarding length or antiquity. Furthermore, factors such as human migration, intermixing, and historical events, such as conquests and displacements, have contributed to the diverse genetic composition of populations throughout history. Nevertheless, the Kurds undeniably possess a deeply rooted and rich historical legacy. The Sumerians documented Kurdistan or 'the land of *Kardo*' or *Karda*, in the first written evidence about Kurds, 3000 BCE.[73]

Ethnicity had a formative role in the self-determination of colonies and anti-imperialism self-determination, but it may play a part in non-colonial encounters because there might be some Kurds who are mixed with other Indo-European groups, such as the Persians, or intermixed with the Arabs. Common origins do not necessarily lead to an identical destiny. However, an ethnic element could be cited for Kurds in Turkey,[74] Iran, Iraq, and Syria, to distinguish them from the Turkish, Arab, and Persian races or free them from racial inequality. Ethnicity can play a decisive role in distinguishing Kurds from other ethnicities with whom they have a shared past and legacy. This applies, in particular, to Persians, as the Kurds may share historical signifiers with them, but shared features are not conspicuous with regard to Arabs and Turks.

71 McDowall (n 4) 9.

72 Major H. M. Burton, 'The Kurds' (1944) 31(1) JRCAS 64.

73 Mansfield (n 65) 23.

74 For Turk's race see Murat Ergin, *"Is the Turk a White Man?": Race and Modernity in the Making of Turkish Identity* (BRILL 2017).

5.1.2.3 History

'Cyrtii' (the Latin form) was identified with Kurds from the second century BCE onward, pointing to 'an amalgam of Indo-European tribes' that had entered the region at different periods from various directions. Cyrtii or Kurtioi, Kortei and Kurt were used by Greek and Roman authors to refer to the people dwelling in the Zagros, concurrently with Semitic tribes.[75] Kurti or Qurtie is first documented in a record dated to the Triumph of the Assyrian King Tiglath-pileser I from 1114–1076 BCE to the south of Lake Wan (the North of Kurdistan). Also, the term was assigned to inhabitants of the Zagros and eastern Taurus ranges 3800 years ago. Indubitably, the appellation 'Kurd' was established by the third century BCE.[76]

Kurds were induced to convert to the new religion of Islam, introduced by Arab Muslims at the time of their triumph in the seventh century CE. The new believers were first called *Kurd/Akrad* from 'Kardu' or 'Kardo'), as a distinct ethnicity by the invaders,[77] and the title has been retained ever since.[78] It is clear that the Kurds have a long historical connection with the Middle East, inasmuch as they are one of the indigenous peoples of the Middle East. Historical ties deepen the national aspiration for creating a nation-state and legitimise the claim for self-determination based upon a distinctive ethnic character. However, territorial claims based on historical ties happen to clash with the territorial integrity of four host states. Thus, the establishment of a segment of the Kurdish areas as an independent state involves historical claims on the remaining three segments.

5.1.2.4 Motherland

Kurdistan has been transfigured over time, mainly due to the lack of an established independent sovereign state over the full extent of Kurdistan as well as the demographic changes brought about by empires and current states. For almost 4,000 years, Kurds have inhabited the contiguous regions of the 200,000 square miles of their stronghold — the natural, lofty mountains that straddle five states — with their own culture, language, customs, and kingdoms.[79] Persianisation, Arabisation, Turkification, deportation, seizure of land, and the migration of non-Kurds to Kurdistan, alongside the continued assimilationist policies and internal

75 McDowall (n 4) 10. The Kurds established the Parthian Empire and the Sassanid dynasty (AD 224). The first Sassanid ruler, Ardashir I, was Kurdish. Eppel (n 19) 5.

76 Mehrdad Izady, 'Exploring Kurdish Origins' (1993) 7(2) Kurdish Life. Also, see Abdul Rahman Ghassemlou, *Kurdistan and the Kurds* (PHC 1965).

77 O'Ballance (n 10) 1. For the Kurdish medieval history (sixth–sixteenth century), see Izady, *Concise Handbook* (n 4) ch 4 and Edmonds (n 45).

78 For the term 'Kurd,' see Godfrey R. Driver, 'The Dispersion of the Kurds in Ancient Times' (1921) 53(4) JRASGBI 563. For 'Kurd' and its philological connections, see Garnik Asatrian, 'Prolegomena to the Study of the Kurds' (2009) 13(1) I&C 1 and Godfrey R. Driver, 'The Name Kurd and its Philosophical Connexions' (1923) 55(3) JRASGBI 393.

79 Brendan O'Leary, 'The Kurds, the Four Wolves and the Great Powers' (2017) 1 JOP 14. For geography of Kurdistan, see Izady, *Concise Handbook* (n 4) Ch 1 and 2.

colonisation adopted by the Kurds' host states, have led to the territorial reduction of Kurdistan (Map 5.2).[80] Documented records evidence the existence of the early residents (circa 10,000 BCE) in that area with a common, distinct 'Halaf' culture, who resided there between 6000 and 5400 BCE,[81] with their own augmented armed force over centuries, which defeated Assyrians, Greeks, and Persians across Anatolia and Mesopotamia.[82]

The term 'Kurdistan' was established in the middle of the twelfth century, pertaining only to the South and East of Kurdistan;[83] however, evidence exists that documents the term's use since the Middle Ages and even before.[84] The land of Karda or *Kurda* was used over the second millennium BCE as in Hurrian or Mitanni's records; as *Kurte* during the Assyrian period; *Gordyne* or *Kordyne* by the Greeks and the Romans; *Beth Qardu* ('Land of the Kurd') by Christian Syriac. This trend was preserved until the Arabs changed it to Jazira (meaning 'Island') after their invasion in the seventh century CE. Under the Umayyad Empire, the Muslim chronicles started to speak about the Kurds and an area called Kordistan/Kurdistan. During the Islamic era, Kurdistan was also called *Iqlim al-Jibal* ('the Mountain Region'), *Kurat al-Jabal* ('Mountain Country'), and *mahat* ('Mede'). In the thirteenth century, the Kurdish Ayyubid Empire was mentioned by Mohammed bin Ibrahim in his book entitled *Tarikh Dawlat al-Akrad* (*The History of the State of the Kurds*).[85] Currently, there is a provincial division named Kurdistan in the East of Kurdistan and a Kurdistan federal, regional government in the South of Kurdistan. The area inhabited by Kurds had been called Kurdistan before it appeared on maps in the sixteenth century.[86] With the arrival of Turkic tribes, *Kurdistan* was first used in 1150 by the Sultan Sandjar of the Seljuk (Mu'zi al-Din Ahmad al-Sinjar) to create a province of that title in 1157 (now Hemedan in the East of Kurdistan),[87] with Bahar as its capital by way of his annexation of 17 Kurdish principalities.[88]

Prior to that, the first map, known as the 'States of the East' in 1057,[89] depicted Kurds as one of the ethnic groups in the region and referred to their land as *Ardh*

80 See Metin Yüksel, 'Kurds and Kurdish Nationalism in the Interwar Period' in Bozarslan, Gunes and Yadirgi (n 2).

81 Izady, *Concise Handbook* (n 4) 32.

82 O'Ballance (n 10) 1.

83 Izady, *Concise Handbook* (n 4) Ch 4.

84 Michael Schiffmann (tr), *Rojava Revolution War and the Future of Syria's Kurds* (Pluto Press 2018) 31.

85 ibid. 76. For Ayyubid Empire, see Gerald Hawting, *The Ayyubid Empire* (EUP 2019).

86 A Kurdish group designed the first detailed Map of Kurdistan in 1947 (Cairo). Maria Th. O'Shea, *Trapped between the Map and Reality: Geography and Perceptions of Kurdistan* (Routledge 2004) 202.

87 Northeast of Ecbatana (the capital of Medes) and composed of the contemporary Kurdish regions of the South and East of Kurdistan. Kendal in Kreyenbroek and Allison (n 63) 10. The province was ruled by the Sultan's nephew, not a Kurd. Guy L. Strange, *Mesopotamia and Persia under the Mongols in the Fourteenth Century AD (From the Nuzhat-al-Kulub of Hamd-Allah Mustawfi)* (RAS 1903), quoted in O'Shea (n 86) 69.

88 Izady, *Concise Handbook* (n 4) 28.

89 By an Arab geographer, Mohammad Al-Kashgari. O'Shea (n 86) 201.

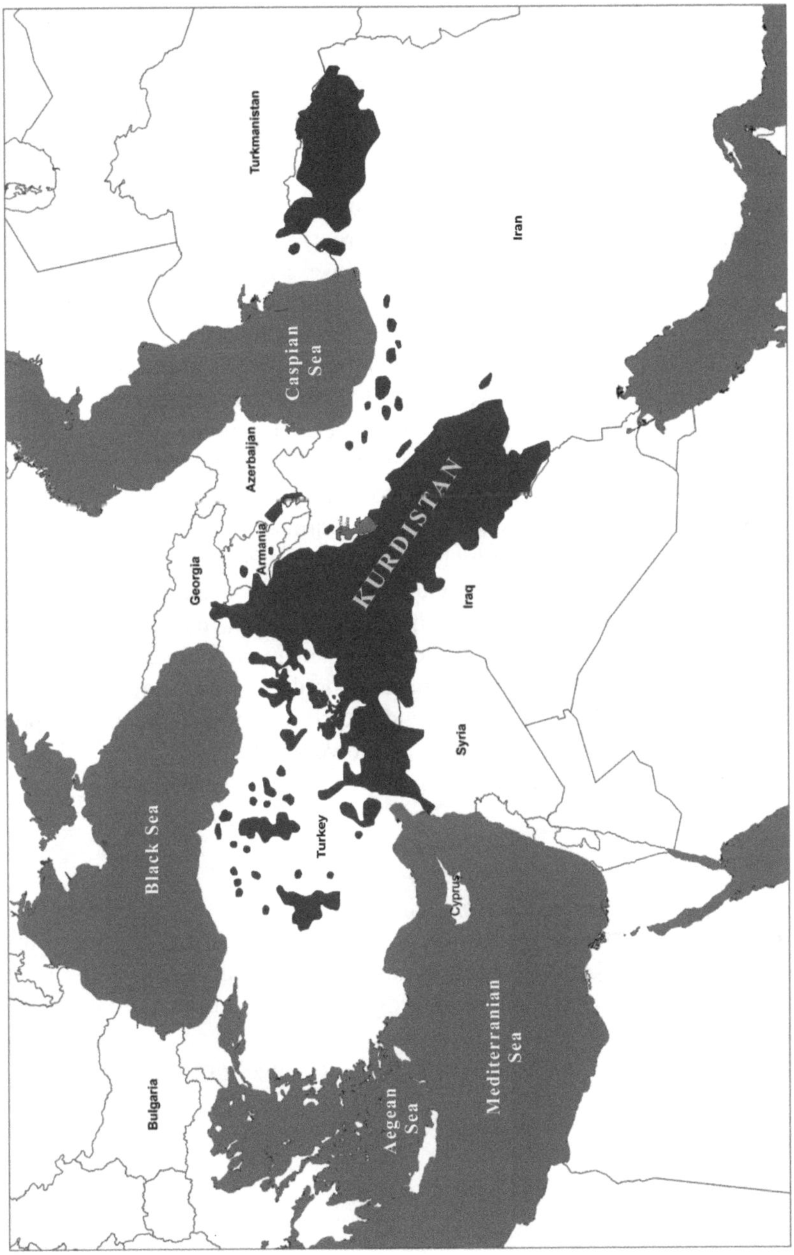

Map 5.2. Kurdistan in the modern Middle East

al-Akrad, which is the Arabic translation of Kurdistan. Created in 1076 CE, the map highlighted the Kurdish presence in the same area aligning with the contemporary Kurdish regions in the South and East of Kurdistan.[90] Before that, Ibn Hawqal (died circa 988) had cited Kurds in his book, *Kitab Surat al-Ard* (*The Face of the Earth*). They are also mentioned in the eminent book *History of Prophets and Kings* by Abu Ja'afar Muhammad al-Tabari (died circa 932).[91] by Abu Ja'afar Muhammad al-Tabari (died circa 932). Furthermore, al-Baladhuri (died circa 892) referred to 'Kurd' in *The Conquest of the Countries*, with regard to their fight against the Arabs in Mosul and Azerbaijan.[92]

Kurdistan is the most concrete expression of being Kurdistani and a justification for claims to statehood as the Kurds have roots in this territory. Autonomous Kurdish governments, sometimes with total sovereignty, ruled Kurdistan until the nineteenth century.[93] Kurdistan is not only a national symbol, but it also connects the Kurds of the four states, rather than separating them. The mountains of Kurdistan do not bar Kurds from moving in or out of their host states. For accommodating the Kurdish population, Kurdistan is a large enough territory to constitute a separate nation-state. The territory plays a critical role in self-determination because territorial units have been the only eligible entities for exercising self-determination. So far, self-determination has been balanced or restricted by territorial integrity and *uti possidetis* principles. Is Kurdistan an established territory? The answer is negative. Since the inclusion of a fragmented Kurdistan into Iran, Iraq, Syria, Turkey, and the former Soviet Union, these host states have pursued a pattern of distinct spatial governance or fractured regionalism so that Kurdistan is not shown as a single contiguous self-determining territory. Fractured regionalism, thus, disrupts the territorial continuity of areas populated by a single group.[94] The states have then cynically and fraudulently depicted the Kurdish people as a population scattered in non-contiguous regions.[95] However, the Kurds and the Kurdish language have survived despite suppressive policies of the states.

5.1.2.5 Language

In Kurdish mythology *Melik Kurdim* (King of the Kurds) of the tribe of Noah, who reigned in Mesopotamia, invented Kurdim as the language of the Kurds thousands of years before Islam.[96] Various vernaculars of Kurdish signify the Kurds' distinct origins. The mountain and plain geography of Kurdistan and the non-centralised Kurds' governing structure account for the occurrence of dialects among the Kurds. Kurdish as a 'macro-language' is a subcategory of the Indo-European

90 McDowall (n 4) 10.
91 Or *The History of Tabari.*
92 Eppel (n 19) 9-10, 15–16.
93 See Chapter 4.1.
94 See Oren Yiftachel, *Ethnocracy: Land and Identity Politics in Israel/Palestine* (UPP 2006).
95 See Hani Sayed, 'The Fictions of the Illegal Occupation in the West Bank and Gaza' (2014) 16 ORIL 79.
96 Bulloch and Morris (n 48) 57.

family of languages. It is verbalised with two main dialects, although there is no rigid border between dialects due to their merger and the geographical dispersion of their speakers, Northern Kurdish (known as Kurmancî), spoken in the north and northwestern section (the West and North of Kurdistan, the north segment of Eastern Kurdistan and north of Southern Kurdistan and Russia), and Central Kurdish (known as Soranî)[97] in the Southern section, including the southern segment of Eastern Kurdistan (Map 5.3).[98] The majority of Kurds speak these main dialects. Although the Kurmancî accent is the language of the majority, both are

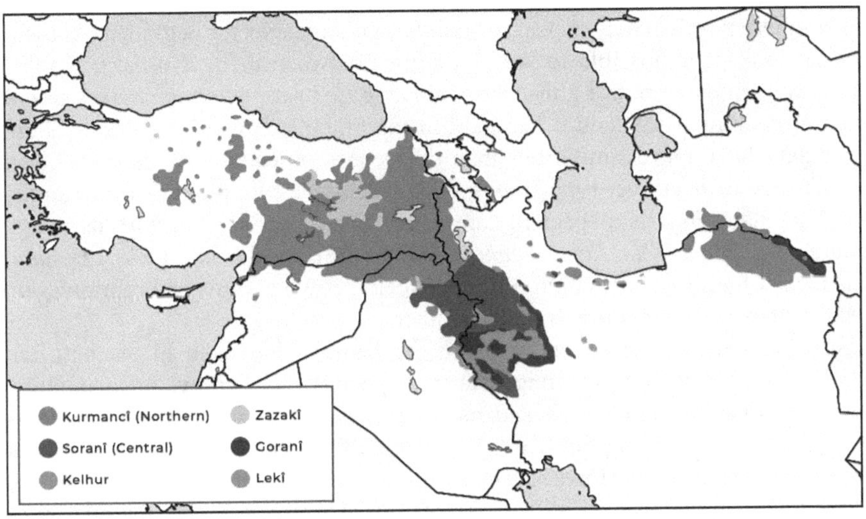

Map 5.3. The Kurdish language and its dialects

97 Another categorisation is Kurmanji and Pahlawâni/Pahlawânik as two main dialects as presented by non-linguists David McDowall and Michael Izady; however, most other scholars stratify the Kurdish language into Kurmanji and Sorani, such as Martin van Bruinessen, 'Kurdish Society, Ethnicity, Nationalism and Refugee Problems' in Kreyenbroek and Sperl (n 7) 47.

98 Bulloch and Morris (n 48) 56. For detailed anatomy of the Kurdish language, see the University of Manchester, *The Dialects of Kurdish* (undated), available at http://kurdish.humanities.manchester.ac.uk/; Orville B. Jenkins, The Kurdish People (upd 2013), available at http://orvillejenkins.com/peoples/kurds.html; Philip G. Kreyenbroek, 'On the Kurdish language' in Kreyenbroek and Sperl (n 7) 53–64; Vladmir Minorsky, 'The Gūrān' (1943) 11(1) BSOAS 75; Ernest McCarus, Kurdish in William J. Frawley, *International Encyclopedia of Linguistics* (2n ed, OUP 2004); Ernest R. McCarus, 'Kurdish Language Studies' (1960) 14 MEJ 325–335 and (1961) 15 MEJ 123; Hemresh Resho, 'On the History and Development of Writing the Kurdish Language in the Latin Alphabet' in *Yearbook of the Kurdish Academy* (The Kurdish Academy 1990) 78–84; Amir Hassanpour, *Nationalism and Language in Kurdistan, 1918–1985* (MRUP 1992); Jaffer Sheyholislami, 'The Language Varieties of the Kurds' in Wolfgang Taucher, Mathias Vogl and Peter Webinger (eds), *The Kurds*: History, Religion, Language, Politics (AFMI 2015); Wheeler M. Thackston, *Kurmanji Kurdish: A Reference Grammar with Selected Readings* (Renas Media 2006); Geoffrey Haig and Yaron Matras, 'Kurdish Linguistics: A Brief Overview' (2002) 55(1) STUF-Language Typology and Universals 3; Jaffer Sheyholislami, Amir Hassanpour, and Tove Skutnabb-Kangas, 'The Kurdish Linguistic Landscape: Vitality, Linguicide and Resistance' (2012) 217 IJSL; Mella (n 62) Part 1, Ch 4; Izady, *Concise Handbook* (n 4).

the formal accents of literature and technology. The vernaculars are divided into sub-dialects. Other dialects with minor speakers are Southern (Kalhur, Lur, Lak), Hawrami, and Zazaki (also controversially known as Gorani) Kurdish.[99]

Despite difficulties of mutual intelligibility with the speakers of Zazaki, as a vulnerable dialect facing extinction,[100] which is due to forbidden development and the lack of any educational institutions, they have been considered as Kurds by themselves and their neighbours.[101] Kurdish vernaculars utilise the forms of a customised version of the Aramaic-Finiqi alphabet (or Arabic alphabet used by the Central Kurdish dialect) with distinct letters specific to Kurdish,[102] Latin/Roman (Northern Kurdish),[103] and Cyrillic scripts in writing.[104] At first glance, Central and Northern Kurdish may appear to be different languages for beginners, but with a closer look, it is possible to see similarities between them; Northern Kurdish can be written using both Latin- and Aramaic-based scripts, which makes it look much more similar to Central Kurdish. In fact, their grammatical structures and vocabulary have more similarities than differences. Furthermore, there has been an exchange of *beyt* over time among both accents despite the lack of a Kurdish sovereign state. *Beyt* is a special genre as folktale or épopée but with its unique features, e.g., *Mem û Zîn*, *Xec û Siyabend* (*Siyamend*), and *Keleha* (*Qelay) Dimdim*. This further highlights the cultural ties between the two accents and reinforces the idea that they are not distinct from each other.

Strict geopolitical obstacles to using the Kurdish language in teaching and learning applied by the sovereign states, especially in Turkey, have inhibited the standardisation of Kurdish and its dialects and linguistic (written and spoken) homogeneity among the Kurds. Kurmancî, for example, has been Turkified through suppression.[105] However, teaching and using both accents and having access to Kurdish music of all four segments on media outlets, including radio and television channels, have paved the way to the standardisation of the Kurdish language with a collective, national, and distinctive identity despite state boundaries which had functioned to widen the estrangement of Kurdish variations, i.e.,

99 See Jamal Nebaz, *Zimanî Yekgirtûy Kurdî* (*Towards a Unified Kurdish Language*) (National Union of Kurdish Students in Europe – NUKSE 1976); Nariman A. Xoshnaw, *Zar û Ziman* (*Tounge and Language*) (2nd ed, Hevi 2014); Foad H. Xorshid, *Zimanî Kurdî û Dialêktîkekanî: Şîkrdneweyêkî Cûgrafyayî* (*Kurdish Language and its Dialects: Geographic Analysis*) (Serdem 2008) and Arash Amani, Mohammad Mohammadamini and Hadi Veisi, 'Kurdish Spoken Dialect Recognition Using X-Vector Speaker Embeddings' in Alexey Karpov and Rodmonga Potapova (eds), *Speech and Computer, SPECOM* (2021 Springer).

100 See Mehemed Malmîsanij, 'The Kırmanjki (Zazaki) Dialect of Kurdish Language and the Issues It Faces' in Bozarslan, Gunes and Yadirgi (n 2).

101 Martin van Bruinessen, 'Kurdish Paths to Nation' in Faleh A. Jabar and Hosham Dawod (eds), *The Kurds: Nationalism and Politics* (Saqi 2006) 25.

102 In the West, East, and South of Kurdistan.

103 In the north of Kurdistan.

104 Cyrillic is used in Russia. Kurdish Latin script was Abdulrezzaq Bedirxan's project initiated in 1914 for uniting the Kurds. Reynolds in Yamane and Naganawa (n 30) 40.

105 International Crisis Group, Turkey's Kurdish Impasse: The View from Diyarbakir (2012).

divide and rule tactics through linguistic regionalism. Nonetheless, the regional variations in Kurdish not only add depth and richness to the Kurdish language itself but also reflect the unique identity and cultural heritage of the Kurdish people. They highlight the vitality and resilience of the Kurdish language throughout its history, testifying to its enduring significance. Social media across Kurdistan's segments and Kurdish radio and television channels based in the South and West of Kurdistan have facilitated contacts among Kurds across the four segments. Both major Kurdish accents are available like other standard languages on Google, Microsoft, and Apple platforms.

There is no doubt that the Kurdish vocabulary has been influenced by other state official languages, state educational systems imposed on the Kurds, and exclusionary and oppressive institutions to incorporate Kurds into non-Kurdish, fictitiously homogeneous nation-states. Also, due to the influence of Islam on the nature of law and government in the region, it is almost impossible to avoid Arabic terminology. This is easy to see in Farsi and Turkish, despite having an established Farsi and Turkish state system. In the face of the states' linguicide policies, the marginalised Kurdish language, nevertheless, persists.

Language is of the utmost importance and plays an appreciable role in distinguishing the speech of Kurds from their neighbours' languages. That is, linguistically, there is a marked difference between the Kurds and their neighbours, each with a rich culture and literature of their own. Despite some similarities and having common words in both Kurdish and Farsi — that could be due to the Indo-European roots of both languages — there is no mutual understanding between speakers of these languages, especially when Kurds utilise Kurdish words. There might be mutual borrowings as well. The extent of borrowing needs a separate study, but what is clear is that modern Farsi has overwhelmingly borrowed from Arabic and Kurdish and other languages within Iran as well, despite the Farsi chauvinist state language policy adopted against the Kurds. This is also the case with the Turkish language's borrowing from different neighbouring languages.

If Kurdish self-determination is exercised on the basis of Kurdish territory (Kurdistan), there will be a dissonance between self-determination and territorial integrity because Kurdish linguistic groups straddle the borderlines of four different states. To preserve political unity, a single language has been imposed by the sovereign states, which has created ethnic conflict since the last century and has fomented the Kurds' resolve to break away from their host states.

5.1.2.6 Religion

Despite some diversity of worship practices due to the absence of a centralised ruling system within Kurdistan, a clear majority of Kurds follow the Shafi'i school (*madhhab*) of Sunni (Sunnite) Islam.[106] This estimate is relative, as there is no

106 For current religion among the Kurds, see Michiel Leezenberg, 'Religion among the Kurds between Naqshbandi Sufism and IS Salafism' in Stansfield and Shareef (n 16). Also, see Michiel Leezenberg, 'Religion in Kurdistan' in Bozarslan, Gunes and Yadirgi (n 2).

official census on the religious persuasion of the Kurds across the various segments of Kurdistan. While the Turks and Arabs of Mesopotamia followed the Hanafi tradition of jurisprudence, in the sixteenth century following the formation of the Ottoman Empire, the Shafi'i school already predominated among Kurds as 'a testimony to [their] independence.'[107]

Êzidîsm (Yazidism), with elements of Judaism, Christianity, and Islam, is an ancient faith of the Kurds based mainly in Şingal (Shengal Mountains) of Southern Kurdistan. Some of them reside in the West and North of Kurdistan and Russia. Alevi is in vogue in most parts of Northern Kurdistan. In the South of Kurdistan, there is the *Ahl-i Haqq* (the 'people of truth') group, which has much in common with Alevi and some elements of Zoroastrianism.[108] They are called *Yarsan* in the East of Kurdistan and are known as *Kakai* in the South (Kirkuk, Xaniqîn) with trivial differences.[109] According to Kakais, Êzidîsm is a branch of Kakaism that later broke off. A dominant sect of Kurdish Alevis and some *Ahl-i Haqq* have selected creeds of Shi'a ideas that are the legacy of the Safavid dynasty, which ruled based on similar heterodox views.[110] The Kurds in the Kirmaşan and Ilam provinces (in the East of Kurdistan) follow the Shi'a doctrines of *Ithna 'Ashari* (twelver), the official religion of the Iranian government. Also, the Fayli Kurds of Kirmaşan were forcibly moved to the East of Kurdistan from the South in the 1970s and 1980s.[111] Ithna 'Ashari Shi'ism was disseminated in Persia during the sixteenth century, but it is not evident when the Kurds were forced to convert to Shi'ism. To avoid repression and enhance their social influence, many Kurds converted to the state religion (Map 5.4).[112] However, this did not change their political or economic status in practice. Kirmaşan and especially Ilam provinces, with their oil fields and other mineral resources, have been two of the most undeveloped and underprivileged divisions under the Iranian regime.

Before Islam, Zoroastrianism prevailed among the Kurds;[113] however, Yarsan and Êzidîsm have much older roots in Kurdistan, while Christianity entered

107 McDowall (n 4) 11.

108 It is scattered mainly in Serpêl Zehaw, Qasrî Şîrîn, Urmîye, and Silêmani, Kirkuk, and Mosul. For *Ahl-i Haqq*, see Philip Mattar, *Encyclopedia Modern Middle East & North Africa* (TG 2004) 82; Cecil J. Edmonds, 'The Beliefs and Practices of the Ahl-i Haqq of Iraq' (1969) 7(1) Iran 89; Ziba Mir-Hosseini, 'Faith, Ritual and Culture among the Ahl-e Haqq' in Kreyenbroek and Allison (n 63) 111–134 and Gunter, *The Kurds* (n 13) 2. For Alevis, see C. M Jacobson, 'The Alevi Religion' in Denise L. Sweetnam (ed), *Kurdish Culture: A Cross-Cultural Guide* (VKW 1994) 209–217 and Erdal Gezik, 'The Kurdish Alevis: The Followers of the Path of Truth (Raa Haq/Riya Heqi)' in Bozarslan, Gunes and Yadirgi (n 2).

109 For Yarsan and Kakai, see Philip G. Kreyenbroek and Khanna Omarkhali, ''Kurdish' Religious Minorities in the Modern World' in Bozarslan, Gunes, and Yadirgi (n 2).

110 McDowall (n 4) 12.

111 For the *Fayli* Kurds, see Munir Morad, 'The Situation of Kurds in Iraq and Turkey: Current Trends and Prospects' (2005) in Kreyenbroek and Sperl (n 7) 90–104.

112 McDowall (n 4) 13.

113 Bulloch and Morris (n 48) 59.

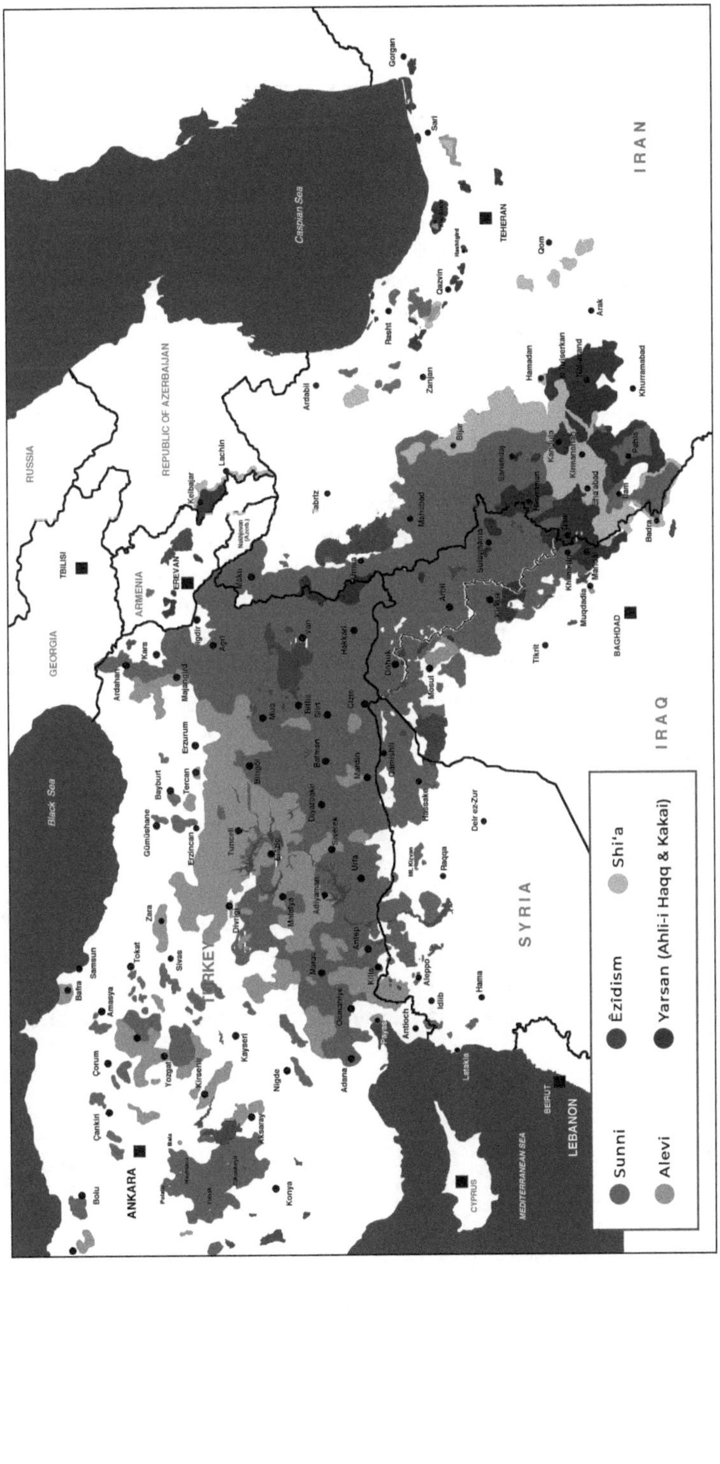

Map 5.4. Kurdistan's Religious Makeup

Kurdistan in 64 CE.[114] For more than two millennia, there has been a symbiosis between Jews and Kurds in many cities of Kurdistan, such as Zaxo, Amêdî, Hewlêr, Silêmanî, Serdeşt, Qamişlo, Urmîye, and many other Kurdish cities. In the 1950s, under the Sunni Arab government of Iraq and before and after the 'Islamic revolution' (1979) in Iran, many Kurdish Jews had to migrate to Israel while retaining their Kurdish identity.[115] Christian Kurds are also cited by al-Masudi in 'Muruj al Dhahab' in the middle of the tenth century.[116] Additionally, Christians have been numerous in Kurdistan, with Armenians and Assyrians. Christian and Jewish minorities within Kurdistan, despite speaking Kurdish, may or may not self-designate themselves as Kurds.

Although Kurdistan is host to important religious minorities, religion is another chief factor shared among the Kurds that marks the difference between them and their host states. Kurds use religion as an identifier of their Kurdish identity to justify their self-determination but not to define their political borders, because Turks, Arabs, and most Kurds follow Sunni Islam, although of different schools. Most citizens of Iran are devotees of Shi'a Islam. The unity of 'brothers' (Kurds and Turks), with common Islamic elements, was weaponised by Turks to consolidate Turkish territory against Christians, other minorities, and the Allied powers. Since the partition of Kurdistan, Kurds have used Sunni Islam to promote shared values and accentuate their national ties. Kurdish Alevis, including Seyyid Riza and Hassan Mekki, also spearheaded independence movements in the North of Kurdistan. Indeed, Islam as a label, at times, served to reinforce an exclusionary Kurdish national identity as in the late nineteenth century and before and after WWI; in this context, religion was placed coterminous with ethnicity to assert a collective Kurdish ethno-national identity to achieve independence.

Many Kurdish leaders came to regard the Ottoman Turks as oppressive Muslims propagating 'deceptive' Islam and taking advantage of it to enslave the Kurds; '*ulama* of Kurdistan had never considered [the faith] of the Ottomans' as true Islam.[117] Indeed, it can be argued that Kurdish ethnic identity trumped the religious identity of the Kurds and reinforced the growth of national self-assertion, although some contemporary scholars introduced Islam as a wedge-driving factor between Sunni Kurds and Alevi and Shi'a Kurds, obstructing Kurdish political unity through to the end of the Ottoman Empire. Over this period, Islam remained a shared tie bonding Sunni Kurds and Sunni Turks.[118] Backing the Kemalists, however, did not last long, as the Kurds learned of the Turks' objective and hidden

114 Mansfield (n 65) 26.

115 Toi Staff, 'Kurdish Rabbi Dies in Jerusalem, at 117 (apparently)' *The Times of Israel* (7 March 2017).

116 McDowall (n 4) 14. For religion in Kurdistan, see Izady, *Concise Handbook* (n 4), Martin van Bruinessen, 'Religion in Kurdistan' (1991) 4 IJKS 5; Kreyenbroek and Allison (n 63); Bruinessen in Kreyenbroek and Sperl (n 7) 26–52.

117 See Soleimani, *Competing Nationalisms* (n 22) 229, 245, 283.

118 Reynolds in Yamane and Naganawa (n 30) 41.

animus for assimilation and elimination of their identity and their opposition to any reform. This brought about a leap to Kurdish nationalism.

With regard to religion, Kurds follow a different rite of Islam. Although Islam seeks to create a single Islamic state through the ideology of *umma*, being Muslim is secondary to the Kurds. Islam brought no political unity between Kurds and their Islamic leaders, *ulama*, and the Turks due to the lack of a universal interpretation of Islam or the existence of heterogeneous interpretations of it among its followers, including Sunnis or Shi'a, and their respective insistence on the superiority of their version.[119] This caused a competing Islamic nationalism that has persisted. The Kurds' host states have used the *surah* (chapter) names in the Quran in the justification of massacring the Kurds, for example *al-Fath* ('the Conquest' or 'the Victory') or *Jihad* ('Holy War') by the Iranian regime in 1980, *al-Anfal* ('the Spoils') in the 1980s by the Ba'ath regime in Iraq, and *at-Tin wa Zeytun* ('the Fig and the Olive') or the Operation Olive Branch by Turkey against the Kurds in Rojava in January 2018. In the most recent case, the incumbent Turkish president called the Kurds who vote for the pro-Kurdish parties as *'kafir'* ('infidels') and 'pagan' in his election campaign in May 2023.

Despite some divergent forms of worship in Kurdistan, religion has not caused a rift in the Kurdish nationalist movement as Kurdish ethnic identity is more potent than religious ties. This has been evident in the North of Kurdistan, where a secular perception of being Kurdistani has been devoid of Islam as a religion since the 1960s and was promoted instead through literary activism, journalism, and the founding of political parties. Until 1938, religious figures and tribal chiefs played a decisive role in Kurdish uprisings against the Turkification and secularisation of Kemalist Turkey. In the period prior to national self-determination and its aftermath, Kurdish periodicals had a decisive role in the Kurdish awakening by promoting a Kurdish self-perception underscoring a unique history, language, and culture. This perspective promoted the secular identity of the Kurds beginning in the 1960s and reinforced it over the 1970s and 1980s with leftist and socialist groups, e.g., the Kurdistan Workers' Party (*Partiya krêkaren Kurdistanê,* PKK), as pioneers of the view emphasising motherland, literature, language, and origin (the myth of Kawa), and particularly pre-Islamic practices or the national religion of Zoroastrianism as cultural signifiers of being Kurdistani. In the 1980s, the nationalist resurgence was less inclusive, and restricted to linguistic and religious minority persuasions.[120]

By posing a challenge to the forming of Kurdish identity in the late decade of the Ottoman Empire, Islam was subsequently excluded from that process as part of the resistance against religious and tribal structures or sectarianism in Turkey. The Kurds found Islam, in every form, to be an agent of fragmentation and assimilation, a tool of colonialism incompatible with Kurdish culture, and a factor inhibiting a Kurdish ethnic and national identity. This approach was modified in the 1990s in order to include more of the religious Kurdish masses, including Shi'a, Êzdî,

119 Soleimani, *Competing Nationalisms* (n 22) 155–198.
120 van Bruinessen in Jabar and Dawod (n 101) 33–35.

and Alevi, in the ethnic context of the Kurds and to remove religious divisions in constructing a Kurdish identity. To Abdulla Ocalan, the imprisoned leader of the PKK, being a Muslim does not imply being a colony of other Islamic nations but, instead, entails being against domination, as Islam in itself stands against exploitation and colonisation. He promoted a secular 'cultural Islam' as a replacement for centralist Islam in Turkey to address the Kurdistan question. This version prevents Islam from entering politics and keeps it within each individual's space. The approach was adopted as a strategy against the Islamic discourse disseminated by the ruling Justice and Development Party (*Adalet ve Kalkınma Partisi*, AKP)[121] and makes religion and nationalism co-constitutive of the Kurdish identity. The Kurds' host states have attempted to exploit religious divergence to foster cleavage, fuelling hatred among the Kurds. However, aside from a few minor skirmishes, these attempts have ultimately proven unsuccessful. In the independence referendum of 2017, Kurdish Shi'a cities cast the most overwhelming yes vote to separate from Iraq.

A unique calendar is a final and conspicuous cultural element attesting to a secular Kurdish distinctiveness.

5.1.2.7 Calendar

Kurds have their own calendar, which starts on the vernal equinox, the first day of spring. They celebrate the pre-historic *Newroz* (New Year's Day) or *Cejna Serê Salê* (*cejn* ('festival') + *ser* ('head/beginning') + *sal* ('year')) as the most prominent national day and an integral part of the Kurdish national identity on 21 March, incidentally the day on which Zuhak was ousted by *Kawey Asinger* in 603. The Kurdish counting of years starts with the defeat of the Assyrian Empire by the Medes to the north of today's Mosul.[122] Although a special calendar has not been considered by legal scholars or anthropologists as an objective element of peoplehood, it does demonstrate the secular and non-Islamic separateness of the group and marks their particular history. In 2023, Kurds observe their year 2723. The calendar is, thus, a demonstrable feature defining the Kurds as a distinct people. Likewise, Persians use the solar calendar of *Hijri Shamsi* based on pre-Islamic systems and is currently in the year 1402. Its starting point, or the New Year, is in March as is the Kurdish calendar but with emphasis on the renewal of nature. The Islamic lunar calendar (*Hijri Ghamari)* is also common in Iran to mark Islamic beliefs or Muslim holidays and rituals. Arabs use the Islamic lunar calendar. The current Islamic year is 1444 AH (Anno Hegirae, in the year of the *Hijra*), commencing with the migration (*Hijra*) of Muhammad (the founder of Islam) and his followers from Mecca to Medina. Its New Year starts in August. Turkey uses the

121 Kılıç (n 55) 816. Also, see Zeki Sarigil, *Ethnic Boundaries in Turkish Politics: The Secular Kurdish Movement and Islam* (NYU Press 2018) 66–95.

122 Bulloch and Morris (n 48) 50.

Gregorian calendar which is employed also in Iran, Iraq, and Syria for international reckoning.

Together the sundry abovementioned factors, plus common literature, clothes, outfit, *Helperkê* or *Govend* (*Dîlan*; a folk movement or dance as a symbol of resistance) and music and many other shared cultural events across Kurdistan, constitute a strong body of evidence in supporting the existence of a distinct Kurdish people bound by common ethno-anthropological (subjective and objective) ties. But was this identity granted fair consideration in the aftermath of WWI and WWII? Did any legal document then address the Kurds as a nation or people in accordance with Wilsonian principles and the UN epoch?

5.2 The Kurds in Legal Documents

Although self-determination units were addressed as a people in legal instruments, the term *people* had not gained any legal standing by the interwar period for the goal of exercising self-determination. The terms then commonly considered for groups aspiring to independence and statehood were *nation*, *nationality*, *ethnicity*, *people*, and *the governed*.[123] In the Wilsonian epoch, these collectives were called *peoples* and *nationalities* for the purpose of self determination. Wilson, in his Fourteen Points, refers to people and nationality for territorial adjustments in Europe and in the non-Turkish portions of the Ottoman Empire. Meanwhile, Leninist self-determination articulated the right of nations and people to choose their status. That is, both concepts were used and are being used in the Wilsonian and the UN eras.[124]

The Kurds were not an exception. Throughout the interwar period, they were referred to using the same terminology in some legal texts. The King-Crane Commission of 1919 addresses the Kurds as a people at the Paris Peace Conference.[125] Prior to WWI and its aftermath, the Kurdish language, religion (Sunni Islam somewhat overlapping with Turks), and a given social stratum (educated urbanite and a peasantry) were prominent markers in promoting being Kurdistani as an aristocratic-lateral *ethnie*, or a people apart. Identifying as Kurdistani was geographically extended but restricted to certain social strata. After WWI, Kemalism and its suppressive and assimilation policies for the purpose of nation-building dissolved the religious marker between Kurds and Turks. After the war, the factors of language and religion reinforced the identification of being Kurdistani and more non-tribal and marginal peasantry joined nationalist movements. They presented their submissions to the Conference. Ultimately, their national aspirations were heeded in the Treaty of Sèvres (1920), in which they were referred to as peoples for the purpose of independence. Article 64 of the treaty

123 See Chapter 3.2. and 3.3.

124 See Chapter 2.

125 King-Crane Commission, 28 August 1919, Submitted by Charles R. Crane and Henry Churchill King.

deemed 'these [sic] people' capable of acquiring independence and establishing an 'independent Kurdish State' (Article 64). Thus, the nation and the people referred to the same collectivity of individuals.[126] Also, they were titled 'the Kurdish nation' by the Turkish Grand National Assembly in 1922. The Assembly decided to grant 'autonomous administration for the Kurdish nation in harmony with their national customs' on 10 February 1922.[127] The International Commission of Inquiry of the League, in the arbitration of the Mosul *vilayet* (1925–1926), referred to the arguments of the Turkish government concerning the Kurds as 'a compact body of people of an entirely different race and language, [who] obviously required separate treatment.'[128] It advised 'an independent Kurdish State' solely based on ethnic argument for 'Kurds' due to their majority in the *vilayet* of Mosul and refuting the Turkish government argument as 'they are neither Turk nor Arab, and this question of their origin, their history and their ethnical relationship to the other races which surround them is naturally of the highest importance.'[129] To the Commission, 'officials of Kurdish race' should have been able to administer their region. The Kurds, as a people, and their views were of great importance in the Mosul case but without any outcomes for them.[130]

In the 1920s, the Kurds became subject populations of dominating *ethnies* (Persian, Arab, and Turkish) that created their own nation-states through 'bureaucratic incorporation' of other communities. The integration into the Turkish, Iraqi, and Persian identities has been significant in the development of Kurds into a vertical-demotic *ethnie*. In other terms, they became a community in which most individuals were united by a shared descent, culture, origin, and religion with a sense of solidarity in a given territory, but the ethnic category lacked political unity. The feeling of ethnic unity was strengthened and continued after WWII.

In the UN era, the term *nation* was replaced by *peoples*. In the first attempt after the founding of the UN, to demonstrate further evidence of their peoplehood and Kurdish identity toward creating a sovereign Kurdistan, the Kurds in the East of Kurdistan announced the short-lived Kurdish Republic of Kurdistan in 1946, underscoring their right to self-determination. Four years after the adoption of the ICCPR and ICESCR, the March Manifesto of 1970 conceded autonomy to the Kurds in Iraq, addressing them as a 'people' (Articles 3(A), 5, 10(A), 14, and 15).[131] In the 1960s and 1970s, Kurds from Christian, Êzdî, Shi'a creeds as well as Assyrians and Arabic-speaking Faylis supported and participated in national movements.

126 See Chapter 3.2.

127 The decision was never put into practice. Robert Olson, *The Emergence of Kurdish Nationalism and the Sheikh Said Rebellion, 1880–1925* (UTP 1989) 40. No concessions were supposed to be granted to the Kurds as they were opposed to the sovereignty of the new Turkey founded on the ideology of Turkish Kemalism.

128 Frontier between Turkey and Iraq (n 66) 15.

129 ibid 57.

130 ibid 18, 57, 76–77.

131 See Martin Short and Anthony McDermott, *The Kurds* (MRG 1975) 23–24.

The Peace Accord between the Kurds and the Iraqi government in 1970 agreed to amend the Iraq Interim Constitution to incorporate 'the Kurdish Nationality' and the *national rights of the Kurdish people* (emphasis added) (Article 10A). Also, in the Law for Autonomy in the Area of Kurdistan, the Kurds are alluded to as a distinct people, though as 'an integral part of the Iraqi people' (Article 1 A and D).[132] Later, the Interim Constitution of 1971 recognised 'the national rights' of the Kurds, and regarded Iraq as consisting of 'two principal nationalisms: The Arab Nationalism and the Kurdish Nationalism' (Article 5b).[133] In these instruments, Kurds are referred to as a people distinct albeit part of the whole people of a state. This means they were recognised as a minority-people in accordance with the common interpretation of a people at the time, and with the caveat that minorities of already established sovereign states were not entitled to external self-determination. This opinion is still prevalent in legal scholarship, which was corroborated by the UN Security Council (UNSC) 20 years later in considering the situation in Iraq. Concerned by the plight of the Kurds in Iraq, the UNSC Resolution 688 (1991) demanded that Iraq end its repression of the 'Kurdish population,' which allegedly was a threat to international peace and security in the region.[134] The term *population* refers to the total of individuals occupying Kurdish-populated areas as part of Iraq or a group of individuals inhabiting a particular locality and having a quality or characteristic in common, i.e., being Kurdish. Nothing more could be conceivable in the context of taking note of a domestic conflict within a state.

Kurds have been referred to in international reports as an ethnic minority of four states, as in the UN Human Rights Situations and Reports of Special Rapporteurs and Representatives,[135] Human Rights Watch (HRW),[136] the UN Office of the High Commissioner for Human Rights (OHCHR),[137] and the European Court of Human Rights (ECtHR).[138] A few state reports focusing on the human rights situation of the Kurds allude to Kurds as a people. In one of these reports, compiled by the Immigration and Refugee Board of Canada (1996), the New Democracy Movement (YDH), as a Turkish political party in Turkey, asks for the recognition of Kurds 'as a people whose culture is officially recognized on a par with the Turkish culture.'[139] In another report by the United Kingdom Home Office about the state treatment of Kurds in Iran, Iraq, and Turkey, Kurds are referred to as a people. The report grounded its reasoning on a report conducted in 2013 by the Danish Immigration Service, the Norwegian Landinfo, and the Danish Refugee

132 ibid 25.

133 The Interim Constitution, Republic of Iraq, 1971.

134 UNSC Res 688 (5 April 1991).

135 OHCHR, Human Rights Situations and Reports of Special Rapporteurs and Representatives, Iran and Iraq.

136 HRW, Kurds.

137 OHCHR, Report on the Human Rights Situation in South-East Turkey: July 2015 to December 2016 (*OHCHR*, February 2017.

138 EC, The ECHR and Human Rights Violations against Kurds in Turkey, 9 October 2018.

139 Immigration and Refugee Board of Canada, The Situation of the Kurds, 1 February 1996.

Council's fact-finding mission in Tehran, Ankara, and London.[140] However, citing Kurds as a people in these instances is not the same as recognising them as a people entitled to self-determination. The serial reports originating in 2015 are provided by the UK government for use by Home Office decision-makers handling particular types of protection and human rights claims, including asylum claims.[141]

In relation to judicial remedies, Kurds brought their case before the quasi-judicial Permanent Peoples' Tribunal (PPT). Although Crawford calls it 'a private foundation,'[142] it is an international opinion tribunal, independent from any state authority, that investigates the self-determination of marginalised groups based on the 1976 Algiers Declaration of the Rights of Peoples.[143] In July 2017, the PPT was asked to consider and evaluate the evidence and the crimes committed in the conflict between the Turkish state and the Kurdish people from 1 June 2015 to 31 January 2017. One suggested approach was to consider the severity of the conflict and respective responsibilities for systematic violations of fundamental individual and peoples' rights of the Kurdish population, as well as Turkish denial of their right to self-determination. In May 2018, the PPT deliberated on its verdict, recognising Kurds, not only in Turkey but also in other host states, as a people with a clear right to self-determination. The right has been 'understood as a threat and met with State repression.' The PPT stipulates:

> [t]he Kurdish People is the subject and bearer of the right of self-determination, both as a people which is ethnically homogenous and based in a defined settlement area and as a minority in the states between which its settlement area has been divided. The fact that the Kurdish People only settle in the individual States as an ethnic minority does not reduce its right of self-determination to mere individual protection of individual members. The Kurdish People of all the States are entitled to the right as a collective right.

140 Landinfo, DIS and DRC, FFM Report, February 2013.

141 UK HO, Country Information and Guidance - Iran: Kurds and Kurdish Political Groups (May 2022); UK HO, Country Policy and Information Note Iraq: Opposition to the Government in the Kurdistan Region of Iraq (June 2021); UK HO, Country Policy and Information Note Turkey: Kurds (February 2020).

142 James Crawford (ed), *The Rights of Peoples* (OCP 1988) 187.

143 The Tribunal was established in Bologna in 1979 as a direct continuation of the Russell Tribunals on Vietnam (1966–1967) and Latin America (1973–1976). It 'is built around an international network of experts, social actors and scholars from several countries of Europe, South America, Asia and Africa, recognized for their independence and competence.' The PPT is a platform to give recognition, visibility and a voice to the peoples suffering violations of their fundamental rights, victims who, according to the Universal Declaration of the Rights of Peoples, proclaimed in Algiers in 1976, were marginalised in international law, which had increasingly become the guarantor of the interests of the public and private holders of political and economic powers. The jurisdiction of the Tribunal is restricted to 'any international crime, specifically on crimes against peace and humanity, genocide, any infringement of the fundamental rights of peoples and minorities, grave and systematic violations of the rights and freedoms of individuals,' whether committed by states, by authorities other than states, or by private groups or organisations.

Despite addressing the Kurds as a people, the Tribunal did not enter the debate of presenting a definition or description of a people. However, it referred to 'the great complexity' of the Kurds' ethnic, religious, historical, and cultural identities.[144] In a qualification of the facts, the Tribunal added that their right to self-determination is 'violated.'[145] The definitive verdict of the Tribunal is recommendatory. The Tribunal identified the Kurds of the four states as a people entitled to the right to self-determination. But a question arises in this context: do the Kurds of the four segments fit within the contemporary framework of self-determination?

5.3 A Territorially Fragmented People

Although the Kurds have been dispersed among the different states of Iran, Iraq, Syria, Turkey, and the Soviet Union since 1926, Kurds continued to connect and interact with one another throughout Kurdistan as a contiguous region, regardless of the political borders separating them. That is, the imposed political boundaries are insignificant for the Kurds.[146] Most Kurds use *Rojava* ('where the sun sets') for the West of Kurdistan (in Syria), *Rojhilat* ('where the sun rises') for the East of Kurdistan (in Iran), *Bakûr* (North) for the North of Kurdistan (in Turkey), and *Başûr* (South) for the South of Kurdistan (in Iraq). Kurds also utilise the term *binxet* ('below the line') to refer to geographical regions of the West of Kurdistan and *serxet* ('above the line') to the North of Kurdistan.[147] *Ewdîw* or *bara dî* ('the other side') is another common term alluding to the geographic segments of the South and East of Kurdistan.

It cannot be denied that transnational interactions were sometimes inhibited due to regional alliances among their host states aimed at containing the Kurds. But transnational socio-economic connections and transborder trade have, nevertheless, played a critical role. There have been exchanges among the four segments despite severe difficulties at times. A few recent prominent instances of coordination and of collaborating organisations are worth mentioning. One example was the arrival of Kurdish forces from the West of Kurdistan on 3 August 2014 to rescue Kurdish Êzdîs during the ISIS invasion into Şingal, under the Kurdistan Regional Government (KRG). In late 2014, *Peshmerga* convoys from the South of Kurdistan arrived in Rojava with heavy weaponry to back the local Kurds in their battle against ISIS which besieged the mainly Kurdish border town of Kobanê (Kobani) for 134 days.[148] A recent instance of Kurdish transborder collaboration

144 PPT, Session on Alleged violations of International Law and International Humanitarian Law by the Turkish Republic and its Officials in their Relations with the Kurdish People and their Organisations, 15–16 March 2018, 5.

145 ibid 7–10.

146 Michael M. Gunter, *Out of Nowhere: The Kurds of Syria in Peace and War* (C. Hurst & Co. 2014) 9.

147 ibid.

148 Loqman Radpey, 'Kurdish Regional Self-rule Administration in Syria: A New Model of Statehood and its Status in International Law Compared to the Kurdistan Regional Government (KRG) in Iraq' (2016) 17(3) JJPS 468.

was the despatching of medical personnel from the KRG in Southern Kurdistan to the earthquake-ravaged areas of the North and West of Kurdistan in February 2023. This was also previously seen between the East and North of Kurdistan in the 2011 Lake Wan earthquake in the North of Kurdistan and the 2017 earthquake in the East of Kurdistan. These instances of cooperation prove that the artificial boundaries, although 'legally' recognised, fail to align with the practical reality of psychological boundaries that continue to define the Kurds' underlying unity unaffected by the imposed divisions.

Kurds have demanded their rights democratically and by establishing political parties within and outside Kurdistan, although the multiplicity of fractious parties has disadvantaged the Kurds. It is not possible to measure the level of the parties' support, and the parties' various stands are tactically political. Dispersal among four states inhibits the adoption of a coordinated stance on the creation of an encompassing Greater Kurdistan. The KDP and the PKK have their own offshoots across the Kurdistani segments. However, Kurds in all segments have attempted to collaborate or run parallel agendas, and that has led to the establishment of a national institution through which they can express their common characteristics and their desire to consolidate their identity. The *Kongreya Neteweyî ya Kûrdistanê* (KNK, Kurdistan National Congress) was originally founded on 14 April 1985,[149] but was re-inaugurated and established 0n 24 May 1999 to 'incarnate the moral unity of the Kurdish nation' and to promote 'the ultimate practice by the people of Kurdistan of their right to self-determination.'[150] The KNK 'consists of representatives of political parties, social, cultural and religious establishments of Kurdistan and independent individuals.' It contemplates 'forming a higher body of the Kurdish people to protect the interests and unity of the nation of Kurdistan,' where 'an international colony' has been created under 'the repressive colonialism of the states of Turkey, Iran and Syria.' Referring to self-determination as a right and its denial by the host states (Point 4 and Point 5d of the KNK Convention), it enumerates its forms for the Kurds as 'autonomy, federalism, confederalism or even independence.' The KNK 'supports the national liberation struggle of Kurdistan in all parts' (Point 6g of the KNK Convention).[151]

That is, Kurds base their national identity as 'a we-group' on their ethnic belonging. Despite the cultural gulf between the Kurds reinforced by their host states through national media, education in the official state languages, military service, and adopted integration policies, the ethnic identity of being Kurdish remains a core belief among the Kurds. That is, the cultural variation within the Kurds — due to their different ecological environments — has not weakened their *ethnie*. Their diversity is a form of adaptation and survival. This characterises and

149 Lokman I. Meho, *The Kurdish Question in U.S. Foreign Policy: A Documentary Sourcebook* (Praeger 2004) 392.

150 The Kurdistan National Congress (KNC), available at http://www.kongrakurdistan.eu/en/.

151 KNC Convention, Endorsed on 26 May 1999.

identifies Kurds as a people and has a determinative role in enhancing Kurdish national consciousness, as a distinguishing marker with their neighbours, and the sense of nationality.

There is no doubt that the absence of a sovereign Kurdish state politically uniting a dispersed people across four states has resulted in the lack of a single standard language and culture. State centralisation primarily shapes linguistic homogeneity. Policies adopted by their host states have tended toward creating a heterogeneous Kurdish community. This, in turn, has led to overlaps with surrounding cultures and languages and even sub-cultures among the Kurds across borders. However, there is no real common bond between the Kurds and Arabs, Turks, and Iranians.

Even when considering Charles Chaumont's notion of 'armed resistance' or collective struggle for liberation against oppression and exploitation as the 'material reality' in action for defining a people, the Kurds unquestionably fulfil this requirement.[152] Since the partition of Kurdistan, Kurds have occasionally challenged their host states through military operations. *Berxwedan Jiyane* ('Resistance is life') is the reality of a people by which the people of Kurdistan have confronted a century of oppression and have persevered for life. Kurdish *berxwedan* — which now has taken on diverse forms, e.g., protests and civil disobedience, grassroots initiatives, political activism, and cultural revival — has also been manifest in their national anthem:

> Hey foe, the nation whose language is Kurdish is alive
> Cannot be crushed by the weapons of any time
> Let no one say Kurds are dead
> Kurds are living
> Kurds are living, our flag will never fall
> We are descendants of the red colour of the revolution.
> ('Ey Reqîb' ('Hey Foe') by Yûnis Raûf aka Dildar)

In the non-colonial realm, a people is defined and predicated on ethnic or national ties, plus the subjective element of distinctness for the common objective of independence. With the consolidation of borders among the four states with Kurdish minorities, nothing changed regarding national ties connecting the Kurds spanning the breadth of ethnic Kurdistan. The 2017 referendum for independence was the most recent event in this saga. It found the Kurds of the South of Kurdistan reaffirming their distinct collectivity and pushing for recognition of their national identity by emphasising their distinctiveness, bolstered by their national ties of history, homeland, ethnicity, language, and religion with a vision to establish an independent Kurdish state. The consensus of the vote was to assert the grassroots notion of

152 Charles Chaumont, 'Le Droit des Peuples à Témoigner D'eux-mêmes' (1976) 2 Annuaire du Tiers Monde 15, quoted in Karen Knop, *Diversity and Self-Determination in International Law* (CUP 2002) 55–61.

independence, in which the religious factor played no part. The referendum acted to foster Kurdistani solidarity across all four states.

The existence of Kurdistan and a single self-representation shared by the entire Kurdish population would still bolster the interpretation that the Kurds constitute a multiterritorial nation, even if half of them supposedly live in Turkey. As a territorially fragmented people, Kurds share, to a large degree, the same origin, language, history, and culture, although the host states have sought to drive wedges or to insulate them and rupture their mutual relations even when these states were at war with each other, e.g., the war between Iran and Iraq (1980–1988). The question here is whether Kurds fall into the category of a people. In legal practice, a people eligible for self-determination has been a minority group in a specific territory.[153] Can we meaningfully say that about the Kurds? Chapter 3 evinced that the conceptualisation of peoples is territorially restricted. Further, a people fragmented across different states is not classified as a people entitled to self-determination. In fact, Kurds are not considered 1) the entire population of an independent sovereign state, 2) the entire population of a territory that has not achieved independence, 3) a population living under foreign military occupation, 4) a people of a colony, or 5) a minority of a single state.[154] As per the existing state of law, peoples meeting these conditions are the beneficiaries and entitled to the right to self-determination.[155] All these peoples are confined to a given territory.

Modern state practice indicates that peoplehood is still interpreted as the whole people of a territorial unit for the purpose of self-determination. However, this can circumscribe a people's self-determination rights. The Badinter Arbitration Commission for the former Yugoslavia rejected 'changes to existing frontiers at the time of independence' when it was supposed that the right of self-determination would be exercised by the Serbs in Croatia and Bosnia-Herzegovina.[156] This was confirmed by the Final Communiqué of the Action Group for Syria (2012) as '[i] t is for the Syrian people to determine the future of the country.'[157] By referring to 'the need for all segments of the Iraqi population to participate in the political process, in inclusive political dialogue, and in the economic and social life of Iraq,' the UNSC underscored the formal or majoritarian formula of peoples in Resolution 2233 in July 2015 pertaining to the presence of ISIS on Iraq and the Kurdish referendum on independence. It also reaffirmed the independence, sovereignty, unity, and territorial integrity of Iraq.[158] Thus, the self-determination unit was interpreted to coincide with the state's borders. In December 2015, the UNSC endorsed the Final Communiqué of the Action Group for Syria through Resolution 2254 and reconfirmed the legal criteria of peoplehood; 'the Syrian people [or the whole people of Syria] will decide the future of Syria.' The Syrian people encompass '[a]ll

153 See Chapter 3.3.2 and 3.3.5.
154 See Chapter 3.4.
155 ibid.
156 ACFY, Opinion No 2.
157 Action Group for Syria, Final Communiqué, available at https://peacemaker.un.org/node/1581.
158 UNSC Res 2233 (29 July 2015).

groups and segments of society,' not only the monolithic majority in Syria.[159] To sum up, the formal criterion is the basis of designating a people that is restricted to a given territory entitled to self-determination. Substantive characteristics are not placed as premium for the purposes of the right of self-determination in determining the existence of a people. Self-determination is indeed a territorial entitlement and applicable to territorial units due to the contradiction between *uti possidetis* and self-determination. But Kurds are now considered minority-peoples spread among four states. The implementation of Kurdish self-determination disrupts the political unity and the territorial framework of four independent states. Kurdish self-determination is, thus, something that is not readily achievable under the current framework of the law. That is, the law of self-determination does apply to the Kurds as a people, but the way that it has been developed makes its application to the Kurdish scenario an uncharted question.

5.4 Summary

A close examination of historico-legal records, focusing on anthropology, reveals that the Kurds have been an identifiable group for thousands of years. Turning to the criterion of national consciousness as a people and with the political will to self-govern or gain independence depending on circumstances, the Kurdish consciousness of being a distinct ethno-political identity existed long before the era of modern nationalism and before self-determination was raised as a political ideal and later as a legal principle. It also predated the political evolution of the Kurds' host states and other modern Middle Eastern nation-states. This is evident in their own empire, kingdoms, and sovereign principalities prior to the modern era. This distinctness is manifested and asserted today by Kurdish territorial entities in the South and West of Kurdistan. Concurrent with historical, economic, and political developments both locally and internationally, Kurds as well as other groups developed their identity through self-consciousness to nationhood and nationalism. The Kurds considered themselves a distinct group through Kurdishness or being Kurdistani hundreds of years prior to their neighbours. Ethnic or national identity has been an issue among the Kurds since the seventh century as a result of a national movement toward self-determination and independence. While being targeted for assimilation aimed at lessening the intensity of Kurdish national consciousness following WWI and the consequent partitioning of Kurdistan and being subjected to Arabisation, Turkification, Persianisation, colonisation, cultural appropriation and exploitation, the host states' fabrication of history through the distortion of Kurdish history, many Kurds still aspire to the ideal of a Western-model nation-state. Developments in the North and South of Kurdistan in the 1960s provided conditions for a re-intensified Kurdish consciousness.

The Kurds possess the basic ethno-anthropological affinities comprising the factual criteria of peoplehood. To implement external self-determination, territory is

159 UNSC Res 2254 (18 December 2015).

understood as the key to defining peoples. Inasmuch as the existing state of the law of peoples confines eligible peoples to a given territory, dispersed peoples do not have a chance to exercise self-determination. No one takes much notice of irredentist peoples. With the partition of Kurdistan, the status of Kurds as a nation changed to that of a minority-people across four states. The current framework does not allow a people who share ethnicity, language, culture, and religion with a separate identity to plot their political status and put an end to their dispersal across four states. Indeed, the principle of self-determination, as codified, is very poorly equipped to grapple with the situation of the Kurds as a territorially divided national group or as a territorially fragmented people. The Kurds, though a people, do not fit either the decolonisation framework or the territorially emphasised concept of a people. In other words, the Kurds fail the legal criteria (*uti possidetis*) of peoplehood for the purpose of external self-determination. Kurdistani territories cannot practice self-determination simultaneously. That is, Kurdistan is not a single established territory but, rather, a territory divided among four separate, potentially self-determined territories. The prevailing practice by self-determined territories does not permit a form of external self-determination amenable to all Kurds or Kurdistan. Whether the Kurds satisfy the injustice or remedial criteria of peoplehood is considered in Chapter 7.

Confined by the territorial integrity of each sovereign state, the exercise of self-determination has been restricted to the existing states' boundaries. Thus, self-determination has been granted only an internal manifestation. The achievement of state sovereignty has been thwarted by the granting of equal access to government by ethnic groups and consulting peoples through an expression of genuine will. But what can satisfy the requirement(s) of internal self-determination? By what means can self-determination be realised for a territorially concentrated ethno-cultural group?

6 The Right to Internal Self-Determination

Peoples might be qualified to exercise the right to self-determination, although some scholars prioritise its internal form. To them, the maintenance of territorial boundaries takes precedence over the external form, i.e., the right to form a new State. But under particular circumstances the failure of internal self-determination can justify the right to form a new State through secession. Thus internal self-determination is not separate from external self-determination.

Based on the Human Rights Covenants, people are granted the internal form of self-determination (the prevailing opinion) that is exercised within the boundaries of states. The internal right of self-determination deals with altering the relations between groups and the state. Given the diverse populations of modern nation-states, power-sharing, the effective participation of minorities in public affairs, and other permutations of political arrangements and mechanisms help in settling or reducing conflicts within societies that are divided along ethno-national lines. Europe, with various minority settlement mechanisms, has advanced the most exhaustive record that can serve as a universal paradigm for the legal justification of internal self-determination.

The accommodation of diversity in a wide variety of situations requires different but appropriate constitutional or democratic political mechanisms. In this view, options of minority representation and participation are encouraged, which promote or guarantee the participation of minorities in the public affairs of their host states. The recognition of ethnic distinction is the first step on the path to the pluralist nation-state and multinational state models. This chapter presages Chapter 7, focusing on secession as one aspect of the Kurdish statehood issue.

6.1 Effective Participation in Public Affairs

Political participation or 'democratic self-determination,' as a procedural right and 'a precondition for a sound minority protection,'[1] signifies 'the actions by

1 Annelies Verstichel, *Participation, Representation and Identity. The Right of Persons belonging to Minorities to Effective Participation in Public Affairs: Content, Justification and Limits* (Intersentia 2009) 65.

DOI: 10.4324/9781003424314-6

which individuals take part in the political process.'[2] Political participation, at the most basic level, means the right to vote and to function as a political actor.[3] Representation in a state's government, as one of the principles of politics, is a relationship through which an individual or groups represent a larger group of people or acts on their behalf.[4] In representative democracies, based on the primary meaning of participation (more than voting), the right to effective participation of minorities signifies that the interests of minorities should be effectively accommodated. Thus, minority participation and minority representation are used interchangeably.[5] The effective participation of minorities in public affairs requires an 'active' element, which is the physical presence of persons representing minorities in decision-making processes.[6] This is called 'mirror representation,'[7] reflecting the ethnic, gender, or class composition of the public. Therefore, minority participation typifies mechanisms for which 'substantive equality' is the ultimate rationale and through which the physical presence of minorities in public affairs is guaranteed.[8] But what is meant by public affairs?

In its General Comment on Article 25 of the ICCPR, which defends and monitors the right to take part in government or the conduct of public affairs, the UNHRC defines public affairs as:

> a broad concept which relates to the exercise of political power, in particular the exercise of legislative, executive and administrative powers... [encapsulating] all aspects of public administration, and the formulation and implementation of policy at international, national, regional and local levels.[9]

Therefore, public affairs can include having a role in parliament, advisory and expert bodies, national self-government, civil service, law-enforcement institutions, public councils, boards and committees, and civil associations.[10] Participation in public affairs is separate from participation in cultural, social, and economic life as per Article 2(2) of the 1992 UN Declaration on the Rights of Persons Belonging to National or Ethnic, Religious and Linguistic Minorities (hereinafter the Declaration on the Rights of Minorities). In any case, participation in public affairs may broadly encompass participation in bodies for trade and industry, agriculture, labour, and other unions or mechanisms for collective representation.[11]

2 Barrie Axford, 'Political Participation' in Barrie Axford and others (eds), *Politics. An Introduction* (Routledge 2002) 120.
3 Verstichel (n 1) 28.
4 Andrew Heywood, *Key Concepts in Politics* (Macmillan 2000) 143.
5 Verstichel (n 1) 30.
6 ibid.
7 ibid 48.
8 ibid 74.
9 UNHRC, 'General Comment 25' (12 July 1996), 'Article 25: "The Right to Participate in Public Affairs, Voting Rights and Equal Access to Public Service,"' [5].
10 Verstichel (n 1) 31.
11 ibid 32.

In whatever way, the physical participation of minorities in the form of influence must be effective. Participation is not effective unless minorities or their representatives have 'influence' on the decision-making process. According to General Comment No. 25 on Article 25, influence can be exercised by public debate and dialogue with an entity's representatives or through its self-organising capability.[12] Therefore, having some reserved seats in parliament does not in itself equate with influence. A minority's vote will likely be defeated by the majority.[13] Effective participation literally thwarts making 'permanent' the situation of groups as political minorities, i.e., participation should change their situation effectively from a minority to a majority. This is possible through radical forms of power-sharing, in the exercise of legislative, executive, and administrative powers, ranging from internal autonomy or self-government to consociational guarantees at the far end of the continuum of presence and influence. The 'counter-majoritarian forms of federal or consociational power-sharing' is the maximalist interpretation of the right to effective participation, which host states have opposed vigorously and in which no political compromise appears possible.[14] Parallel consent, veto rights, and the language(s) used in parliament are other ways of achieving effectiveness.[15] However, these mechanisms are insufficient, as they might not satisfy the respective substantive equality.

On the situation in Syria to determine the future of the country, the UNSC Resolution 2118 notes 'not only inclusive[ness] but also meaningful[ness]' of the participation of all the Syrian people.[16] Thus, pure presence is not enough to realise substantive equality in the decision-making process. Participation is effective if it leads to protecting and promoting the identity of minorities. This might meet the meaningfulness of the participation. Establishing 'appropriate' local or autonomous administrations[17] and other permutations of decentralisation is one way to secure this.[18] Participation in public affairs is the practice of the right to self-determination by every member of a minority. Therefore, minority members may consider it 'the purest form' of self-determination.[19] In this regard, Resolution 1541(XV) in its Principle IX refers to free political institutions, freely expressed wishes, and informed democratic processes.

In some cases, to the UNHRC, consultation can ensure the effective participation of indigenous minorities in decisions which affect them as in the cases of

12 General Comment 25 (n 9) [8].

13 Verstichel (n 1) 33, 70.

14 Will Kymlicka, 'The Evolving Basis of European Norms of Minority Rights: Rights to Culture, Participation and Autonomy' in Marc Weller, Denika Blacklock and Katherine Nobbs (eds), *The Protection of Minorities in the Wider Europe* (Springer 2008) 30.

15 Verstichel (n 1) 33.

16 UNSC Res 2118 (27 September 2013).

17 CSCE, Copenhagen Document (1990), [35].

18 Ulrike Barten, *Minorities, Minority Rights and Internal Self-Determination* (Springer 2015) 246.

19 ibid 252.

Apirana Mahuika v. New Zealand[20] and *Länsman et al. v. Finland*.[21] The Advisory Committee on the FCPNM, in its Commentary on the Effective Participation of Persons Belonging to National Minorities in Cultural, Social and Economic Life and in Public Affairs regarding the 'effectiveness' of participation, perceives a formal provision for the participation of persons belonging to national minorities as insufficient. Their participation should have a substantial influence on decisions which are taken, and, insofar as possible, there should be shared ownership of the decisions taken.[22] Thus, mere consultation is not a sufficient component of effective participation. National minorities should have real opportunities to influence decision-making, the outcome of which should adequately reflect their needs, according to the Advisory Committee.[23] Likewise, a veto-type right is not sufficient to guarantee the proper involvement of minority representatives in issues which do not concern them directly or exclusively. A variety of methods serve as a substitute for, or a complement to, the 'veto' system.[24]

The mechanisms by which minorities could be ensured of effective participation is a context-dependent issue. But, obviously, much decision-making takes place at the national, regional, and local levels. In workable situations of this kind, effective structures are set up to guarantee equilibrium between individuals and to protect marginalised communities. These structures may be related to the right to self-determination. What is the relevance of effective participation by minorities in public affairs for the right to self-determination? The Friendly Relations Declaration while stating international law introduced a new category of self-determination in addition to the three modes introduced by Resolution 1514(XV): 'any other political status freely determined by a people' (Principle 5). Thus, any other political status could comprise any initial or internal form of self-determination.[25] A people may be eligible for the right of self-determination internally and externally, although internal and external forms should be applied in order with *priority* given to the former or the original conception of self-determination.[26] This is due to the precedence of territorial integrity.[27] Furthermore, self-determination is not necessarily the radical form of creating a new independent state for some peoples.[28] One might ask whether internal self-determination satisfies a lingering aspiration of a group to create their own state. The best way is to consult the group itself. In some cases, Catalonia for example, an internal form of self-determination may not put

20 *Apirana Mahuika v. New Zealand* (27 Oct 2000), Communication No. 547/1993, UNHRC.

21 *Länsman et al. v. Finland* (8 November 1994), Communication No. 511/1992, UNHRC.

22 Council of Europe, Advisory Committee on the FCPNM, *Commentary on the Effective Participation of Persons Belonging to National Minorities in Cultural, Social and Economic Life and in Public Affairs* (adopted on 28 February 2008), [18]–[19].

23 ibid [71].

24 ibid [97], [99].

25 Barten (n 18) 197.

26 ibid 194.

27 Ebru Demir, 'The Right to Internal Self-Determination in Peacebuilding Processes: A Reinterpretation of the Concept of Local Ownership from a Legal Perspective' (2017) 8 AOHR 18, 22.

28 Eric Kolodner, 'The Future of the Right to Self-Determination' (1994) 10(1) CJIL 153.

an end to revolutionary or radical nationalism to achieve a sovereign homeland. This might be the case with the Kurds as well. Therefore, the answer to the question is context-dependent, i.e., depending on the extent to which the internal form of self-determination may or may not satisfy the radical, national aspirations of a community. Quebec is worth mentioning as an internal manifestation of self-determination that has settled the Quebec people's aspiration for autonomy within Canada, although a large minority voted for independence in the 1995 referendum. Nonetheless, the violations of the constitutional obligations or unilateral revision or revocation of the agreed construct can be an incentive for the minority group to insist on exercising the external version of self-determination.

6.2 Internal Self-Determination and Effective Participation

A range of different UN bodies have engaged with self-determination, such as the UNESCO, the CERD, and the UNHRC. In 1998, the Division of Human Rights Democracy and Peace as part of UNESCO, held the International Conference of Experts on the Implementation of Right to Self-Determination as a Contribution to Conflict Prevention. In its contribution to the prevention or solution of present and future conflicts, the Conference referred to 'fully participatory democratic pro cesses' to achieve self-determination.[29] Internal self-determination, as a continuous right over a period of time, is the right to self-government. As per the Conference of Experts, the internal right to self-determination as a probable 'peremptory norm of general international law'[30] encompasses 'the right to decide the form of government and the identity of rulers by the whole population of a state and the right of a population group within the state to participate in decision making at the state level.' It also means a people's right to practise territorial political, cultural, linguistic, and religious autonomy within the current state's borders.[31] The governing institutional order and participatory arrangements can guarantee these developments for all segments of a state. They are referred to in Article 1 common to both the ICCPR and the ICESCR.

Effective participation in public affairs is closely connected to and can be guaranteed by internal forms of self-determination, which take various forms hinged on situations concerned and how parties, the state, and the minority reach a compromise. An effective presence in public affairs of a state is the exercise of an internal form of self-determination. The CERD confirmed this in its General Comment No. 21 on the Right to Self-Determination (1996):

29 Report of the International Conference of Experts, *The Implementation of the Right to Self-Determination as a Contribution to Conflict Prevention* (21–27 November 1998).

30 Alain Pellet, 'Kosovo—The Questions Not Asked' in Marko Milanovic and Michael Wood (eds), *The Law and Politics of the Kosovo Advisory Opinion* (OUP 2015) 272.

31 Report of International Conference of Experts (n 29).

> [t]he right to self-determination of peoples has an internal aspect, that is to say, the rights of all peoples to pursue freely their economic, social and cultural development without outside interference.' In that respect, there exists a link with the right of every citizen to take part in the conduct of public affairs at any level, as referred to in Article 5(c) of the International Convention on the Elimination of All Forms of Racial Discrimination (1965). In consequence, governments are to represent the whole population without distinction as to race, colour, descent or national or ethnic origin.[32]

In other terms, internal self-determination links peoples of states to the governments representing them. Representation should be devoid of any discriminatory features.

The internal aspect of Article 1(1) of the ICCPR is choosing legislators and political leaders by the whole population of the state, as a people, free from any manipulation or undue influence on the part of domestic authorities themselves. Thus, it is manifested in other provisions of the Covenant, including freedom of expression (Article 19); the right to peaceful assembly (Article 21); the right to freedom of association (Article 22); the right to take part in the conduct of public affairs, directly or through freely chosen representatives (Article 25(a)); and the right to vote (Article 25(b)).[33] These rights are a necessary precondition for the effective participation of minorities in public affairs.[34] Therefore, Article 1(1) is implicitly relevant to the effective participation of minorities, as part of the 'whole people,' in public affairs through a representative government. Both the UNHRC General Comment No. 12 on Article 1 of the ICCPR (1984) and the General Comment No. 25 on Article 25 of the ICCPR (1996) link Article 1(1) of the ICCPR with Article 25. That is to say, choosing representatives and the right to vote are among manifestations of the right to self-determination within states' boundaries. These rights can be exerted simultaneously at local and national levels.

Internal self-determination is the systematic engagement of all groupings in the national democratic process which allows for 'the preservation of their cultural identity and their development on an equal footing with the majority population.'[35] That is, the minority's opinion carries the same weight as the majority's. Internal self-determination or the internal solution is the accommodation of two ends of self-determination: a right to representative government and the right to territorial unity.[36] In fact, a right to internal self-determination (the conduct of public affairs) is deduced from Articles 21, 22, and 25 of the ICCPR.[37] It is implemented within existing boundaries through a democratic process in which peoples freely

32 CERD, 'General Comment No 21' (23 August 1996), 'The Right to Self-Determination,' [4].

33 Antonio Cassese, *Self-Determination of Peoples; A Legal Reappraisal* (CUP 1995) 53.

34 Verstichel (n 1) 197.

35 Peter Hilpold, *Autonomy and Self-Determination: between Legal Assertions and Utopian Aspirations* (EEP 2018) 43.

36 Christine Bell, *On the Law of Peace: Peace Agreements and the Lex Pacificatoria* (OUP 2008) 206.

37 General Comment 25 (n 9), [2]

determine their political status; self-determination as a process amounts to continuing determination,[38] meaning that one person votes many times. This form is compatible with the dictum of integrity of the state and can have cultural, economic, social, and political aspects.

The political aspect of internal self-determination is a method of devolution of power and joint government for a people with a particular ethnic character living within a larger mother state. These requirements are stipulated in the principle of equal rights and self-determination of peoples of the 1970 Friendly Relations Declaration. This would be a government representing all peoples of the state. In fact, the sovereignty of states is linked to the idea of internal self-determination. A representative or pluralist government 'as a requirement of international law'[39] can be achieved through the participation of a population in public affairs[40] or having 'a say' in the political decision-making process. The participation of citizens in public affairs management may result in a pluralist government of all peoples of a sovereign state. This, in turn, is obtainable through amendment of the constitution, or institutionalised protection, and the establishment of certain forms of governance, such as regional self-government or self-rule and autonomy to be represented in the different legislative, administrative, and judicial bodies of the state. In other words, it is the people's right to engage in the decision-making process. This encompasses the right to exercise political autonomy within the boundaries of the existing state without giving preference to cultural, ethnic, linguistic, or religious identity. That is the traditional Western position on self-determination. Put differently, self-determination and democracy are linked by the people of a territory participating effectively and democratically in the territory's political decision-making processes.

Another body which dealt with self-determination and its implementation is the Vienna Declaration and Programme of Action. The Programme (1993) made reference to 'a Government [sic] belonging to the territory without distinction of any kind.'[41] Unlike the UN Friendly Relations Declaration in its saving clause, the 1993 Declaration does not refer to race, creed, or colour. It considers the continuing right of participation of all inhabitants or 'the whole people' of a state in its political system without discrimination for the purpose of self-determination.

As stated, the effective participation of minorities in public affairs is of relevance to the internal right to self-determination. Integration, representation in a state's government, and autonomous administration can arguably meet the requisite criteria for (internal) self-determination. Choosing any appropriate manifestation of internal self-determination is contingent on the economic, cultural, and social

38 Rosalyn Higgins, *Problems and Process – International Law and How We Use it* (OUP 1994) 120.
39 Jane Wright, 'Minority Groups, Autonomy, and Self-Determination' (1999) 19(4) OJLS 623.
40 General Comment 25 (n 9).
41 Representatives of 171 states adopted the Action. Subsequently, the UNGA endorsed this declaration in Resolution 48/121 (14 February 1994). As it is a declaration and not a treaty, the status of it is not monitored by the UN Secretary-General. And contemplating the declaration was adopted by acclamation at the conference, and then the UNGA resolution was adopted without a vote, it is not possible to say how many countries have joined or approved it.

contexts of the particular state and peoples, as there are no definite 'forms and procedures'[42] of realising the free wishes of peoples. In some situations, internal self-determination for the purpose of effective participation is also realised by guaranteeing political rights, which are stipulated by international legal instruments.

6.3 International Human Rights Law on Political Rights

The International Bill of Rights entails international law provisions that expressly deal with minorities' effective participation in public affairs. Self-determination implies a territory's political status without the interference of others. Nevertheless, participation denotes sharing status with others (those governing) and with consent, that is, a 'balance of interests' between majority and minority wishes.[43] The right to popular engagement or inclusion in government, which is an established norm of international law,[44] is the internal political aspect of self-determination.[45] It comprises autonomous administrations or self-rule to promote and protect the ethnic, cultural, linguistic, and religious identity of minorities and the new law of hybrid self-determination or recasting sovereignty, which protects minority rights.[46] Hybrid self-determination aims to reconstruct the unitary sovereignty of a state or redefine a state. Principle VIII of the Helsinki Final Act of 1975 affirms the right of all peoples to have a role in sovereignty.

Articles 21 and 22 of the ICCPR guarantee the right to freedom of assembly and the right to freedom of association, respectively. According to General Comment No. 25 on Article 25 of the ICCPR, the following freedoms must exist in an environment of full enjoyment and respect for the rights guaranteed in the articles: 1) freedom to engage in political activity individually or through political parties and other organisations, and 2) freedom to debate public affairs, to hold peaceful demonstrations and meetings, to criticise and oppose, to publish political material, to campaign for election, and to advertise political ideas.[47] At the European level, Article 11 of the ECHR also guarantees both rights stipulated in Articles 21 and 22 of the ICCPR. These political rights are necessary but not sufficient[48] to ensure that minorities have an effective role in matters affecting them.

The right to participate (or the right of political participation) in the conduct of public affairs, or 'substantive self-determination,'[49] directly or by means of freely

42 *Western Sahara (Advisory Opinion)* [1975] ICJ Rep, 36.
43 Barten (n 18) 251.
44 Valerie Epps, 'The New Dynamics of Self-Determination' (1997) 3(2) ILSA JICL 433.
45 Antonio Cassese, 'Political Self-Determination — Old Concepts and New Developments' in Antonio Cassese (ed), *UN Law/Fundamental Rights: Two Topics in International Law* (Sijthoff and Noordhoff 1979) 137–165.
46 Bell (n 36) 227.
47 General Comment 25 (n 9) [25].
48 Verstichel (n 1) 200.
49 James Anaya, 'Contemporary Definition of the International Norm of Self-Determination' (1993) 3 TLCP 131, 145.

chosen representatives, is a well-established right. It is expressed, in general terms, in Article 21 of the UDHR (the right to take part in the government) and Article 25 of the ICCPR. Article 25 of the ICCPR recognises the right of every citizen to take part in the conduct of public affairs, vote and be elected, and have access to public services. Article 3 Protocol No. 1 of the ECHR requires states to 'undertake to hold free elections at reasonable intervals by secret ballot, under conditions which will ensure the free expression of the opinion of the people in the choice of the legislature.'

The right to participate is a form of 'self-government' through 'meaningful choice' for electing representatives. This idea of the involvement of groups gained significant backing from the 1990s.[50] It is referred to as 'effective participation in public affairs' (Paragraph 35) for national minorities in the 1990 Document of the Copenhagen Meeting of the Conference on the Human Dimension of the Conference on Security and Co-operation in Europe (CSCE).[51] Effective participation in public affairs transcends political participation and is a foundational and substantive right without which fully democratic governance is not realised.[52] The right to effective participation is also stipulated in Article 2(2) and (3) of the UN Declaration on the Rights of Minorities[53] and Article 15 of the Council of Europe's FCPNM 1995.[54] Other instruments referring to this right are Article 21 of the UDHR (1948), the Flensburg Recommendations Towards Effective Participation of Minorities (1994),[55] and the soft legal standard[56] of the 1999 Lund Recommendations on the Effective Participation of National Minorities in Public Life (hereinafter the Lund Recommendations).[57]

Part IV of the Copenhagen Document concerns questions relating to national minorities, which can only be satisfactorily resolved in a democratic political framework based on the rule of law, with a functioning independent judiciary (Paragraph

50 Milena Sterio, *The Right to Self-Determination under International Law: "Selfistans," Secession and the Rule of the Great Powers* (Routledge 2013) 13.
51 Now OSCE. Copenhagen Document (n 17) [35].
52 Marc Weller, 'Creating the Conditions Necessary for the Effective Participation or Persons Belonging to National Minorities' (2004) 10 IJMGR 265.
53 Art. 2(2): 'Persons belonging to minorities have the right to participate effectively in cultural, religious, social, economic and public life.' (3). 'Persons belonging to minorities have the right to participate effectively in decisions on the national and, where appropriate, regional level concerning the minority to which they belong or the regions in which they live, in a manner not incompatible with national legislation.' UNGA Res 47/135 (18 December 1992).
54 Art. 15 of FCPNM: The Parties shall create the conditions necessary for the effective participation of persons belonging to national minorities in cultural, social and economic life and in public affairs, in particular those affecting them.
55 Or the Central European Initiative Instrument for the Protection of Minority Rights (19 November 1994).
56 Weller (n 52).
57 The Lund Recommendations on the Effective Participation of National Minorities in Public Life. Participation here includes participation in decision-making (in the central government, elections and proportional representation in parliament, advisory and consultative bodies) and self-governance (non-territorial or territorial autonomies).

30). The fundamental political rights in the Document are Paragraphs 6–9.3. The Document is especially concerned with the effective participation of minorities in public affairs, aiming at the protection and promotion of the identity of minorities, in Paragraph 35, through establishing 'appropriate local or autonomous administrations corresponding to the specific historical and territorial circumstances of such minorities and in accordance with the policies of the State concerned.' The paragraph, though only a recommendation, refers to local or autonomous administrations as the means by which the referenced aims are achieved. However, the policies of states might restrict the implementation of those aims.

As political rights incorporated in general international human rights are not enough to ensure and claim minorities' effective participation and representation, special conditions are required to promote or guarantee that minorities engage in the public affairs which affect them. The hereinabove rights are prerequisites for the participation of minorities; however, they do not actually guarantee the effective presence of minorities in the decision-making process. In other words, these rights might influence some outcomes of the decision-making process, but the degree of influence might not be adequately and substantively effective. Therefore, they should be supplemented by extra measures with minority participation and representation of a state's governing body which defines their express objective. A question is posed here: is there an international legal framework for securing minority participation?

6.4 The Legal Basis of Effective Participation of Minorities in Public Affairs

Article 1 of the Human Rights Covenants recognises internal self-determination for all peoples. The bias toward territoriality has led many states to maintain a conservative stance on granting internal self-determination to their people to avoid the possibility of disruption. The UNHRC in its General Comment No. 12 Article 1 (The Right to Self-Determination of Peoples) calls for taking positive action to facilitate the realisation of and respect for the right to self-determination under the UN Charter. However, the UNGA was not widely successful in promoting the internal self-determination of ethnic groups within sovereign states.

The UN Secretary-General submitted the study on 'popular participation in its various forms as an important factor in the development and in the full realization of human rights' to the UN Commission on Human Rights in 1985.[58] The study mentions the elements of popular participation including, *inter alia*, the right to self-determination. The 1986 Declaration on the Right to Development adopted by the UNGA also emphasises popular participation as an important factor in the full

58 United Nations, *Study by the Secretary-General on Popular Participation in its Various Forms as an Important Factor in Development and in the Full Realization of Human Rights* (1984) UN Doc. ElCN.411985110.

realisation of all human rights.[59] In the case of a disavowal of an active role for a segment of a state, the assertion of external self-determination may be a telling way to guarantee meaningful participation.

The UN Commission on Human Rights, in its Commentary on the Declaration on the Rights of Minorities, presents 'a list of good practices' pertaining to effective participation,[60] including representation in legislative, administrative, and advisory bodies and more generally in public life. These practices can be implemented through minority representation mechanisms such as proportional representation systems and different forms of preference voting.

Regarding national minority rights, the moderate approach between Article 1 (to determine political status and to enjoy the right to choose a nation's form of constitution or government) and Article 27 (a right to enjoy and maintain one's culture, to profess and practise religion, or to use one's own language) of the ICCPR is a right to 'effective participation' in public affairs directly affecting them (Article 25 of the ICCPR, the right of individuals to participate in settling political status).[61] This right appeared in the minority rights regimes of the 1990s.[62] The Copenhagen Declaration (1990) endorsed it and, based on this right, recommended territorial autonomy, although that was dropped in later declarations.[63]

With regard to effective participation, the Report of the CSCE Meeting of Experts on National Minorities (1991), in its Section III, considers the effective opportunity of minorities, 'in accordance with the decision-making procedures of each State.' The Member States consider that the 'appropriate democratic participation of persons belonging to national minorities or their representatives in decision-making or consultative bodies constitutes an important element of effective participation in public affairs.'[64] Section IV, Paragraph 7 lists a few measures that yield 'positive results': advisory and decision-making bodies in which minorities are represented, in particular, with regard to education, culture, and religion; elected bodies and assemblies of national minority affairs; local and autonomous administration; and autonomy on a territorial basis. Other features that should be included are the existence of consultative, legislative, and executive bodies chosen through free and periodic elections; self-administration by a national minority of components for maintaining identity in situations where autonomy on a territorial underpinning does not apply; and decentralised or local forms of government.[65] The politics of Organization for Security and Co-operation in Europe (OSCE) Member States are bound and shaped by these provisions.

59 Art. 8(2), UNGA Res 41/128 (4 December 1986).

60 UN Commission on Human Rights, *Commentary of the Working Group on Minorities to the United Nations Declaration on the Rights of Persons Belonging to National or Ethnic, Religious and Linguistic Minorities* (30 May–3 June 2005), UN Doc. E/CN.4/Sub.2/AC.5/2005/2, [42], [44], [45].

61 Kymlicka in Weller, Blacklock and Nobbs (n 14) 28.

62 Verstichel (n 1) 2.

63 Kymlicka in Weller, Blacklock and Nobbs (n 14) 28.

64 Report of the CSCE Meeting of Experts on National Minorities, 19 July 1991.

65 ibid Sec IV, [7].

The Lund Recommendations constitute another instrument aiming at the interpretation and elaboration of existing international rules regarding the effective participation of minorities in public affairs. The Recommendations were published by the Foundation on Inter-Ethnic Relations in 1999. They were developed by 18 experts on international law, political science, and sociology, illustrating ways to improve the participation of national minorities in public life. These recommendations bind no state legally or politically;[66] however, they are 'a quality of authoritative interpretation' of the relevant standards.[67] Their first general principle states that the effective participation of national minorities in public affairs is a *sine qua non* component of a peaceful and democratic society.[68] The respect for human dignity, equal rights, and non-discrimination are principles that affect the rights of national minorities to participate in public affairs and to enjoy other political rights, according to its Principle 2. The next general principle is expressed in Parts II and III of the Lund Recommendations, which enumerate arrangements for effective participation of minorities in public affairs and self-governance, respectively, and which include a reserved number of seats in one or both chambers of parliament or parliamentary committees allocated to members of national minority cabinet positions, seats on the supreme or constitutional court or lower courts, and positions on nominated advisory bodies or other high-level organs, personnel addressing minority concerns, special measures for minority participation in the civil service as well as the provision of public services in the language of the national minority.

The UN document concerned specifically with minority issues is the Declaration on the Rights of Minorities, which shared elements in the CSCE Copenhagen Document.[69] It was adopted through UNGA Resolution 47/135 of 18 December 1992 by consensus. Thus, it could be categorised as *opinio juris*. Whether the necessary state practice exists is controversial. In any case, as a cardinal resource for the UN, the Declaration establishes basic criteria to safeguard the rights of individuals belonging to minorities. It provides advice to states in managing diversity and assuring non-discrimination as well as to minorities themselves in their quest for equality and participation. It was inspired by Article 27 of the ICCPR. According to the Declaration, the promotion and protection of the rights of persons belonging to national or ethnic, religious, and linguistic minorities contribute to the political and social stability of states. The rights to identity and non-discrimination are incorporated in Articles 1 and 2(1) of the Declaration.

At the UN level, the right to the effective participation of minorities in public affairs is incorporated in Article 2(2) and (3) of the Declaration:

66 Verstichel (n 1) 214–215.

67 John Packer, 'The Origin and Nature of the Lund Recommendations on the Effective Participation of National Minorities in Public Life' (2000) 11(4) HM 29, 41.

68 Lund Recommendations (n 57), General Principles, 1.

69 UNGA Res 47/135 (18 December 1992).

> 2. Persons belonging to minorities have the right to participate effectively in cultural, religious, social, economic and public affairs. 3. Persons belonging to minorities have the right to participate effectively in decisions on the national and, where appropriate, local level concerning the minority to which they belong or the regions in which they live, in a manner not incompatible with national legislation.

The first clause, compared to other documents and other provisions within the Declaration, has not been confined to limitations, such as 'where appropriate' and 'wherever possible.'[70] Also, it has not been confined to political participation, while Article 2(3) of the Declaration confines effective participation to 'where appropriate.' At the national level, participation is implied to be 'always obligatory and not subject to the appropriateness criterion.'[71] In addition, minorities should not participate in a manner incompatible with national law. Whatever the case, there could be no national law directed against the protection and promotion of a minority's identity.[72]

Internal self-determination in its theory and practice is typically associated with 'the European liberal tradition.'[73] With different minority situations, Europe has been a legal laboratory for adopting different approaches to guarantee internal self-determination or the effective participation of minorities in public affairs. The most comprehensive and legally binding document on minority protection is the Council of Europe's FCPNM 1995.[74] However, this is a regional instrument that could be a potential blueprint for other plural states across the world. The right to effective participation of minorities in public affairs is stipulated generally in Article 15 of the Framework as hard law[75] regarding participation effectively, fairly, and fully in cultural, religious, social, economic, and public affairs — known as a third-generation minority right. It is listed after the right to protection against discrimination and the right to develop and maintain ethnic, linguistic, and religious identity.[76] According to the FCPNM, the protection of national minorities and persons belonging to such minorities constitutes an integral part of the international protection of human rights (Article 1). Apart from effective participation in public affairs, Article 15 also guarantees effective participation in cultural, social, and economic life. These are interrelated as socio-economic difficulties frequently impact the effective participation of minorities in public affairs.

The Advisory Committee of the Framework (ACFC) interpreted Article 15 as a central provision of the Framework Convention in its commentary in February

70 Verstichel (n 1) 251.
71 ibid 251.
72 Thornberry, quoted in ibid.
73 Karen Knop, *Diversity and Self-Determination in International Law* (CUP 2002) 19.
74 FCPNM (n 54).
75 Weller (n 52).
76 ibid.

2008.[77] The Commentary perceives three corners of a triangle which, together, form the main foundations of the Framework Convention: Article 4 (promote full and effective equality between persons belonging to a national minority and those belonging to the majority with taking due account of the specific conditions of the persons belonging to national minorities), Article 5 (promote the conditions necessary for persons belonging to national minorities to maintain and develop their culture and to preserve the essential signifiers of their identity, namely their religion, language, traditions, and cultural heritage) and Article 15.

Article 4 requires the right of equal protection of the law and before the law and the prohibition of any form of discrimination. The right to effective participation, as enshrined in Article 15, makes it possible that the concerns of persons belonging to minorities regarding full and effective equality (Article 4) and their right to preservation and development of their specific identity (Article 5) are heard and effectively taken into account.[78]

Effective participation is the central idea of the Lund Recommendations. It is a way to democratically avoid national self-determination. However, its flexible vagueness has made it popular.[79] Its minimalist interpretation is one of implementing political rights in a non-discriminatory manner, while its robust interpretation is achieving 'some degree of *representation* in the legislature' but precisely in proportion to a minority's share of the overall population.[80] However remedial the intent, non-discrimination and representation do not directly address the actual sources of ethnic conflict.[81]

The 1994 General Comment No. 23 on Article 27 of the ICCPR mentions the effective participation of minorities:

> [w]ith regard to the exercise of the cultural rights protected under article 27, the Committee observes that culture manifests itself in myriad forms, including a particular way of life associated with the use of land resources, especially in the case of indigenous peoples. That may include such traditional activities as fishing or hunting and the right to live in reserves protected by law. The enjoyment of those rights may require positive legal measures of protection and measures to ensure the effective participation of members of minority communities in decisions which affect them.

According to the comment, the enjoyment of cultural rights may require measures to ensure the effective participation of members of minority communities. But what measures? This reflects the perception that states would decide on the kind of measures. Of course, this should be in consultation with the respective minority.

77 Commentary on Effective Participation of Minorities (n 22) [8].
78 ibid [8].
79 Kymlicka in Weller, Blacklock and Nobbs (n 14) 29.
80 ibid.
81 ibid 30.

Together, all the abovementioned instruments add a strong degree of normative force to claim effective participation and clear obstacles to effective participation in order to implement internal rights of self-determination. The right to effective participation in public affairs as stipulated in the instruments stated hereinabove can be implemented through a range of options and mechanisms at the national level including federalism, territorial autonomy, non-territorial engagement, devolution, and decentralisation (local or autonomous administrations).

Depending on the context, mechanisms include, but are not limited to, inclusion in elections (electoral privileges for minority parties and minority representatives), parliamentary committees for minority Issues, ombudspersons in parliament, participation in the executive and the judiciary (ministerial posts, government commissioner, minority representatives, and minority parties in legislative bodies), round tables, advisory and consultative bodies, liaison committees, federalism, territorial and non-territorial autonomy, and self-government arrangements. Special representation rights ought to supplement these mechanisms.[82] States may resort to different measures to involve minorities in effective participation.

6.5 Constructs to Implement Internal Self-Determination

Democratic elections and legislatures are not sufficient in all situations for fulfilling the conditions of self-determination. In some situations, self-determination needs to be translated into forms of power redistribution. Internal self-determination is a delegation of state functions (power-sharing) to peoples or minorities within a state.[83] Disintegration of power,[84] delegation, diffusion, dislocation, disaggregation, division, and transfer of political and territorial power at the levels of the central government or sub-state governance are employed to achieve first political unification and then national identity to accommodate diversity in a modern nation-state. These governmental and territorial power-sharing arrangements can sometimes also reduce conflict and deliver peaceful dividends in contrast to circumstances where they are not present.[85] To live up to representative (joint) government or decentralised power, federal entrenchments are devices for this process within an entity,[86] which could take myriad political permutations, such as cultural home rule, administrative autonomy, associate status, local administration or self-government (with its own law and central bank), representation in the national legislature, and parliamentary independence. These are mechanisms in which the centralising tendencies are counterbalanced or compromised by considerable autonomy in some matters. A power-sharing model for excluded or marginalised groups could be a mix of some, or all, of these

82 Will Kymlicka, *Multicultural Citizenship. A Liberal Theory of Minority Rights* (OUP 1995) 108, 115.

83 See Chapter 2.6.1.

84 Bell (n 36) 106.

85 See Lars-Erik Cederman, Simon Hug and Julian Wucherpfennig, *Sharing Power, Securing Peace?: Ethnic Inclusion and Civil War* (CUP 2022).

86 Daniel J Elazar, *Exploring Federalism* (UAP 1991) 39.

types. These constructs are constitutional designs or the layering of public authority to facilitate effective participation of minorities in the state form[87] and subsequently the implementation of internal self-determination.

There are also forms of electoral representation, quotas, and other mechanisms for this purpose. One of the power-sharing forms is the territorial stratum of public authority. Effective participation in public affairs is facilitated for minorities territorially clustered in the regions they reside or according to the geographical distribution of the minority, which could be implemented in various forms, from a confederal to a federal system or devolution. This was referred to in Article 14 of the *Proposal for a European Convention for the Protection of National Minorities* (1993).[88] Autonomy is one of these arrangements. However, the phrase 'where they live' was removed from the final draft of the convention. Despite this, Article 15 of the Explanatory Report of the Framework encourages states to promote 'effective participation of persons belonging to national minorities in the decision-making processes and elected bodies both at national and local levels; [and] decentralised or local forms of government.'[89] This is in conformity with Article 4(3) of the European Charter of Local Self-Government.[90] Also, the OSCE's Lund Recommendations include non-territorial or territorial arrangements, self-governance, or a combination of both for the purpose of effective participation of minorities in public life.[91]

Given the existence of majorities in the respective sub-state, federalist, autonomous, and self-government arrangements, this principle could provide the greatest or most extreme form of effective participation in public affairs for minorities such as the Kurds, as these forms encourage broad control over a minority's own affairs. Governmental control should be linked with a special representation mechanism at the national decision-making level. The allocation or devolution of power, 'devolutionary self-determination,'[92] could take various forms, from a complex ruling system to territorial autonomy to cultural autonomy. The grassroots features of these constructs and their relevance to the right to effective participation in public affairs are relevant.

6.5.1 Autonomy

Autonomy is an inconclusive legal concept that should be made concrete in each situation.[93] Its multiple definitions contribute to its flexibility, which makes it mal-

87 Weller (n 52).

88 Art. 14. EC for Democracy through Law, *Explanatory Report on the Proposal for a European Convention for the Protection of Minorities* (18 March 1991).

89 FCPNM and Explanatory Report, Art. 15 (February 1995), H (95) 10.

90 '[P]ublic responsibilities shall generally be exercised, in preference, by those authorities which are closest to the citizens.'

91 Lund Recommendations (n 57) [14].

92 Gerry Simpson, 'The Diffusion of Sovereignty: Self-Determination in the Post-Colonial Age' (1996) 32 SJIL 255.

93 Hans-Joachim Heintze, 'On the Legal Understanding of Autonomy' in Markku Suksi (ed), *Autonomy: Applications and Implications* (KLI 1998) 13.

leable in the negotiations between governments and groups that demand greater control over their own affairs. Its malleability, over time, enables the substantive positive and negative results to be offset.[94] Autonomy, as an 'ultimate tool,' is a mechanism through which minorities have effective participation in matters affecting them and to which they can adapt their own nation-building policies.[95] Autonomy in actuality is an 'alternative' to and a limited expression of self-determination.[96] It is a constituent part of internal self-determination or two sides of the same coin.[97] Self-determination belongs to members of national, religious, ethnic, or linguistic minorities and, perhaps, to minority groups themselves. In other words, self-determination is consonant with minority rights. It protects the 'existence' and develops the 'identity' of the groups.[98]

Autonomy was first granted to groups to implement equality (as a counterbalance to or parity with the rights of the majority),[99] minority protection, and conflict resolution in some treaties after WWI.[100] It is the primary type of self-determination for minorities.[101] However, there is no positive general right to minority autonomy. It is rather a privilege which is granted by states.[102] The right, nevertheless, may be recognised by special treaties, but they do not generate a positive right to autonomy.[103]

Autonomy has not been recognised as a right pursuant to self-determination. However, international human rights law makes it legally valid, i.e., it recognises the legitimacy of the claim to autonomy. The 1993 Additional Protocol on Minorities to the ECHR recognises 'appropriate local or autonomous authorities' or

94 Fernand de Varennes, *Towards Effective Political Participation and Representation of Minorities* (UNWP 1998) 6.

95 Verstichel (n 1) 66–67

96 Hilpold (n 35) 44; Louis B. Sohn, 'The Concept of Autonomy in International Law and the Practice of the United Nations' (1980) 15(2) ILR 180.

97 Gnanapala Welhengama, 'The Legitimacy of Minorities' Claim for Autonomy through the Right to Self-Determination' (1999) 68(4) NJIL 431.

98 Marc Weller, 'Why the Legal Rules on Self-determination Do Not Resolve Self-determination Disputes' in Marc Weller, Barbara Metzger, and Niall Johnson (eds), *Settling Self-Determination Disputes: Complex Power-Sharing in Theory and Practice* (BRILL 2008) 20.

99 Joseph Marko, *Equality and Difference: Political and Legal Aspects of Ethnic Group Relation*, quoted in Wright (n 39) 613.

100 As in the Religious Peace of Augsburg, the Peace of Westphalia, Versailles Peace Treaty (1919), Sèvres Peace Treaty (1920), Self-Government Act of Åland (1920), Peace Treaty between the Republic of Finland and the Russian Socialist Federal Soviet Republic (1920), Treaty of Kars (1922), Lausanne Peace Treaty (1923), Treaty of Peace with Italy (1947), Camp David Accords (1978), and Friday Agreement of 1998. Markku Suksi, *Autonomy* (MPEPIL updated 2013).

101 Gudmundur Alfredsson, 'The Right of Self-Determination in International Law' in Olgun Akbulut and Elçin Aktoprak (eds), *Minority Self-Government in Europe and the Middle East: From Theory to Practice Studies in International Minority and Group Rights* (BRILL 2019) 22.

102 Joel Feinberg, *The Moral Limits of the Criminal Law: Volume 3: Harm to Self* (OUP 1989) 49.

103 The Paris Convention concerning the Territory of Memel (1924) and the De Gasperi-Gruber Agreement of 1946 on South Tyrol are two examples. Gaetano Pentassuglia, 'State Sovereignty, Minorities and Self-Determination: A Comprehensive Legal View' (2002) 9(4) IJMGR 303.

'a special status' for national minorities.[104] Nonetheless, the 2007 UN Declaration on the Rights of Indigenous Peoples in its Article 4 recognises both the (internal) right to self-determination and the right to autonomy or self-government (institutional arrangements) for indigenous peoples in matters relating to their internal and local affairs, as well as ways and means for financing their autonomous functions.[105] It implies varying shades of liberation from a rugged central grasp on the life of the people.[106] Full autonomy as a devolution of power in a unitary state for exercising the internal aspect of self-determination[107] is compatible with the integrity and political unity of sovereign states and countervailing or taming secessionist movements[108] and avoidance of new state formation followed by the redrawing of existing external boundaries. It is an open-ended reference ranging from territorial autonomy with legislative power, political autonomy, personal autonomy (e.g., the use of the freedom of association), functional autonomy or functional layering of public authority (linguistic units within national, regional, or local organisations), and cultural autonomy.[109] Put differently, it is the rule by the minority over its own exclusive concerns.[110]

Autonomy stands in contrast to full national sovereignty; it is a diminished or re-division of sovereignty.[111] As such, it alters the relations between minority groups and their host states. Some legal instruments such as the 1990 Copenhagen Document on the Human Dimension of the CSCE interpret autonomy as 'one of the possible means' to support and 'to protect and create conditions for the promotion of the ethnic, cultural, linguistic and religious identity of certain national minorities' within independent states.[112] Local or autonomous administration corresponding to territorial conditions is one of the possible means of autonomy. The Lund Recommendations refer to it as self-government.[113] Also, the Congress of Local and Regional Authorities of Europe recommends local, provincial, or regional ties of government in territories where national minorities represent a substantial

104 Art. 11, PACE, 'Recommendation 1201 on an Additional Protocol on the Rights of Minorities to the ECHR' (19 January 1993), CoE Doc. Doc. 6742, 1403-15/1/93-2-E.

105 UN Declaration on the Rights of Indigenous Peoples (13 September 2007).

106 Joshua Castellino, *International Law and Self-Determination: The Interplay of the Politics of Territorial Possession with Formulations of Post-Colonial National Identity* (MNP 2000) 50.

107 Also, as 'the liberal' aspect of self-determination, but nationalism does not limit self-determination to 'an internal right.' James Summers, *Peoples and International Law* (MNP 2007) 343.

108 Yash Ghai, 'Public Participation, Autonomy and Minorities' in Zelim A. Skurbaty (ed), *Beyond a One-Dimensional State: An Emerging Right to Autonomy?* (MNP 2005) 13–14.

109 Suksi (n 100).

110 Arend Lijphart, *Democracy in Plural Societies: A Comparative Exploration* (YUP 1977) 41.

111 Feinberg (n 102).

112 Document of the Copenhagen Meeting of the Conference on the Human Dimension of the CSCE (29 June 1990), 20 [2].

113 Lund Recommendations (n 57) [19], [21].

part of the population[114] to guarantee the right to effective participation of persons belonging to national minorities in public affairs affecting them.[115]

The UN Working Group on Minorities, in its Commentary to the UN Declaration on Minority Rights, introduces autonomy to protect the identity of minorities and to ensure their effective participation that can be 'territorial, cultural and local, and can be more or less extensive.'[116] To the Council of Europe's Advisory Committee on the FCPNM, territorial autonomy 'can foster a more effective participation of persons belonging to national minorities in various areas of life.'[117] These offer normative support to the claim for territorial autonomy. That is, the abovementioned instruments legitimise the claim to autonomy. Otherwise, there is no direct right to autonomy pursuant to the right to internal self-determination.

6.5.1.1 Territorial Autonomy

Territorial autonomy or spatially focused self-governance is the vesting of a territory or an entity of sizeable or concentrated national minorities with all rights, excluding the rights to engage in independent external affairs and the establishment of regional armed forces.[118] It could incorporate various degrees of self-government, ranging from administrative autonomy to full self-government. Entities with administrative autonomy possess independent executive institutions and elected representatives, but they are subject to the central legislature.

On the other hand, a territory with full self-government has the right to elect its own legislative and judicial power and is granted executive and administrative functions. Foreign, defence, financial, and immigration affairs are an exception to this rule. In any form of autonomy, the constitutional framework of the unitary state is preserved, with the autonomous entity or entities as an integral part of the host state.[119] As a possible solution to self-determination claims, maximum autonomy is introduced, which is understood as having the ability to wield internal sovereignty over the areas of culture, education, language, religion, finance, judicial administration, public safety, industry, energy, infrastructures, and enhanced freedom to engage with other states, sub-states, and international organisations (self-governance and regional integration).[120]

114 Recommendation 43 (1998) on 'Territorial Autonomy and National Minorities.'

115 Local law/Special Status, Draft reply to Recommendation 70 (1999) of the Congress of Local and Regional Authorities of Europe, (CM/Del/Dec(2002)781/10.1, 794/10.3, 795/10.3 and 796/10.6, CLRAE Rec 70 (1999), PA REC 1201 (1993)).

116 Commentary on Declaration on the Rights of Minorities (n 60) [20].

117 Commentary on Effective Participation of Minorities (n 22) [133]–[134].

118 Barten (n 18) 245.

119 Stefan Wolff and Marc Weller, 'Self-Determination and Autonomy: A Conceptual Introduction' in Stefan Wolff and Marc Weller (eds), *Autonomy, Self-Governance and Conflict Resolution, Innovative Approaches to Institutional Design in Divided Societies* (RTFG 2005) 12.

120 Wolfgang F. Danspeckgruber, 'Self-governance Plus Regional Integration: A Possible Solution to Self-Determination Claims' in ibid 32–33.

The 1990 CSCE Copenhagen Declaration endorsed territorial autonomy in its Article 35, albeit as a recommendation:

> [t]he participating States note the efforts undertaken to protect and create conditions for the promotion of the ethnic, cultural, linguistic and religious identity of certain national minorities by establishing, as one of the possible means to achieve these aims, appropriate local or autonomous administrations corresponding to the specific historical and territorial circumstances of such minorities and in accordance with the policies of the State concerned.[121]

The Parliamentary Assembly of the Council of Europe (PACE) reiterates the similar endorsement but as 'a right,' though not legally binding, for persons belonging to a national minority 'in the regions where they are a majority' to have 'appropriate local or autonomous authorities or to have a special status, matching this specific historical and territorial situation and in accordance with the domestic legislation of the State.'[122]

According to the European Charter of Local Self-Government,[123] local self-government 'denotes the right and the ability of local authorities, within the limits of the law, to regulate and manage a substantial share of public affairs under their own responsibility and in the interests of the local population.' Transferring power from a central government to an autonomous authority could include a certain degree of executive, legislative, and judicial powers, short of full sovereignty and the redrawing of new external boundaries or a decentralisation in administrative matters — such as in France, self-government with certain legislative powers; Italy (Bolzano), and an independent administrative, legislative, and judicial system; and Finland (the Åland Islands). Autonomies for the Åland Islands in Finland; South Tyrol, the Valle d'Aosta, Trentino-Alto Adige and Friuli-Venezia Giulia in Italy; Puerto Rico in the United States; the Azores and Madeira in Portugal; Catalonia, the Basque Country, Galicia, and the Canary Islands in Spain; Corsica in France; Flanders in Belgium; Northern Ireland, Scotland, and Wales in the United Kingdom; the Faeroe Islands in Denmark; the Atlantic Coast in Nicaragua; the Inuit majority in Greenland; and the Chittagong Hill Tracts in Bangladesh are many examples worthy of mention. This trend is now 'universal' in Western democracies.[124]

Regional self-government or autonomy could take various sub-state governance forms for a concentrated minority or community, including constituent entities at the federal level to decentralised administration at the local level. Functional or non-territorial autonomy with respect to language, education, religion, and culture is granted to distinctive dispersed groups that do not have to form a majority in a

121 Conference on Human Dimension of CSCE (n 112).

122 Recommendation 1201 (n 104).

123 European Charter of Local Self-Government states it clearly in Art. 3.

124 Kymlicka in Weller, Blacklock and Nobbs (n 14) 19.

delineated territory.[125] In the first model, the existence of regions is secured either by the constitution or by a federal agreement and is not a matter of question without the consent of the people involved. Belgium, Germany, the Russian Federation, and Switzerland are a few examples of this model. In the second model, their existence is not secured. Both these models have the primary legislative power. Spain and the United Kingdom (Scotland and Northern Ireland) follow the second construct. The Czech Republic and Hungary have regions in which the very existence of a specific minority is secured by the national constitution. In their case, minorities have been granted legislative power in conformity with a set framework of national legislation (third model). There are regions in Poland and the United Kingdom (e.g., Wales) which have the power to enact laws and regional legislative acts in conformity with a framework set by national legislation; however, their existence is not secured by the constitution (fourth model). Also, there are other models as in Denmark, France, Sweden, and the United Kingdom in which regions have decision-making power, though without legislative power, and councils are directly elected by the population or the local authorities (as in Finland and Latvia).[126] Self-government refers to various organisational structures at the sub-state level. Regional self-government is a manifestation of self-government, although self-government does not qualify by virtue of meeting territorial autonomy requirements.

Territorial autonomy may be delimited as far as a region is concerned, but not if one looks at the rights of individuals. Thus, the issue of who belongs to the minority is not addressed either by the officials who carry out the prerogatives of self-rule or by the people concerned. On the off chance that a specific minority (or minorities) may be conceded local autonomy, the territory should be defined and established so that it ensures majority status for the minority, and that usually involves many minority individuals. In any case, the boundaries of the autonomous territory that belongs to the minority may comprise members of the majority. The autonomous territory can be allowed to monitor immigration not only from international countries but also from other areas of the state.[127] Such a monitoring system is to ensure that the local majority status of the national minority is retained.

Unlike federalism, autonomy does not provide for institutionalised participation in the national legislative process.[128] Representation at the centre, particularly when the autonomous territory is small and its primary issues are local, is often trivial. Examples are the Åland Islands, Puerto Rico, and the Sami in Finland and Norway. It is, however, necessary to forestall the one-sided modification or termination of an autonomy agreement if one aims at significant representation of a minority at the national level or in a state's governing administration. The Åland Islands is an example in which, without the approval of both the national and the Åland

125 Tom Hadden, 'Integration and Autonomy: Minority Rights and Political Accommodation' in Ian O'Flynn and David Russell (eds), *Power Sharing: New Challenges for Divided Societies* (Pluto Press 2005) 38.

126 Markku Suksi, *Sub-State Governance through Territorial Autonomy* (Springer 2011) 123–124.

127 Verstichel (n 1) 469–470.

128 Joseph Marko, quoted in ibid 471.

legislatures, the autonomy agreement laws cannot be altered. This representation could be accomplished through advisory bodies to the authorities, not necessarily by institutional representation in the national lawmaking body. Another method for being associated with the national decision-making process is that of conceding to the leader of the autonomous locale a position of authority in the government or granting the autonomous authority the power of presenting bills to the national parliament on subjects that fall under the purview of the national government — such as Gagauzia in Moldova and the Åland Islands in Finland, respectively.[129]

6.5.1.2 Federalism

Internal self-determination is aligned with some forms of government within existing boundaries of states, ranging from federalism, confederalism, a canton system, local government or popular sovereignty, political equality, autonomy concerning the protection of minorities, exclusive control over education, and a variety of social and cultural matters. Among this variety of possible exercises, federalism — as a territorial power-sharing practice[130] — is a political order for the integration of people by a 'shared government' to preserve and protect the 'identity and distinctiveness' of different peoples of a state. Federalism, as a normative concept, advocates setting aside individual 'preferences' to constitute a 'joint action' or to establish 'self-government of the constituent units.'[131]

The Forum of Federations, an intergovernmental organisation that develops and shares comparative expertise on the practice of federal and decentralised governance through a global network, perceives federation as the 'best' means of safeguarding distinct groups or minorities that 'are geographically concentrated in such a way that they may achieve self-governance as a majority within a regional unit of government.'[132] The overarching term 'federal political systems' refers to 'self-rule plus shared rule'[133] in political organisation, including unions, constitutionally decentralised unions, federations, confederations, federacies, associated states, condominiums, leagues, and joint functional competencies and hybrids.[134] It encompasses two divisions: a geographical division of the state into various units and a division of powers in a state among sub-state units, each of which has jurisdiction within the region assigned to it, and a central government controlling the whole territory. In this system, there is no hierarchy that singles out the central

129 Yash Ghai, *Public Participation and Minorities* (MRGI 2001).

130 Brendan O'Leary, 'The Logics of Power-sharing, Consociation and Pluralist Federations' in Weller, Metzger, and Johnson (n 98) 56.

131 Ronald L. Watts, 'Federalism, Federal Political Systems, and Federations' (1998) 1(1) ARPS 117, 118, 120.

132 The Forum of Federations, Models of Federal Power Sharing (Conference Paper 1999). Its mission is 'to strengthen inclusive and responsive governance, including pluralism and gender equality, in federal, decentralized, and transitioning countries.'

133 Elazar (n 86) 12.

134 Watts (n 131) 120.

government and the sub-state governments.[135] All are equally subordinate to the Constitution.

A federation is conventionally symmetrical; all members have equal competencies.[136] However, situations can require asymmetric structures. In the asymmetric construct, one or more federated bodies are granted unique powers that are not given to other members for the protection of its people's culture and language.[137] The United States, Germany, and Austria are examples of the former, while Quebec in Canada, Kashmir in India, and Kurdistan in Iraq have adopted the latter structure.

Federalism includes both autonomy for the member-states and, through a bicameral parliamentary structure, involvement in the legislative process at the national level. While the lower house is commonly based on proportional representation of the population, the upper house is typically focused on equality of representation on the part of the different sub-state bodies regardless of population size. Moreover, Member States also have a significant voice in matters of constitutional reform.[138]

Another feature is the potential for sub-states, such as cantons in Switzerland, to initiate federal legislation.[139] The central government and the various sub-state governments have a wide scope of consultation and cooperation structures. Moreover, regular power-sharing arrangements can be introduced between the 'constituent pieces' of the federation. These features are seen in Belgium, Bosnia and Herzegovina, and Switzerland.[140]

Federation, as one of the federal political systems, comprises a compound of 'constituent units and a general government.'[141] Both polities and the government — elected by citizens — have their own constitution, which delegates legislative, administrative, and taxing powers (the dispersion of constitutional powers) to them and has the power of dealing with people directly. In a confederation, the component governments or communities have delegates in 'the institutions of shared rule.'[142] This is the interplay between shared institutions and the governments of constituent units as they operate indirectly on the citizens.

Federalism associates peoples consensually to form a single dynamic, powerful unit for 'common ends' and as an 'alternative to the center-periphery model.'[143] This is a way of restraining the nationalist aspirations of ethnic groups for political

135 Yoram Dinstein, 'The Degree of Self-rule of Minorities in Unitarian and Federal States' in Catherine Brölmann, René Lefeber, and Marjoleine Zieck (eds), *Peoples and Minorities in International Law* (BRILL 1993) 222.

136 Kristian Myntti, *A Commentary on the Lund Recommendations on the Effective Participation of National Minorities in Public Life* (AAU 2001) 48.

137 ibid.

138 Verstichel (n 1) 467.

139 Walter Kalin, 'Federalism and the Resolution of Minority Conflicts' in Günther Bächle (ed), *Federalism against Ethnicity? Institutional, Legal and Democratic Instruments to Prevent Violent Minority Conflicts* (Ruegger 1997) 178.

140 Verstichel (n 1) 468.

141 Watts (n 131) 121.

142 ibid.

143 Elazar (n 86) 13, 33.

decomposition,[144] ameliorating internal conflicts,[145] and recognising distinct groups in multiethnic states.[146] This political organisation sustains 'the existence' of distinct polities[147] yet upholds internal integrity-diversity and the sharing of common policy making and administration by right[148] through non-centralised dispersion of political power, constitutionally or by covenants and a host of other contracts. For ethnic groups with aspirations to sovereign nationhood, federalism has its own strictures.[149]

There are two types of federations: integrative and pluralist. The former is centralised, that is, the federal government and judiciary have considerable powers over inhabitants and over the member-units of the federation.[150] It works with 'homogenized people' and is based on the ideas of liberal democracy of sharing power. The United States and federations in Latin America are integrative. On the contrary, pluralist bodies are decentralised and are composed of the member-states with significant policymaking and legal powers that can withstand infringements by the federal branches of government.[151] More than one nation or people is recognised in this model. It is consociational in the federal executive, legislature, and judiciary. Belgium, Switzerland, and Canada exemplify pluralist societies. The host states of the Kurds are also pluralist; however, they follow a different system of ruling.

6.6 Summary

The international right of individual members of minorities to effective participation in public affairs, with the ultimate goal of substantive equality, is incorporated in the minority rights instruments. Substantive equality leads to the protection and promotion of a minority's identity. Effective participation and representation of minorities are prerequisites to minority protection. The recognition of difference is the first step in this process, which could be without assimilation (through integration to reverse discrimination) and segregation (through autonomy to reverse assimilation). The presence of minorities in these mechanisms could be represented on a two-pole scale denoting the individual's right to vote and to stand for election and the equal representation of groups. Mechanisms which ensure minority representation are situated in-between. Influence also could be on the same scale: from non-binding advice to absolute veto power. Mechanisms that provide the right to legislation, majority voting, double majority voting, or suspensive veto powers, are located in-between.

144 Murray Forsyth (ed), *Federalism and Nationalism* (LUP 1989) 284; Siegfried Weissner, 'Federalism: An Architecture for Freedom' (1992) 1(2) NELR 42.

145 Watts (n 131) 131.

146 Daniel J. Elazar, 'International and Comparative Federalism' (1993) 26(2) PS: PSP 190, 195.

147 Watts (n 131) 132.

148 Elazar (n 86) 5–6.

149 See Robert Howse and Karen Knop, 'Federalism, Secession, and the Limits of Ethnic Accommodation: A Canadian Perspective' (1993) 1 NELR 269.

150 O'Leary in Weller, Metzger and Johnson (n 98) 57.

151 ibid.

Minorities should not only be present in these mechanisms but should also have an influence on the decision-making process. The participation of minorities in public affairs should be effective, meaning their ability to bring about substantive equality in the decision-making process on matters which impact upon them while they exert control over their own cultural, political, economic, and social matters. This process, in turn, impacts upon their identity. The participation of minorities and representation mechanisms is relevant in parliament, the administration, and the judiciary. To this end, the political rights contained both in the ICCPR and the ECHR are not sufficient for participation in public affairs as a broader concept. Effectiveness is ensured by the presence of minorities at different possible mechanisms ranging from insignificant to broad via a combination of territorial and non-territorial autonomy.

The effective participation of minorities in public affairs is directly related to the right to internal self-determination, which is in agreement with the territorial integrity of states. Depending on the situation, this form of self-determination is achieved through power-sharing mechanisms, veto power, and the devolution of power to a minority-people within a parent state or by forming a representative government of all peoples of the state so that states can invoke their territoriality, i.e., granting internal self-determination through sharing power can protect the sovereignty of states. Integration, representation in a state's governing body, and autonomous governance can satisfy the requirement of (internal) self-determination.

The right to effective participation can be implemented by similar structures and a minority-people is generally involved in the decision-making process of national, regional, or local level of self-governance or autonomy constructs. Territorial mechanisms of internal self-determination are truly and regionally reflective of effective representation and participation of territorially concentrated ethno-cultural groups on the local level. Territorial autonomy constructs enable them to exercise legislative and executive power more effectively at a local level. This model has been a workable framework of internal self-determination in states with regionally concentrated minorities. Substantive equality and effective participation in public affairs embodied in the form of local autonomy, enhanced by providing additional mechanisms of representation at the national level, including liberal-democratic representative institutions such as a national parliament and non-territorial autonomy, can put into effect or satisfy internal self-determination for a regionally dense community as a minority-people. Such mechanisms can counter structural segregation, inequality, and discrimination in multiple fields of public affairs and eliminate the underrepresentation of minorities.

A question can arise in the context of non-recognition or denial of a minority-people's right to internal self-determination: does it pave the way to secession? The failure of internal self-determination, in modern international law, predicates external self-determination which is essentially the question of a right to secede.[152]

152 Knop (n 73) 18.

7 Secession

Implications for Kurdistan

Non-negotiable external borders can occasionally be redrawn if a people agitates for self-determination externally along national lines. This process will amount to secession or secessionist self-determination, that is, the seceding people remove themselves from the authority of their mother state to self-govern outside the confines of the state. But are peoples at liberty to detach territorially or does international law forbid it? When, how, and to what extent can self-determination justify the separation of component parts of sovereign states to establish new states?

7.1 Secession in Legal Scholarship

Secession or state-breaking, in the modern literature, is the implementation of external right of self-determination of peoples that requires geopolitical re-organisation of existing states, that is, the separation of a *de jure* part of the host state for the purpose of creating a new independent state or integrating with another existing state based on the wishes of the affected group.[1] Secession can be unilateral without the consent of or prior negotiations with the parent state. If any change is precluded, the right is not realised. The goal of moulding new independent states is the foundation of the right, and a right of secession is 'simultaneously' the right of self-determination. However, it has not been codified as self-determination in the practice of states, although a restricted form of it does exist. In this context, the state from which the entity secedes does not yield the possession or control of the territory involved.[2]

New states are also formed by revolution and subsequent secession. After WWI, secessionist local units successfully carried out with consent or without opposition of the former administration or against the assent of the sovereign (the dismemberment of a defeated power) and by means of armed conflict or threat to use force. Another mode of secession can be a combination of occupation, armed conflict, and later accorded independence, as occurred in the cases

1 David Raič, *Statehood and the Law of Self-Determination* (KLI 2002) 308.

2 Jörg Fisch, *The Right of Self-Determination of Peoples: The Domestication of an Illusion* (CUP 2015) 42–43.

DOI: 10.4324/9781003424314-7

of Indonesia, North Korea, South Korea, North Vietnam, Bangladesh, Guinea-Bissau, and Eritrea.

There are two kinds of secession in the present century: secession within a larger state and the secession of a self-determination unit. In particular, the latter case might involve a non-self-governing territory. Self-determination reinforces the secession of a self-determination unit and its assertion of statehood when the mother state precludes it. However, international law protects the territorial integrity of states against external use of force and intervention 'though not to the point of providing a guarantee.'[3] In any case, self-determination must be applied through a free and genuine expression of the will of the peoples of the self-determination territory.[4] A negative example worth citing in this context is Southern Rhodesia, which disparaged the right to self-determination.

Several states with distinct minority-peoples or nations residing densely in a specific territory recognise a permissive right to secession in their constitutions. Some constitutions go even further by embedding a perspicuous provision that legitimises the holding of a referendum for the purpose of external self-determination. Thus, the 'right' of unilateral exit is granted under national law or should be sought directly from the central government. The secession of Singapore from Malaysia (1965) and the secession of Eritrea from Ethiopia (1993) occurred in the absence of such a provision. On the other hand, in the absence of an express reference in the form of a rule of law to a referendum, the parent state, on occasion, acquiesces to the separation of an entity in advance. Cases involving an ad hoc acceptance of referenda include Ottawa with respect to a Quebec referendum (1995), Khartoum with respect to South Sudan (2011),[5] and London with Scotland (2014). By this approach, according to the Supreme Court of Canada in *Reference re Secession of Quebec* (1998), the outcome can have both international legitimacy and domestic 'democratic legitimacy,'[6] which other parties will have to recognise. Indeed, the groups are granted 'an implied constitutional self-determination status'[7] or an agreed political change between the parent state and the sub-population, such as an agreement on the configuration of decolonisation between the colony and its former sovereign administrative power. In some recent cases, there were illegal and unilateral referenda as in Catalonia or Crimea[8] and in east and southeastern Ukraine (Luhansk, Donetsk, Zaporizhzhia, and Kherson) controlled by Russia and pro-Russian forces on the question of becoming part of Russia.

3 James Crawford, *The Creation of States in International Law* (2nd ed, OUP 2006) 383–384, 387.

4 *Western Sahara (Advisory Opinion)* [1975] ICJ Rep 32.

5 Its independence was consensual grounding in constitutional provision and consent of the parent State on waiving its territoriality. See Øystein H. Rolandsen, *A History of South Sudan; from Slavery to Independence* (CUP 2016).

6 *Reference re Secession of Quebec* [1998] 2 SCR 217, [3].

7 Marc Weller, 'Why the Legal Rules on Self-Determination Do Not Resolve Self-determination Disputes' in Marc Weller, Barbara Metzger, and Niall Johnson (eds), *Settling Self-Determination Disputes: Complex Power-Sharing in Theory and Practice* (BRILL 2008) 39.

8 See Christian Marxsen, 'The Crimea Crisis – An International Law Perspective' (2014) 74(2) HJIL 367.

A few states have formally codified and acquiesced to secessionist self-determination, conceding an unambiguous permissive right of secession for subnational minorities,[9] which is tantamount to saying that it is normalised. The express and undisputed recognition and allusion in state constitutions of a right to self-determination in the form of secession are the Ethiopian constitution of 1994 (Article 39(1)): '[e]very Nation, Nationality [sic] and People in Ethiopia has an unconditional right to self-determination, including the right to secession'; the South Africa constitution Chapter 14, Section 235;[10] the 1921 Principality of Liechtenstein constitution (Article 4(2));[11] the conditional secession in the Law on the Special Legal Status of Gagauzia of the Republic of Moldova;[12] the 1947 Constitution of the Union of Burma under Chapter X;[13] the Preamble of the 1968 Constitution of Czechoslovakia to the point of separating the Slovak and Czech nations; the 1984 Constitution of Saint Christopher and Nevis (Article 113); and Articles 70 and 72 of the Constitution of the Soviet Union of October 1977. Constitutionalised self-determination detracts from the sovereignty of the state insofar as it nullifies one of the state's prerogatives. But what if a people claim a right to self-determination in the form of unilateral secession under international law but in the absence of the abovementioned means? Is a unilateral political divorce legal? And if so, what constitutes the foundation of justified secessionist units?

A majority vote of independence of a people in a given territory has not been considered significant for recognition by states. However, implementing constitutional processes and the consent of the government of the relevant state have been decisive in secession and the achievement of independence. This is in compliance with the safeguard clause of the Friendly Relations Declaration of 1970, in which any representative government mirroring the whole people of its territory has the right to preserve its cohesion. Yet the assent of a dismantling state is not required for the separation of its constituents, as the state in question no longer represents all the people. The successful separation of the constituent republics of the former Socialist Federal Republic of Yugoslavia (SFRY) is a rare case[14] and cannot vindicate a general right of secession under international law. Regarding independent states, secession is allowed as a legal remedy in certain circumstances, including the non-existence of a sufficiently representative government of a sovereign independent state or the political exclusion of part of its population and severe violation

9 Some had special provision for it, including the constitution of the Caribbean islands Saint Kitts and Nevis (1983) and Burma (1947 to 1974).

10 The right of the South African people as a whole to self-determination, as manifested in this Constitution, does not preclude, within the framework of this right, recognition of the notion of the right of self-determination of any community sharing a common cultural and language heritage, within a territorial entity in the Republic or in any other way, determined by national legislation.

11 The 2003 Constitutional Reform.

12 Arts. 1(4) and 5(2). The Law on the Special Legal Status of Gagauzia (Gagauz Yeri) (23 December 1994).

13 The Constitution of the Federal Republic of the Union of Burma (24 September 1947).

14 Crawford (n 3) 417–418.

of human rights. These are labelled 'medium' and 'extreme' violations. In either case, the oppressive state loses its authority to stop the group from secession should it wish to.[15]

The right to remedial secession has been referenced in the Report of the Rapporteur to the United Nations Sub-Commission Against the Discrimination and the Protection of Minorities on Possible Ways and Means of Facilitating the Peaceful and Constructive Solution of Problems Involving Minorities (1993),[16] and the General Recommendation XXI adopted in 1996 by the CERD. The CERD did not recognise a general right of peoples to unilaterally secede from states, although this, to the CERD, can be arranged by 'free agreements of all parties concerned.'[17]

In 2005, the Commentary of the Working Group on Minorities, which serves as a guide to the understanding and application of the UN Declaration on the Rights of Minorities, deals with a link between the right of persons belonging to minorities to effective political participation and the right of peoples to self-determination. Paragraph 19 states that

> [i]f participation is denied to a minority and its members, this might in some cases give rise to a legitimate quest for self-determination. If the subpopulation claims a right to external self-determination and challenges the territorial integrity of the State, it would have to stake a claim to be a people, and that claim would have to be based on Article 1 common to the [Human Rights] Covenants and would therefore fall outside the Declaration on Minorities.[18]

Referring to Article 8(4) of the Declaration, nothing therein may be construed as permitting any activity contrary to the purposes and principles of the UN, including sovereign equality, indivisibility, and political independence of states. In the case of exclusion from the representative government of national or ethnic, religious, and linguistic groups as a minority-people, secession could be an *ultimum remedium*[19] so that there is no sensible potential of consolation but secession.[20] Aside from Bangladesh with its *sui generis* character, state practice is not able to validate remedial secession.

15 Joseph Blocher and Mitu Gulati, 'A Market for Sovereign Control' (2017) 66(4) DLJ 797.

16 UN Sub-Commission on the Promotion and Protection of Human Rights, *Possible Ways and Means of Facilitating the Peaceful and Constructive Solution of Problems Involving Minorities: Report*, Submitted by Asbjorn Eide, E/CN.4/Sub.2/1993/34/Add.4, 11 August 1993.

17 CERD, 'General Recommendation No 21' (1996), 'Right to self-Determination,' UN Doc. A/51/18.

18 Economic and Social Council, Commission on Human Rights, Sub-Commission on the Promotion and Protection of Human Rights, Commentary of the Working Group on Minorities to the UN Declaration on Rights of Persons belonging to National or Ethnic, Religious and Linguistic Minorities (4 April 2005).

19 Annelies Verstichel, *Participation, Representation and Identity: The Right of Persons Belonging to Minorities to Effective Participation in Public Affairs: Content, Justification and Limits* (Intersentia 2009) 186.

20 Allen Buchanan, *Secession: The Morality of Political Divorce from Fort Sumter to Lithuania and Quebec* (Westview 1991) 44.

7.2 Secession under International Law

Would-be secessionist communities must appeal to international law to legitimise their claim in the absence of a domestic provision on secession and when a state is the perpetrator of abuses. International law has evinced its role as external intervention either to mitigate a humanitarian disaster or grave injustices as in the cases of East Timor, Somalia, Bosnia, Rwanda, Haiti, the South of Kurdistan, Kosovo, and South Sudan.[21] Despite these interventions, according to the Fact-Finding Mission to Georgia, 'secession is not accepted in state practice.'[22] It should be noted that the Mission conducted its work in the wake of the Russia-Georgia armed conflict of 2008. States have not legally acquiesced in the principle of secession, and secession is condemned in practice by the UN, including aUNSC, as the right to self-determination has been narrowed down and could be invoked only by the whole people of a state not a minority within that state.

Thus, the unrestricted right of self-determination has been limited. Being a people is now insufficient to advance a claim to secession. Under international law, if a party (i.e., a state ruling the territory which is claiming the right) is not committed to its obligation and abuses a people, suppressing them through genocide or ethnic cleansing, the claimant can demand the implementation of secessionist self-determination. This is not the right of self-determination accorded to every people (Article 1 of the ICCPR), which does not have this limitation. It is 'conditional' on the treatment by the state which opposes the right; therefore, it is not categorical.[23] In other words, the right to secession is generated as a result of 'adverse conduct' by the central government.[24] This is the shift from a right to 'an *ultima ratio.*' By virtue of this thesis, distinct nations within a state with objectively different ties and sharing the subjective feeling of being distinct do not have a right of secession, though they may have the right to utilise their own language and a restricted form of autonomy. Refusal of such rights, along with oppression by the state, could lead to armed conflicts. In these situations, the state would not be able to honour and grant the rights, ultimately causing and propelling the separation of the territory — as it fears that an armed clash might end in genocide — to determine its political status through the right to self-determination for its 'survival' in this situation. Accordingly, only 'unjustly treated people' qualify to lay a claim to external self-determination.[25]

With regard to secession, international law has been influenced by scholarly debate, which is often open to qualified secession in positive international law;

21 For Secession and external intervention. See Georg Nolte, 'Secession and external intervention' in Marcelo G. Kohen (eds), *Secession: International Law Perspectives* (CUP 2006).

22 Report of the International Fact-Finding Mission on the Conflict in Georgia vol II, September 2009.

23 Fisch (n 2) 47.

24 Weller in Weller, Metzger, and Johnson (n 7) 39.

25 Fisch (n 2) 47–50.

however, its empirical foundation is rather thin but not entirely lacking.[26] The literature has developed around this interpretation. Secession is not 'an established international law standard' as the Canadian Supreme Court held,[27] neither as a general right nor as a remedial right in oppressive circumstances. International law does not address the substance of secession, as it is an internal matter, but it deals with its procedure and its result if it leads to statehood. This is due to its collusion with a normative procedure or 'due process' of international rules at a higher level which steers the procedure.[28] Once secession is a factual result, its consequences shall be regulated by international law. First, due process starts with ascertaining the legitimacy of secession; it must not take place with any form of military support by third states. Only liberation movements are entitled to this kind of support. Secession conflicts, as an internal matter, are ruled by international human rights and humanitarian law. Second, the legitimation of secession is attained through public consultations, e.g., a referendum or plebiscite requested by the international community. Third, the principle of *uti possidetis* is applied throughout the process of secession. That is, pre-existing (administrative) boundaries shall be the external boundaries of the new state.[29]

Due to the paramount importance of political unity and sovereignty, states have been opposed to according the right of secession to racial or national minorities.[30] Also, in the discussion of self-determination at Versailles following WWI, there was no universal acceptance of the right to secede for ethnic groups. In the Åland Islands case, the Rapporteurs, while denying the existence of any absolute rule of separation for a minority of the population of a state, upheld the theory of secession not in consonance 'with the very idea of State,' since withdrawing from the mother state would give rise to 'destroy [the] order and stability' of states and 'anarchy' in international relations. Likewise, it would detract from the 'State as a territorial and political unity.'[31] The Commission of Jurists, however, observed that

> [p]ositive international law does not recognize the right of national subpopulations, as such, to separate themselves from the State of which they form part by the simple expression of a wish, any more than it recognizes the right of other States to claim such separation.[32]

26 Donald L. Horowitz, 'Self-Determination: Politics, Philosophy, Law' in Margaret Moore (ed), *National Self-Determination and Secession* (OUP 1998) 201.

27 *Quebec* (n 6) [135].

28 Antonello Tancredi, 'A Normative "Due Process" in the Creation of States through Secession' in Kohen (n 21) 189–190.

29 ibid 190–192.

30 Antonio Cassese, *Self-Determination of Peoples: A Legal Reappraisal* (CUP 1995) 122.

31 Report Presented to the Council of the League of Nations by the Commission of Rapporteurs (16 April 1921), LN Council Doc b7/21/68/106, 4, [17].

32 Report of the International Committee of Jurists Entrusted by the Council of the League of Nations with the Task of Giving an Advisory Opinion upon the Legal Aspects of the Aaland Islands Question, LNOJ (1920–1946), Special Supplement 3, 3–[vi]. Self-Determination as Applied to *de Facto* Situations. its Forms, 5.

Unlike the Jurists, the Rapporteurs reasoned that separation would be an 'exceptional solution' as a last resort when the incumbent state 'lacks either the will or the power to enact and apply just and effective guarantees.'[33] This standing was vindicated by the UN and international practice in the cases of Katanga (1961) in Congo,[34] Biafra in Nigeria (1967–1970),[35] and Bangladesh in Pakistan (1971).[36] In all these cases, the emphasis was on the intangibility of the territorial integrity of the mother states. In the event of a severe infringement of human rights and divestment of minority-peoples striving for internal self-determination, the implementation of the right of self-determination would take an external form of separation of the territorial people, hence secessionist self-determination.[37] Where racial minorities were concerned, the situation was different.

Although the practice of sates and the UN evinces that there is no right to external self-determination for ethnic minority groups of sovereign states, the right is conferred to on racial minorities. The right to internal self-determination accrues to all peoples of independent states — as it is universal — and this is conceived in the qualifying or balancing clause (between self-determination and territorial integrity) of Paragraph 7 of Principle V of the Friendly Relations Declaration. The Declaration is the only international instrument which refers to secession. As the most authoritative statement to the International Commission of Jurists on East Pakistan,[38] the Paragraph elaborates:

> [n]othing in the foregoing paragraphs shall be construed as authorizing or encouraging any action which would dismember or impair, totally or in part, the territorial integrity or political unity of sovereign and independent States conducting themselves in compliance with the principle of equal rights and self-determination of peoples as described above and thus possessed of a government representing the whole people belonging to the territory without distinction as to race, creed or colour.

It is worth noting that the safeguard clause is a departure from the law on secession. The 1993 Vienna Declaration also implicitly refers to separation through reversed reading.

The 1993 UN World Conference on Human Rights held in Vienna interpreted the clause somewhat differently: any government representing its whole people 'without distinction of any kind' observes self-determination, and its territorial

33 Commission of Rapporteurs (n 31) 4, [17].

34 The Congo Question. UNSC Res 169 (24 November 1961); *Katangese People's Congress v. Zaire* (1995) ACHPR, Doc. Communication 75/92.

35 The UN did not deal with the case, but the Organization of African Unity (OAU) discussed the conflict in Res 51(IV) (September 1967), OAU Doc AHG/51(IV).

36 UNSC Res 307 (21 December 1971).

37 See Dietrich Murswiek, 'The Issue of a Right to Secession – Reconsidered' in Christian Tomuschat (ed), *Modern Law of Self-Determination* (MNP 1993).

38 International Commission of Jurists, *East Pakistan Staff Study* (1972) vol 8 ICJR 23, 44.

integrity is preserved in accordance with both the Friendly Relations Declaration and the Charter of the UN,

> this shall not be construed as authorizing or exhorting any action, which would dismember or impair, totally or in part, the territorial integrity or political unity of sovereign and independent States conducting themselves in compliance with the principle of equal rights and self-determination of peoples and thus possessed of a government representing the whole people belonging to the territory without distinction of any kind.[39]

The UNGA's Declaration on the 1995 Occasion of the Fiftieth Anniversary of the UN confirms this standing.[40]

In the drafting of the Friendly Relations Declaration, most states took a strong stand against secession. The initial draft commencing with the principle of self-determination (Western version) was replaced with the final draft (socialist version), with the principle of territorial integrity in the beginning. Therefore, any breakaway movement is to be considered very rigidly.[41] However, having not abided by equality makes the party's ruling illegal.[42] The literal translation of the saving clause would then be the effective government should represent 'the whole people belonging to the territory without distinction as to race, creed or colour' in which the aspirations of all peoples are expressed. All residents, thus, would have equal access to government and the political decision-making process. In independent states that deny this right, secession is allowed 'indirectly' for discrete peoples as a legal atonement or remedial secession,[43] or in cases of political injustice in certain circumstances, including non-existence of a sufficiently representative government of a sovereign independent state, grievous persecution or political persecution, territorial injustice,[44] economic discrimination and exploitation,[45] and when a group's culture is under the peril of extinction by the state, the right exists.[46] Furthermore, the term *creed* encompasses 'religious beliefs' but not political views as every political sub-population which is not represented by the government would have a right to secession, which is unlikely to the point of being inconceivable. Therefore, the right to internal self-determination is vested only in racial and religious groups. Two possible reasons are cited for this: first, some par-

39 Vienna Declaration and Programme of Action (25 June 1993).

40 UNGA Res 50/6 (24 October 1995).

41 Cassese (n 30) 112.

42 Fisch (n 2) 203.

43 Remedial secession is available against them, but in concurrence with certain conditions and requirements, not automatically. Crawford (n 3) 119.

44 Fernando R. Tesón, 'Introduction: The Conundrum of Self-Determination' in Fernando R. Tesón (ed), *The Theory of Self-Determination* (CUP 2016) 10.

45 For the economic cause of secession, see Pau Bossacoma, *Morality and Legality of Secession: A Theory of Self-Determination* (Palgrave Macmillan 2020) 130–134.

46 Lord Avebury, 'Self-Determination and International Law: The Kurdish Case' (1994) 7 IJKS 7, 13.

ticipating countries intentionally countenanced religious communities and second, conferring the right on these groupings would not destroy or derange the integral structure of the sovereign state. But territorial integrity would fail by vesting the right of external self-determination on other collectivities such as cultural, ethnic, and linguistic groups. Access to government could probably block legislation, thus leading to unfair and unequal treatment. Thus, equal access to government does not necessarily mean equal rights.[47]

The Western proposals (by the United States and the United Kingdom) focused on the universal facet of self-determination for all geographically distinct and ethnically or culturally diverse populations of independent states.[48] These drafts had the support of Australia, Canada, France, Japan, and the Netherlands, but they were opposed by a majority of developing and Socialist Bloc nations, as they assumed that the text prompted separationist movements and impaired the political unity of sovereign states.[49] Italy then offered a conflation of the US and UK proposals, which holds that:

> States enjoying full sovereignty and independence, and possessed of a government representing the whole of their population, shall be considered to be conducting themselves in conformity with the principle of equal right and self-determination of people as regards that population. Nothing in the foregoing paragraphs shall be construed as authorising or encouraging any action which would impair, totally or in part, the territorial integrity, or political unity, of such States.[50]

In spite of having the backing from most states, Lebanon suggested inserting the phrase 'including the indigenous population and without distinction as to race, creed or colour,' to the Friendly Relations Declaration draft. It intended to restrict the line of Italy's proposed draft, as that country's phrasing could include any group living within the territory of an independent state. The proposed phrase had appeared in the 1959 amendment but was removed from the UN Resolution 1514(XV) of 1960 regarding the attainment of independence by colonial countries and peoples.[51] By prioritising the principle of territorial integrity in Paragraph 7 of Resolution 2625(XXV), any disruption of the integral unity of state was constricted. However, a representative government or institution could guarantee and express the legitimate proclivities of separate minorities as well as their identities.

But what if there is no representative government? What would constitute a legal or non-legal remedy given the non-existence of such a government? Does the Declaration grant a right to external self-determination to detach from a

47 Cassese (n 30) 114–115.

48 The US and the UK proposals are accessible from UN Doc. A/AC.125/L.32, 2 and A/AC.125/SR.69.

49 UN Doc. A/AC.125/L.32, 2 and A/AC.125/SR.69, 115–116.

50 UN Doc. A/AC.125/L.80.

51 Cassese (n 30) 117.

non-democratic state? When and under what conditions is the unity of a state disrupted? To what extent is the integrity of that state kept safe under the Declaration? The Friendly Relations Declaration, as evidence for the *opinio iuris* of states, has played a decisive role in the development of customary international law. The legal effects of the Declaration could be on the content of international law or on constituting evidence for the legal assertions in the Declaration.[52] The use by the ICJ of the Friendly Relations Declaration in the *Corfu Channel* as well as *Nicaragua* judgements is evidence of *opinio iuris* on the prohibition of the use of force and the principles of non-intervention. Thus, the Declaration can be accepted as an expression and formulation of already existing rules of customary international law.[53] But what is the value of the Declaration for the evolution of the norm on self-determination? Concerning the principle of self-determination, the ICJ quotes two paragraphs of the Declaration in its *Western Sahara* opinion.[54] Thus, the Declaration is evidence of *opinio iuris* and, thus, the expression of self-determination.

The territoriality of states has not been a peremptory norm for states that are able to cede their territory and peoples which have been able to secede from pre-existing states. Although the territorial integrity of states must be of the foremost import, its impairment is conceivable; i.e., territorial integrity is a rebuttable presumption that can be invoked by states that adhere to or behave in conformity with self-determination. By connecting and safeguarding the territorial integrity of independent states through representative government in Paragraph 7 of Resolution 2625(XXV), secession is possible if various populations of the territory are not represented in the government of that state or if part of its population is excluded,[55] i.e., the presumption ceases to exist. This situation encourages the population or group to establish a representative government through secession.

The final part of the paragraph is construed strictly and confines secession to certain conditions. First, the central government of a state persistently denies the right of religious and racial collectivities to participate in the decision-making process. Second, the government 'grossly' and 'systematically' encroaches on their human rights. Third, settling disputes within that state is unlikely.[56] In other words, divesting these groups of internal self-determination could lead to an external form of self-determination or secession or the constitution of a new state. This position had been confirmed by Héctor Gros Espiell, the Special Rapporteur of the Sub-Commission on Prevention of Discrimination and Protection of Minorities (1980).[57] Some have a similar stance, as they perceived the paragraph to call for

52 Ian Sinclair, 'The Significance of the Friendly Relations Declaration' in Vaughan Lowe and Colin Warbrick (eds), *The United Nations and the Principles of International Law: Essays in Memory of Michael Akehurst* (Routledge 2002) 8–13.

53 Helen Keller, *Friendly Relations Declaration (1970)* (MPEPIL updated 2009), [38]–[39].

54 *Western Sahara* (n 4) [58]. Declaration by Judge Nagendra Singh [81].

55 Crawford (n 3) 119.

56 Cassese (n 30) 109–125.

57 The Right to Self-determination Implementation of United Nations Resolutions Study Prepared by Hector Gros Eapiell Special Rapporteur of the Sub-Commission on Prevention of Discrimination and Protection of Minorities, 10, [60].

'defence' of the territoriality of a state if it represents its whole population — but in any case of violation of human rights or excluding minorities, the reparation 'lies within the state.' In any case, secession has not been established in international law, although Paragraph 7 acknowledges a qualified or remedial right of secession within existing states under certain qualifications by linking the internal self-determination to its external form by the transgression of the former by the parent state.

The balance of self-determination in the form of secession with representative government is expressed in different international instruments, such as the report by the International Commission of Jurists on Bangladesh's secession[58] and the CERD's General Recommendation XXI(48) of 1996. This idea also has been confirmed by the UNHRC in the case of Hong Kong.[59] Based on General Comment No. 12 and 25 of the UNHRC, States Party to the Human Rights Covenants 'should describe the constitutional and political processes which in practice allow the exercise of this right.'[60] The Human Rights Covenants make no mention of territorial integrity and do not restrict self-determination. This was not their remit. However, territorial integrity is a *jus cogens* norm. The Canadian Supreme Court confirmed the existence of a legitimate qualified or conditional right of secession (see below).

The Declaration of Friendly Relations is an agreement among states, recognising that encroachment on the right of self-determination by a governing state with respect to its own minority-peoples and the legitimacy of a secessionist attempt by the suffering group would pave the way to the lawfulness of third state support of the group in the form of an 'action.' In other words, the situation is of international importance.[61] To what extent should the degrees of severity in the situation draw the international community of states' attention? Is there any threshold for secession?

7.3 The Threshold for Secession

It is self-explanatory that the degrees of oppression inflicted upon a particular group can vary. Accordingly, not every degree of oppression leads to the ultimate remedy of secession. What accounts for the legal success of a secessionist movement? At a certain point, mistreatment by a state validates a right to secession. The conceptual purpose of the right of self-determination is to develop and preserve the collective identity of a people along with the effective enjoyment of individual human rights. Guaranteeing the right of self-determination logically involves ensuring the freedom and existence of that people. Therefore, a conditional right of

58 '[I]f one of the constituent peoples of a State is denied equal rights and is discriminated against, it is submitted that their full right of self-determination will revive.' The Events in East Pakistan, 1971: A Legal Study by the Secretariat of The International Commission of Jurists (1972) 69.

59 UNHRC, 'CCPR Hong Kong Special Administrative Region (SAR)' (1999) CCPR/C/HKSAR/99/1, 5.

60 UNHRC, 'CCPR General Comment 12,' Art. 1, [4].

61 Raič (n 1) 319–320.

unilateral secession should be included in self-determination: if it is not there, then the overriding purpose of self-determination is not met. This is in alignment with the non-existence of international legal remedies for minority-peoples deprived of their right to self-determination. Then the *ultimum remedium* is obvious in the form of unilateral divorce.[62]

The threshold to the territorial separation of a people within a larger state can be determined by internal colonialism. In line with this approach, the central authorities view a people inhabiting a discrete territory within their state in such a manner that they are, in fact, as regards the remainder of the state, a non-self-governing territory. In this context, the arrangement between the state and the territory will be one that unilaterally puts the latter in a subordinate role or status with discriminatory policies exercised over the people owing to factors of ethnicity or separateness.[63] The adopted discriminatory measures lead to the denial of political and social equality and are detrimental to the cultural identity of the subordinate people. This can be within a framework of decolonisation, albeit not as a general right, through separation of the respective territory.[64] Internal colonisation appears to advocate a qualified right to secession by acknowledging an egregious violation of the subordinate people's human rights.[65]

The arguments concerning a restricted right of self-determination as a counterpart to the territorial integrity of states call for the inclusion of an uncontested qualified or remedial right of secession in the right of self-determination. In the light of documented practice, the following standards are imperative for unilateral secession or a conditional variant of self-determination. They are a set of legal requirements that are formulated through research and observation, inferring from historical cases, scholarly debate, and existing practice and materials:

1. The existence of a territorially clustered, inhabited sub-national minority with the attributes of peoplehood. The holder of any right of secession is an ethnic minority in the sense of a people with the full right of self-determination.[66] In most cases of secession, however, there are minorities within the seceding group, such as Serbian enclaves inside Kosovo and Anglophones and aboriginal minorities in Quebec.[67] Therefore, the secessionist group is frequently not ethnically homogeneous. In any case, a non-people community is not eligible for a conditioned right to secession.

62 ibid 326.

63 James Crawford, 'Outside the Colonial Context' in Allan W. J. Macartney (ed), *Self-Determination in the Commonwealth* (AUP 1988) 13–14.

64 Thomas M. Franck, 'Postmodern Tribalism and the Right to Secession' in Catherine Brölmann and others (eds), *Peoples and Minorities in International Law* (BRILL 1993) 13–14.

65 Raič (n 1) 328.

66 ibid 308.

67 Mancini, quoted in Michel Rosenfeld and András Sajó (eds), *The Oxford Handbook of Comparative Constitutional Law* (OUP 2012) 495.

2. A defined territory. It is important to establish a link between the people involved and a recognisable territory for a right of secession to exist. In other words, a people should constitute a majority within a certain territorial unit. Indeed, the application of a right to secession is limited to a geographically recognisable territory.
3. An unrepresentative government which applies discriminatory policies. It would not be sufficient to bring up or establish a right to separation simply due to the absence of a representative government. The threshold is higher. Special circumstances may exacerbate a state's inherent lack of representativity.
4. The collectivity must be a victim of misconduct by the host state in the forms of extreme human rights violations and denial of internal self-determination. Judge Wildhaber identifies this standard as in *Loizidou vs. Turkey,* a 1997 judgement of the ECtHR.[68] Self-determination is a feature of the international architecture of safeguarding human rights.[69] In other words, human rights and self-determination are interconnected. Unlike the legal exercise of external self-determination, a right of unilateral divorce does not require the pre-condition of respecting internal self-determination. On the other hand, denying a people's right to internal self-determination entitles the people to exercise the right of unilateral exit. As was explored heretofore in Chapter 6, internal self-determination is realised in action when people within a state exercise their right to self-government, political autonomy, or cultural, religious, and linguistic freedoms. Persistent encroachment on internal self-determination also provides grounds for the transmogrification of internal self-determination into the external dimension, taking the form of unilateral secession. But how is the right of internal self-determination breached? A violation is identified by
   a. Formal denial of a people's right to internal self-determination,[70] through, for example, a coup or permanent suspension of the parliament in which a minority has a majority, and non-recognition of an acceptable type of effective participation in public affairs for a sub-national minority.
   b. Application of indirect discriminatory policies against the collective identity of a minority-people by according the right of internal self-determination but withholding its exercise in practice, as in the case of Bangladesh. Forcible assimilation, for example, through cultural genocide, under-representation in decision-making processes, and blocking a people from participating effectively in matters affecting them are true antitypes of discrimination.

68 See *Loizidou v Turkey (Concurring Opinion by Judge Wildhaber and Judge Ryssdal)* (1997) 23 EHRR (Concurring Opinion of Judge Wildhaber, joined by Judge Ryssdal).

69 John Morss, '"Mars for the Martians?": on the Obsolescence of Self-Determination' in Tesón (n 44) 189.

70 Allen Buchanan, *Justice, Legitimacy, and Self-Determination: Moral Foundations for International Law* (OUP 2007) 353.

c. Grievous abuses of human rights,[71] e.g., the right to life through genocide or ethnic cleansing[72] so that a people's physical or cultural survival is imperilled.

A constitutional provision should guarantee a people effective political participation at all levels. This is conditioned on respecting the people's human rights. If their basic rights are excessively ignored or violated, they are not able to freely determine their political status. Any transgression through the use of force is a significant challenge to the existence and development of the group's identity, which is achieved through the exercise of self-determination. This is also the case when the cultural survival of the community is threatened, for example, by forbidding the use of its language as with the suppression of the Kurdish language in Turkey.[73] Furthermore, the prospect of pursuing the right to secession is likely to be denied for a group unjustly treated.[74] If denied, they are not able to give effect to the qualified right. Kurds exemplify this situation (see 7.6.).

In the case of a secessionist attempt, disproportionate use of force, in the forms of massacre, rape, ethnic cleansing, and plundering, is not justified to maintain a state's territorial integrity.[75] In the case of a normal situation, such violations of human rights should have a 'consistent pattern of gross and reliably attested' occurrence, according to the Economic and Social Council Resolution 1503(XLVIII), 27 May 1970 regarding the procedure for dealing with communications relating to violations of human rights and fundamental freedoms. The right of a state to preserve its territoriality comes about through its consistent respect for the self-determination, human rights, and humanitarian welfare of its people. Breaching these is the equivalent of abusing its sovereign power.[76] Secession is still not the automatic punishment.

5. All remedies should be exhausted for the implementation of self-determination before relying on the last resort of secession. Separation as the *ultimum remedium* approach to external self-determination requires that the harmed group seek other legally possible options for advancing its internal self-determination before rushing to the last resort. This process grants the secession legitimacy. Possible alternatives are national and international judicial remedies. Nonetheless, no judicial remedies are available under contemporary international law, and such judicial solutions are extremely uncommon or unusual at the national level.

71 Nielsen in Moore (n 26) 111.
72 Buchanan, *Justice* (n 70) 331–353.
73 Nielsen in Moore (n 26) 111.
74 Margaret Moore, *The Ethics of Nationalism* (OUP 2001) 147.
75 Raič (n 1) 370.
76 Tancredi in Kohen (n 21) 176.

Therefore, to exhaust all remedies, the political alternative of negotiation is reliable for finding a solution that is carried out within the respective state boundaries. The practices of Bangladesh and Croatia confirm this process. Non-fulfilment of this requirement constitutes a general abuse as well as abuse of the specific right to self-determination. However, any grave violation of basic human rights acts as a catalyst by which both requirements of infringement of the right of internal self-determination and exhaustion of all remedies (judicial and political) are fulfilled.[77] Unilateral secession, an activist form of self-determination, without the parent state's consent is 'a possible avenue for self-help' or self-defence in an emergency.[78] In fact, a deliberate policy of breaching a group's human rights is tantamount to the accused state's 'forfeit[ing] the protection it enjoys by virtue of international law.'[79]

6. Implementation of the right of self-determination should be congruent with the free, genuine, and collectively expressed will and desire of all the people who would qualify for secession; i.e., secession necessitates the application of certain democratic tenets to be followed.[80] Changing the legal status of territory must not be imposed without the participation of its people. This is confirmed by the ICJ in the *Western Sahara* case.[81] This criterion can be met by means of a referendum or the existence of a representative body of all residents who support the will of the respective people. A clear expression accords legitimacy to the secession-formed state, strengthens its legality, and facilitates the process of its recognition by the international community.[82] Southern Rhodesia[83] and the South African Bantustans[84] failed to fulfil this requirement. In the case of the Bantustans, the consent of the South African government to the impairment of its territoriality did not result in the pursuit of new states inasmuch as consensual secessions were in breach of self-determination and the outcome of the adoption of racist policies.

The above standards are seen among the standards formulated by Schachter for determining the peoples entitled to secession.[85] In sum, if these requirements coalesce, the component of the people that would like to detach is highly likely to

77 Raič (n 1) 368–372.
78 Morss in Tesón (n 44) 188.
79 Christian Tomuschat, 'Secession and Self-Determination' in Kohen (n 21) 41.
80 Jure Vidmar, *Democratic Statehood in International Law: The Emergence of New States in Post-Cold War Practice* (HP 2013) 140–141.
81 *Western Sahara* (n 4) [55].
82 Georges Abi-Saab, 'Conclusion' in Kohen (n 21) 473.
83 UNGA Res 747(XVI) (27 June 1962); UNSC Res 202 (6 May 1965); UNGA Res 2022(XX) (5 November 1965).
84 UNSC Res 402 (22 December 1976); UNSC Res 407 (25 May 1977); UNGA Res 37/43 (3 December 1982), and UNGA Res 37/69A (9 December 1982).
85 Oscar Schachter, 'Sovereignty–Then and Now' in Ronald St. J. MacDonald (ed), *Essays in Honour of Wang Tieya* (MNP 1994) 684.

succeed. The ultimate success of secession, according to the Supreme Court of Canada, would be contingent on its legality and legitimacy, which are likely the bases of recognition by the international community.

This is not the case with colonies. Decolonisation, i.e., self-determination from metropolitan European control and exploitation, was not regarded as a case of secession. Resolution 1514(XV) did not recognise a right of secession for minorities within colonies on the supposition that decolonisation occurs once and for all. However, the secession of sub-administrative territories later led to the dismemberment of several already decolonised states, each of which lost parts of their original territory. As per Paragraph 6 of Resolution 1514(XV), territorial integrity is used to restrict separation. Despite this, since the adoption of the Resolution in 1960, while the UNGA has insisted on the territorial integrity of non-self-governing entities, it has not been entirely consistent in its approach. Examples are the Gilbert (Kiribati) and Ellice (Tuvalu) Islands and Micronesia (Palau and Marshall Islands), in which territorial integrity was not honoured. The chapter does not address colonial secessions owing to the Kurds' split condition among decolonised states and the non-colonial setting the Kurds are in for the purpose of boundary-alteration. The abovementioned requirements have been tested and applied in non-colonial contexts.

7.4 Non-Colonial Secession

Secession is in pursuance of self-determination or violation of it. It would be in advancement of self-determination when it is denied by a metropolitan state.[86] In the pre-1945 period, a group securing control over territory and seeking to withdraw from a state could achieve statehood, sometimes through a long drawn-out armed conflict. However, this was not a unilateral right approved or conferred by international law. The secessionist movements of Katanga and Rhodesia were considered 'illegally carried out' as 'contrary to the *Loi fondamentale* and Security Council decisions,'[87] and by an 'illegal racist minority regime,'[88] respectively. However, according to the Canadian Supreme Court, 'this does not rule out the possibility of an unconstitutional declaration of secession leading to *de facto* secession.'[89] Also, it usually would be opposed by the government of a mother state. Read as intervention in the internal affairs, third states would remain indifferent to the situation. However, international law would recognise the firmly established independence of a seceding entity in cases of effective control of the territory.[90]

Nonetheless, there is no rule in international law prohibiting secession in a non-colonial context. First, the seceding entity is considered as a subject of international

86 Crawford (n 3) 385.
87 UNSC Res 169 (24 November 1961), [1], [8].
88 UNSC Res 216 (12 November 1965), [2].
89 *Quebec* (n 6) [155].
90 Crawford (n 3) 388–389.

law in resolutions, although it may have acted contrary to law. The resolutions do not refer to any international law rule which bans secession; rather, reliance is on the municipal law of the mother states. Resolutions reflected international concerns by referring to foreign influences in the Katanga insurgency[91] or the peril to international peace and security in Southern Rhodesia owing to the invalid unilateral declaration of independence made by a racist minority which succeeded in usurping power,[92] not an international law rule. In other words, international law remains neutral toward secession; i.e., it does not 'condemn rebellion or secession aiming at the acquisition of independence.'[93] However, it is 'a legally neutral act' and its consequences are regulated by international law.[94] The ILC affirms this in the principle of non-recognition of territorial acquisition by illegal force.[95]

The opposition of a government to secession makes the international community disinclined to recognise unilateral secessions since the establishment of the UN, and subsequent breakaway entities have not been admitted to the organisation. Bangladesh was admitted after its recognition by Pakistan. Non-colonial situations which led to accomplished secessions or resulting from state demise or state breakdown are Senegal (1960), Singapore (1965), Bangladesh (1971), Armenia, Azerbaijan, Belarus, Georgia, Kazakhstan, Kyrgyzstan, Moldova, Tajikistan, Turkmenistan, Ukraine, Uzbekistan (1991), Slovenia, Macedonia, Croatia, Bosnia-Herzegovina, Serbia and Montenegro (1991–1992), the Czech Republic and Slovakia (1993), and Eritrea (1993).[96] Among these entities, Eritrea, Bangladesh, and Kosovo are the rare situations that met the standards for a conditional right to secession. These are the closest cases comparable to the Kurdistani segments. The failed cases of Northern Cyprus and Quebec are also illustrative for Kurdish secession and its relevant arguments.

7.4.1 Eritrea

The historical and contextual situation of Kurdistan, at least its southern segment, is comparable to Eritrea. Occupied by Great Britain after 1941 (later subject to the Italian Peace Treaty of 10 February 1947), the Italian colony of Eritrea (from 1890)[97] was united with Ethiopia as a federal unit in 1952 under the aegis of the UN. Before that, it was variously under the control of the Ethiopian Empire, Egypt,

91 See Georges Abi-Saab, *The United Nations Operation in the Congo 1960–1964* (OUP 1978).

92 UNGA Res 2024(XX) (11 November 1965); UNSC Res 216 (12 November 1965) and UNSC Res 217 (20 November 1965).

93 Hersch Lauterpacht, *Recognition in International Law* (CUP 2012) 8.

94 Crawford (n 3) 389–390.

95 YILC 1950, vol I, Article 18: Non-recognition of Territorial Acquisitions Obtained by Force, 111–112.

96 Crawford (n 3) 391.

97 See Gerald K.N. Trevaskis, *Eritrea, a Colony in Transition: 1941–52, Issued Under the Auspices of the Royal Institute of International Affairs* (OUP 1960) 18.

and the Ottoman Empire without unity, government, or name.[98] After 1947, the Four Powers (Britain, France, the United States, and the USSR) did not achieve an agreement regarding the final disposition of the land. Therefore, the issue was referred to the UNGA according to the Treaty of 1947. Ultimately, a federation was formed on 11 September 1952 'on the principles of democratic government' (UNGA Res 390A – Para. 12), and Britain ended its occupation on 15 September.[99] However, displeased with many articles of the Eritrean constitution, the new Ethiopian constitution (1955) did not mention the federation; one single Ethiopian language was announced in 1956 for the whole country.[100]

Ethiopia abrogated the federation on 14 November 1962 and annexed Eritrea as its fourteenth province. After back-and-forth clashes in the 1970s and 1980s, the Tigrean People's Liberation Front (TPLF) of Ethiopia and the Eritrean Peoples Liberation Front (EPLF) won substantial victories against the Ethiopian army in May 1984 and took Addis Ababa and Asmara. The EPLF formed the provisional government in Eritrea.[101] Striving for independence throughout this long run-up, the EPLF co-opted the Ethiopian movement of TPLF or the Ethiopian People's Revolutionary Democratic Front (EPRDF) to beat down the military regime of Ethiopia. The victorious Transitional Government of Ethiopia recognised the right of self-determination of the people of Eritrea, who voted in favour of independence (99.8%) in a plebiscite for 'the future status of Eritrea' in April 1993 under the United Nations Observer Mission to Verify the Referendum in Eritrea (UNOVER).[102] The Ethiopian government recognised Eritrean independence on 29 April and assisted its admission to the UN on 28 May 1993.[103] Self-determination was never mentioned in international consideration of the situation.[104] There was no reference based on Italian law, British law, Eritrean law under the federation, or Ethiopian law (after the disintegration of the federation) to a right to self-determination or secession for Eritreans.[105] Under international law, there are three feasible claims for the separation of Eritrea from Ethiopia.

First, Eritrea like other colonial territories had a right to independence after 1945. This case was little more than a postponed case of decolonisation and a normal exercise of self-determination rather than secession.[106] According to Chapter XII of the UN Charter, Eritrea was a territory detached from the enemy state of Italy (pursuant to the peace treaty of 1947) as a result of WWII. Thus, it should have been included in the post-war trusteeship system by virtue of Article 77(1)(b).

98 Gregory Fox, 'Eritrea' in Christian Walter, Antje von Ungern-Sternberg, and Kavus Abushov (eds) *Self-Determination and Secession in International Law* (OUP 2014) 273–274.
99 ibid 276–277.
100 ibid 277–278.
101 ibid 278–279.
102 Authorised by UNGA Res 47/114 (16 December 1992).
103 UNSC Res 828 (26 May 1993) and UNGA Res 47/230 (28 May 1993).
104 Crawford (n 3) 402–403.
105 Fox in Walter, Ungern-Sternberg and Abushov (n 98) 280.
106 Fisch (n 2) 210.

It would then develop 'towards self-government or independence.' Also, as a colonial or overseas non-self-governing territory, self-determination was applicable, as was enshrined in the Charter of the UN.[107] Even then, as the ICJ held in the *Status of South West Africa* case, there is no obligation to designate a colony as a mandate territory[108] and, in such cases, self-determination is promoted based on Chapter XI. UNGA Resolution 1514(XV) conceded that the goal of self-determination is complete independence, provided that the people of a given territory desire it. On the other hand, the Eritreans were not truly consulted as the other colonies voted for decolonisation in a UN-supervised referendum from 1945 to 1960. According to the Commission of Inquiry, the people of Eritrea were mired in a dilemma of becoming independent or attaching themselves to Ethiopia. The Commission recommended four alternatives. The UNGA voted 46 to 10 in favour of federation with Ethiopia with its own constitution and full-fledged autonomy over matters not vested in the federal government. The federation was ratified following the passage of Resolution 1514(XV) of 1960. The problem was that it remained for the Four Powers 'to take appropriate measures for giving effect'[109] to the recommendation of the UNGA as specified in the peace treaty.[110] In other words, the Four Powers, not the UN, were to determine the status of Eritrea.

Second, to atone for Ethiopia's annulment of the federation (approved by the UN) in 1962, the Eritreans could secede from their mother state. However, the Eritreans' claim to independence was not supported by the international community.[111] This was so even though the annexation of Eritrea was in breach of both the Resolution of 1950 and the Ethiopian Federal Act. However, there are some points to mention: UNGA resolutions do not normally possess binding force, including 'broad dispositive powers under the Charter.'[112] Ethiopia — whether under the obligations of *erga omnes* or the Four Powers — must be bound to the federal model. Under the general entitlements of international law, mandating the federation did not nullify the inalienable right to self-determination, and the federation would continue its existence even after its termination. Ethiopia's historic title to Eritrea was disavowed[113] as a valid counterbalance to the efforts by non-self-governing territories to claim the right to self-determination by non-self-governing territories. Self-determination had already been recognised and affirmed in UNGA Resolution 1654 (1961) at the time of abrogation of the federation (1962). The

107 Also, see *Legal Consequences for States of the Continued Presence of South Africa in Namibia (South West Africa) notwithstanding Security Council Resolution 276 (1970) (Advisory Opinion)* [1971] ICJ Rep 16, 31.

108 *International Status of South West Africa (Advisory Opinion)* [1950] ICJ Rep 128, 139.

109 Italian Peace Treaty, Annex XI, [3].

110 Fox in Walter, Ungern-Sternberg and Abushov (n 98) 282–284.

111 Tomuschat in Kohen (n 21) 28.

112 Crawford (n 3) 551–552.

113 Regarding historic title, see *Western Sahara* (n 4) 34–36.

resolution was addressed to self-determination-seeking units within those states that found the right unacceptable.[114]

Third, having been exposed to flagrant abuses of human rights for almost 30 years of striving for independence, Eritreans were legally entitled to an assertion of curative secession while accosting the post-colonial trend of rebuffing unilateral secessions by relying on state practice and the territorial integrity or political unity of sovereign and independent states stipulated in Resolution 1514(XV) (1960) and 2625(XXV) (1970).[115] The degree and scope of the violation of rights are controversial, but some interpret the severity as 'extreme and unremitting persecution and the lack of any reasonable prospect for peaceful challenge,'[116] while other reports refer to 'genocide, the exclusion of a minority from the political process, or the outbreak of armed conflicts or despotic governments suppressing the rights of minorities.'[117] Eritrea is a case which meets most requirements for secession. However, a critical factor in Eritrea is that the parent state ultimately consented and validated the secession.

7.4.2 Bangladesh

Bangladesh is the closest example matching the situation in the North of Kurdistan. East Bengal (erstwhile East Pakistan) was a part of the state of Pakistan (created in 1947 as a result of the partition of India).[118] Pakistan was geographically divided (1,200 kilometres of Indian territory stretched between them). The two Pakistani segments were separate in terms of language, culture, and history, but Islam united them. The central government in Islamabad applied systematic discrimination politically and economically against the people of East Pakistan, despite the triumph of an absolute majority of the Awami League of Bengalis in the National Assembly elections of December 1970. The League had stood for a decentralised Pakistan through federation. Nevertheless, its suspension by the government on 1 March 1971 led to martial law in East Pakistan and, consequently, to repression, genocide, and crimes against humanity. Millions of Bengalis fled to India. As a last-ditch measure, the Awami League declared the independence of Bangladesh on 10 April 1971 retroactive to 26 March. India intervened. A large-scale two-week-long war between India and Pakistan ended on 17 December with the surrender of the Pakistani army in East Bengal. Pakistan recognised Bangladesh on 22 February 1974; 28 states had granted prior *de jure* recognition. Although there was local support for Bangladesh separatism as well as a Bengali insurgency, Indian intervention was the decisive factor in the emergence of Bangladesh. Despite a case

114 Fox in Walter, Ungern-Sternberg and Abushov (n 98) 285–287.

115 ibid 287–288.

116 Cassese (n 30) 120.

117 Fact-Finding Mission to Georgia (n 22) 139.

118 According to Lahore Resolution (1940) to create the independent Muslim States. Subrata R. Chowdhury, *The Genesis of Bangladesh, A Study in International Legal Norms and Permissive Conscience* (Asia Publishing House 1972).

of illegal intervention by a third state (violation of the UN Charter), India's effective and continued presence materially furthered the recognition of Bangladesh as a new member of the international community — unlike other cases. Another instrumental factor was the evidence of misconduct, genocide, and crimes against humanity committed by the Pakistan army and state.[119] Internationally, the USSR played an important role by supporting India against Pakistan.[120]

The insurgency for autonomy and independence was buttressed substantially by Bengalis. East Bengal was not a non-self-governing territory by 1971, although it was geographically separate and was distinct ethnically and/or culturally from the country administering it (Principle IV of Res 1541(XV)).[121] However, the West Pakistan state arbitrarily placed the East in a position or status of subordination (GA Res 1541(XV), Annex, Principle V), which, in turn, denoted its post-colonial status. In fact, Bangladesh was *carence de souveraineté* after 25 March 1971,[122] and the genocide carried out by Pakistan, together with the facts of territorial and political contiguity of East Bengal in 1971, identified East Bengal as a self-determination-seeking entity. The UNGA Resolution 2793(XXVI) of 7 December 1971 did not refer to the right of self-determination. In any case, Bangladesh and its people, as an ethnic minority, satisfied all criteria for the right of unilateral secession, especially the vital requirement that available remedies had been exhausted by peaceful negotiations with the governing state.

To this argument, as mentioned before, some argue against Bangladesh as a good example of the qualified secession doctrine since Bangladesh was not universally recognised prior to Pakistani consent in 1974. Bangladesh was legally suspended between 1971 and 1974. To this group of scholars, the creation of Bangladesh was a political process. Put differently, its legal status (statehood) was a consequence of a political process (universal recognition). The oppression inflicted on Bengalis had an indirect role, that is to say as an initiator, in the country's acquisition of statehood, although it gave rise to the universal acceptance of Bangladesh.[123] The Bengalis' situation has not served as a precedent for other secessionist movements. Since the 1920s, Kurds in the East and North of Kurdistan have endured ongoing flagrant human rights abuses, suffering for longer than Bengalis, but a question arises as to whether every scenario must proceed to a clear stage of gross human rights abuses before the international community of states comes to the aid of a threatened people.

119 Crawford (n 3) 141–142.
120 Fisch (n 2) 210.
121 Chapter XI of the UN Charter.
122 Crawford (n 3) 126.
123 Vidmar (n 80) 163–164.

7.4.3 Kosovo

The ICJ, in its advisory opinion titled *Accordance with International Law of the Unilateral Declaration of Independence in Respect of Kosovo*, did not address the self-determination of peoples outside the context of non-self-governing territories, peoples subject to alien subjugation, domination, and exploitation.[124] Also, it did not deal with the extent of the right of self-determination and the existence of any right of remedial secession or the right to separate from a state, as it was 'not necessary' and was 'beyond the scope of the question posed by the General Assembly.'[125] Therefore, the ICJ contemplated only the lawfulness of declarations of independence by the Kosovars under international law. Ultimately, by considering numerous instances of declarations of independence in colonial contexts and state practice during the eighteenth, nineteenth, and twentieth centuries, it concluded that 'the act of promulgating the declaration' is not regarded as contrary to international law. In the non-colonial context, there is no 'rule prohibiting the making of a declaration of independence.'[126] The Court then concluded that since general international law contains no applicable prohibition of declarations of independence, the declaration of independence of 17 February 2008 did not violate general international law.[127]

The Court's decision prepared the ground for the legality of declarations of independence and secession from a state without any restraint. Can we conclude that 'anything that is not prohibited is allowed' or 'anything that is not expressly allowed is prohibited'?[128] The Declaration of Independence was promulgated on 17 February 2008, but the violent process referred to in the Declaration goes back to 1991. The 1991 independence of the Republic of Kosovo was not buttressed by the international community despite 'the excessive and indiscriminate use of force by Serbian security forces and the Yugoslav Army' which had resulted in numerous civilian casualties (UNSC Res 1199, 23 September 1998) from the early 1990s, the termination of Kosovo's autonomy in March 1989, the suspension of the Kosovo Assembly in July 1990, the abolition of the Kosovo Constitutional Court in late 1990, and the replacement of Kosovars by Serbs in all sectors.[129] These measures indicated an aversion to secessionist claims by ethnic communities. They were engaged sufficiently in internal self-determination quests. However, it is not contested that Kosovo Albanians were denied the ability to exert internally their right to self-determination.

124 *Accordance with International Law of the Unilateral Declaration of Independence in Respect of Kosovo (Advisory Opinion)* [2010] ICJ Rep.

125 ibid [82]–[83].

126 ibid [79].

127 ibid [84].

128 For more details on the *Opinion*, see Christian Walter, 'The Kosovo Advisory Opinion: What It Says and What It Does Not Say' in Walter, Ungern-Sternberg and Abushov (n 98) 13, 26–27.

129 Photini Pazartzis, 'Secession and International Law: The European Dimension' in Kohen (n 21).

To Ahtisaari, the Special Envoy of the UN Secretary-General, the Declaration was rooted in the *sui generis* situation of Kosovo, under a legal regime created by Resolution 1244 supported by the UNMIK and the KFOR, which was 'irreversible.'[130] Regarding the secession of Kosovo, earned sovereignty was decisive by which Kosovo sought separation and showed its capability of being a sovereign state to engage in international relations.[131] Furthermore, the language of Resolution 1244 regarding autonomy for a group emanates from the existence of the right of self-determination in international law, a right of secession based on the right of self-determination. The resolution constituted the first formalised decision of the international community acknowledging the enjoyment of the right of self-determination of a human community within a sovereign state under specific circumstances.[132] Before this, the Canadian Supreme Court had recognised the same right for ethnic groups within states, *under special circumstances* (emphasis added). The special circumstances of Kosovo were established by the UNSC itself. Non-fulfilment of special circumstances results in failure.

Serbia likewise had no effective authority over Kosovo for several years, so the non-existence of a representative government was also not the case, nor was it a matter of internal self-determination. How could the incumbent 2008 Serbian state have been responsible for the oppression inflicted on Kosovars by the 1991 SFRY? The Declaration ended no gross breaches of human rights, and, therefore, secession did not qualify as a last resort measure. Kosovo, therefore, did not meet the criteria for a qualified unilateral declaration. The situation in Kosovo very much resembles that of the South of Kurdistan before 2003 in Iraq, albeit with a different outcome (see 7.6.2.).

7.5 Failed Cases

There have been numerous failed endeavours by groups or territories to break away from states since 1945, including Tibet (China), Katanga (Congo), Biafra (Nigeria),[133] Kashmir (India), East Punjab (India), the Karen and Shan states (Burma),[134] the Turkish Federated State of Cyprus (Cyprus), Mayotte (France), Tamil Eelam (Sri Lanka), Somaliland (Somalia), Bougainville (Papua New Guinea), Republika Srpska (Bosnia and Herzegovina), the Chechen Republic of Ichkeria (Russian Federation), Abkhazia (Georgia), South Ossetia (Georgia),

130 Martti Ahtisaari, the Special Envoy of the UN Secretary-General, UN Doc S/2007/168 (16 March 2007), [7].

131 James R. Hooper and Paul R. Williams, 'Earned Sovereignty: The Political Dimension' (2003) 31(3) DJILP 355.

132 Tomuschat in Kohen (n 21) 34.

133 Based on the parameters for secession, Biafra was a legitimate case of secession. However, it was not recognised owing to the political consideration of the disruption of Nigeria and the other African States. Raič (n 1) 335.

134 The constitutional guarantee for secession was denied and suspended in 1962. See Li-ann Thio, 'International Law and Secession in the Asia and Pacific Regions' in Kohen (n 21).

the Republic of Serbian Krajina (Croatia), Anjouan (the Islamic Republic of the Comoros), Gagauzia (Moldova), the Republic of Artsakh (Nagorno-Karabakh between Armenian and Azerbaijan), the Democratic Republic of Yemen (Yemen), and Catalonia and the Basque Country (Spain). Some of these entities are still vying for secession. Scottish secession could be considered a failed case but not for falling short of meeting the remedial secession standards. The failure is rather due to the vote of refusal by Scots in the 2014 referendum. Despite that, the ruling Scottish National Party is pushing for a second independence referendum as a result of the UK's Brexit withdrawal from the European Union (EU) two years after the Scottish refusal in the 2014 referendum. In November 2022, the UK Supreme Court refused Scotland's entitlement to a right to external self-determination because its people enjoy internal self-determination. Also according to the ruling, the Scotland Act 1998 as a constitutional settlement establishes a carefully calibrated scheme of devolution powers. To the UK Court, the principle of (external) self-determination is simply not in play here, as Scotland is neither a colony nor under foreign occupation, and the Scottish people have not been denied meaningful access to government to pursue their political, economic, cultural, and social development. The Scottish government, thus, needs to seek UK government approval as in the 2014 independence vote to hold a second independence referendum.

Regarding the Serbian population in Bosnia-Herzegovina and Croatia, the Arbitration Committee hedged the right to self-determination to 'existing frontiers' by insisting on the exclusive principle of *uti possidetis juris*. It only sanctioned the right to 'recognition of their identity under international law,' and it considered subsidiary ethnic communities as 'minorities' with their 'national and international guarantees.' Additionally, the Committee perceived the right to self-determination mentioned in Article 1 of the two 1966 International Covenants as a choice of 'nationality' for the Serbs in Bosnia-Herzegovina and Croatia.[135] In other words, they were deemed ineligible for secession.

Although humanitarian law has been transgressed in these situations, the international community of states has tended to support the territorial integrity of states with secessionist movements. These cases confirm the non-existence of an unlimited right of secession for minority ethnic communities despite meeting all the necessary requirements of peoplehood and being a people separate from the majority people. International practice forthrightly denies it.

As a norm, the contention that self-determination will give rise to unilateral secession has not been recognised for peoples or groups outside of the colonial context or within independent states. There is also no record of admitting a new member to the UN outside the colonial realm against the importunate wishes of the government of the parent state opposed to the secession of part of its territory. Bangladesh is the only exception, although not as a case of self-determination but, rather, as a *fait accompli* owing to military intervention by a third state. Other cases could not be counted as unilateral secession because the concerned

135 ACFY, Opinion No 2.

parties had given their consent before recognising independence as in Senegal, Singapore, the Baltic States, and Eritrea. International recognition of secessionist independence came about as the result of an agreement, as in the Soviet Union and in Czechoslovakia. The breakup of the SFRY was a matter of fact, and the constituent republics did not have the right to secession by means of self-determination.[136] These instances cannot also be categorised under the remedial right to secession owing to the component entities' failure to establish an agreement on institutional revisions, just as the main reason for dismantling the federal state was not an irremediable act by the SFRY.[137]

Granting cultural rights or internal self-government to peoples of an independent state should not be interpreted as a right to secede.[138] In any case, the reason for unsuccessful attempted unilateral secessions may be that they did not have or have not qualified for a right to secession as they did not satisfy the manifold criteria for it. The condemnation of the attempt and the confirmation of the right of territorial integrity of parent states substantiate the existence of the previously mentioned criteria for an accomplished unilateral secession.

A significant failed case of secession is Quebec. Concerned about being a subordinate appendage of English-speaking Canada, some of Quebec's inhabitants have striven for independence since 1968 through the *Parti Québécois.*[139] But French, perhaps *de jure*, but arguably not *de facto*, was already an official language of Canada, enjoying fully coequal status with English. The mostly French-speaking people of Quebec conducted two referenda in 1980 (almost 60% against independence)[140] and again in 1995. The latter referendum found 49.4% of the Quebec population in favour of independence on 30 October 1995. Therefore, the Canadian Parliament asked the Supreme Court of Canada in 1996 to advise on the constitutional and international legality of the *Reference by the Governor in Council Concerning Certain Questions Relating to the Secession of Quebec from Canada*. The non-colonial secession of Quebec sheds light on the threshold for a qualified right to secession and its required standards. The Court, while distinguishing external from the internal form of self-determination, observed that if the right of the people to internal self-determination is 'totally frustrated,'[141] the people are entitled to secession. It recognised a right to external self-determination in situations of 'former colonies; where a people is oppressed, as for example under foreign military occupation; or where a definable group is denied meaningful access to government to pursue their political, economic, social and cultural development.'[142] To put it another way, the Court tacitly confirms that the right to independence through secession exists in the event of denial of totally frustrated

136 Crawford (n 3) 401, 416.

137 Tancredi in Kohen (n 21) 187.

138 Crawford (n 3) 417–418.

139 ibid 411.

140 Thomas D. Musgrave, *Self-Determination and National Minorities* (OUP 2000) new introduction.

141 *Quebec* (n 6) [135].

142 ibid [138].

internal self-determination to a people. But it 'remains unclear whether this third proposition actually reflects an established international law standard.'[143] The Court did not reach a determination because the Quebec case did not approach such a threshold.

In cases that are non-colonial in context, the Court determined that people are entitled to external self-determination when they are deemed 'subject to alien subjugation, domination or exploitation.'[144] However, by referring to the safeguard clause of the Declaration of Friendly Relations and the final statement of the CSCE Vienna meeting (1989),[145] it rejected the assertion of the Quebec people. Referring to the 'great importance' of territorial integrity of states, the Court made it clear that

> [t]here is no necessary incompatibility between the maintenance of the territorial integrity of existing states, including Canada, and the right of a 'people' to achieve a full measure of self-determination. A state whose government represents the whole of the people or peoples resident within its territory, on a basis of equality and without discrimination, and respects the principles of self-determination in its own internal arrangements, is entitled to the protection under international law of its territorial integrity.[146]

The UK Supreme Court applied the case of Quebec with equal force to Scotland and its people within the United Kingdom. However, unlike the case of Quebec, it does not question whether the UK government represents the people of Scotland, on an equal, non-discriminative basis.

Since the Québécois were 'equitably represented in legislative, executive, and judicial institutions,' the Canadian government is 'representing the whole people belonging to the territory without distinction' and the Québécois possess 'prominent positions within the government,' 'freely' making 'political choices' and pursuing 'economic, social and cultural development within Quebec, across Canada, and throughout the world.'[147] The Court rendered the right to unilateral secession or external self-determination possible in a situation: when 'a people is blocked from the meaningful exercise of its right to self-determination internally, it is entitled, as a last recourse, to exercise it by secession.'[148] In the end, it held that the people of Quebec had not reached that 'threshold.'[149]

Thus, the Quebec people were enjoying and exerting their rights to internal self-determination and, accordingly, the Court rejected any entitlement to detach unilaterally from Canada under the international law defining rights to self-determination.

143 ibid [135].
144 ibid [133].
145 ibid [126].
146 ibid [130].
147 ibid [136].
148 ibid [134].
149 ibid [135].

However, the Court recognised negotiated secession based on democracy, the rule of law, federalism, and respect for minorities.

The Kurds in Kurdistani segments have endured a different legal climate from that in which the Québécois find themselves in Canada. Their circumstances may be more comparable to those faced by Kosovars and Bengalis in their respective struggles.

7.6 The Secession of Kurdistan

The Kurds are currently divided among four separate states. As a result, their quest for recognition and self-determination unfolds across four distinct yet interconnected environments within a single regional space. This struggle involves shaping their destiny within four different state frameworks and asserting a 'majority' status through the rejection of externally imposed borders. In the light of the doctrine of a qualified right of secession, the Kurds in the four states meet the first two standards of a qualified right to secessionist self-determination. Based on the circumstances presented in Chapter 5, the Kurds as sub-minorities of the states of Iran, Iraq, Syria, and Turkey would qualify as a minority-people in each.

As was detailed in Chapter 6, local autonomy can fulfil self-determination internally in the case of a territorially concentrated group and combined with other representative mechanisms at the national level. Functional autonomy could be one of supplementary mechanism for Kurds outside of the majority Kurdish territories of their host states. A constitutional provision may secure a people effective political participation, but there might be other non-constitutional and political processes which, in practice, allow the recognition of minorities. To investigate this, the political model adopted in the states is examined to see whether Kurds are recognised and their right to internal self-determination is fulfilled or respected. A relevant question is whether they exercise autonomy of governance within the respective territorial states. In addition, to qualify for unilateral secession, it should be examined whether Kurds have enjoyed representative and non-discriminatory governments at any point in time after the partition of Kurdistan among four states. Here, only major breaches are noted among the many consistent grave human rights violations against Kurds by the host states.

7.6.1 The Secession of Rojhilat (East) from Iran

7.6.1.1 Representative Government

To establish a qualified right to secession, the lack of a representative government is necessary. The current constitution of the Islamic Republic of Iran has been effective since 3 December 1979 and was amended in July 1989.[150] Although minorities are a constituent part of the state, there is no constitutionally guaranteed

150 Constitution of the Islamic Republic of Iran.

representation or mechanism for the effective participation of minorities in public affairs. Moreover, minorities do not participate in the sovereignty of the state. Article 5 of the constitution presupposes the doctrine of the *vilayat-i faqih* (supreme spiritual leader), who exercises ultimate sovereignty over all affairs.

The right of participation of Kurds in elections has not been formally blocked by Iranian governments, but they have had no role in the decision-making processes of their host state. The government of Iran denies their fundamental human rights but does not formally deny them a representative government. For instance, legislative and local representation is guaranteed, but they are also subject to *de facto* and *de jure* discrimination. In legislative and local elections, Kurdish candidates are filtered by state bodies, including the Guardian Council and intelligence agencies, to guarantee the seats for already selected representatives in the Islamic Consultative Assembly and local councils. Indeed, the so-called elected representatives are actually appointees and do not represent the Kurdish people but, rather, the state. Also, their effective participation in public life in existing forms of proportional representation, including local self-government bodies, is not guaranteed. Thus, the Kurds are not able to make their own decisions concerning the fulfilment of their rights.

Iran ratified the ICCPR in 1975.[151] Although Article 19 refers to enjoying equal rights of the people of Iran regardless of the ethnic group or tribe, in reality, the post-revolutionary leaders of Iran have applied considerations of race, language, and religion to all aspects of the political, social, and economic life of the population of the state. In other words, minorities are not responsible for the state structure. It is noteworthy that Iran ratified the Convention on the Elimination of Discrimination in 1968. There has never been a representative government in Iran including any Kurds serving as a minister or deputy of the presidency. Kurds are particular victims of discriminatory policies, since they are mainly Sunni as in the provinces of Urmîye and Kurdistan. Even Shi'a affiliation, as exists mostly in the provinces of Ilam, Kirmaşan, and Xorasan and partly in Kurdistan province, has not dispelled adverse discrimination. In a few cabinets, a Shi'a Kurd did occupy a ministerial position albeit not as a representative of the Kurds in the government. There is also no federal structure in the state that, if violated, can be viewed as a denunciation of the constitutional provisions leading to secession. Briefly put, no special participatory mechanisms have been set up for minorities. In any case, current practices still would not induce secession. As per the threshold for secession, unrepresentativeness and denial of internal self-determination should be complemented by extreme human rights violations.

7.6.1.2 Human Rights Record

To carry out a direct takeover in 1934, Persia followed Kemalist Turkey's linguistic policy, declaring Persian (Farsi) as the sole official language and restricting the use of the Kurdish language. Most of the Kurdish chiefs were imprisoned and

151 Ratification of 18 International Human Rights Treaties, available at https://indicators.ohchr.org/.

poisoned from 1929 to 1937, and their titles as *agha*, *emir*, and *beg* were outlawed. Many Kurds were exiled to other non-Kurdish cities.[152]

Kurds constitute one of the prominent national minority-peoples in Iran; however, there is no article or principle in the constitution referring to the Kurds. Under the pretext of a principle in Islam indicating no 'difference' between 'brothers' (Article 11), the term 'minorities' was omitted in the final draft of 1979, which accentuated and recognised the eternally unchangeable religion of the Twelver Ja'fari school of Shiism (Principle 12) as the official religion of the state and even required the President to be Shi'a (Articles 12 and 115, respectively). Nonetheless, other Islamic schools of thought, such as the Hanafi, Shafi'i, Maliki, Hanbali (the four schools of Sunnism), and Zaydi, are recognised, and their followers are entitled to perform their 'religious education and training and personal status' (Article 12). Disputes over religious education and personal status (marriage, divorce, inheritance, and will) are considered in the courts in consonance with their own jurisprudence (*fiqh*). Where followers of these schools constitute a majority, 'local regulations, within the domain of the council's jurisdictions, are set according to that school of thought so long as the rights of the followers of other schools of religion are maintained' (Article 12). The Kurds of Urmîye and Kurdistan, and parts of Kirmaşan provinces follow the Shafi'i school. Yet no Sunni mosque has been allowed to be built in Shi'a-majority cities. By virtue of Article 13, Zoroastrian, Jewish, and Christian Iranians are the only recognised non-Muslim religious groups, who, within the limits of the law, are free to exercise matters of personal status and religious education. They can 'perform their religious rites and ceremonies.' They are numerically small and are geographically dispersed. This is the only type of minority recognition in the constitution.

Despite the prevalent multilingual context of Iran, Farsi has been designated the sole official language of the state and, as per the constitution, '[o]fficial documents, correspondence, and texts, as well as text-books, must be in this language and script' (Principle 15). The same principle authorises the use of other regional and ethnic languages and their teaching in schools alongside Farsi. Nonetheless, this principle has not been implemented in practice. As a right of language instruction, a governmental rule was adopted in September 2015 to teach Kurdish language and literature as an undergraduate university subject at the University of Kurdistan, based in Sinne.[153] But this does not secure any right for instruction in Kurdish throughout the educational system. On the contrary, by securitisation of education, Kurdish activists are convicted and imprisoned for teaching the Kurdish language to children, as in the cases of Zara Muhamadi, Mojgan Kawosi, Keyvan Minooi, Idris Minbari, Xidir Muhamadi, Omid Soleimani, Ferîde Weysi, Sîrus and Azad Abbasi, Sirwe Rahmanipoor, Kiomars Latifi, Alireza Nosrati, Soma Pourmohammadi, Sirwe Purmohammadi, Varan Mohammadnejad, Seywan Ebrahimi, and many

152 David McDowall, *Modern History of the Kurds* (IB Tauris 2021) 225–231.

153 BBC, 'University of Kurdistan Admits Students for the Kurdish Language for the First Time' (*BBC*, 25 June 2015).

others across Rojhilat were detained and placed under surveillance by the Iranian security and intelligence organs.[154] To sum up, the language is govermentalised as the Iranian state follows a racially exclusive (Persian) and homogenised vision of the nation mandating the Farsi language and Shi'a Islam as its religion. Persia's name change to 'Iran' in 1935, in fact, led to the subjugation, assimilation, and suppression of all other national and ethnic groups, e.g., the Baluch people, Kurds, Qashqais, Armenians, Azeris, Tabaris, Talesh, Arabs, Turkmens, Gilaks, and other ethnic minorities, under the pretext of an Iranian nation-state. The Iranian state has been acting as an occupier of their homelands.

The Perso-Shi'a regime has not tolerated discussion of human rights or issues concerning the self-determination of minorities even when any change of existing boundaries is ruled out. It securitises minority issues. After the 'Islamic Revolution' in 1979, the Kurds of the East, under the leadership of Foad Mostafa Soltani (known as kak Foad), founded the first resistance movement there with a march against the threats and presence of the regime's forces. This move encouraged Kurds in other cities to openly oppose the new power in Tehran. The Kurds' demand for autonomy led to the issuance of *Jihad* (holy war) fatwa against them by the Ayatollah in August 1979, the reconquest (*fath-e*) of Kurdistan from the brief secular sovereignty which lasted for two and half years, and the subsequent numerous persecutions and summary executions of Kurds, resulting in the deaths and executions of almost 10,000 Kurds.[155] The Kurds boycotted the referendum for the 1979 constitution to express their disapproval and to compel acceptance of their circumstances. The new regime in Iran perceived the autonomy demanded by the Kurds in Rojhilat as a call for separation from the state. The end of the Iran-Iraq war provided an opportunity for resuming negotiations between the Kurds and the Iranian regime in 1988. While waiting for an Iranian delegation, the Secretary-General of the Democratic Party of Iranian Kurdistan (PDKI), Dr Abdul Rahman Ghassemlou, his deputy Abulla Qadri, and the intermediary Dr Fazil Rasul were assassinated in Vienna by the Iranian regime's negotiators in July 1989, according to the Austrian Public Prosecutor. Sediq Kamangar, a senior member of *Komala* (the Society of Revolutionary Toilers of Iranian Kurdistan),[156] met the same fate the next month. On 18 September 1992, Dr Sadiq Sharafkandi, Ghassemlou's successor, was murdered along with Fattah Abduli and Homayun Ardalan (the

154 HOHR, Zahra Mohammadi (Zara), Kurdish Language Teacher's 5 Years Imprisonment Sentence Confirmed; HOHR, Kurdish Language Teacher and Cultural Activist Anisa Jafarimehr, Arrested in Kermanshah; HOHR, The Arrest of at least 12 Kurdish Language Teachers in One Year by Iranian Government Forces. Also, see Kurdistan Human Rights Association (KMMK) and Kurdistan Human Rights Network.

155 UN Press Release, 7 September 1979, No. HR/178, 'Sub-Commission Demands Cessation of Summary Executions of Kurds in Iran' [FCO 8/3394]. Anita Burdett, *Records of the Kurds: Territory, Revolt and Nationalism, 1831–1979: British Documentary Sources*, vol 12 (CUP 2015) 688. For the demand for autonomy by the Kurds in the East of Kurdistan and the Iranian regime's brutal response, see Allan Hassaniyan, *Kurdish Politics in Iran: Crossborder Interactions and Mobilisation Since 1947* (CUP 2021) 98–125.

156 Komala was established in 1969.

deputies of the PDKI in Europe and Germany) and Nouri Dehkordi at the Mykonos restaurant in Berlin. According to the ruling of the German court, the Iranian government was 'directly involved' in the 'political' assassinations. As per the arrest warrant of March 1996 issued by the Chief Federal Prosecutor, the Iranian Minister of Intelligence, Ali Fallahian, is wanted internationally. More arrest warrants were obtained for two Iranian Ministry of Intelligence agents who had been heavily involved in the planning of the Mykonos operation from the beginning of the process. In April 1997, the Berlin Court of Appeal upheld that 'Iran's political leadership ordered the crime.'[157] Since early 1988, Kurds have conducted occasional military operations inside Iran. The June 2021 presidential election was boycotted by the Kurds as another expression of their dissidence.

UN Special Rapporteurs have expressed deep concern over the Kurdish community being persecuted, arrested, and sentenced to death for their political affiliation or beliefs.[158] According to their 2018 report on the Situation of Human Rights in the Islamic Republic of Iran, the Kurds are being detained

> on charges related to various activities, such as environmental activism, eating in public during the month of Ramadan, working as *Kulbars* (border couriers)[159]..., or cheering for the results of the referendum held in neighbouring Iraqi Kurdistan in September 2017, among others.[160]

They are also charged with 'political or security-related crimes, often for engaging in civic activism or because of their membership in Kurdish political parties.' They include workers, teachers, Kolbars, artists, and human rights activists. This report referring to the OHCHR states that the Kurdish people have 'endured the largest number of executions (64) of all ethnic minority groups.'[161] That is confirmed, as a disproportionately high number of Kurdish political prisoners received the death penalty and were executed as specified in the 2019 report.[162] This continues to be the case in 2023 as well. For decades, the regime has refused to deliver the bodies of executed political individuals and activists after decades, rendering them in the status of forced disappearance. Discrimination is illustrated by the disproportionate number of arrests and convictions of Kurds.

157 See Mykonos Urteil [Mykonos Judgement], Urteil des Kammergerichts Berlin vom 10. April 1997 [Judgement of the Court of Appeal of Berlin on April 10, 1997], OLGSt Berlin, (1) 2 StE 2/93 (19/93).

158 OHCHR, Special Rapporteur on Iran, available at https://www.ohchr.org/en/hrbodies/sp/countries-mandates/ir/pages/sriran.aspx.

159 Those who transport goods on their backs between the South and East of Kurdistan.

160 Report of the Secretary-General, 'Situation of Human Rights in the Islamic Republic of Iran,' 4 September 2019, A/HRC/37/24, [49].

161 Report of the Secretary-General, 'Situation of Human Rights in the Islamic Republic of Iran' (12 March 2018).

162 Annual report of the UN OHCHR and Reports of the Office of the High Commissioner and the Secretary-General, 8 February 2019, A/HRC/40/24, [14].

The Kurds reportedly are subjected to more severe physical punishment or torture than other prisoners, regardless of the type of crime for which they are accused.[163] The UN Special Rapporteur, in the July 2021 report, referred to the number of executions between 2010 and 2020 in Iran of which '53 per cent were Kurdish' charged with 'alleged involvement in political groups.' The Rapporteur noted that 'these figures are likely underestimates, given that the official acknowledgement of executions of minority prisoners is less (only 21 per cent in 2020) and owing to minority prisoners often being executed outside their home province.'[164] This level could be considered an egregious violation of human rights for the purposes of secession.

The 2018, 2019, 2020, 2022, and 2023 Reports of the Special Rapporteur referred to the 'excessive use of force against and systematic, extrajudicial killings' of Kurds, especially *Kolbars*.[165] Also, violations of the economic, social, and cultural rights of minorities are commonly noted in almost all UN reports on the human rights situation in Iran.[166] There are exploitative relations between the Kurds and the central authorities of Iran in managing natural resources and allocating profits. The state has not fairly shared revenue derived from the Kurdish regions' natural resources in oil, gold, and other minerals, constituting a violation of economic self-determination by the Kurds' host states as the Kurds have no control over their wealth and resources. It increases economic and social despair and neglects the impoverished Kurdish provinces, beset with the highest rate of unemployment in a form of internal economic colonialism.[167] Even nature and the ecosystems of Rojhilat have been securitised and are not immune from Iranian state ecocide policies. The regime has dried up and depleted the region, endangering the lives of Kurds living there.[168] Alongside these policies, many environmental activists have faced imprisonment, charged with political offenses, and are under the regime's security monitoring. The Iranian regime has adopted the internal colonialism approach, putting Kurdish areas into a subordinate status with discriminatory policies exercised over them based on factors of ethnicity and religion. The

163 US Department of State, '2018 Country Reports on Human Rights Practices: Iran.'

164 Situation of Human Rights in the Islamic Republic of Iran, Note by the Secretary-General, 16 July 2021, A/76/160, [68].

165 Situation of Human Rights in the Islamic Republic of Iran, A/73/398, 27 September 2018; Report of the Special Rapporteur on the Situation of Human Rights in the Islamic Republic of Iran, A/74/188, 18 July 2019; Report of the Special Rapporteur on the Situation of Human Rights in the Islamic Republic of Iran, 28 January 2020, A/HRC/43/61, [43] and 14 May 2021 A/HRC/47/22; Report of the Special Rapporteur on the Situation of Human Rights in the Islamic Republic of Iran, Javaid Rehman, A/77/181, 18 July 2022.

166 OHCHR, Iran (Islamic Republic of), available at https://www.ohchr.org/EN/Countries/MENARegion/Pages/IRIndex.aspx.

167 See Kamal Soleimani and Ahmad Mohammadpour, 'The Securitisation of Life: Eastern Kurdistan under the Rule of a Perso-Shi'i State' (2020) 41(4) TWQ 663.

168 See Allan Hassaniyan, 'Environmentalism in Iranian Kurdistan: Causes and Conditions for its Securitisation' (2020) 20(3) CSD 355 and Gordyaen B. Jermayi, 'In the Mountains of Kurdistan, Iran Fosters an Environmental Crisis' (*KPI*, 22 February 2023).

East of Kurdistan is viewed as a non-self-governing territory despite regime claims to be anti-colonialist and anti-imperialist. The adoption of internal colonialism by the state is another justification for the secession of the East of Kurdistan from Iran.

The regime in Iran does not deny the existence of the Kurds within the country's borders. Nevertheless, to strip almost all attributes of being Kurdistani, it has applied a set of sophisticated security policies. Cultural genocide has been an integral part of the host states' policies against Kurds over the last century. These range from the Perso-Shi'ification of state education, the division of Eastern Kurdistan into separate provinces and concurrently altering their names, militaristic tribalisation and Persianisation and Shi'ifying the Kurdish space, to militarisation and strictures of Kurdish life. By these means, the regime has 'otherised' the Kurds ethnically and religiously.[169]

The outrage sparked by the brutal murder of *Jîna Emînî* at the hands of the 'morality police' in Tehran — under the pretext of a skewed hijab — sparked protests started in Jina's hometown, Seqqiz, and shortly spread across Iran after her funeral procession on 16 September 2022. Anguish was transformed into a sustained uprising in the *Jina Revolution* under the banner of *Jin, Jiyan, Azadî movement.*[170] As of October 2023, more than 137 Kurds were murdered, and more than 8,000 injuries were reported. This is in indication of the over-representation of the Kurds in killings. In the ongoing mass arrests, more than 6,000 people including women and adolescents have been jailed, their fate at serious risk. In addition, more than 300 juvenile students were kidnapped. Some of them have been sentenced to death on the charge of 'enmity against God' or *muharebeh* ('waging war against God') and 'disrupting national security,' and ten were murdered under torture.[171] The Kurds have endured more losses than any other national and ethnic group within the geographic boundaries of Iran, and this process is continuing. Systematic sexual violence has been deployed by the Iranian authorities against most prisoners.[172] For months, many Kurdish cities endured a vicious crackdown even during

169 Soleimani and Mohammadpour (n 167).

170 On the streets and campuses, protesters chant *'Jin, Jiyan, Azadî.'* It literally means 'woman, life, freedom,' but the scope is broader, and the impact strikes much deeper. Thus, the slogan's genesis is best preserved untranslated. As a motto, its roots trace to the Kurdish women's liberation movement in Northern Kurdistan against the Turkish state in the early 1980s, later to appear mentioned and interpreted in the writings of Abdulla Ocalan. The bedrock foundation of *Jin, Jiyan, Azadî* underlies the people in the East of Kurdistan; there, women and men have long stood equally alongside as manifested in female organisations established in the twentieth century by Kurdish parties there including the PDKI and Komala. Other Kurdish parties followed suit. Women have exercised a decisive role in Kurdish movements over the last century. In Rojava, the Kurdish self-ruled area in the West of Kurdistan, the female military force of YPJ and other female parties across Kurdistan have voiced this slogan. The slogan means free life is unachievable without women's freedom and without eliminating discrimination and inequalities in the society.

171 See HOHR, 'enmity or war against God.' Also, see Situation of Human Rights in the Islamic Republic of Iran — Report of the Special Rapporteur, Javaid Rehman, A/HRC/52/67, 7 February 2023.

172 Tamara Qiblawi and others, 'How Iran's Security Forces Use Rape to Quell Protests' (*CNN*, 21 November 2022).

mourning ceremonies. What was happening was reminiscent of the state-sponsored massacre and extrajudicial executions of the Kurds after the 'Islamic Revolution' in 1979. Unable to quell the uprising, the regime's retaliation, as always, is to strike at civilian targets, including an elementary school in a refugee settlement and the Eastern Kurdistan parties' headquarters (*Partî Azadî Kurdistan*, PAK), PDKI, and Komala) based in the South of Kurdistan. These attacks were carried out with three bombardments using the suicide drones and missiles, which led to the killing of 20, among them a pregnant woman and her infant, and more than 50 injuries. By international standards, Tehran has long since forfeited its legitimacy in the East of Kurdistan. Both the previous and incumbent governments have trampled on the Kurds' political, social, and cultural rights. In addition to being denied any political power, the Kurds of the East had no part in putting these governments in place.

The situation remains dire. As a victim of misconduct by their host state owing to human rights violations and denial of internal self-determination, the Kurds in Iran may meet the required standards for qualified unilateral secession. But there are two issues in this regard. First, with respect to the requirement that all remedies be exhausted, the Kurds of Rojhilat have already reached a dead-end point at which they realise that political alternatives are not viable. Non-recognition or suppression of ethnic differences is the primary reason for this stalemate. Second, their expressed will for secession is difficult to demonstrate because a referendum under the control of the Shi'a theocratic, Persian chauvinist Islamic Republic of Iran is inconceivable. The ability of Kurds in the East to exercise their right to self-determination internally is totally frustrated. Their brethren in Başûr are in a different situation.

7.6.2 The Secession of Başûr (South) from Iraq

7.6.2.1 Representative Government

After almost eight decades of coups and crackdowns in Iraq, the processes of federalisation and political pluralism started in 2003 with the Shi'a Arab majority and the two minorities of Kurds and Sunni Arabs. The federated representative democracy evolved from the erosion of a state which was originally monarchical (from 1925–1958) and later became a one-party (Ba'ath Socialist) unitary and centralised state (from 1958–2003). After the US-led invasion in 2003, Iraq was governed under the laws issued by Paul Bremer, the first US civil administrator in Iraq,[173] from 2003 to 2005. The Iraqi pre-eminent permanent Constitution introduced a republican, democratic, federal, representative, parliamentary (Constitution of Iraq, Article 1) system for the people of Mesopotamia in a multiethnic, multiconfessional and multisect state (Article 3).

173 Saad Jawad, 'The Iraqi Constitution: Structural Flaws and Political Implications' (01. LSE MEC Paper Series 2013) 8.

Iraq has ratified both the Convention on the Elimination of Discrimination and the ICCPR in 1970 and 1971, respectively.[174] To achieve a representative government, Article 20 of the constitution stipulates the right to participate in public inasmuch as 'Iraqi citizens, men and women, shall have the right to participate in public affairs and to enjoy political rights including the right to vote, elect, and run for office.' That is, the people of Iraq directly (their representatives to the parliament) or indirectly (the Prime Minister and the Council of Ministers) elect their representatives to govern the state.

After the adoption of the Iraqi constitution in 2005, a *de facto* autonomous Kurdish entity was formed within Iraq. Since then, there has been an Iraqi representative government of all people residing on Iraqi territory. The Council of Representatives is elected through a direct secret general ballot. The representation of all components of the people shall be upheld in it (Article 49). No provincial electoral districts have been introduced. The Kurdish alliance usually gets almost 20% of the seats in the Council of Representatives, roughly equal to the Kurdish population in Iraq. The Speaker of the Council of Representatives, by convention, is filled by the Sunni parties approved by the largest bloc in the Council.[175] The Speaker has a Kurdish deputy. The Council of Representatives shall elect the President of the Republic from among the candidates (Article 70 First). At the level of the federal government, the Kurds are guaranteed the symbolic post of President of the Republic, a deputy prime minister, and three ministerial posts in the government; in practice, these are granted to Kurdish parties. Jalal Talabani, the leader of the Patriotic Union of Kurdistan (PUK), was the first non-Arab President of Iraq from 2006 to 2014. The post of Prime Minister (nominated by the largest bloc to form the government cabinet or the Council of Ministers), by convention, is filled by a Shi'a candidate.[176] The constitution fails to specify in what manner the Kurdish adherence of the ministers should be determined. Nonetheless, the rule of equal representation means that the Council of Ministers, which includes 15 members at most, comprises two to five Kurds as ministers in the federal government. This has always been debated and opposed by the appointed prime ministers since 2003. There should be guarantees for the Kurdish minority on the federal level regarding effective participation in public affairs in the broadest sense of the term: political participation plus effective participation in the executive and the judiciary. The rules pertaining to the composition of the Council of Ministers and the decision-making authority should guarantee the Kurds equal participation in the federal executive power. Thus, the Kurds in the South of Kurdistan do not meet the standard of non-representation for the purpose of secession.

174 Ratification of Treaties (n 151).

175 Renad Mansour, 'Iraq's 2018 Government Formation: Unpacking the Friction between Reform and the Status Quo' (LSE MEC Report 2019) 7.

176 ibid 8.

The Iraqi federation is an example of self-rule and shared rule; in effect, it is autonomy vis-à-vis the federal government.[177] The constitution not only recognises the sufferings of racial oppression in the massacres of Halabja, Barzan, Anfal, and the Fayli Kurds (The Preamble) but also provides territorial autonomy to the Kurds in Başûr. This asymmetric, quasi-federal regionalism and decentralised system recognises 'the region of Kurdistan' (which now comprises four governorates) as a federal region (Article 117(1)) that enjoys a higher degree of autonomy. The region is authorised to adopt its own constitution defining the structure of powers of the region (Article 120) for exercising executive, legislative, and judicial powers in accordance with the Constitution (Article 121(1)).

Regarding the laws of central and local governments, '[t]he priority goes to the regional law in case of conflict between other powers shared between the federal government and regional governments,' according to Article 115. Also, in case of any contradiction between regional and national legislation in matters outside the exclusive powers of the federal government, the regional authority shall have the right to amend the application of the national legislation within that region' (Article 121(2)). To secure and thwart the unilateral revision or revocation of the powers of the Kurdistan region, articles of the Iraqi constitution

> may not be amended if such amendment takes away from the powers of the regions that are not within the exclusive powers of the federal authorities, except by the approval of the legislative authority of the concerned region and the approval of the majority of its citizens in a general referendum (Article 126(4)).

This could be construed as a veto power granted to the Kurds over any constitutional amendment that is contrary to their interests.

The KRG shall have the right to exercise executive, legislative, and judicial powers in consonance with this Constitution, except for those authorities stipulated as the exclusive authorities of the federal government (Article 121(1)). It is allocated an equitable share (17%) of the national revenues sufficient (Article 121(3))[178] with its own internal security forces (Article 121(5)). The KRG shall have offices in embassies and diplomatic missions to follow cultural, social, and developmental affairs of interest to Kurdish society (Article 121(4)). Since the autonomy was *de facto* established in 1992, the Iraqi constitution confirmed the validity of the legislation, decisions, and contracts validly enacted under the government of the region of Kurdistan since 1992 (Article 141).

177 John McGarry and Brendan O'Leary, 'Iraq's Constitution of 2005: Liberal Consociation as Political Prescription' (2007) 5(4) IJCL 670, 676.

178 The central government has used financial pressure as a point against the KRG, as the federal government consider signing deals with foreign companies and exporting the oil to be illegal and unconstitutional.

7.6.2.2 Human Rights Record

Before 2003, the South of Kurdistan might have, at some points, met the threshold for remedial secession. After the annexation of Southern Kurdistan to Iraq in 1923, no political or cultural rights were afforded to the Kurds, despite pledges made by the International Commission of Inquiry.[179] Iraq's non-adherence to the overdue pledges outraged the Kurds. Therefore, the Kurds did not accept the status imposed on them and initiated their determination to challenge the status quo, resulting in eight decades of human rights abuses by the Iraqi government.

Concurrent with the situation of Bengalis in East Pakistan, the termination of the Kurds' autonomy established by the March Manifesto of 1970 and the subsequent widespread Iraqi violence against the Kurds was for nought, as in this case, there was no third state intervention. In the 1980s, the expansion of the Kurdish region in the South of Kurdistan gave Saddam Hussein the pretext to retaliate. Hence, the Kurds turned to guerrilla warfare, which led to the savage government response of using chemical weapons in March 1987 against the PUK's positions. The Iraqi Army had the goal of extinguishing 'any human being or animal present' in Kurdistan.[180] Everyone who championed negotiation or reconciliation was abducted. The Iraqi regime bombarded the town of Serdeşt in the East of Kurdistan with mustard gas on 28 June 1987 near the end of the Iran-Iraq war. Two-thirds of its population (almost 8,000 people) was exposed to the deleterious effects of chemical weapons, leaving more than 130 dead. Following the signing of a peace deal between Iran and Iraq, Zerde, a village located in Dalahoo (Kirmaşan) along with a few nearby villages were also poisoned a few days later. This heinous act led to the loss of 275 lives and left more than 1,100 injured. Both Iran and Iraq have accused each other of using chemical weapons in the Kurdish regions. However, to this day, no state official other than Ali Hassan al-Majid, an Iraqi security figure commanding the Anfal ('Spoils') campaign against the Kurds in Başûr, has been brought to trial for these crimes. Ali Hassan al-Majid, aka Chemical Ali, was sentenced to death by hanging. In 2005, the District Court of The Hague convicted Frans Cornelis Adrianus van Anraat, a Dutch businessman, of complicity in violations of the laws and customs of war for selling chemicals to Iraq, making a contribution to the attacks that were aimed at the destruction of the Kurds. He was consequently sentenced to 15 years in prison.

In January 1988, when advancing Iranian troops captured Halabja, the Kurdistan question was supposed to be solved by *Operation Anfal*[181] by which the Kurds were to be eliminated. Nearly 5,000 civilians perished, and thousands were maimed by

179 See Chapter 4.3.10.

180 Joost R. Hiltermann, A *Poisonous Affair: America, Iraq, and the Gassing of Halabja* (CUP 2007) 99.

181 The name of a *Surat* or chapter of the Quran. HRW, *Iraq's Crime of Genocide: The Anfal Campaign against the Kurds* (YUP 1995). Also see Joost R. Hiltermann, *The 1988 Anfal Campaign in Iraqi Kurdistan* (Arras Erbil 2008).

the chemical onslaught on Halabja on 16 March 1988,[182] which, as of that date, was 'the worst' violation of the Geneva Protocol 1925. In the *Anfal* operations numbered II, III, IV, V, VI, VII, and VIII from March to September,[183] thousands upon thousands of Kurds were disappeared, executed, or suffocated, and 4,000 villages were razed.[184] It was reminiscent of Nazi atrocities but, on this occasion, was aimed at 'the atomization' of Kurds. Over 400,000 Kurds crossed the border to seek refuge in Rojhilat and Bakûr only to be poisoned twice in June 1989 and January 1990 in the Turkish camps. Turkey worried about the emergence of 'Kurdistan' on Turkish territory.[185] Still, the international community underwrote Saddam by taking no action to deter Baghdad. The UNSC passed Resolution 620 on 26 August 1988 which 'condemns resolutely the use of chemical weapons' and asked the Secretary-General to take 'appropriate and effective measures.'[186] Later, it became evident that France, Germany, Italy, and the Netherlands had provided chemical materials to Baghdad.[187] The Anfal campaign has been recognised as genocide against the Kurds by the parliaments of Norway, South Korea, the UK, and Sweden.

Resolution 688 (April 1991) recognised 'a massive flow of refugees towards and across international frontiers and to cross-border incursions' and the suffering of the Kurds 'from the repression in all its forms inflicted by the Iraqi authorities' which threatened international peace and security in the region. The international community was '[d]eeply disturbed by the magnitude of the human suffering involved.' However, it did not recognise the Kurds' right to self-determination. Instead, the UNSC hoped that 'an open dialogue will take place to ensure that the human and political rights of all Iraqi citizens are respected.'[188] This resolution and the subsequent no-fly zone were decisive in the establishment of the Kurdish Autonomous Area (KAA) regime.

Since then, Iraq has had no effective authority over the South of Kurdistan, although the special circumstances of the Kurds, unlike Kosovo, did not culminate in any form of state creation. The Kurds of the South underwent actual genocide or ethnic cleansing owing to the deliberate *Anfal* campaign of the Iraqi Ba'ath regime to destroy their identity; that is, the physical survival of the Kurds was threatened by the actions of the Ba'athist regime in 1988. The Kurds had a strong claim to secession owing to the Iraqi government's nerve-gas attack. It amounted to the

182 For Halabja, see Nicole F. Watts, 'Re-Claiming Halabja' in Gareth Stansfield and Mohammed Shareef (eds), *The Kurdish Question Revisited* (OUP 2017).

183 HRW, 'Genocide in Iraq, The Anfal Campaign against the Kurds; A Middle East Watch Report' (HRW 1993).

184 For a list of villages bombarded with chemical weapons, see Gérard Chaliand (ed), *The Kurdish Tragedy* (trans Philip Black, ZB 1994).

185 John Bulloch and Harvey Morris, *No Friends but the Mountains: The Tragic History of the Kurds* (OUP 1992) 29.

186 UNSC Res 620 (26 August 1988).

187 McDowall (n 152) 354–362.

188 UNSC Res 688 (5 April 1991).

forfeiture of Iraq's political legitimacy and its demonstrable failing to fulfil its trusteeship function.[189] In cases where states utilise their powers to the detriment of a section of their population and employ a policy of oppression against their peoples, they are 'badly misgoverned' and 'alienated';[190] that is, the mother state has forfeited its right to sovereignty.

Looking at the current situation, however, is the incumbent government responsible for what the previous regime did? There was a prevailing national movement at the time, but did the Kurds have effective control over Kurdish territory? Should the answer be assumed in the affirmative, they might not have been able to mount a prolonged resistance, since they needed third-state intervention, as in the case of Bangladesh. No neighbouring state backed them because, to the neighbours, the Kurds' ultimate claim would transcend state borders. The recognition of any Kurdistani entity would affect the neighbouring states having sympathetic Kurdish populations within their territories.

The current situation of Başûr closely resembles that of Quebec in Canada. The Kurds have been represented in the Iraqi federal government from 2003 to the present time, although there are conflicts between the Kurds and Baghdad on matters such as oil resources and the distribution of income resulting from selling oil.[191] For various reasons, among them the right to self-determination, KRG's authorities chose the pathway to independence presented by a referendum held in September 2017. After establishing autonomy for the Kurds, the KRG held a planned independence referendum on 25 September 2017 in its region and other Kurdish-controlled but disputed areas,[192] including Kirkuk — a multiethnic city with a Kurdish preponderance. The referendum took place with 92.73% (of 72.2% of the electorate) voting in favour of independence. One of the main drives for holding the referendum just when the ISIS was threatening to overwhelm Iraq was the central government's budget policy. Thousands of Kurdish Êzdîs were killed, captured, and enslaved by ISIS in the Şingal Mountains on 3 August 2014. This amounted to genocide as described in the OHCHR report to the UN, followed by a dozen states thus far.[193] Kurdish complaints of discrimination originate with the Iraqi governments' practice since February 2014 of cutting the KRG's budget.[194] Surprisingly, Arab regions under the rule of ISIS did not suffer any budget cuts from Baghdad, but the South of Kurdistan never received its allotted share of the

189 Moore, *Ethics of Nationalism* (n 74) 150.

190 Crawford (n 3) 111.

191 Ed Butler, 'Iraqi Kurdistan's Battle with Baghdad over Oil Revenues' (*BBC*, 10 April 2015).

192 Two unofficial referenda had already been held in February 2004 and in January 2005, called for independence unanimously (98.8%, 1.7 million signatures), but the Kurdish leaders rendered it unpractical due to the time and the neighbours' policy toward the KRG. See David Romano, *The Kurdish Nationalist Movement: Opportunity, Mobilization and Identity* (CUP 2006) 216.

193 OHCHR, 'UN Commission of Inquiry on Syria: ISIS is Committing Genocide against the Yazidis' (*OHCHR*, 16 June 2016). The European Parliament, Belgium, the Netherlands, the UK, Canada, the US, and Germany have recognised the ISIS treatment of Kurdish Êzdîs as genocide.

194 KRG Cabinet, 'Official KRG Response to Statements Made by Prime Minister of Iraq, Haider al-Abadi' (*KRG*, 17 February 2016).

federal budget.[195] Baghdad also divested the *Peshmerga* forces' equipment. In the meantime, the KRG encountered an economic crisis with an exodus of almost 2 million displaced persons from the West of Kurdistan, Syria, and other parts of Iraq.

In addition, Kurdish authorities pointed out the non-enforcement of Article 140 of the Iraqi constitution on the disputed areas previously belonging to Kurdistan, including Kirkuk. Article 140 proposes a census concluding 'with a referendum in Kirkuk and other disputed territories to determine the will of their citizens [to stay within Arab control or the control of the KRG], by a date not to exceed the 31st of December 2007.' The failure to implement Article 140 is one of the cardinal factors driving the Kurds to call for independence.[196] Kurds are still being expelled from these areas. To the Kurds of Southern Kurdistan, Iraq is a 'free union,' which has been formed 'freely and by choice' (Preamble to the Iraqi constitution 2005), but this union is not their choice any longer. Indeed, to the Kurds, the multiple violations of the Iraqi constitution made the maintenance of the union impossible.[197] However, the constitution does not provide a legal basis for secession and independence. Iraq's Supreme Federal Court declared the independence referendum as unconstitutional, rendering the results null and void.

The referendum took place despite all the concerned and opposing countries including Turkey, Iran, Iraq, and the United States.[198] Israel was its only supporter.[199] A majority voted in favour of separation; however, the entity was faced with jointly punitive economic and military measures and embargoes by the neighbours and by Baghdad.[200] The 2017 referendum was not followed up by an immediate declaration of independence. Instead, the KRG authorities expressed their intention to take advantage of the referendum as leverage against Baghdad to negotiate independence and other recurrent issues.

The factual foundation and the rationale for conceding a right to external self-determination based on extreme violations of human rights of the Kurds in the 1980s have since been surpassed. In contemporary Iraq, there is currently no indication of the practice of flagrant, systematic, and persistent discrimination of Kurds that would justify the secession of the KRG. Therefore, the international community is not likely, either now or in the foreseeable future, to approve the secession of the Kurds in Başûr. The situation for the Kurds in Bakûr is significantly different.

195 Alistair Lyon and Suadad al-Salhy, 'Iraq's Maliki Threatens to Cut Funds if Kurds Pipe Oil to Turkey' (*Reuters*, 12 January 2014); Reuters World News, 'Iraqi Kurdish Deputy PM Says Deal with Baghdad 'Easy' if Salaries Paid' (*Reuters*, 16 February 2016).

196 For the disputed territories, see Mohammed Ihsan, 'Arabization as Genocide: The Case of the Disputed Territories of Iraq' in Stansfield and Shareef (n 182) 375–391.

197 Hawre H. Hama, 'Iraqi Kurdistan's 2017 Independence Referendum: The KDP's Public and Private Motives' (2020) 51(1) AA 109.

198 Tulay Karadeniz and Tuvan Gumrukcu, 'Kurdish Independence Referendum: Turkey, Iran and Iraq Unite in Opposition to 'Kexit' Vote' (*Independent*, 22 September 2017).

199 Jeffrey Heller, 'Israel Endorses Independent Kurdish State' (*Reuters*, 13 September 2017).

200 Maher Chmaytelli, 'Iraqi Kurds Face more Sanctions after Calling Elections' (*Reuters*, 3 October 2017).

7.6.3 The Secession of Bakûr (North) from Turkey

7.6.3.1 Representative Government

Remedial separation, as a last resort, would apply in the context of a misgoverned territory that has endured a policy of oppression for a century. Since the inception of Mustafa Kemal's regime in 1923, with its monist nation-building project, the Turkish government, as per its constitution, has denied the very existence of the Kurds as a separate people, although he had earlier conceded the existence of Kurds, referring to 'every kind of right, racial, social and geographical' for them 'in sincerity or in deceit.' At the same time, he stressed that Kurds and Turks as two peoples would unite into one whose interests are together with a common 'Islamic element.'[201] Islam was, indeed, used to obfuscate others, namely the Armenians. The new policy had the effect of erasing Kurdish identity. In the North of Kurdistan, Turkification metastasised to convert Kurds to 'good Turks'[202] through the establishment of the so-called People's Houses (*Halkevleri*) which aimed to assimilate the Kurds by offering educational, cultural, and sports initiatives.[203]

No minority has been recognised in the Turkish constitution. None of the constitutional changes included any amendments concerning the status of the Kurds. The constitution affirms the 'Turkish Motherland and Nation' as the indissoluble unity of the Sublime Turkish State (Preamble). Ataturk nationalism, Turkishness, and the 'TURKISH NATION' (as in the original text) are principles that stand out in the preamble of the constitution. The supremacy of the Turkish language is decreed (Article 3). This is deemed non-amendable and non-negotiable (Article 4). Articles 9 and 70 further reinforce the same identity for the purpose of entering into public service and the exercise of juridical power respectively by '[e]very Turk' and 'the Turkish Nation.'

With Turkey's transition to electoral democracy and a multiparty system initiated in the 1950s, the Kurds' legal status did not change. The ensuing coup in 1960, the 1961 Constitution, and subsequent liberties re-activated Kurdish nationalism, but the Kurds and their organisations were not immune from extralegal and judicial persecution. The 1971 coup and the subsequent extensive state violence stimulated the Kurds' quest for independence, once again spearheaded by the PKK. The Turkish government's repressive policies toward any Kurdish political participation led to the establishment of the PKK with the founding goal of creating an independent Kurdish state comprising all Kurdistani segments in Turkey, Iraq,

201 Statement made on 1 May 1920, Grand National Assembly records, quoted in *Sacak,* No 39, April 1987; *Hakimiyet-i-Milliye,* 6 May 1921, in *Bulletin Piriodique,* 12 April–25 May 1921, quoted in Hamit Bozarslan, 'Les Révoltes Kurdes en Turquie Kémaliste (Quelques Aspects)' (1988) 151(6) Guerres Mondiales Et Conflits Contemporains 107, 121.

202 McDowall (n 152) 207–216.

203 Dilek Kurban, *Limits of Supranational Justice: The European Court of Human Rights and Turkey's Kurdish Conflict* (CUP 2020) 89.

Iran, and Syria.[204] Kurds were portrayed as 'Mountain Turks.'[205] To the Turks, the Kurds were 'of Turkish origin and there was no such thing as the Kurdish nation' while paradoxically, and even worse, they did not have 'the faces of human beings' and should be expelled to 'Africa to join the half-human half-animals who lived there.'[206] The Turkish government had already launched its program of intimidation, coerced assimilation, and the denial of Kurdish particular ethnicity. At the start of 1971, the Kurds of Bakûr initiated a guerrilla resistance to which the government responded by imposing intermittent martial law.[207]

The Law on Political Parties (Law 2820), adopted in April 1983, provides that '[p]olitical parties shall not uphold the aim of changing the principle of the unity of the State' (Article 80). Article 81 adopts a more restrictive measure by banning political parties from using languages besides Turkish and 'creating minorities within the country of the Republic of Turkey through preserving, developing or spreading languages and cultures other than the Turkish language and culture.'[208]

As in Article 3, Article 14 of the constitution prohibits activities which violate 'the indivisible integrity of the State with its territory and nation.' In its interpretation of these articles, Turkey's Constitutional Court held:

> [n]o concessions can be made with regard to this fundamental principle… The Constitution, which is based on the principle of unitary state, does not permit [a] federal state. Therefore, political parties cannot include [a] federal system in their programs, and cannot advocate such a structure…As the principle of nation-state does not permit the notion of multi-national state, there is no room for a federal structure in such a system.[209]

Kurds have been integrated into the mainstream Turkish political parties' ranks for delivering Kurdish votes.[210] Indeed, the Kurdistan issue has not been looked into as an ethno-political question.[211] Turkish parties raising the Kurdistan question as a priority and overtly Kurdish parties have frequently been closed down since the establishment of the first one in 1987, under the charges of being separatist, inciting

204 Thomas Phillips, 'International Legal Perspectives on Aspects of Self-Determination in North Kurdistan and Turkey: Kurdish Language Education, and Political Participation' (PhD Thesis, University of Liverpool 2020) 202.

205 İsmail Beşikçi, *M. Kemal Ataturk, UNESCO and Destruction of Kurdish Identity in Turkey* (CDK 1986) 5.

206 Quote from *Otuken* Journal. McDowall (n 152) 406, 409.

207 ibid 410–416.

208 Turkey, Law on Political Parties (amended in April 2018).

209 Constitutional Court Decision, E. 1993/3, K. 1994/2, 16 June 1994, *Anayasa Mahkemesi Kararlar Dergisi* (AMKD) [Constitutional Court Reports] 2, No. 30: 1201, 1199, quoted in Ergun Özbudun, 'Party Prohibition Cases: Different Approaches by the Turkish Constitutional Court and the European Court of Human Rights' (2010) 17(1) Democratization 125.

210 Hamit Bozarslan, 'Political Crisis and Kurdish Issue in Turkey' in Robert Olson (ed), *The Kurdish Nationalist Movement and its Impact on the Middle East in the 1990s* (Lexington 1996) 135.

211 Phillips (n 204) 198.

minorities against the political unity of the 'Turkish nation,' recognising the Kurds and their identity, speaking Kurdish in their campaigns, advocating federalism or territorial autonomy, or recently under the excuse of supporting 'terrorism.'[212] Kurdish parties are not tolerated and are considered illegal, leading to their dissolution even before they start their activities.[213]

Contesting before the ECtHR has not had a significant outcome. On one hand, the ECHR has hindered the effectiveness of the ECtHR, and on the other hand, in relation to the Turkish state violence in the Kurdish region, the Court has never made full use of its review authority and jurisprudential instruments.[214] However, there were clandestine Kurdish parties.[215] Concurrently, Kurdish politicians could win a few seats in the Grand National Assembly of Turkey (GNAT) through a coalition with a Turkish socialist party in 1987. Later, the expelled members established the first pro-Kurdish political party, the People's Labour Party, which was closed down in 1993. Since then and with the dissolution of the Democratic People's Party, People's Democracy Party, the Democracy Party, and the Democratic Society Party, Kurdish representatives were banned from political activities, stripped of their immunities, and sentenced to imprisonment or faced extrajudicial execution. In some cases, the parties' buildings were bombed. But for those Kurds integrated into the ruling parties, speaking in Kurdish for their constituencies has had no criminal consequence,[216] implying that those who acquiesce to voluntary assimilation will be immune, i.e., identifying as 'Turkish' offers the possibility of ascending to the highest ranks within the government. Simply put, Kurds can be anything but Kurdish.

Although Kurdish candidates did pass the threshold in Kurdish provinces, their parties could not meet the threshold for entering the GNAT. Their seats were given to candidates from other parties with far fewer votes. During this period, Kurdish mayors governing Kurdish cities were on the rise. In 2007 and 2011, Kurds entered the GNAT by running with independent candidates at a high financial cost.[217] Civil disobedience campaigns demanding social and political rights and the release of the members of Kurdish parties and mayors failed to achieve results. Article 33 of Law on Political Parties No. 2839 on Parliamentary Elections maintains the threshold to enter parliament at 10% of the valid votes cast on a national basis.[218] The ECtHR found the threshold 'excessive'[219] as it is the highest in Europe. To the

212 See *United Communist Party of Turkey and Others v. Turkey* (ECtHR, 30 January 1998); *Socialist Party of Turkey v. Turkey* (ECtHR, 8 July 1998) and *HADEP and Demir v. Turkey* (ECtHR 14 March 2011).

213 Kurban (n 203) 110.

214 For Kurdish and pro-Kurdish political party dissolutions before the ECtHR, see ibid 110–113.

215 Phillips (n 204) 201.

216 Kurban (n 203) 99–101.

217 ibid 102, 105.

218 Opinion on Amendments to the Electoral Legislation and Related 'Harmonisation Laws,' (March and April 2018).

219 See *Yumak and Sadak v. Turkey* [GC] (ECtHR, 8 July 2008) No 10226/03.

Committee on the Elimination of All Forms of Racial Discrimination, Turkey's electoral threshold is indirect discrimination and acts as 'an obstacle to the equitable representation of minority groups in political affairs and a State's governing board, in particular in elected bodies.'[220] Law No. 739 of March 2022 has lowered the electoral threshold to 7%. However, it still remains among the highest in the OSCE region and is still in place as an effort to impede the access of smaller parties, including the Kurds, to the GNAT and the legislature. Additionally, the amendment has imposed stricter eligibility requirements for political parties to participate in parliamentary elections, which has been denounced by both the Office for Democratic Institutions and Human Rights (ODIHR) and the Council of Europe's Venice Commission as 'excessive' and 'discriminatory.'[221]

Despite the policy of cultural annihilation pursued by the Turkish government since 1924, the Kurds have gained seats through the People's Democratic Party (*Partiya Demokratîk a Gelan* known as HDP) in the national parliamentary elections of June and November 2015 and 2018 by exceeding the 10% obstacle. The HDP is considered as a pro-Kurdish party though not mainly oriented toward Kurdish concerns. It reclaimed Kurdish heartlands in the municipal elections of March 2014 and 2019, despite the arrest and long imprisonment of candidates and the removals of Kurdish mayors through extralegal measures prior to the elections.[222] Almost 55 out of the 59 HDP deputies were stripped of their parliamentary immunity collectively by a 'special process' and have been imprisoned after the coup attempt in 2016, convicted of using the terms '"Kurds" and "Kurdistan", mediating between the AKP, calling for democratic autonomy for the Kurdish region,'[223] including the co-chair of the HDP, Selahattin Demirtaş and Figen Yüksekdağ. Before them, Leyla Zana faced a 15-year prison sentence from the State Security Court. Her offense? Speaking a sentence in the Kurdish language within the Turkish parliament and subsequently testifying about human rights abuses in Turkey before the Helsinki Commission of the UK Congress. Her testimony before Congress was charged as an 'act of treason.' Among many other Kurdish parliamentarians who were sentenced to long imprisonment are Gültan Kisanak, Orhan Doğan and Vedat Aydın (the head of the People's Labor Party (HEP) who was murdered in July 1991.

On 22 December 2020, the Grand Chamber of the ECtHR ordered Demirtaş's 'immediate release' due to a lack of relevant and sufficient grounds.[224] Unsurprisingly, the Turkish government held the ruling 'hypocritical' and 'entirely

220 CERD, *Concluding Observations on the Combined Fourth to Sixth Periodic Reports of Turkey*, UN Doc. CERD/C/TUR/CO/4-6, 11 January 2016, [31].

221 Joint opinion of the Venice Commission and the OSCE/ODIHR on the Amendments to the Electoral Legislation, CDL-AD(2022)016-e, 20 June 2022.

222 Serhet Tutkal, 'Trustees Instead of Elected Mayors: Authoritarian Neoliberalism and the Removal of Kurdish Mayors in Turkey' (2021) NP 1. Also, see Nicole Watts, *Activists in Office: Kurdish Politics and Protest in Turkey* (UWP 2010).

223 Kurban (n 203) 108–109.

224 *Selahattin Demirtaş v. Turkey* [GC] (ECtHR, 22 December 2020) No 14305/17.

political.'[225] In 2022, ECtHR also deemed the imprisonment of 13 HDP members of parliament as political, which violated the freedom of expression, the right to vote and stand for election, and Article 18 of the ECHR. It refused to hear an appeal in April 2023 and ordered Turkey to pay a remedial €184,600. Most Kurdish mayors-elect were sacked by governmental orders and arrested on allegations of politically motivated 'terrorist' offences. They were replaced by the government's appointees for longer than the tenure set by law. As of October 2023, this process is continuing, and the Chief Public Prosecutor has appealed to the Constitutional Court to ban the HDP. It is charged with destroying 'the indivisibility between the state and the people,' while its members are being stripped of their parliamentary immunity and are facing imprisonment. Less than three weeks before the 2023 election, the Turkish state made a significant number of arrests, including 110 top officials of the HDP, as well as pro-Kurdish lawyers, journalists, and artists. To mitigate the risk of being closed and as a precautionary measure, the HDP made the decision to participate in the parliamentary elections of 2023 by running under the banner of the Green Left Party (YSP), which managed to exceed the 7% threshold. The YSP was renamed to the Peoples' Equality and Democratic Party (HEDEP) in October 2023.

The closure of political parties is the government's response to any demand for Kurdish cultural, linguistic, and educational rights. The Turkish Constitutional Court, in contemplating the closure of the *Sosyalist Parti* (Socialist Party) stated that 'there is no community in Turkey which has an original/authentic sociological structure.'[226] To this court, the Kurds do not meet a minority characteristic, let alone a nation, as they do not 'possess qualities compatible with a minority's sociological and legal definition.' It also denied the Kurds 'scientifically' due to the lack of 'the necessary characteristics and elements to be considered as a minority.' The Court believed that 'there is no certain area or city which has natural or administrative borders which might be considered as the Kurdish origin [sic] people's land or only populated by them.'[227]

Hostility by the Turkish central government is evident in its denial to federal or sub-state units of effective and meaningful representation in the legal and political structure of the state. Therefore, Kurdish ethnic recognition and the formation of a government representative of the Kurds is far from achieving reality. While successive central governments of Turkey have not restricted the participation of Kurds in elections, the Kurds have participated to only a trivial extent in Turkey's decision-making processes or in matters that affect them directly.

7.6.3.2 Human Rights Record

The Turkish state has continuously abused its sovereign power to the detriment of the Kurds of Bakûr. The identity of the Kurds under Turkish rule is at stake on

225 BBC, 'Erdogan Attacks Europe Court's Order for Demirtas's Release' (*BBC*, 23 December 2020).

226 *Sosyalist Parti* (Socialist Party)-1992, quoted in Derya Bayir, *Minorities and Nationalism in Turkish Law* (Routledge 2016) 211.

227 ibid 211–213.

several counts that may entitle them to qualified secession. As with other minorities in Turkey, the denial of their existence by an ultra-nationalist state is one of these aspects. Fascism is embedded in the Turkish state.[228] This is the case with other minorities, but Kurds are the largest in Turkey. Indeed, any challenge from any minority to the Turkish identity has been suppressed. But the Turkish state has long repressed the Kurdish language and culture, particularly, as is well documented elsewhere, involving a long background of grave human rights violations.

On 17 February 1923, Mustafa Kemal made no reference to the Kurds in his remarks to the Izmir Economic Congress,[229] which was held after battering his external enemies. He had already recognised the ethnic and cultural rights of the Kurds in the Amasya Protocol (1919) and in a public interview,[230] but soon Turks were assigned to all senior administrative posts in Kurdistan. Mentions of Kurdistan were obliterated from official Turkish correspondence, and replaced by Turkish names. March 1924 marked the climax of a process by which the Kurdish language was prohibited in courts and schools. Simply put, linguicide and ethnocide became the genesis of progressive colonisation.[231]

The extent of the subsequent persecution of the Kurds by Turkey is revealed by Law No. 1850, which legalised '[m]urders and other actions committed individually or collectively, from the 20th of June 1930 to the 10th of December 1930,...during the pursuit and extermination of the revolts' in Kurdish areas. The Minister of Justice, Mahmut Esat Bozkurt, also stated in 1930:

> [w]e live in a country called Turkey, the freest country in the world...I believe that the Turk must be the only lord, the only master of this country. Those who are not of pure Turkish stock can have only one right in this country, the right to be servants and slaves.[232]

In accordance with this belief and perception, the Zilan Valley massacre of July 1930 was orchestrated by the Turkish state to suppress the independence movement, resulting in the brutal murder of up to 50,000 people. Additionally, the Turkish state decimated 220 villages in the Zilan area during this episode. Another incident, known as the Thirty-three Bullets incident on July 28, 1943, entailed the summary execution of 33 Kurds from the Özalp district of Wan without trial. They

228 See Firat Demir, 'From Islamic Renaissance to Neo-Fascism in Turkey' (2016) 50(2) RMES 186.

229 He never mentioned the Kurds after proclaiming the new Republic. Andrew Mango, *Ataturk: The Biography of the Founder of Modern Turkey* (1st ed, John Murray 1999) 253.

230 'In accordance with our constitution, a kind of local autonomy is to be granted. Hence, provinces inhabited by the Kurds will rule themselves autonomously.... The Grand National Assembly of Turkey is composed of the deputies of both Kurds and Turks and these two peoples have unified their interests and fates.' Mesut Yeğen, 'The Kurdish Issue in Turkey: Denial to Recognition' in Marlies Casier and Joost Jongerden (eds) *Nationalisms and Politics in Turkey: Political Islam, Kemalism, and the Kurdish Issue* (Routledge 2011) 67–84.

231 Bulloch and Morris (n 185) 172.

232 Quoted in Nezan Kendal, 'The Kurds under the Ottoman Empire' in Gerard Chaliand (ed), *A People without a Country: The Kurds and Kurdistan* (1st 1980, rev and updt, ZB 1993) 65.

were charged with providing support for the Kurdish separatist movement, primarily through smuggling goods to Iran. One of them survived and sought refuge in Rojhilat.

As a long-term policy up to the 1980s, using Kurdish names as tribal names and surnames was banned by the 1934 Surname Law. Registrar authorities appended 'Turk' or 'Ozturk' to the Kurds' surnames. Certain Kurdish names and surnames were also banned. This process was mirrored in the East of Kurdistan where state officials assigned ethnically or racially oriented names to the Kurds, e.g., 'Irannezhad,' 'Mihandoost,' 'Iranpour,' 'Mihanparast,' 'Iranparast,' and 'Irandoost,' or Persianised Kurdish surnames while issuing property documents and identity certificates. By enacting Law No. 2510 in June 1934, the Turkish government elected to assimilate the non-Turkish population into the Turkish language and culture and abrogate all recognised Kurdish tribes. Its objective was to coerce Kurds to lose their majority and their identity.

Turkey still follows 'the lines of the principles and reforms of Kemal' especially in education, which should be conducted in '[n]o language other than Turkish' as a mother tongue to all Turkish citizens (Article 42), who are 'Turk' (Article 66). The 1980 coup and the 1982 Constitution promoted the suppression of Kurdish political and cultural rights by extensively banning the Kurdish language, in particular.[233] Turkey's Law 2932 decreed on 19 October 1983 that the Kurdish language and Kurdish names for children are forbidden and illegal. The following year this ban was extended to almost every aspect of life.[234] Many journalists and intellectuals were arrested, and Kurdish villages were given Turkish names. Since then, Kurdish political rights have been subjected 'to the realm of counterterrorism laws' by which Kurds, including politicians and activists, were charged with violating Turkey's national security and were tried by ad hoc courts. The State of Emergency Law (No. 2935) was introduced on 25 October 1983. In 1984, the State Security Courts were reinstated, ostensibly to try terrorism offences but actually to repress the Kurds through confessions achieved under torture.[235] The State of Emergency Law was annulled in 2002 despite the ending of the state of siege in 1987. However, the Regional Governorship of the State of Emergency was established and empowered 'carte blanche' to act in violation of social, civil, and political rights and banish political dissidents and civil servants from the affected regions.[236] This led to the darkest days for the Kurds of the North, with 200,000 civilians killed.[237] Despite EU pressure, the Anti-Terror Law has remained the legal

233 Kurban (n 203) 90–93.

234 ibid 93. For the use of the Kurdish alphabet in official documents before the ECtHR, see ibid 119–122.

235 UNCHR, Report of the Special Rapporteur on Torture and Other Crel, Inhuman or Degrading Treatment or Punishment, Mr. Nigel S. Rodley, E/ CN.4/1996/35, 9 January 1996, [38]. ibid 96.

236 ibid 80, 96–97.

237 See Hamit Bozarslan, 'Dark Times: Kurdistan in the Turmoil of the Middle East, 1979–2003' in Hamit Bozarslan, Cengiz Gunes and Veli Yadirgi (eds), *The Cambridge History of the Kurds* (CUP 2021).

framework to suppress Kurdish opposition. These actions and subsequent Turkish state practices meet the threshold for justifying Kurdish secession.

In 1987, Prime Minister Turgut Özal (later President) established the OHAL Region ('Governorship of Region in State of Emergency') as a large region in Kurdistan under a special governor.[238] These measures led to demonstrations and protests by families of PKK members and victims in 1990. The PKK then targeted state checkpoints and police stations. In return, the government censored the media and savagely razed and evacuated Kurdish villages. While the Turkish state removed the ban on using the Kurdish language in 1991 and the Kurds were allowed to celebrate Newroz, the Law on Combatting Terrorism (No. 3713) was introduced in April to prosecute Kurdish politicians for using the Kurdish language in political domains.[239] Legal actions were brought against Kurdish politicians and mayors for using the Kurdish language and the banned Kurdish letters x, q, and w. Any clothes and scarves of red, yellow, and green suggesting the Kurdish flag are not allowed.

In November 1991, the PKK suggested a federal entity for Kurdistan, to which Ankara turned a deaf ear. A unilateral ceasefire was instituted by the PKK from 21 March to 15 April 1993, while stressing the unity of Turkey, waiving self-determination, but demanding 'cultural freedoms and the right to broadcast in Kurdish.' Aiming to exterminate the guerrillas, the government resumed its draconian policy and refused negotiations. The death toll continued unabated, but Turkey's influence over the north of Kurdistan did not go unchallenged; for instance, President Özal called the Kurds' program 'a coherent national movement' which was nothing less than the 'gravest threat yet' to Turkish unity. Özal, with a desire for EU membership and its induced reforms, attempted to resolve the Kurdistan question. But he died of an alleged 'heart attack' on 17 April 1993. Ankara continued a campaign of military crackdown, systematic deportation, and abduction as well as the stripping of Kurdish delegates of parliamentary immunity by applying the emergency rule and ruthlessly following a 'capture and kill' strategic plan.[240] But even this level of violation of Kurdish human rights did not gain international support for the secession of the Kurds in Bakûr.

The constitutional ban on using the Kurdish language in speech and broadcasting was lifted in 2001 by approving Law No. 4709, Articles 9 and 10. The ban was expanded to private media in 2003,[241] while faced with the suspension of their license.[242] But this process was not meant to concede the identity of the Kurds. Although these changes were 'significant,' according to the European Commission, their enforcement, however, faced 'considerable restrictions.'[243] With the transition

238 Michael Gunter, *The Kurds: A Modern History* (MWP 2016) 35.
239 Kurban (n 203) 94.
240 McDowall (n 152) 419–441.
241 Law on the Amendment of Various Laws, No. 4928, 15 July 2003.
242 Kurban (n 203) 124.
243 EC, 2004 Regular Report on Turkey's Progress towards Accession, SEC (2004) 1201, 6 October 2004, 18.

from the individual nature of Kurdish rights, including linguistic rights, to a collective right of democratic confederalism for Bakûr in the mid-2000s, thousands of Kurdish mayors and active Kurds in national movements were targeted by the Turkish judicial system and charged with the alleged crimes of 'terrorism' and involvement in Kurdish groups within Turkey and other states to build 'an independent state structure.'[244] Celebrating Newroz, attendance at non-violent demonstrations, reference to the PKK's written materials in their articles, and, in the case of lawyers, petitions to the ECtHR were among the evidence used against those charged. In 2006, thousands of Kurdish minors were treated as adults as per the amendment to the Anti-Terror Law and were tried for 'participating in pro-PKK demonstrations.'[245] Since 2010, the Kurdish movement has proposed the establishment of 'democratic autonomy' in the Kurdish region as a solution to the Kurdistan question.[246] But it was refuted by the Turkish state. Rejecting federalism or any kind of autonomy or self-rule to a people is one of the requirements that has led to successful cases of secession. The Kurds rejected the government's constitutional reforms and boycotted a national referendum in September 2010.[247] The reforms were restricted to linguistic rights, although the Kurdish parties still had to use the Turkish language.[248]

On 28 December 2011, 34 mostly teenage Kurdish civilians crossing the border between the South and North of Kurdistan were killed in a bombing carried out on the presumption that they were PKK militants transporting weapons — a frequent story for the Kurds in the North of Kurdistan that shows the consistent pattern of gross violations of human rights, fulfilling the criteria for remedial secession. The incident was sanctioned by the government, and the case, known as the *Roboski Massacre*, was dismissed by a military prosecutor two years later as an unintentional mistake. That decision indicated impunity for the perpetrators, as in previous cases.[249] Roboski families faced charges and sentences. The ECtHR cited 'the failure to carry out an effective investigation into the bombing.'[250] However, the order of the Turkish Constitutional Court did not challenge the impunity of the government officials in murdering civilians.

The last ceasefire between the PKK and the Turkish state, known as the Resolution Process, was initiated by Ocalan in December 2012. Over this time, linguistic rights were expanded by the Turkish government, but other Kurdish expectations were denied, including legal reforms and public education in Kurdish, the dropping of the electoral threshold, and the reconsideration of the Anti-Terror Law.[251] Following the ISIS siege of Kobanê in Rojava, the peace negotiations

244 Kurban (n 203) 103.
245 ibid 126.
246 ibid 104.
247 ibid 102–104.
248 ibid 127.
249 ibid 288.
250 *Benzer and Others v Turkey* (ECtHR, Final 24 March 2014) No 23502/06, 51.
251 Kurban (n 203) 128.

abruptly stalled in February 2015 despite a promulgated reconciliation agreed by both parties. Between July 2015 and December 2016, Turkish security forces, under the pretext of a curfew and counterterrorism legislation, flattened the Kurdish cities in the Nisêbîn district, including Mêrdîn, Cizîr, Silopî, Sur, and Gever. The attacks led to carnage, serious human rights violations, excessive use of force, and the displacement of half a million Kurds. A UN report referred to 'up to 189' civilians who were trapped in basements of buildings 'without water, food, medical attention and power' before being massacred by the Turkish forces.[252] The total number of victims was undoubtedly understated. Despite all this, secession was still not considered a remedy for this situation.

In May 2018, the PPT in its verdict:

> note[d] that the Kurds [had] been systematically excluded from the economic and political decision-making process, their culture and language banned from public usage, and their political parties, media, journalists, and activists targeted [for persecution]. [...] The Prosecution has, therefore, requested that the PPT establishes that the root cause of the War and State crimes alleged was the denial of the right to self-determination of the Kurdish people.[253]

Turkey is a party to the Convention on the Elimination of Discrimination and the ICCPR. However, it entered reservations to both conventions. In relation to the Convention on the Elimination of Discrimination, Turkey does not contemplate itself as being bound by Article 22 of this Convention egarding representation at the consideration of implementing provisions of the Convention.[254] Provisions cannot be enforced without the explicit consent of the state. With regard to the ICCPR, Turkey reserves the right to interpret and apply the provisions of Article 27 in accordance with the related provisions and rules of the Constitution of the state and the Treaty of Lausanne (1923) and its appendixes.[255]

The Turkish state is best delineated by a complex mix of functionally and territorially democratic and authoritarian features.[256] Its democracy, legality, and citizenship rights disappeared in the North of Kurdistan, and its entrenched emergency rule with a discriminatory framework, under different names since the 1920s, has targeted ethnically conscious Kurds. If Kurds demand equality and political representation at the national and local levels, they must assimilate voluntarily into

252 OHCHR, 'Report on the Human Rights Situation in South-East Turkey' (*OHCHR*, February 2017).

253 PPT, Alleged Violations of International Law and International Humanitarian Law by the Turkish Republic and its Officials in Their Relations with the Kurdish People and their Organisations, 15–16 March 2018.

254 Art. 22: 'The specialized agencies shall be entitled to be represented at the consideration of the implementation of such provisions of the present Convention as fall within the scope of their activities. The Committee may invite the specialized agencies to submit reports on the implementation of the Convention in areas falling within the scope of their activities.'

255 Ratification of Treaties (n 151).

256 Guillermo O'Donnell classifies Turkey as a 'brown' country. Quoted in Kurban (n 203) 79.

the Turkish community.[257] Otherwise, they are denied equal political participation. Are their grievances likely to be remedied, at the hands of an essentially authoritarian regime, short of full independence after a century of living under suppression and denial? Is separation just? The Kurds have resisted assimilation at their own expense while they have tried to seek a democratic solution. They are being murdered simply for expressing their cultural identity through singing or listening to Kurdish music, as well as for their resistance to performing Turkish nationalist songs. Their petitions to domestic or international judicial bodies have been ineffective and have resulted in the ECtHR overseeing state violence, a negative effect on political rights and Kurdish legal mobilisation, despite limited gains in linguistic rights.[258] The proposal put forth since the 1990s by the Kurdish movement for a model of internal self-determination, which included the concept of democratic autonomy to facilitate effective participation in public affairs, has been fully suppressed by the Turkish state. No remedy remains to pursue. Thus, the Kurds of the North meet all requirements for a qualified unilateral secession, and their right to self-determination internally is totally frustrated. The aftermath of the deadly 6 February 2023 earthquake in the North of Kurdistan is the most recent example of the Turkish government's planned misrule over the region, and the incessant Turkish oppressive policy through blocking and confiscating relief aid to the Kurds was followed by their forceful evacuation and dispossession as in the aftermath of the 2011 Wan earthquake. Turkey also prevented assistance to the occupied Kurdish regions of the West of Kurdistan that were severely affected by the quake. The challenges facing the Kurds in Bakûr are far more difficult to overcome than the situation of their compatriots in Rojava.

7.6.4 The Secession of Rojava (West) from Syria

7.6.4.1 Representative Government

Like the other host states of the Kurds, Syria was founded on the denial of the minorities within its boundaries, via its Arabic nation-building plan. The ending of the French mandate in the Levant and Syria's independence in the 1940s again brought no practical benefit to the quest for Kurdish rights. However, Kurds retained their presence in the ranks of the Ministry of the Interior and the Syrian army. Some also were elected to the parliament in 1947–1949 and 1954–1958, and some held ministerial posts in 1949–1957. Husni Za'im, Sami Hinnawi, and Adib Shishakli could be considered as Kurdish presidents. One might argue that they represent the integration of the Kurds in Syria, since they never declared their background, while they proclaimed Syria to be an Arab state. The Ba'ath party, with its Alawite sectarian dominance, finally put an end to the power of the Sunnis and Kurds in March 1963.[259] The Kurds' demands were subsequently brushed aside.

257 ibid 80, 129.
258 ibid 109–132.
259 Jordi Tejel, *Syria's Kurds: History, Politics and Society* (Routledge 2009) 29–46.

From 1970 to 1990, the Kurdish Muslim Brotherhood and sheikhs bonded the Kurds to the regime by allowing certain Kurdish elites to hold military positions in the Alawite Shi'a Ba'ath sect as atonement for the oppressive measures taken against them, but, in fact, the actual purpose was to politically smother the Arab Sunnis. However, Kurdish candidates won parliamentary seats in the election of May 1990, and this ameliorated the economic conditions of Western Kurdistan.[260]

Syria's Permanent Constitution (1973) was amended on 15 February 2012, when the 2011 uprising was one year old. Like its predecessor, the amended text introduces the 'Arab identity' of people that strives for 'the unity of the Arab nation' as the country is considered to be an 'integral part of the Arab nation,' 'the beating heart of Arabism,' (Preamble) and 'part of the Arab nation' (Article 1).[261] The educational system is accountable for preserving this identity (Article 28). The principle of political pluralism was promulgated as the underpinning of the political system of the state, and power was exercised 'democratically through the ballot box' (Article 8(1)). Only '[l]icensed political parties and constituencies shall contribute to the national political life,' by honouring 'the principles of national sovereignty and democracy' (Article 8(2)). However, any political activity or forming any political parties or groupings 'on the basis of religious, sectarian, tribal, regional, class-based, professional, or [featuring] discrimination based on gender, origin, race or color' is unacceptable (Article 8(4)). In practice, policies of non-representation in decision-making processes and of blocking the Kurds from participating effectively in public affairs have been followed by the Syrian state.

The constitutional provisions of 2012 contain no measures offering special benefits to minorities. The system of governance is republican (Article 2) with Arabic as the official language (Article 4). Concerning language as the identifying criterion of a minority, the law provides no language rights in fields such as education, administration, the judiciary, and media. As a republican system, the Syrian Constitution declares the religion of the President of the Republic to be Islam (Article 3), with an emphasis on protecting and respecting the 'personal status of religious communities.'

Although there has never been a representative government of all peoples of Syria, the constitution obligates the citizens 'to maintain' national unity (Article 47). Under these circumstances, how does the state deter its minority-peoples from secession? Since it perceives the population of Syria to be Arab, as its name suggests, the constitution does not refer to, recognise, or single out any minority or ethnic group. As with all other minorities in the multiethnic Syrian state, Kurds are not recognised per se and cannot benefit from any article of the constitution. There is, thus, no legal instrument at the national level granting the Kurds an effective role in public affairs. Although there are a few general provisions, including Articles 23 and 49, concerning the contribution made by the people of Syria in political affairs, in practice, there is no specific consultative mechanism set up to allow or

260 ibid 54-59, 107–121.

261 Constitution of the Syrian Arab Republic 2012.

institutionalise effective Kurdish participation for playing a role in matters affecting them. No inclusive government for all Syrians has ever existed. Since 2011, the Kurds of Rojava have unilaterally established a form of democratic confederalism which the Syrian regime, however, has not recognised.

7.6.4.2 Human Rights Record

The Kurds, as silent victims in Syria, have never struggled against the central government.[262] They have not been able to engage in negotiations with the regime to claim their rights,[263] just as they have never sought secession;[264] their parties have been perceived as 'marginal actors' and 'outsiders.'[265] Before 2011, HRW investigated their 'minority' status in 1990, 1992, 1993, and 1996[266] noting the eras when they were under the rule of the Ottoman Empire (up to 1918),[267] France (up to 1946), and the Arabs (since 1946). The Kurds in the West of Kurdistan meet human rights violation requirements of a qualified right to secession over these eras.

The High Commissioner of the mandatory power, France, adopted a regressive policy toward the autonomy of minorities in Syria in its declared constitution of 1930, contemplating the integrity of the country through underscoring individual rights. Kurds petitioned three times for administrative autonomy to evince their support for the French administration rather than a will to gain specific cultural or political rights for Kurdish regions. But France was not prepared to concede autonomy to the Kurds.[268]

In post-mandate Syria, the process of economic development was the start of the intervention of militants and dictators in the political life of Syrians. Several political upheavals led to the emergence of pan-Arabism with the creation of the federal United Arab Republic (UAR of Egypt and Syria) as its embodiment. The UAR was founded by Gamal Abdel Nasser on 1 February 1958. The Kurdistan question, thus, became a side issue. Pan-Arabists adopted a policy of suffocation, denial, and discrimination against minorities, especially the Kurds, whom they regarded as recruited agents opposed to Arabism.[269] After the disintegration of the UAR on 28 September 1961, the Arab Syrian Republic was proclaimed; however, the coup

262 See Michael M. Gunter, *Out of Nowhere: The Kurds of Syria in Peace and War* (C. Hurst & Co. 2014) ch 2 and Kerim Yildiz, *The Kurds in Syria: The Forgotten People* (Pluto Press 2005).

263 For the Kurds' rights under the Syrian Constitution, see Yildiz (n 262) ch 8, 9, and 10.

264 Ziadeh Radwan, 'The Kurds in Syria: Fueling Separatist Movements in the Region' (Special Report 2009).

265 Tejel (n 259) 85.

266 HRW, 'World Report on Syria' (1990, 1992, 1993, and 1996).

267 Gunter, *Out of Nowhere* (n 262) 7.

268 Martin Strohmeier, *Crucial Images in the Presentation of a Kurdish National Identity: Heroes and Patriots, Traitors and Foes* (BRILL 2003) 131.

269 Tejel (n 259) 40–42. For UAR, see Elie Podeh, *The Decline of Arab Unity: The Rise and Fall of the United Arab Republic* (SAP 1999).

of 8 March 1963 engineered by the Ba'ath party brought about a turning point in Syrian policy. The regime became authoritarian, leading to aggravated Arabisation.

Forcible assimilation is one of the standards justifying secession. However, the Kurds' host states have pursued policies of cultural genocide in hostile response to the Kurdistan cause. Despite its international obligations, the Syrian regime has tried to erase Kurdish names anywhere it found them. Decree No. 93 on 23 August 1962 and its subsequent 'census' of Cizîr (in Hesekê province) in November 1962 divested 120,000 Kurds of Syrian nationality. [270] Twenty per cent of the Kurds in the West of Kurdistan at this time were affected.[271] The government regarded them as illegal immigrants from Iraq and Turkey plotting to establish a 'Kurdish State.' Only 'true' Syrians received new identity cards, and the unregistered or those registered as foreigners became stateless. A common response to requests about the fate of individuals was that '[they] had no name [and were] not on the registration lists of Syrian Arabs.'[272] About 154,000 'alien' and 160,000 unregistered Kurds lived in a legal vacuum.[273] They were deprived of human rights and were rendered officially non-existent.[274] Some members of a single family might acquire Syrian nationality; others did not.[275] Arabic slogans singled out the Kurds: 'Save Arabism from Jazira' or 'Fight the Kurdish Menace.'[276] Despite all this, the Kurds of Rojava did activate the last resort (secession) in the absence of international support. There was no legally possible alternative for them.

A security report on Cizîr ('Jazira'), published on 12 November 1963 (publicised in 1968) by a former agent of the Secret Services[277] refuted the 'history,' 'civilization,' 'language,' and 'even [the] definite ethnic origin' of the Kurds.[278] It even denied their existence. Later, the author advocated liquidation of all 'enemies,' linking them to Israel: 'there is no difference between them and Israelis, for Judistan and Kurdistan, so to speak, are of the same species.'[279] The agent dubbed the Kurds 'a malignant tumor' and a 'danger' within the Arab world, which should be eradicated through 'excision.' He adopted the following measures against them: 1) the displacement of Kurds from their lands to the interior, 2) the denial of education, 3) the handing over of 'wanted' Kurds to Turkey, 4) the denial of employment possibilities, 5) an anti-Kurdish propaganda campaign, 6) deportation of Kurdish

270 Within 'one day' and without prior notice. Yildiz (n 262) 33.

271 HRW/Middle East, 'Syria; the Silenced Kurds Vol.8, No.4 (E)' (1 October 1996).

272 ibid.

273 KurdWatch, Report 5, 6 and 9.

274 See Gunter, *Out of Nowhere* (n 262) ch 2 and Maureen Lynch and Perveen Ali, *Buried Alive: Stateless Kurds in Syria* (Refugees International 2006).

275 Loqman Radpey, 'Kurdish Regional Self-rule Administration in Syria: A New Model of Statehood and its Status in International Law Compared to the Kurdistan Regional Government (KRG) in Iraq' (2016) 17(3) JJPS 468; Amir Hasanpour, 'The Language Policy of Syria' (1991) KT.

276 Tejel (n 259) 48–52.

277 Muhammad Talab al-Hilal.

278 Study of the National Social and Political Aspects of the Province of Jazira 1963.

279 The report is quoted in Ismet Ch. Vanly, 'The Kurds in the Soviet Union' in Philip G. Kreyenbroek and Stefan Sperl (eds), *The Kurds: A Contemporary Overview* (Routledge 1992) 122–170.

religious *ulama* (clerics) who would be replaced by Arabs, 7) the implementation of a 'divide-and-rule' policy against the Kurds, 8) the colonisation of Kurdish lands by Arabs; 9) the militarisation of the 'northern Arab belt' and the deportation of Kurds from this area, 10) the creation of 'collective farms' for the new Arab settlers, 11) the denial of the right to vote or hold office to anyone lacking knowledge of Arabic, and 12) the denial of citizenship to any non-Arab wishing to live in the area.[280] The report also suggested establishing an 'Arab belt.'

The Syrian Arab Republic ratified the ICCPR and the Convention on the Elimination of Discrimination, both in 1969. Again an interparty rift between the Ba'athists ended with another coup on 13 November 1970 by Hafez al-Assad, who took up what was called a 'corrective movement' policy. Syria's Permanent Constitution was proclaimed on 13 March 1973, and it remained in force until 15 February 2012,[281] following the March 2011 uprising. The Constitution declared that Syria was a Republic of the 'Arab nation' and was devoted to the power of the 'Arab masses' and to 'Arab unity' (the Preamble of the Constitution).[282] The Arabisation fiat was proclaimed in May 1977 (Directive No. 15801)[283] under which 332 Kurdish villages and towns were renamed.[284] The regime even ordered the rewriting of Arab history in 1975 so as to integrate the minorities and 'non-national' groups into 'Arabness' as the 'unanimist ideology.' The Kurdish language and music were outlawed at workplaces, meetings, festivals, and ceremonies by decree No. 1012/S/25, 1986.[285] The installed policy of assimilation and denial of minority rights lingered on for non-Arab ethnic groups under the rule of Hafez al-Assad for 30 years. Up to his death in 2000, he adopted an 'agrarian reform' programme to ruin the Kurds and seize their land.[286]

By virtue of Decree No. 50 (September 2001), publishing in the Kurdish language was restricted in Syria. A certain number of Kurds were charged and sentenced for distributing Kurdish materials in 2002.[287] On 25 June 2003, the Syrian government arrested the Kurds who demonstrated for civil and political rights on World Children's Day. Also, protests on 6 October 2003 and 10 December 2003 before the Syrian Parliament led to the arrest of Kurdish demonstrators. Kurds and Arabs marked the Declaration of Federalism in Iraq, simultaneously with World Women's Day, as a pretext for celebration on 8 March 2004. The vicious reaction of the regime led to the imprisonment of members of the *Yekîtî* (union) party.

After 2004, the Syrian regime evinced some degree of malleability toward Kurdish cultural rights, but suppression of Kurdish leaders continued up to the

280 ibid.
281 It is still in effect. The government simply amended the text of 1973. English version of the Constitution 2012.
282 Peter B. Heller, 'The Permanent Syrian Constitution' (1974) 28(1) MEJ 53.
283 Yildiz (n 262) 117.
284 Tejel (n 259) 56.
285 David McDowall, *The Kurds of Syria* (KHRP 1998) 47.
286 Tejel (n 259) 59–68.
287 HRWWR, Middle East & North Africa, 'Human Rights Developments, Syria' (2002).

2011 uprising. Maashouq Khaznawi, an outspoken Kurdish cleric, was kidnapped on 10 May 2005 and found dead three weeks later. His assassination sparked the Kurdish demonstrations that followed.[288] In October 2005, the Syrian opposition appealed for 'a fair democratic solution' to the Kurdistan issue to secure the equality of all Syrians and the 'national minorities' and their diverse rights under 'a unified Syrian state,'[289] but this declaration had no practical effect. On 7 October 2011, another Kurdish leader, Mishaal Tammo,[290] was assassinated in Qamişlo,[291] and six demonstrators were shot dead at his funeral.[292] All these events culminated in the 2012 Qamişlo revolt (*serhildan*)[293] further splitting the Kurds from Damascus and inducing a drift in the policy of the government toward the Kurds. But these events did not advance a Kurdish claim to secession.

With the removal of Syrian state control from Rojava and the establishment of Kurdish self-rule there since 2012, no reports of human rights violations have come to light while the incumbent Syrian state is still accountable for the oppression inflicted on the Kurds before the 2011 civil war. The situation of occupied regions under Turkey and its supported insurgents is different. Turkey launched Operation Olive Branch on 19 January 2018,[294] with the deployment of Turkish troops into the Kurdish canton of Efrîn (Afrin) in Rojava. The argument put forward by the Turkish government to justify the operation was that the intervention was necessary to 'counter' the PKK, other Kurdish groups, and ISIS and to prevent an alleged 'terrorist threat.'[295] Many Kurdish civilians were killed during the operation. Later, Turkey occupied Efrîn without objections from any third-party country or international organisation. Turkey then escalated the intervention beginning on 9 October 2019; the new phase operated under the code name Peace Spring and engaged the help of the Free Syrian Army (FSA) and former members of ISIS. The operation followed the US decision to withdraw its troops from Kurdish regions, after which the Turkish Army penetrated deeper into Rojava. Turkey justified its invasion in a series of letters to the UN in which it claimed its right to self-defence against a 'direct and imminent threat' under Article 51 of the UN Charter and contended that it 'will carry out this operation in support of efforts to facilitate the

288 David L. Phillips, *The Kurdish Spring: A New Map of the Middle East* (Routledge 2017) 151. Also, see Nicholas Blanford, 'A Murder Stirs Kurds in Syria' (*Christian Science Monitor*, 16 June 2005).

289 Syrian Opposition, 'Damascus Declaration for National Democratic Change' (*Documents on Democracy*, 16 October 2005).

290 He was the leader and speaker of the Syrian 'Kurdish Future Movement.'

291 BBC, 'Syrian Kurdish Activist Mishaal al Tammo Shot Dead' (*BBC*, 7 October 2011).

292 Dominic Evans, 'Syrian Kurdish Anger Smolders after Activist Death' (*Reuters*, 15 October 2011).

293 HRWWR, 2004, 'Syria Events of 2004' (2005); HRW, 'A Wasted Decade, Human Rights in Syria during Bashar al-Asad's First Ten Years in Power' (July 2010); HRW, 'Group Denial Repression of Kurdish Political and Cultural Rights in Syria 2009' (26 November 2009).

294 Ali K. Akan, 'Turkish Army Announces "Operation Olive Branch" in Afrin' (*Anadolu Agency*, 20 January 2018).

295 Identical letters from the Chargé d'affaires a.i. of the Permanent Mission of Turkey to the UN addressed to the Secretary-General and the President of the SC, S/2018/53, 22 January 2018.

safe and voluntary return of displaced Syrians to their homes of origin.'[296] Both the US[297] and Turkey relied on the same international law framework, although the former supported the Kurds militarily in their fight against ISIS, while the latter tried to eliminate the material underpinning of the Kurds' right to self-determination. Turkey's actions have incontrovertibly led to the mass displacement of people, summary executions tantamount to war crimes, and unlawful attacks, as reported by the OHCHR[298] and Amnesty International.[299]

Since the 2018 invasion, occupied districts have been administered directly by Turkish governors. The Turkish government has established public schools using a curriculum similar to that of the Turkish Ministry of Education, opened branches of the Turkish postal service, built a new regional campus of Turkey's Gaziantep University, and imposed Turkish state symbols in the public space. Turkey and its allies have also weaponised water against the Kurdish regions of northern Syria by cutting and restricting water supplies during the pandemic. Since 2018, ethnic cleansing of Kurds and demographic change through settling many thousands of non-Kurds, including Arab Palestinians, into occupied areas have been steady policies of Turkey in Efrîn, Serê Kaniyê, Tell Halaf, Girê Spî, and elsewhere under Turkish occupation.[300] Cutting down thousands of olive and forest trees has been another heinous violation of Turkish-backed factions.[301] These are just some of the many egregious violations of rights imposed by the Turkish occupation.

Rojavan self-rule is yet to be formally recognised. The Kurds' demand for its recognition has been rejected by Damascus. Syrian state control over the region might yet be restored with Russian support if the Syrian crisis is to be forcefully resolved. The revocation of Rojava self-rule, albeit not unconstitutional, may then encounter Kurdish resistance. The outcome is not predictable, as the level of conceivable oppression or violation of human rights of the Kurds by the Syrian state might or might not lead to the ultimate remedy of secession. Thus, the secession of the West of Kurdistan from Syria does not yet qualify as a last resort measure for the time being.

296 Letter from the Permanent Representative of Turkey to the UN addressed to the President of the SC, 9 October 2019, S/2019/804.

297 Letter from the Permanent Representative of the United States of America to the UN addressed to the Secretary-General. (2014). S/2014/695.

298 OHCHR, Turkey's Syria Offensive Could Spark another Catastrophe, Warn Humanitarians (2019).

299 Amnesty International, 'Syria: Damning Evidence of War Crimes and other Violations by Turkish Forces and their Allies' (2019).

300 See SOHR, 'Palestinian Donations Fund Arab settlement on Kurdish Land in Northern Syria' (SOHR, 3 September 2022), SOHR, 'Ongoing demographic change in Afrin' (SOHR, 10 May 2022) and The Syria Report, 'Palestinian Aid Group Builds Settlement for Displaced Syrians in Afrin' (9 May 2023).

301 Loqman Radpey, 'The Violations of Sovereignty and the Right to Self-Determination in Rojava and Ukraine' (2022) OpinioJuris.

7.7 Summary

Geopolitical mutation at the state-level through separation is rare, but it is fairly simple to carry out. Secession remains an internal matter, and, as Crawford notes, 'if the metropolitan state wishes to oppose the secession by whatever lawful means, other states will stand aside and allow it to do so.'[302] However, international practice is in contravention when secessionist movements have some elements of external intervention, e.g., if they are encouraged by a third state or receive foreign support.

The principle of territorial integrity is peremptory in the relations between states, rather than states vis-à-vis seceding entities as confirmed by the ICJ in Kosovo.[303] Therefore, secession under international law without the consent of the state is not unlawful, as the seceding entity has no duty to honour the territoriality of its mother state. But states do have that duty. In the context of derivation from a dissolving state, as in the case of Yugoslavia, the absence of a claim to territorial integrity by a parent state results in the emergence of new states. Also, the violation of an internationally recognised status by a state, as in the case of autonomy for Eritrea, negates the territorial integrity principle.

Within the basic status of the right of territoriality of states, it cannot be argued that a general limited right to territorial separation of distinct ethnic communities from their host state exists. That is, the international legal system has adopted a conservative stance, nearly a ban, toward the primary right of secession for non-colonial peoples and territories. This standing is the dominant approach to unilateral secession. In any case, positive international law dissuades secession, classifying it as an internal matter. Within this framework, secession is absolutely prohibited, and oppressed peoples must be respectful of existing state boundaries while they are left at the mercy of states prone to violating their rights.

Under specific circumstances, including the threat to the existence or identity of a people, enforcing self-determination in the form of unilateral separation from the responsible state is unavoidable. Most successful secessions have led to the creation of new states only when the pursuit of secession occurred through peaceful means. The international community tends to disfavour secession if the assent of the state involved is lacking. Indeed, the requirements for exercising the qualified right to secession are not met, are disputed, or are not recognised by the international system. This right remains morally justified as, in this case, external self-determination is not an inherent or positive right but a type of reparation. Secession can also be consensual. Currently, an anti-secessionist attitude rules the international community. There is no enunciated vestige of secessionist self-determination in legal instruments about the right to outright secession for oppressed communities, although this topic has strong backing in some legal literature. But the presence of a legitimate right to secession has been acknowledged as accepted under modern international law.

302 James Crawford, 'Response to Experts Reports of the Amicus Curiae' in Anne F. Bayefsky (ed), *Self-Determination in International Law* (KLI 2000) 160–161.

303 *Kosovo* (n 124) [80].

A people possesses the right to a unilateral boundary-alteration when its circumstances reveal a breach of its right to internal self-determination after systematic abuses of its basic human rights. The existence of a qualified right to secessionist self-determination is not disputed when state practice verifies it. It is argued that, under some exceptional situations and at least comparable conditions represented in concrete form by the cases of Bangladesh and Croatia, a minority-people's right to unilateral independence occurs beyond the colonial context. Cases of secession suggest that a right to unilateral secession exists, is recognised, and conceded, only if the total requirements are satisfied. Where the people concerned have tried seriously but fruitlessly to find means of successfully enforcing their right to internal self-determination within that state, the respective people shall have the freedom to exercise it unilaterally, through secession, in their own right to self-determination as the ultimate remedy.

Since 1920, the Kurds have remained unrecognised as minority-peoples, except in the Iraqi constitution. Inspecting the human rights record of their host states shows that the Kurds are arguably, at some points, justified to detach conditionally. The host states contrived a *Staatsvolk* in which they have valorised and dominated their own single ethnicity of Fars, Turk, and Arab, while denying the recognition of Kurds within their boundaries. These systemic disadvantages remain the present reality. Given the doctrine of a qualified right to secession, various legal arguments, taking into account different and appropriate considerations bearing directly on the issue, argue for or against the right of the Kurds to unilateral secession.

Kurds have tried to coexist within the host states' framework, exhausting peaceful efforts while suffering physical insecurity. Their host states have failed to address the Kurds' concerns about self-determination, and, therefore, the Kurds appear to qualify for unilateral secession, as they have exhausted most remedies and realistic political arrangements for the purpose of realising the right of internal self-determination. The legitimacy of states is called into question due to the exclusion of minority groups.[304] This then may trigger their rights to seek external self-determination as in the cases of Kosovar Albanians and the South Sudanese. But the Kurds have been given no legal and peaceful means to withdraw while their host states do not treat them well or equally. The states have been incessant in breaching the Kurds' human rights. If we contemplate the recurrence of one of the two violations (human rights violations and rejection of internal self-determination), it would suffice to confer on them the right to secede as they meet other required criteria for a qualified right to justify the claim to outright secession. In any case, they need the predecessor states to recognise their secessionist units, but the host states are averse to any Kurdish secessionist claims.

Although the consent of the predecessor state has not always been an indispensable condition for the legality of secession, the secessionist movement might need a victory in an armed conflict with the state. The clear denial by Turkey, Iran, and

304 See Micha Germann and Nicholas Sambanis, 'Political Exclusion, Lost Autonomy, and Escalating Conflict over Self-Determination' (2020) 75(1) IO 178.

Syria of proposals for political and territorial autonomy within the context of a federal arrangement indicates that the Kurds cannot pursue practical approaches to the settlement of the dispute. Also, there is no case of recent states' revocation of autonomy arrangements or a diminished degree of territorial self-rule administration or loss of power at the national level. Indeed, these have not been sanctioned since the border changes in the 1920s. Attempts at negotiation and agreement have failed. Also, pursuing secession through an amendment to the states' constitution is not tenable. Therefore, if the Kurds decide to withdraw, the central governments in Iran, Syria, and Turkey could not rely on territorial integrity to impede secession, as the Kurds have exhausted all available mechanisms for settling the dispute.

Recent developments in the Kurds' host states have led to the establishment of Kurdish self-rule *de facto* entities in the South and West of Kurdistan in Iraq and Syria, respectively, while Kurds in the North and East of Kurdistan have not achieved any form of control. Are the Kurdish entities entitled to statehood? Any entity staking a claim to statehood must satisfy international legal requirements to activate this process.

8 Kurdistan Statehood

Many ethnic and national groups desire to found their own nation-states. The birth of states is intricately linked to the right to the external expression of self-determination or 'full self-determination,' which leads to the rare phenomenon of state creation. Internal self-determination is the curtailed determination of the political status of a people. The exercise of external self-determination is not the only process of state formation. Basically, external self-determination is a principle which relates to the right to be a state, and the available probative practice certifies this connection. The secession of an oppressed people to create their own state is crowned as a quintessential goal of the self-determination principle.

Self-determination, statehood, and recognition are inextricably interconnected in state creation. The right to self-determination can have an explanatory or a creative role in state formation (see 8.5.).

8.1 The State

Although the 'state,' in its contemporary form, is a recent phenomenon,[1] as the full or unlimited legal person of international law,[2] it has not been straightforwardly defined. Any effort to define it would be in vain[3] because the issue has not given rise to long-standing disputes. From the perspective of the international legal system, debate about the concepts of sovereignty and government is more prominent.[4] This has led to considerable controversy, for its definition has not been agreed by international authorities.

Since the seventeenth century, depictions of the doctrine of statehood have changed from philosophical and abstract ones to legal ones with political and sociological aspects. The doctrine of the state was never definitively rendered in nineteenth-century international law, as it was something of concern only to existing

1 Jan Klabbers, *International Law* (2nd edn, CUP 2017) 74.

2 David Raič, *Statehood and the Law of Self-Determination* (KLI 2002) 23.

3 ILC Rep, 'Report of the International Law Commission on the Work of Its First Session,' (12 April–9 June 1949), A/925, A/CN.4/13 and Corr., 1–3.

4 James Crawford, *Brownlie's Principles of Public International Law* (8th ed, OUP 2012) 127–128.

DOI: 10.4324/9781003424314-8

states that had the authority to deal with the issue of statehood.[5] Statehood received its steady and current sense in the early twentieth century.[6] In the twentieth century, a state was simply defined as 'a corporate group that has compulsory jurisdiction, exercises continuous organisation, and claims a monopoly of force over a territory and its population, including all actions taking place in its area of jurisdiction.'[7] Thus, force played an important role. In the twentieth century, priority was also given to juridical power. This is seen in the definitions of some international legal scholars such as Ian Brownlie.[8]

With the above in mind, a state has some exclusive and general legal characteristics such as 'equal' status compared with other states. Like them, it can make treaties, control internal affairs, give its consent to international agreements, exercise freedom of action,[9] contribute to custom, make law, and form state practice and *opinio juris*.[10] The Yugoslavia Arbitration Commission in its Opinion No 1 (November 1991) framed a state based on the principles of public international law: 'the State is commonly defined as a community which consists of a territory and a population subject to an organized political authority; that such a State is characterized by sovereignty.'[11] To put it another way, a state is a territorial political authority composed of human beings and institutions in an organised way. It is a real entity that is legally discernible from the people making it up.[12] This entity possesses, as the ICJ held, 'the totality of international rights and duties'[13] and other relations;[14] this is a totality of rights and duties that every state accordingly may claim for itself and take protective action to retain. In sum, a state is a territorially political entity with a full international legal personality (with the attribution of right and duty) or statehood status. Theoretical justifications dominate scholarly debates on territorial state formation.

8.2 Tests of Statehood

Two different underpinnings of the declaratory and the constitutive theories of state or theories of recognition dominate the classic doctrines of statehood. These schools are methods of acquiring statehood known as the effectiveness-only view and the recognition-only view, respectively. The declaratory (*de facto*) doctrine is basically founded on factual attributes or factors of effectiveness of an entity

5 James Crawford, *The Creation of States in International Law* (2nd ed, OUP 2006) 5–6. Also, see Rowan Nicholson, *Statehood and the State-Like in International Law* (OUP 2019) 39–85.

6 Nicholson (n 5) 86–91.

7 Max Weber and A.M. Henderson, *The Theory of Social and Economic Organization* (Free Press 1964) 156.

8 Ian Brownlie, *Principles of Public International Law* (OCP 1979) 73–76.

9 Crawford (n 5) 37.

10 Nicholson (n 5) 102, 105.

11 ACFY, Opinion No 1.

12 Daniel P. O'Connell, *International Law*, vol 1 (S&S 1970) 81.

13 *Reparation for Injuries Suffered in the Service of the UN (Advisory Opinion)* [1949] ICJ Rep 10.

14 See Nicholson (n 5) ch 3.

claiming statehood referred to in the Montevideo Convention: a defined territory, a permanent population, a government, and the capacity to enter into international relations.[15] Thus, if the effectiveness test is passed by an entity or the declaratory view is fulfilled, statehood is automatically acquired with subsequent rights, duties, and other legal relations. Under this theory, effectiveness is necessary while recognition is not necessary and is viewed as 'a political act' or solely symbolic gesture without any effect on the legal aspects of statehood; existing states are free to recognise a newly created entity as a state ('contractual view of statehood'),[16] and their refusal does not change the legal status of the state or its legal claim to statehood. Under this view, a state may recognise a newly created entity as a state despite disqualification under the effectiveness attributes.

On the other side, the constitutive (*de jure*) test of statehood is rather arbitrary in its doctrinal bases.[17] Under this standing, the criterion of recognition is regarded as a constitutive feature of statehood, although it is not a legal theory; statehood cannot be accomplished until other states accord recognition to a state.[18] Under this view, entities claiming statehood do not have statehood relative to non-recognising states, but they are defined as states relative to recognising states. It was applied in special political circumstances during the interwar period as well as earlier, especially in excluding non-European powers and in order to deny the legality of situations raised by the illegal use of force, such as Japan's occupation of Manchuria in 1931 (and the subsequent creation of the state of Manchukuo).[19] This era gave birth to *de facto* recognition as a temporary expedient for hesitant states concerning a newly created state. It was a revocable decision.[20] The legal doctrine mostly supports the declaratory viewpoint; however, reality is with the constituent perspective, as recognition, regardless of its being a political or legal act, explicitly influences the attainment of statehood.[21] That is, it delivers legal effects as respecting the sovereignty of the recognised state.

A third test toward statehood concedes an intermediary position to recognition. It affirms recognition as a political (declaratory) act but not as a statehood characteristic. States have an obligation to accord recognition and the legal label of statehood to an emerged state if it fulfils the effectivity criteria.[22] However, state

15 Edward McWhinney, *Self-Determination of Peoples and Plural-Ethnic States: Secession and State Succession and the Alternative, Federal Option* (MNP 2007) 15.

16 Nicholson (n 5) 118.

17 It is described as 'a family of theories,' of which the strictest one (the 'recognition-only' view of statehood) renders recognition as both necessary and sufficient for statehood. Another theory upholds that effectiveness is necessary, but recognition is, in some way, also necessary for statehood or 'effectiveness-plus-recognition.' ibid 113–114, 123.

18 Milena Sterio, *The Right to Self-Determination under International Law: "Selfistans," Secession and the Rule of the Great Powers* (Routledge 2013) 48.

19 McWhinney (n 15) 16.

20 ibid 21.

21 Sterio (n 18) 48.

22 ibid 49.

practice does not support this view as recognition has been regarded as a discretionary act.[23] Another rule of creating statehood is 'the effectiveness-or-recognition view,' that is, some entities can acquire statehood by effectiveness and others by recognition but no entity can acquire it by both methods, or the same entity can be subject to both rules simultaneously. If entities acquire statehood through this rule, recognition repairs any shortages of the effectivity criteria. Somalia, the Vatican City, Monaco, Palestine, and the recognition of new states in Eastern Europe and in parts of the former Soviet Union in the 1990s are mentioned as examples of this rule.[24] There are limited exceptions to the abovementioned tests that are dealt with in statehood forms. However, effectiveness and recognition play an instrumental role in any entity claiming the right to self-determination for acquiring statehood.

8.3 Self-Determination, Statehood, and Recognition

Under international law, the right to self-determination is separate from the attainment of statehood. However, the right to self-determination is associated with statehood, though not always.[25] External self-determination and statehood are inseparable. When a self-determined entity claims its right to create and to become recognised as a new state, the law of self-determination and the law of statehood interconnect. If the people of the entity seek to implement its external self-determination, the legal inquiry on the qualification of the criteria of statehood might be necessary in the eyes of the international community at the time of state formation.[26] If the people striving for the external self-determination cannot attain statehood due to illegality or illegitimacy, for example, their self-determination is not accomplished, i.e., *ex iniuria ius non oritur* (law would not arise from unlawfulness). In other words, statehood is instrumental in enabling peoples to accomplish their right to external self-determination. Then, the law of statehood is applied in this context, although self-determination is not legally contingent on statehood. However, as will be shown in various forms of state creation, this is not always the case. In reality, statehood appears to be contingent on recognition, even if, according to the Montevideo Convention, '[t]he political existence of the state is independent of recognition by the other states.'[27] In other words, recognition is instrumental and has a bearing on the entity's claim for statehood, whereas meeting the Montevideo Convention requirements has not always resulted in the attribution of statehood. Conversely, non-qualification of the criteria has led to statehood, as in the case of Palestine. Indeed, state creation has become so opaque and political

23 Nicholson (n 5) 125.

24 ibid 128–130.

25 Yaël Ronen, 'Palestine in the ICC: Statehood and the Right to Self-determination in the Absence of Effective Control' (2020) 18(4) JICJ 947. Palestine was a non-member of the UN with observer status in 2012. Also, see Michelle Burgis-Kasthala, 'Over-Stating Palestine's UN Membership Bid? An Ethnographic Study on the Narratives of Statehood' (2014) 25(3) EJIL 677.

26 Sterio (n 18) 46.

27 Art. 3, Convention on the Rights and Duties of States (Montevideo Convention), 26 December 1933.

that presenting a single argument is unlikely. East Timor, Kosovo, South Ossetia, Abkhazia, and South Sudan are recent cases revealing unevenness in the application of the effectiveness criteria of statehood.[28] States can recognise entities that do or do not comply with the four classic criteria of statehood, since recognition is a political act.

The capacity to enter into relations with other states connects to recognition, as the willingness of other states enables the entity claiming statehood to enter into such relations.[29] For this purpose, the entity should be accorded the sovereign label. Thus, insofar as relationships with the recognising state are concerned, recognition is constitutive 'in nature' even if it is a declaration of an already existing fact.[30] By promoting recognition as a legal act, unrecognised entities stand in the position of suspension.

In the 1990s, new states in Europe were created through the exercise of external self-determination and remedial secession. The European Community (EC) introduced guidelines on the recognition of new states. Their recognition hinged on the respect of human rights and the protection of minority rights through granting the right to internal self-determination to peoples and minorities within the territory of entities claiming statehood. The EC accorded external self-determination only in the case of availability of already granted internal self-determination. The new and a few other unusual criteria, such as changing the name of the entity and inserting a provision in the constitution of Macedonia, are neither universal nor considered as part of customary law of statehood.[31] These requirements are considered additional to the Montevideo attributes, suggesting that entities meeting the characteristics are more legitimate and worthy of sovereignty than that of others that do not exhibit these characteristics, especially when an eligible people is accorded the right to exercise their external right to self-determination to establish their sovereign state. A state would possess some important constitutive attributes. In general, throughout the twentieth and twenty-first centuries, the classic requirements of statehood have shaped legal research and court judgements.

8.4 Attributes of a State in International Law

Once a self-determination-seeking entity separates from its parent state and demands recognition as a new state, it must have satisfied customary international law, that is to say, the applicable classic requirements of statehood as depicted in Article 1 of the Montevideo Convention on the Rights and Duties of States (1933). The classical criteria of statehood include 1) a permanent population, 2) a defined territory, 3) a government, and 4) the capacity to enter into relations with

28 Sterio (n 18) 47.

29 ibid 48.

30 Robert Jennings and Arthur Watts KCMG QC (eds), *Oppenheim's International Law*, vol 1 (9th edn, Longman 1996) 133.

31 Sterio (n 18) 45–49.

the other states.[32] The Badinter Arbitration Commission for the Former Yugoslavia describes a state with the same elements in its first Opinion.[33] These are known as traditional constitutive features that must be met before a geographical entity is qualified to be considered an effective territorial entity. The customary law criteria are based on the concept of effectiveness.[34] To the traditional criteria, Crawford added further modern or legal criteria, such as independence, sovereignty, permanence, willingness and ability to observe international law, a certain degree of civilisation, recognition, and compliance with the principle of self-determination.[35] The modern requirements are based on legality (international law). An entity enjoying the factual criteria, as mentioned earlier, can, in theory, stake a claim to statehood since its formation, in Oppenheim's terms, is 'a matter of fact, and not of law.'[36] The individuals making up its population are regarded as the first constitutive characteristic of any entity.

8.4.1 Permanent Population

A collectivity of individuals, as inhabitants, is a necessary element of territorial entities. Deserted territories cannot qualify as states. In Oppenheim's view, the community of individuals 'may belong to different races or creeds, or be of different colour.'[37] Therefore, it may not necessarily be a people in the sense of international law. The constituent populace may consist of more than one people. No minimum quantity of population has been articulated although their presence must be permanent.[38]

Two conditions must be fulfilled for the purpose of permanency. First, the respective territory must be suitable for habitation. Second, the people must have the desire to stay in the territory; moving elsewhere to pursue financial gain is not a matter of statehood. Displaced people or refugees who are expectant to return to their homeland cannot make up a permanent identifiable population. Nonetheless, nomads, as in Somalia, travelling within and outside of the country do not disqualify an entity from its aspirations for statehood; the country will still have permanent individual residents.[39] Despite lacking a permanent population, the Vatican City is recognised as a state due to the special reason of 'the strength and influence of the government' which compensates for the other criteria.[40] Population is both the

32 Art. 1, Montevideo Convention.
33 ACFY, Opinion No 1.
34 Jure Vidmar, *Democratic Statehood in International Law: The Emergence of New States in Post-Cold War Practice* (HP 2013) 39.
35 Crawford (n 5) 37.
36 Oppenheim, quoted in ibid 16.
37 Lassa Francis L. Oppenheim, *International Law: A Treatise*, vol 1 (2nd ed, Longmans 1955) 108 (online).
38 Crawford (n 5) 52.
39 Raič (n 2) 58–59.
40 Nicholson (n 5) 112.

subject of the authority of a state and a beneficiary of its sovereignty. After all, the main purpose for the creation of the state is to further the prosperity and emancipation of the individuals comprising its subjects on a defined territory.[41]

8.4.2 Defined Territory

A state cannot be a state without its people occupying a portion of the earth's surface or an identifiable geographical area. Sovereignty cannot occur without territory. In other words, territory is the basis for exercising governmental powers. As in the case of population, the size of the region is of no concern provided that the sovereign entity possesses a rightful claim[42] and real or effective jurisdictional power over the territory. The territory of a state can be non-contiguous, as East Pakistan (later Bangladesh) demonstrated when it was not physically adjoined to West Pakistan before 1971. Sovereignty exists in various types and measures. Fragmented territory or its small quantity or intensity is not an obstacle to claim statehood. Claims to the territory of an existing or a nascent state do not tarnish the state's identity or existence. The claim could be about the entire territory of a new state or the boundaries of the state. In 1949, the boundaries of Israel were not defined. However, it qualified by reason of the attribute of territory and was admitted to the UN.[43]

The 'sufficient consistency' of territory is enough, as the ICJ holds, 'even though its boundaries have not yet been accurately delimited, and the State actually exercises independent public authority over that territory.'[44] In other words, there is no need for 'fully delimited and defined' or agreed frontiers.[45] The PCIJ had confirmed this proposition in its Advisory Opinion on the *Monastery of Saint Naoum* (*Albanian Frontier* 1924).[46] Also, uncertain boundaries and fluctuating effective control, for example, as the result of substantial military conflicts are not impediments or challenges to statehood as long as they are not of 'a serious nature.'[47] In any case, to avoid the likely infringement of the territorial sovereignty of a state, the border it asserts must be made known to the international community of states. This applies in cases of emerging states.[48] State territory may not be fixed and can

41 Matthew Craven and Rose Parfitt, 'Statehood, Self-Determination and Recognition' in Malcolm Evans (ed), *International Law* (5th ed, OUP 2014) 195.

42 ibid 196.

43 Crawford (n 5) 46–49.

44 *North Sea Continental Shelf (Federal Republic of Germany v. Denmark) (Judgement)* [1969] ICJ Rep 3, [32]. This was reconfirmed in *Deutsche Continental Gas-Gesellschaft v Polish State* [1929] 5 ILR 11, quoted in ibid 50.

45 *Case Concerning the Territorial Dispute (Libyan Arab Jamahiriya/Chad) (Judgement)* [1994] ICJ Rep 6, 22, 26, [44], [52].

46 *Question of the Monastery of Saint-Naoum (Albanian Frontier) (Advisory Opinion)* [1924] PCIJ Rep B09.

47 Higgins, quoted in Crawford (n 5) 51.

48 Raič (n 2) 61–62.

shift over time. An organisation should effectively govern the inhabitants and the territory of a would-be state to maintain a level of order.

8.4.3 Government

An effective government is the main element of statehood. Government, exemplified by the exercise of power in the territory of the state over both its people and territory, is a bedrock of independence. An entity of this type exercises such power or has the right to exercise it in relation to other states. Governing power with respect to territory is territorial sovereignty. The exercise of might or territorial jurisdiction is effectiveness. As all other requirements rely on the government, it should be considered the main attribute of a state. Interstate relations (legislative, executive, or judicial) are based on this authority.[49] The lack of governmental effectiveness may lead to non-recognition of a state, although, as in the case of the Republic of the Congo in 1960, it can also lead to premature or precipitous recognition,[50] i.e., recognition despite the lack of an effective government. Recognition by other states was constitutive of Congo's statehood.[51]

Any entity claiming statehood has some form of government in control of its territory. International law sets out no particular necessities with regard to the nature and scope of this control[52] or its conformity or non-conformity with the right of self-determination of peoples,[53] except that the government must provide 'some degree of maintenance of law and order and the establishment of basic institutions'[54] — that is, stable institutionalised structures (political, administrative, and executive organisations)[55] and unrivalled government. The maintenance of legal order helps to stabilise a factual situation (the respective entity) and the international legal order.[56]

In certain cases, an entity's statehood may be contrary to international law; a new state may be created, or an entity may attempt to detach from an existing state in violation of certain international norms. In such cases, one expects the effectiveness factor, as a legal requirement, to be enforced more stringently on the

49 Crawford (n 5) 55–56.
50 ibid 57.
51 Nicholson (n 5) 174.
52 This changed at the time of the recognition of new states in Eastern Europe and in the Soviet Union (1992) on which new States should 'respect for...the commitments subscribed to in the Final Act of Helsinki and in the Charter of Paris, especially with regard to the rule of law, democracy and human rights.' These documents refer to democracy as the only system of government of European nations. See Vidmar (n 34) 78–155.
53 Raič (n 2) 62.
54 Crawford (n 5) 59. For types of control that counts as law and order, see Craven and Parfitt in Evans (n 41) 203–204.
55 Report of the International Committee of Jurists Entrusted by the Council of the League of Nations with the Task of Giving an Advisory Opinion upon the Legal Aspects of the Aaland Islands Question (Special Supplement, LNOJ 1920–1946) 14.
56 Raič (n 2) 52.

government claiming authority over the territory. Thus, illegality may lead to the non-attribution of statehood status with its legal rights and obligations. Indeed, the entity's actual characteristics are not legally constructed. Unsuccessful secessions, including Biafra, fall into the last category in which entities lack authority or their effectiveness is imperfect. Also, the duration of an effective government in North Korea contributed to its statehood and the recognition of two states: North Korea and South Korea.[57] Therefore, the government in a territory demonstrates the existence of a certain legal status. By and large, effectiveness is a relative or context-dependent prerequisite for statehood, although, of all the classical criteria of statehood, effective government takes the lead. In any case, effectiveness is the power to hold and enforce legal rights and commitments throughout the territory and over the people inhabiting that territory.[58] It then allows for international legal personality. This ability has to be acquired together with consideration of the realities and developments of any situation before international law validates statehood.[59]

To this rule, there can be exceptional circumstances, for example, when a treaty or an exclusive right of external self-determination (as for colonies or in a non-colonial context) is the bedrock of statehood. In the case of decolonisation, however, there is no consistent and universal practice. Despite the supportive role of the right to self-determination, the withdrawal of a colonial power from a colony has not always been followed by automatic recognition of the territory claiming statehood due to competing claims over the territory. In other words, self-determination falls short of fully advancing decolonisation, as it only applies partially and selectively to some colonies. Angola, Timor Leste, and Western Sahara are examples worth mentioning.[60] Any substantial or total lack of effectiveness is cured by means of exercising the right to statehood. Put differently, the law is adapted to specific factual situations. Bangladesh, Croatia, and the former Soviet republics of Georgia and Moldova are factual situations that were recognised as states despite the existence of ineffective governments.[61]

A breach of a peremptory norm (prohibition on the use of force) by India was consequential in realising the effectivity criteria by Bangladesh, but the Pakistani government's forcible denial of the Bengalis' right to self-determination was the decisive pre-condition for making the recognition of Bangladesh legal. In this case, law arose from unlawfulness 'to vindicate self-determination.'[62] In this context, the consideration of effectiveness is discarded or mitigated by reliance on the right to external self-determination and the legal status of statehood is acknowledged. This approach was used by the Office of the Prosecutor of the International Criminal Court (ICC) to recognise Palestinian statehood for a ruling on the Court's territorial

57 Crawford (n 5) 59.
58 Raič (n 2) 50.
59 ibid.
60 Yaël Ronen, *Transition from Illegal Regimes under International Law* (CUP 2011) 55.
61 Raič (n 2) 67, 402–406.
62 Nicholson (n 5) 184.

jurisdiction in Palestine. The pre-trial Chamber affirmed the Prosecutor's view in its decision on 5 February 2021.[63] It seems there are two laws here: the underlying self-determination right as the super norm which then requires specific legal signifiers to be more flexible when classifying facts in a given case.

In other words, traditional international law fails to provide an explanation of these situations. This is a lacuna where politics steps in. This is also the case with unilateral secession if certain conditions have been fulfilled. In this context, a right of secession is a further criterion for the acquisition of statehood. The Republics of Abkhazia, South Ossetia, and the Serb Republic of Bosnia-Herzegovina (i.e., the Republika Srpska, which was supported by Serbia-Montenegro in its exercise of control) are examples of unsuccessful unilateral secession in 1999.[64] These entities did not qualify in terms of a right to secede (i.e., the last resort against serious or persistent injustices), despite meeting the classic criteria of statehood, including governmental effectiveness and independence. In this context, facts (effective control) might be acknowledged but the legal status (of statehood) is denied. Unlike these cases, the Turkish Republic of Northern Cyprus, according to the ECtHR, has no effective overall control over northern Cyprus.[65] Thus, it fails the effectiveness criteria, including independence, as it is Turkey and its military presence that actually run the government. Thus, it is not a state. Moreover, Turkey breached a peremptory norm (prohibition on the use of force) by using force on the territory of Cyprus. Also, Republika Srpska and the Russian annexation of the 'Republic of Crimea'[66] in 2014 and other regions of Ukraine in 2022 by using force fall into this category: law does not arise from unlawfulness.

The continuity of government is the continuity of the state and, as a result, the continuation of conducting internal and international relations which may encourage reinforcement of the status and recognition by the international community. On its negative side, a persistent shortfall of governmental effectiveness disqualifies the territory from being a state — especially in the case of a newly established state, if statehood is not the result of the unlawful conduct of a third state. In another situation, the new state may become extinct.[67] This is not the case with already established states, even in the situation of temporary or prolonged grossly ineffective government. The prolonged period of ineffective government resulting from civil wars in Syria and Yemen has not led to the extinction of the international personality of these states. This is the case with the occupation of a part of the state as well. On occasions, civil unrest has led to a failed state, as in the case of Somalia, Somalia has legally survived and preserved its international personality, although it failed the criteria of effectiveness for almost two years. International law favours

63 *Decision on the 'Prosecution Request Pursuant to Article 19(3) for a Ruling on the Court's Territorial Jurisdiction in Palestine'* (*Pre-Trial Chamber*) [2021] ICC Rep. Also, see Ronen, 'Palestine' (n 25).

64 UNSC Res 1255 (30 Jul 1999); UNSC Res 1287 (31 Jan 2000).

65 *Cyprus v Turkey* (2002) 35 EHRR 30, [77].

66 UNGA Res 68/262 (27 March 2014).

67 Crawford (n 5) 60–61.

the presumption of the continuity of states' international personality in the absence of a successor, dramatic changes of government, or if there is still a way forward with the incumbent state.[68] Only newly created and not fully established states are subject to the requirements of statehood.[69] However, there are states which ceased to exist after their creation without the withdrawal of recognition through consent or dissolution, as in the cases of Yugoslavia and Czechoslovakia. In the case of Somalia, 'recognition becomes a much more useful guide' than the effectiveness criteria and their application.[70] The exclusive right to govern the territory should be exercised without interference by any external state; this is implicit in the capacity of a new state to initiate relations with other states.

8.4.4 Capacity to Enter into Relations with Other States

A state, as an original foundation, must prove that it is basically independent. A vital proof of independence is to evince that the aspiring entity has the capacity to enter into relations with other states, for example through diplomatic agreements facilitating interstate interaction, trade agreements enabling interstate commerce, etc. Engaging in relations with other states is not an international obligation but, rather, a voluntary act.[71] If any state is not willing to enter into relation with the entity claiming statehood, the respective state 'merely denies an entity the *opportunity* to enter into relations.'[72] But, the capacity to establish ties with other existing states is crucial.[73] This capacity is not a criterion for statehood; rather, it is a variable result predicated on the respective situations of the entities involved. It is partially contingent on the power of the territory's government to fulfil its international commitments. It also depends, in part, on the entity itself, as the purpose of conducting and having responsibility for foreign affairs is that it must be independent of any other state. In other terms, the competence to have relations with other subjects of international law is 'a conflation' of government and independence.[74] It, thus, does not necessarily entail recognition by other states.[75] This competence has been extended to international organisations and federal constituents of federations. Non-state actors or *de facto* unions have also sought out that capacity although not on an equal footing with states. The Rojava self-rule is an example worthy of mention. However, this does not imply their achievement of statehood. Only an independent state can demonstrate that it has such a capacity.

68 Raič (n 2) 71–72.
69 Robert McCorquodale, 'The Creation and Recognition of States' in Samuel K.N. Blay and others (eds), *Public International Law: An Australian Perspective* (OUP 2005) 192.
70 Nicholson (n 5) 112–113.
71 Vidmar (n 34) 41.
72 Talmon, quoted in Nicholson (n 5) 126.
73 Raič (n 2) 73.
74 Crawford (n 5) 61–62.
75 Nicholson (n 5) 127.

8.4.5 Independence

As the central criterion for statehood, the exercise of independence means the ability to act as the sole governmental authority, i.e., manifesting 'the exclusive competence of the State' regarding the affairs of its territory, as the Permanent Court of Arbitration (PCA) noted in the *Island of Palmas Case*.[76] Effectiveness is a norm to accord entities statehood, but the effectiveness criteria do not encompass 'prior possession of the right to exclusive jurisdiction' and 'prior possession of *any* right or duty.'[77] If an entity is not independent, it is regarded as an inseparable segment of a state. Alternatively, a partially independent entity, in some instances, may become an agent of another state for certain purposes.

Independence has different meanings in different contexts. In the context of secession from an existing state, 'substantial independence' is required as an initial requirement for statehood — otherwise, it will not be considered a 'definitively created' state.[78] For an existing state, e.g., one undergoing civil war, an inability to exercise authority over a substantial amount of time is trivial, as international law protects its sovereignty.

Classically, independence is the existence of a separate state which is not subject to the authority of any other state or group of states. In other words, a state has authority insofar as it possesses uncontested sovereignty or governmental competence. Likewise, the respective state is not the enlarged scope of action of another sovereign state. That is, an independent state is not under the legal authority of another state, and no superior state can legally impose its will on an inferior or subject state.[79] Two scenarios are possible here. First, an entity, while not formally independent, has considerable genuine independence in regard to its domestic and foreign relations. Second, an entity, though officially independent, may, in reality, be a puppet in the hands of another state so that its independence is 'nugatory or meaningless.'[80] Therefore, 'formal' (or nominal) and 'actual' independence are discernible.

If the powers of a government over territory are conferred upon the separate authorities of the state, that state is formally independent. Formal independence is a fact, not a right. It is referred to as legal independence, implying being subject to international law but 'not to the laws of any other State.'[81] In this regard, the incumbent constitution or any other legislation may distribute powers to other state agencies, such as defence and a department or ministry of the interior. These powers can also be granted to an agency or individual by the previous sovereign. The power can be trammelled by the constitution. A coup or revolution can also

76 *Island of Palmas Case (Netherlands vs USA)* (1928) PCA, 2 RIAA 829, [838].
77 Nicholson (n 5) 96.
78 Crawford (n 5) 61–62.
79 *Customs Regime between Germany and Austria (Individual Opinion of Judge Anzilotti)* [1931] PCIJ Rep Ser A/B no 41, 81–84.
80 Crawford (n 5) 66.
81 Talmon, quoted in Nicholson (n 5) 96.

discontinue the independence of a state. Some developments do not derogate from the formal independence of the states, such as constitutions, coups or revolutions, military bases or other territorial concessions, the exercise of governmental competence on the bedrock of agency, possession of joint organs for certain purposes, or membership of international organisations possessing coercive authority. On the other hand, the existence of a particular claim of the right to exercise governmental authority over the putative state and discretionary authority to intervene in the internal affairs of the putative state do derogate from formal independence.[82] However, the criterion of independence does not mean the freeing of a state from any outside interference.[83] This would be an unlikely outcome in the modern legal system. Also, it does not deny the exertion of political pressure on another state to achieve a political or economic objective — for example, manipulation in the price of oil in energy markets.

If formal independence persists, actual or genuine independence is in question. It is gradable or quantitative. Actual independence amounts to the governmental authority at its most basic level of a state that needs to be classified as 'independent.' This degree is minimal and factual.[84] Factors such as diminutive size and resources, political alliances, policy orientation between states, belligerent occupation, and illegal intervention do not detract from actual independence. Nevertheless, substantial illegality of origin, entities formed under belligerent occupation — e.g., the Japanese invasion of the Chinese provinces of Manchuria[85] — and substantial external control of the state (protected states, puppet states, and governments as in the case of the South African Bantustans, purported grants of colonial independence) clearly derogate from actual independence.[86] An actual independent state is 'its own'[87] and is held accountable and liable for its actions under international law.

Formal and actual independence are related. The coexistence of these concepts is not an issue. However, an entity is not regarded as a state if its formal independence or its internationally recognised status veils the absence of actual independence. This connection is more complicated where an entity is not found to have formal independence yet enjoys substantial *de facto* independence. Taiwan is an example of this situation. Here, a few scenarios are possible. First, for the purposes of international law, an entity should basically be treated as a state if it exists as a separate territory and has a certain degree of real authority over its territory. Rojava could be a good example of this scenario. Second, if an entity has formal independence, and its original creation was neither dubious nor illegal, independence ought to be assumed for reasons of statehood. Nevertheless, independence is not presumed if the entity is created out of serious illegality, or a new system is established in occupied territory by or under the auspices of the occupant. Here,

82 Crawford (n 5) 67–71.
83 Raič (n 2) 75.
84 Nicholson (n 5) 96.
85 '[T]he sovereignty over Manchuria belongs to China.' League of Nations Res (24 February 1932).
86 Crawford (n 5) 72–87.
87 Raič (n 2) 78.

the entity may or may not be formally independent. Third, the statehood of extant states is not tainted, even though they may lose actual power for a long time. This is a solid assumption. Fourth, when the former metropolitan state concedes full formal independence to a territorial unit, independence is assumed for the entity.[88] A formal and actual independent entity is qualified to be a state. The sovereignty of such an entity can hardly be disputed.

8.4.6 Sovereignty

Sovereignty is a distinct feature of states and is inseparable from statehood.[89] It is sometimes substituted for independence in the context of statehood.[90] Nevertheless, sovereignty is 'an incident or consequence of statehood, namely, the plenary competence that States prima facie possess,' while independence is a pre-condition or requirement for achieving statehood. Consequently, sovereignty is 'plenary authority' with respect to internal and foreign affairs,[91] that is, internal (law-making and law-enforcing authority) and external sovereignty. Independence denotes sovereignty in relations between states, as the PCA held.[92] In other words, it is a capacity to enjoy rights and to be bound to and to bind other states to international obligations.

In the *Corfu Channel* case, Judge Alvarez, in his individual opinion, defined sovereignty as 'the whole body of rules and attributes which a state possesses in its territory, to the exclusion of all other states, and also in its relations with other states.'[93] In other words, sovereignty refers to the totality of competencies or full personality, which is granted by international law.[94] Sovereignty has also another meaning, in Judge Anzilotti's perspective: *suprema potestas* or highest authorities.[95] Though limited by international law, this interpretation holds that no supreme authority supersedes others or gives them total competence.[96] Thus, it is also different from government. In the international legal system, states are equal and autonomous, but nothing in the system is endowed with legal systemic supremacy.[97] It follows that sovereign entities are subjects that possess full international legal personality or have acquired statehood. State sovereignty can sometimes, in practice, be undermined as a result of a civil revolt, such as in the case of Syria.

88 Crawford (n 5) 88–89.
89 Raič (n 2) 19, 25.
90 ibid 75.
91 Crawford (n 5) 89.
92 *Island of Palmas* (n 76) 838.
93 *Corfu Channel (United Kingdom of Great Britain and Northern Ireland v. Albania) (Separate Opinion of Judge Alvarez)* [1949] ICJ Rep 39, 43.
94 Raič (n 2) 25–26.
95 Judge Anzilotti (n 79).
96 See Antony Anghie, 'Rethinking Sovereignty in International Law' (2009) 5(1) ARRLSS 291.
97 Raič (n 2) 26.

There are recorded instances in which entities have not achieved statehood status despite satisfying the abovementioned traditional requirements of statehood. The effectiveness normally does not by itself justify statehood with its subsequent rights or give *de facto* situations a legal status. The reason may be sought in a series of recent negative cases, e.g., the South African Bantustans, in which statehood was rejected by the international community of states due to non-entitlement to statehood or so-called illegality.[98] In other words, the customary criteria of statehood are sometimes inadequate. This occurs when an entity claiming statehood is located within the boundaries of an already established state but does have a qualified right to be a state. That is, law does not arise from unlawfulness.

Crawford's modern criteria, such as 'permanence (continuance of the requirements of statehood),' 'willingness and ability to observe international law,' 'a certain degree of civilisation,' 'recognition,' and 'legal order' (of government), are useful and necessary for statehood.[99] He argues that this list has been updated by attributes of 'a political or moral character,' including in accordance with the principle of self-determination, not by use of force in violation of Article 2(4) of the UN Charter, and not in the pursuance of racist policies.[100] It is submitted that these are not founded on effectiveness but on the legality of the procedure through which a state is formed. The British colony of Southern Rhodesia,[101] the Bantustan territories (South Africa),[102] and Northern Cyprus[103] are instances in which the original creation of a state was substantially illegal. Their illegality or deviation from international rules certainly led to the non-attribution of statehood. Bantustans, created in violation of the prohibition of racial discrimination, were also present in South West Africa, which later gained independence as Namibia. The ICJ dealt with it in a landmark case.[104]

Unlike the context in which a non-effective entity with entitlement to the right to self-determination attains statehood, the law in these cases is not adjusted to a factual situation. Simply put, illegality or nullity rules out the existence of a factual situation. Therefore, legality is considered a constitutive requirement of state formation.[105] Satisfying the customary criteria for statehood upgrades the situation of a geographical area to an effective *de facto* entity without legal effect. If it is

98 Vidmar (n 34) 39, 61.

99 See Crawford (n 5) 90–95.

100 David J. Harris and Sandesh Sivakumaran, *Cases and Materials on International Law* (S&M 2015) 88. Also see, Blay and others (n 69) 191.

101 UNSC Res 202 (6 May 1965); UNSC Res 216 (12 November 1965); SC Res 217 (20 November 1965); UNSC Res 221 (9 April 1966); UNSC Res 232 (16 December 1966); UNSC Res 424 (17 March 1978).

102 UNSC Res 181 (7 August 1963); UNGA Res 1899(XVIII) (13 November 1963); UNSC Res 418 (4 November 1977).

103 UNSC Res 541 (18 Nov 1983); UNSC Res 550 (11 May 1984).

104 *Legal Consequences for States of the Continued Presence of South Africa in Namibia (South West Africa) notwithstanding Security Council Resolution 276 (1970)* (*Advisory Opinion*) [1971] ICJ Rep.

105 Raič (n 2) 153.

legally formed, that is, its establishment is not followed or is not the result of an infringement of any basic rules of international law, then international law invests it with legal personality; hence, the entity is recognised as a state. Modern criteria are classified as the obligations to respect grassroots rules of international law.[106] These norms are of a *jus cogens* character.[107] Among them, for the purpose of state creation, are the violation of the right of self-determination of peoples (in the colonial context at least) and the prohibition of aggression[108] and systematic racial discrimination, including the prohibition of Apartheid.[109] The modern qualifications are derived from recent state and UN practice and were originally developed in other fields of international law.[110]

Under the law of statehood, entities claiming statehood must satisfy both sufficient (effectiveness) and necessary (legality-based) criteria[111] because customary law cannot establish whether an entity is a state objectively.[112] The rationale behind the additional criteria of statehood, therefore, is applied if the creation of an effective entity is linked to territorial illegality. The cases of Southern Rhodesia, the South African Bantustans, and Northern Cyprus are specific cases on which this rationale is based. In the non-colonial context or the post-Cold War epoch, the territorial status quo of metropolitan states is a barrier that entities must face despite meeting both categories of statehood criteria. Indeed, the principle of territorial integrity is delineated as 'oneness' or 'wholeness' of the state in terms of its territory,[113] effectively meaning the non-applicability of the right to independence. That hurdle is reversible through consent of the metropolitan state or international engagement. State establishment in contemporary international law does not represent a fulfilment of conventional or additional statehood requirements but, instead, a resolving or waiving of territorial borders. The practice of post-Cold War state creation confirms this. Therefore, the achievement of statehood can be acquired through different forms of state creation. Statehood generally depends on the realisation of the Montevideo criteria, but some cases depart from those requirements. Despite falling short of fulfilling all the criteria, statehood has been recognised where a right to self-determination existed. Also, in some cases, additional criteria were added to the Montevideo standards albeit without establishing a rule of customary international law.

106 ibid 153–154.
107 *Accordance with International Law of the Unilateral Declaration of Independence in Respect of Kosovo (Advisory Opinion)* [2010] ICJ Rep, [122]. The ICJ 'does not link the illegality of a state creation exclusively to *jus cogens*.' Vidmar (n 34) 42.
108 See Art. 11 of the 1933 Montevideo Convention; Art. 17 of the Bogotá Charter; UNGA Res 2625(XXV); UNGA Res 3314(XXIX) (14 December 1974), and Principle IV of the CSCE Helsinki Final Act.
109 Raič (n 2) 156.
110 Blay and others (n 69) 191.
111 Martin Dixon, Robert McCorquodale, and Sarah Williams, *Cases and Materials in International Law* (OUP 2017) 144.
112 Vidmar (n 34) 61.
113 Samuel K.N. Blay, *Territorial Integrity and Political Independence* (MPEPIL updated 2010) [1].

8.5 Statehood Models Achieved via Self-Determination

As was clarified heretofore, statehood is directly linked to external self-determination. In modern cases and with the extension of the right of self-determination beyond the colonial context, self-determination has been applied peripherally in various situations concerned with statehood; it is pressed into service so as to enhance the effectiveness of the territorial unit. In other words, the right to self-determination has been, on occasion, creative of statehood or has played an explanatory role in state creation. Also, the principle operates to create a local unit — for example,[114] to avert its exercise by other units which are usually larger, such as in the case of the Bantustans in South Africa. In situations where the metropolitan state prevents a self-determination unit by force from seceding, the principle of self-determination reinforces secession. Also, there is a situation in which self-determination would stunt the creation of a state if the entity were created by infringing self-determination, notwithstanding the effectiveness of its government.[115]

Southern Rhodesia, as a non-self-governing territory under Chapter XI, is an example, in which an 'illegal racist' white minority regime[116] declared independence in November 1965[117] in 'a systematic denial [of the black majority] in its territory of certain civil and political rights, including in particular the right of every citizen to participate in the government of his country.'[118] In other words, Rhodesia's 'structure' was not in congruence with the right or principle of self-determination in some looser sense that did not as such constitute a violation of the duty to honour external self-determination.[119] To attribute responsibility to Rhodesia for acts of aggression on Zambia and other infringements of international law,[120] some regard Rhodesia as a *de facto* entity or regime. But for these acts, Rhodesia should be a state — under the effectiveness norm — yet it was not recognised due to its 'racially discriminatory structure' or its suppression of the achievement of external self-determination and its impingement of Zambia's territoriality.[121]

Non-entitlement to the right of external self-determination is the reason behind the non-acquisition of statehood or denial of their claim to statehood by the

114 Jan Smuts described establishing separate native institutions as 'separate representation' and 'development' to exercise equal political rights. This 'territorial segregation' was adopted in South Africa (1948) in the Cape Colony. To Smuts, this is not a violation of self-determination, but its realisation by a backward people of differing capacity. Jan C. Smuts, 'Native Policy in Africa' (1930) 29(115) JRAS 248, 261, 264, 265.

115 Crawford (n 5) 128–129.

116 UNSC Res 216(1965) (12 November 1965) [2].

117 For Rhodesia, see Albert J. Coetzee, *The Sovereignty of Rhodesia and the Law of Nations* (TP 1970).

118 Citing the Universal Declaration, the Colonial Declaration and UNGA Res 648(VII) (10 December 1952). James E.S. Fawcett, 'Security Council Resolutions on Rhodesia' (1965-1966) 41 BYBIL 103.

119 Nicholson (n 5) 176.

120 UNSC Res 455 (23 November 1979).

121 Nicholson (n 5) 179–180.

effective *de facto* entities of the republics of Abkhazia, Serbian Krajina, Anjouan, and Bougainville. This occurred, although each of these republics met the classic criteria of statehood and did not infringe *jus cogens* rules. They did not meet the required criteria for a qualified right to external self-determination and independence. The recent successful cases of Kosovo and South Sudan indicate the crucial role of the right to (external) self-determination both in the process of state formation and the legality of statehood.

There are several ways by which a modern nation-state is created. If there is a correlation between ethnic groups and states — that is, if political and cultural boundaries coincide — the outcome of the political expression of the peoples concerned is a nation-state. The outgrowth is, thus, a combination of cultural (nation) and political (state) units.[122] Numerous states hitherto have emerged, through implementing decolonisation and exploiting the dissolution of metropolitan states in the post-colonial time, and some have used the process of secession (Chapter 7), either violently or peacefully. The discussion of statehood incarnations cannot depart from the classical or effectiveness criteria of state formation. In some cases, nonetheless, they are inadequate to justify the attainment of statehood by a self-determination entity. The independence of former colonies comprises the first context of implementing self-determination after this process was consolidated as a legal right in 1966. Decolonisation is not directly relevant to Kurdistan. However, the Kurds are fragmented among decolonised states. Thus, how their host states achieved statehood is of relevance.

8.5.1 Decolonisation

Former colonies exercised their right to self-determination and, consequently, achieved statehood after WWII. The right of peoples to decolonisation is an 'axiomatic' principle in natural law based on which seizing overseas territories and colonising them is illegitimate and not only prohibited by law but, according to a UNGA resolution, also 'a crime.'[123]

The right to self-determination has been recognised in international law for colonies which is known as decolonisation. It, in principle, is a matter of 'justice' in which a legislative majority has no role, although, in a small number of cases, a majority vote in a plebiscite played a confirmatory role in achieving independence.[124] Justification for exercising self-determination was based on overturning past illegalities such as '[being] subject to exploitation and unjust domination,'

122 Alfred Cobban, *The Nation State and National Self-Determination* (rev. and ed., Crowell 1970) 35.
123 Art. 1, UNGA Res 2621(XXV) (10 October 1970).
124 Jörg Fisch, *The Right of Self-Determination of Peoples: The Domestication of an Illusion* (CUP 2015) 54, 206.

'serious injustices,'[125] 'alien subjugation, domination and exploitation,'[126] 'colonial domination and foreign occupation,'[127] and 'colonial domination and alien occupation and against racist régimes.'[128] Later, the 1970 Friendly Relations Declaration declared tacitly illegal any logic of colonial rule and unequal domination.

The criteria for decolonisation are based on the principle of *uti possidetis*, for both the first (1776–1826) and second (1945–1989) eras of decolonisation,[129] which was also countenanced by the ICJ in the cases of *Frontier Dispute* (Burkina Faso/Republic of Mali) of 1986[130] and the *Chagos Archipelago* of 2019.[131]

Standards concerning self-determination of colonial territories are:

1) All peoples of non-self-governing territories have the right to self-determination, i.e., they can 'freely determine their political status and freely pursue their economic, social and cultural development.'[132]
2) This right subsumes the external expression of self-determination, i.e., complete independence and freedom.
3) The provision of Paragraph 6 of Resolution 1514(XV) denies the right to ethnic minorities within colonial territories, as any alteration of colonial boundaries 'is incompatible with the purposes and principles of the Charter of the United Nations.' In other words, territorial integrity and *uti possidetis* prevail over self-determination, which has led to many current problems in different corners of the world. The upshot of establishing self-determination must be a single (territorial) 'self,' to preserve the colonial borders.
4) Based on the Principle VI of Resolution 1541(XV), the final resultant of exercising self-determination by colonial peoples can take three forms: a) sovereign independent state, b) association with an independent state, or c) integration into an independent state.

By abandoning the sovereignty of colonisers over colonial territories, the first form is realised. However, the other two forms can be accomplished through free and voluntary choice, democratic means, and constitutional processes. For integration, this process should be activated 'with full knowledge of the change in their status, their wishes having been expressed through informed and democratic processes, impartially conducted and based on universal adult suffrage.'[133]

125 Allen Buchanan, *Justice, Legitimacy, and Self-Determination: Moral Foundations for International Law* (OUP 2007) 339.

126 Declaration on the Occasion of the 50th Anniversary of the UN, UNGA Res 50/6 (9 November 1995) and Vienna Declaration and Programme of Action (25 June 1993).

127 UNGA Res 55/2 (18 September 2000).

128 Art. 1(4) of the Additional Protocol I of 1977 to the 1949 Geneva Conventions.

129 Fisch (n 124) 206.

130 *Frontier Dispute (Burkina Faso v. Republic of Mali) (Judgements)* [1986] ICJ Rep.

131 *The Chagos Archipelago (Advisory Opinion)* [2019] ICJ Rep.

132 UNGA Res 1514(XV) (14 December 1960) [2].

133 Principle IX(b). UNGA Res 1541(XV) (15 December 1960).

Statehood attributes of decolonisation are a point of departure from the Montevideo criteria. In the absence of a permanent population, a relatively known territory, effective government, and independence, an entity is not validated as a state. Nevertheless, this is irrelevant to decolonisation as non-fulfilment of effectiveness criteria does not bar the acquisition and validation of statehood. Governmental effectiveness is of the utmost importance, and its lack ends in the non-existence of an entity. The serious absence of effective jurisdiction over the vast majority of the population or the lack of actual exercise of authority over territory is compensated for by the applicable and highly acknowledged or categorical right to external self-determination as *jus cogens* in the context of decolonisation. Namely, the inhabitants of colonial territories have the qualified right to external self-determination and independence in the colonial context. Indeed, the colonial power's illegal act results in the absence of any actual exercise of authority or governmental powers; colonisation clearly prevents a colonial people from exercising self-determination. Colonisation was not illegal at the time, but its continuation in the post-1945 era became illegal once the prohibition against conquest and foreign rule emerged.[134]

As per Resolution 1541(XV), colonial peoples, holders of the right, and territories were entitled to determine their political status by establishing an independent state, as they were considered to be valid self-determination units. This stand is tenable in granting independence to most colonies. The legal right to external self-determination is the rationale for the exclusive right to exercise control over the territory (effectiveness) by a representative government following a declaration of independence. Algeria, Guinea-Bissau, Angola, and Congo exemplify this situation. In many colonial territories, the transfer of sovereignty to colonies or their recognition by colonial powers does not take place, as many colonies acquired statehood before the powers in charge of their administration acknowledged their independence.[135]

Briefly put, if an exclusive right to exercise authority is based on a treaty provision or another rule of international law, the lack of the exercise of actual control does not withhold an entity from forming a state. In this context, the entitlement to exercise authority through implementing external self-determination cures and overrides the shortfall of effectiveness, and statehood is created even if the administering state refuses the implementation of the right to external self-determination. By denying a people's right to external self-determination and refusing the establishment of a representative government of that people, the administering state loses its right to territorial integrity as per the Principles of Friendly Relations Declaration. The recognition norm can also operate in this context. There is room for dissolution of multinational states, especially if nations and ethnic groups are denied their right to self-determination. This is not imminent for the Kurds' host states, but going forward, it could not be ruled out.

134 Raič (n 2) 95.
135 ibid 96–103.

8.5.2 Dissolution

Self-determination outside the decolonisation paradigm has been contentious; nevertheless, the development of the theory of self-determination during the twentieth and twenty-first centuries has led to a new form of the formation of states — dissolution — prominent in the 1990s in Eastern Europe. In this passage, the parent state is dissolved totally followed by the emergence of multiple new or successor ones. This fundamental departure from the traditional Western position on self-determination has encouraged many ethnic groups to exercise self-determination within one section of a state's territory to create their own state. Nonetheless, the exact parameters of self-determination have remained unclear. Dissolution is not only another context of departure from classic attributes of statehood but also creative of new guidelines for achieving statehood. In this context, the international law of statehood has been inconsistently applied for entities claiming statehood. There are two special cases of the consensual or contested dissolution processes in international law: the Soviet Union and the Socialist Federal Republic of Yugoslavia and (though still controversial).

8.5.2.1 The Soviet Union

The USSR was administered ethno-territorially as a federal unitary state resulting from applying the Bolsheviks' view of national self-determination to put an end to imperial Russia's oppression of indigenous and bordering nations.[136] Despite the application of strictly centralised rule over the republics, the mere facts of inter-republican economic relations and constitutional endorsement of self-determination paved the way for peripheral ethnic groups to promote their aspirations.[137]

In 1918, the Russian Soviet Federated Socialist Republic recognised the sovereignty of Lithuania, Latvia, and Estonia. In 1921, the three Baltic republics joined the post-war League of Nations. In 1940, early in WWII, the Soviet government annexed them pursuant to the secret Molotov-Ribbentrop Accords concluded just prior to the outbreak of war in 1939. Despite wartime and immediate post-war summit meetings which the USSR claimed were tantamount to *de jure* recognition, the Allied Powers and numerous UN and international organisations never recognised the 1940 annexation. Ultimately, beginning in 1989, Soviet occupation forces withdrew from each of the states in question, and the USSR acknowledged the restoration of their sovereignty. In 1990 and 1991, the Baltic States declared independence based on the illegality of the secret Molotov-Ribbentrop pact of 1939 and the illegitimate occupation of their lands in 1940. They refrained from referring to the right to self-determination under international law. In their view, their *de jure* sovereignty must have carried on their exercise of external self-determination as peoples subject to foreign occupation. These states also refrained from the right

136 Thomas D. Musgrave, *Self-Determination and National Minorities* (OUP 2000) 38.
137 Veljko Vujačić, *Nationalism, Myth, and the State in Russia and Serbia* (CUP 2015) 10.

to escape the procedures for secession of a republic prescribed in a Soviet law of 1990. By virtue of that law, two-thirds of the respective republic's population had to approve secession. The appreciable Russian minorities within these states and the improbable results of hypothetical referendums persuaded the states to eschew the formal procedures of self-determination.[138]

Lithuania, Estonia, and Latvia promulgated their unilateral independence and statehood on 11 March 1990, 20 August 1991, and 21 August 1991, respectively. The Soviet Union recognised their independence on 6 September 1991. Six days later, their admission to the UN was recommended by the (UNSC. Prior consent and recognition on the part of the metropolitan state were significant and effective in the eventual recognition by the Member States of the UN. Nevertheless, their applications for recognition had been delayed. As their independence was 'suppressed,'[139] they had the right to self-determination and could have exercised it if they had chosen to do so. The implosion of the Soviet Union in the early 1990s led to the creation of 15 new states. Twelve Soviet republics declared independence after the Baltic republics. While the Baltic republics were eligible under international law to exert their right to self-determination and recuperate their interwar independence, other republics relied on the Soviet constitution to do the same.

Based on Article 72 of the Soviet Constitution (1977), the Union republics had 'the right freely to secede from the USSR.' This right was also recognised in the constitutions of 1924 (Article 4) and 1936 (Article 17). Having no precedents in applying this article, a new law was passed to hold a referendum on secession by the republics. It was 'the first' detailed procedure on how to implement the process of secession in a national constitution. The law had no chance of being applied, since the abrupt collapse of the Soviet system led to the *de facto* independence of the republics outside of municipal law.[140] Nonetheless, the republics held referendums for secession but not on the basis of Article 72. They took advantage of 'a fair and widely used application' of self-determination[141] through referendums to legitimise their breaking away.

The EC legitimised the breakup of the Soviet Union in December 1991 based on self-determination by publishing the Declaration on the Guidelines on the Recognition of New States in Eastern Europe and the Soviet Union on 16 December 1991 (hereinafter EC Guidelines). This document referred to 'the principles of the Helsinki Act and the Charter of Paris, in particular, the principle of self-determination' to accede their commitment 'in particular [to] the principle of self-determination.'[142] The Paris Charter (November 1990) 'reaffirm[s] the equal rights of peoples and their right to self-determination in conformity with the Charter of the United Nations and with relevant norms of international law, including those

138 Antonio Cassese, *Self-Determination of Peoples: A Legal Reappraisal* (CUP 1995) 258–268.
139 ibid 262–263; Crawford (n 5) 394.
140 Cassese (n 138) 264–266.
141 ibid 266.
142 Declaration on the Guidelines on the Recognition of New States in Eastern Europe and in the Soviet Union (16 December 1991).

relating to territorial integrity of States.'[143] The Community (of 12 members) justified 'the progressive' dissolution of the Soviet Union as 'a realization of the political principle of self-determination,' by which a 'people should freely choose its international political status.'[144] The recognition of those new states was preconditioned upon observing the 'rule of law, democracy and human rights,' as well as guaranteeing the rights of 'ethnic and national groups and minorities.'[145] Simply put, the external aspects of self-determination and their statehood would be recognised only if the republics 'fully' respected the principle of 'representative democracy,' i.e., 'internal self-determination.'[146] The super-sovereign states, thus, imposed a 'novel theory of recognition' on nascent states.[147] But this requirement was not applied in later diplomatic relations between these new states and the EU, and it did not affect their status at the UN.

The Russian Federation recognised the independence of 11 states of the former Soviet Union, as a continuing personality of the Soviet Union. Later, most of them were admitted into the UN in March and May 1992 without dissent.[148] Belarus and Ukraine were already founding Members of the UN.

8.5.2.2 The Socialist Federal Republic of Yugoslavia

As of 1990, the SFRY was a federal state consisting of six republics (Bosnia-Herzegovina, Croatia, Macedonia, Montenegro, Serbia, and Slovenia) and two autonomous provinces (Kosovo and Vojvodina). Later, the republic of Bosnia and Herzegovina, composed of Serbs, Croats, and Bosnian Muslims, was created.[149] Following the breakup of the central government of the SFRY, Croatia, Bosnia and Herzegovina, Macedonia, and Slovenia separated from the SFRY. The Federal Republic of Yugoslavia (FRY) as the successor of the SFRY was created by the merger of Vojvodina and Kosovo, Montenegro, and Serbia. While the international community dwelled on the dissolution of the SFRY or the secession of Bosnia and Herzegovina (15 October 1991), Croatia (25 June 1991),[150] Macedonia (17 November 1991),[151] and Slovenia (25 June 1991)[152] following their referendums, Montenegro and Serbia perceived it as secession, and other entities espoused dissolution.[153] The Yugoslav constitution did not clarify whether the right to self-determination belonged to republics or peoples. It was

143 Charter of Paris for a New Europe (21 November 1990).
144 Cassese (n 138) 267.
145 Guidelines on New States (n 142).
146 Cassese (n 138) 268.
147 Sterio (n 18) 39.
148 Crawford (n 5) 395.
149 Vujačić (n 137) 10–12.
150 The referendum was held in May 1991. It was suspended on 7 July, but was confirmed on 8 October.
151 The referendum was held in September 1991. It declared its association 'within…Yugoslav states.'
152 The same day as Croatia. The referendum was held in December 1990.
153 Sterio (n 18) 32–33; Crawford (n 5) 396.

not clear-cut whether national groups outside of their prospective republics had the right to self-determination. For example, could Serbs from Croatia vote only for or against Croatia's independence, or could they vote in their own referendum for an autonomous entity of their own or secession from Croatia?

Following the International Conference on the Former Yugoslavia (ICFY) on 27 August 1991, the EC established the Badinter Arbitration Commission of experts in August 1991 to clarify whether Yugoslavia was in the process of dissolution or secession. In its Opinion No 1 (29 November 1991), the Arbitration Commission concluded that the former Yugoslavia was in an incomplete 'process of dissolution' without reference to self-determination,[154] and that was endorsed by UNSC Resolution 757 on 30 May 1992.[155]

Based on the EC Guidelines, the Arbitration Commission recognised Slovenia on 15 January 1992,[156] and Croatia on the same day, with double constitutional amendments for the protection of minorities[157] despite not having control over a considerable portion of its territory.[158] Macedonia was recognised on 16 December 1993 ('unduly' due to the similarity of its name to a province in Greece),[159] followed by Bosnia-Herzegovina on 6 April 1992.[160]

The FRY of Serbia and Montenegro promulgated its new constitution as a continuation of the Socialist Federal Republic on 27 April 1992. Slovenia, Croatia, and Bosnia-Herzegovina were admitted to the UN on 22 May 1992 and Macedonia on 8 April 1993 after Serbia-Montenegro renounced any territorial claim to the territory of the other four republics. Serbia and Montenegro were not admitted to the UN until 2000,[161] as the UN concluded that the SFRY 'has ceased to exist' (UNSC Res 757(1992), 30 May 1992 and UNSC Res 777, 19 September 1992). Moreover, the FRY 'has not been generally accepted.' The Arbitration Commission had reaffirmed the 'dissolution' of Yugoslavia in its Opinion No 8 of 4 July 1992, and it considered the process 'complete.'[162] The process of the breaking up of the Yugoslav Federation as a 'matter of fact' was inevitable. As most of its constituent republics were in the process of dissolving, there was no 'effective power' over 'communities that possess a degree of autonomy.'[163] Also, sizable ethnic conflicts and consequent atrocities had paralysed the pre-existing single state.[164]

154 ACFY, Opinion No 2.
155 UNSC Res 757 (30 May 1992); UNSC Res 777 (19 September 1992) and UNSC Res 1022 (22 November 1995).
156 See ACFY, Opinion No 7.
157 4 December 1991 and 8 May 1992. Protecting Minority Regime beyond Current International Law. Crawford (n 5) 397–398.
158 ACFY, Opinion No 5. A point of strongly criticised.
159 Crawford (n 5) 400. ibid Opinion No 6.
160 ACFY, Opinion No 4.
161 UNSC Res 1326 (31 October 2000); UNGA Res 55/12 (1 November 2000).
162 ACFY, Opinion No 8.
163 ibid Opinion No 1.
164 Crawford (n 5) 400.

In the post-colonial context, modern legal attributes for statehood constitute grounds for recognition of an entity as a state. Creation of a state in breach of an underlying norm of international law precludes an effective entity from being a state under international law. In this context, the criteria for statehood are not the same as the conditions for recognising a factual situation. Statehood was coupled with international recognition. The EC Guidelines comprise a modern checklist of statehood for such situations. In addition to traditional criteria, the declaration adds more general criteria based on democratic principles, the acceptance of appropriate, international obligations, and good-faith negotiations committed to a peaceful process:

- respect for the provisions of the Charter of the UN and the commitments subscribed to in the Final Act of Helsinki and in the Charter of Paris, especially with regard to the rule of law, democracy[,] and human rights;
- guarantees for the rights of ethnic and national groups and minorities in accordance with the commitments subscribed to in the framework of the CSCE;
- respect for the inviolability of all frontiers which can only be changed by peaceful means and by common agreement;
- acceptance of all relevant commitments with regard to disarmament and nuclear non-proliferation as well as to security and regional stability; and
- [a] commitment to settle by agreement, including where appropriate by recourse to arbitration, all questions concerning State succession and regional disputes.[165]

Although these requirements were meant 'to clarify the sort of policies the new States were expected to follow after recognition,'[166] they conditioned the attribution of statehood on fulfilment of the abovementioned requirements. In fact, these are regarded as 'political conditions for recognition' but not statehood attributes.[167] What if republics failed to comply with one of these conditions? They would not be recognised by the member states of the EC. Such entities would, therefore, not come into existence as states. If they adhered to these requirements, however, they would qualify for recognition as legal personalities. Despite this, the republics were recognised as sovereign states. These criteria may not necessarily apply to other potential cases of dissolution because the international community's response in each instance may vary from its reactions in prior instances.

It seems that there was little or no objection to the legal solution of creating new states,[168] but this has become complicated after the decolonisation period. Do the Kurds have any place or opportunity to press their case for statehood? An investigation of their status reveals to what extent they comply with the legal characteristics of statehood.

165 Guidelines on New States (n 142).
166 Raič (n 2) 166.
167 Talmon, quoted in Nicholson (n 5) 131.
168 Crawford (n 5) 12.

8.6 Kurdistan's Statehood

With the law of self-determination closing off or narrowing down since 1945, its application to the Kurds has been complex. Nonetheless, on occasion, radical alterations in the territorial arrangements of their host states have occurred in the wake of political unrest. The US-led invasion of Iraq in 2003 and the 2011 uprising in Syria have led to some forms of effective Kurdish control over Kurdistani regions, namely, a federal KRG and a self-governed democratic confederation known as Rojava. In the process of creating these entities, segments of Kurdistan have fallen out of the control of existing states. The Kurds have an opportunity, however uncertain, to take advantage of the forms of self-determination that may emerge in the future for establishing Greater Kurdistan. In any case, their statehood will be contingent on the fulfilment of the Montevideo criteria plus the 'contemporary' requirements and may be coupled with international recognition. Their prospects for statehood need to be considered. This section reflects developments as of October 2023.

8.6.1 The Kurdistan Regional Government of Southern Kurdistan

Upon the expulsion of Saddam Hussein's regime from the South of Kurdistan in 1990, the Kurds gained some respite from the Iraqi state's oppressive rule. Nevertheless, the Republican Guards, backed by airpower, hit back with mass killings of civilians. The UNSC reacted with Resolution 688 on 5 April 1991.[169] The West evinced the gravity of its response by creating two separate no-fly zones (the thirty-sixth parallel) over the South of Kurdistan (protecting Kurds)[170] and the south (protecting Shi'as) of Iraq in April.[171] Subsequently, Saddam withdrew from Başûr in October 1991, and the KAA was established.[172] After the collapse of the Ba'athist regime in 2003, a Transitional Administrative Law was proclaimed on 8 March 2004 to establish federalism in Iraq.[173] It was approved by the UNSC in June 2004.[174] Iraq's permanent constitution was approved by the people of Iraq on 15 October 2005; it recognised the KRG as a *de jure* federal entity, 'the regional government' within the federal Iraqi state (Iraqi constitution, Article 116).

Within the context of the Iraqi federal constitution, the KRG has its own constitution, much like any state within a federal state, under which it controls its territory and maintains its governance.[175] The KRG approved the Kurdistan draft

169 UNSC Res 688 (5 April 1991).

170 Global Security, 'Operation Northern Watch' which then was renamed 'Operation Provide Comfort' (OPC).

171 ibid 'Operation Southern Watch.'

172 Or the Kurdish Autonomous Region (KAR). Maria Th. O'Shea, *Trapped between the Map and Reality: Geography and Perceptions of Kurdistan* (Routledge 2004) 1.

173 US General Accounting Office, 'Iraq's Transitional Law' (USGAO, 25 May 2004).

174 UNSC Res 1546 (8 June 2004).

175 See the Kurdish Regional Constitution in Michael J. Kelly, 'The Kurdish Regional Constitution within the Framework of the Iraqi Federal Constitution: A Struggle for Sovereignty, Oil, Ethnic

constitution (the Provisional Constitution of the Federal Republic of Kurdistan) on 24 June 2009, which was approved by parliament two days later. But the referendum promised by the constitution for its approval has not been held. The KRG may be able to move down the path to complete autonomy as it continues to meet the previously mentioned criteria of statehood. Through utilising its power beyond the central government, the KRG implicitly demonstrates its independence from the centre, though it has never explicitly expressed or confirmed it.

The KRG meets the first criterion of statehood with a permanent population of 6,033,814 in 2019, according to the Kurdistan Regional Statistics Office (KRSO).[176] Before the 2017 referendum, its population had grown to more than 8 million after the recapture of disputed Kurdish cities from the ISIS forces. Thus, according to demographic data, the population of the South of Kurdistan surpasses the population of the smallest recognised states.[177] The KRG, as a territorial entity,[178] currently exercises its authority over an area of 46,861.41 square km, including the four governorates of Hewlêr, Duhok, Silêmanî, and Halabja.[179]

The Kurdistan *Peshmergas* fought against the ISIS 'caliphate' and captured the greater part of the Kurdish-disputed areas. *Peshmergas* controlled these territories as of 2014 when the Iraqi army fled in the face of the insurgent ISIS peril. On 15 October 2017, subsequent to the September referendum, the central government won back the disputed Kurdish areas, oil fields, and other facilities and infrastructure with the help of Iranian forces and the Shi'a militia of the Popular Mobilization Forces (*al-Hashd al-Shaabi*).[180] Hewlêr lost control of a significant chunk of 40% of the entire territory it held *de facto* from 2014. The KRG still, nevertheless, meets the defined territorial qualification. Even though its boundaries are not fully demarcated, it clearly governs a substantially consistent Kurdish area.

The South of Kurdistan is run by a parliamentary and democratic system (Constitution of the KRG Article 1), which exercises KRG authority throughout the region with respect to the people and the land that sustains them. After 20 October 1991 and despite a full-fledged blockade by Saddam, the first multiparty elections (National Assembly and the presidency) were held peacefully on 19 May 1992 in Başûr. The KRG was formed, and a parliament was established with all parties represented. Since then, four general elections have been held (1992, 2005, 2009, and 2013), with the last parliamentary elections in September 2018.[181] Since 1991, the Kurdish authorities of the KRG have exercised governmental functions, and Baghdad exercises no control over the Kurdish regions. The Kurdistan government controls and protects the borders of the Kurdistan region by deploying

---

Identity, and the Prospects for a Reverse Supremacy Clause' (2010) 114(3) PSLR 707.

176 KRSO, Population.

177 UNFPA, World Population Dashboard.

178 Constitution of Iraq, Arts. 4(Third), 117(First).

179 KRSO, Kurdistan Region.

180 See Patrick Cockburn, 'As the Wars End' (2017) 39(24) LRB.

181 The Kurdistan Parliament.

the *Peshmerga* forces (Constitution of the KRG Article 13).[182] Baghdad sought to retake control of the external borders of Iraq after the September independence referendum. However, it did reach an agreement with the KRG's Kurdish officials in Hewlêr.

In September 2006, the South of Kurdistan set up a Department of Foreign Relations (DFR), headed by a minister, to advance the interests of the Kurds and the Kurdistan Region in the international community.[183] The KRG exercises effective authority in the conduct of foreign affairs and international relations with other states (entering into contracts for oil and gas exploration and exploitation) and intrastate relations (legislative, executive, or judicial). The KRG, independently of the federal government, regulates the oil and water assets of the area (Constitution of the KRG Articles 113 and 17) and sets tax levels (Constitution of the KRG Article 93). In February 2022, the Iraqi federal court deemed the 2007 Kurdish oil and gas law unconstitutional, ruled on the handing over of all crude from the KRG and neighbouring areas to the federal government, and declared KRG oil contracts with oil companies, foreign parties, and states invalid. The judicial council of Southern of Kurdistan defied the ruling as per Article 112 of the Iraqi constitution. The KRG exports oil through Turkey which flares tensions between the KRG and the Iraqi government. Iraq won a legal case against Turkey over Kurdish oil exports at the Paris-based International Chamber of Commerce's International Court of Arbitration in March 2023. The following month, the KRG and Baghdad reached an agreement on resuming crude oil exports from KRG to Turkey. Under the agreement, Kurdistan's oil exports will be supervised jointly by Erbil and Baghdad, while the management of oil sales will be handled by the Iraqi state-owned SOMO. The revenues generated from these exports will be deposited in an account at the Iraqi Central Bank, with control over the funds entrusted to the KRG. In the June 2023 federal budget bill passed by the Iraqi parliament allocated for the years 2023, 2024, and 2025, Kurdish provinces can directly request their share if they feel they are being unjustly treated by Hewlêr. In that case, the Iraqi prime minister would take necessary actions, which may include directly funding the provinces. The parliament also passed an article in the bill to export the KRG's oil in coordination with the Iraqi government and to hand over its non-oil revenues to Baghdad. In other words, the Iraqi state will have the authority to monitor and audit the KRG's income from its oil and gas resources. These indications might be the initial steps toward undermining the autonomy of the KRG.

Sovereign states have recognised the KRG, which is now host to more than 40 diplomatic missions and representations. In other words, the KRG is regarded in international law as having an international personality *sui generis*. It has diplomatic representation in 14 countries, including the EU, Germany, the United Kingdom, and the United States. The DFR pursues Kurdistan's foreign policy without reference to the federal government. However, this does not mean that the KRG is in

182 KRG, Ministry of Peshmerga.
183 KRG, Department of Foreign Relations, Foreign Representations in the Kurdistan Region.

full control of Southern Kurdistan's external affairs. Hewlêr is the primary destination of visits by members of the US Congress and other countries' presidents, as well as foreign and defence ministers. The South of Kurdistan is far more than a region of Iraq. The KRG's *Peshmerga*, trained, equipped, and partially funded by the United States and Europeans, is a partner of the Global Coalition against Daesh (or ISIS)[184] as well as the combined Joint Task Force-Operation Inherent Resolve (CJTF-OIR),[185] and has played a decisive role in defeating this extremist Sunni force in Iraq. Exercising power concerning foreign policy and affairs is a sovereign act of states not of just an entity of a state.

The KRG has a demonstrated capacity for statehood as it follows the classic criteria of state designation. However, satisfying legal requirements is necessary but insufficient. The KRG enjoys substantial *de facto* independence under the current arrangements, yet it is not fully independent in relation to Iraq as confirmed by the aftermath of the 2017 referendum and the consequent loss of control over parts of its previously controlled territory confirms that fact. Thus, the KRG remains legally part of Iraq and the foundation on which the Kurdish government administers the territory is the Iraqi constitution. The government in Hewlêr has not become independent from Iraq, especially regarding budgetary issues, although it raises taxes and exacts customs and duties. The ISIS onslaught and the budget cut by Baghdad in 2014 led to sporadic, desperate financial and social crises for the KRG which have continued up to this date; the transfer of budget share (12.6% as agreed with Baghdad) is blocked, and wages are suspended time and again due to halted payment to the Kurdistan region by Baghdad. The regional parliamentary and presidential elections, which were supposed to be held simultaneously on 1 November 2017, were postponed to September 2018. The 2022 elections are yet to be held, and this time they are being organised by the Iraq's Independent High Electoral Commission with a scheduled date in February 2024.

Regarding the willingness and ability to observe international law as a requirement of statehood, the Kurdish autonomous self-rule in the South has, in practice, demonstrated its scrupulous compliance. The KRG 'guarantees…all the civil and political rights' mentioned in its Constitution 'as well as in…international treaties and conventions' (Constitution of the KRG, Preamble), and considers '[c]onventions, agreements and international declarations regarding human rights… complementary provisions' of its Constitution (Constitution of the KRG, Article 69). It also recognises 'freedoms and rights decided in the international treaties, conventions and agreements' for foreigners (Constitution of the KRG, Article 70).

The KRG is in a *de facto* status as the territory of a state, the government of which does not exercise state administrative control over it. It can be treated as a state, though with a limited personality short of statehood, because it exists on a separate territory and has a certain degree of real authority over that territory, but it has not yet reached the legal status of statehood or a sovereign or fully independent

184 The Global Coalition against Daesh, available at https://theglobalcoalition.org/en/.
185 CJTF-OIR, available at https://www.inherentresolve.mil/.

state. The presence of Turkish military forces deep within its territory, ostensibly aimed at countering Kurdish guerrillas, poses a significant challenge to the KRG's effective control and independence. In any case, the KRG must acquire a qualified right of secession if its withdrawal is to attain legitimacy and be deemed successful. It is noteworthy that no declaration of independence has been adopted so far.

8.6.2 The Democratic Confederal Self-Rule of Rojava (Western Kurdistan)

Recent developments triggered by the 2011 Syrian uprising, including the rise of ISIS, its onslaught against Kurdish cities, and the resistance of the *Yekîneyên Parastina Jin* (YPJ, Women's Protection Units) and the *Yekîneyên Parastina Gel* (YPG, People's Protection Units) have resulted in the West of Kurdistan's Kurds asserting *de facto* confederalism within the Syrian state to retain independent control over their internal and external affairs. This *de facto* united state is situated along the border adjacent to the KRG.

In the aftermath of the Syrian insurgency that began in March 2011 and upon the precipitous retreat of Syrian security forces in the summer of 2012 (19 July), the Kurds living in Rojava or now the Autonomous Administration of North and East Syria (AANES) replaced Syrian flags with their own. In July 2012, they assumed control of state institutions through the implementation of an agreement with Damascus.[186] The Democratic Union Party (*Partiya Yekîtiya Dêmokrat*, PYD) and the Kurdish National Council (KNC or *Encûmena Niştimanî ya Kûrdî li Sûriyê*, ENKS) of 16 Kurdish parties established the Supreme Kurdish Council followed by their adoption of 'The Social Contract of Rojava Cantons in Syria.' This was established as the constitution of a self-proclaimed union of Kurdish autonomous cantons. They thereby initiated a process of developing a decentralised federal Syrian state, culminating in a unilateral declaration of democratic federalism on 17 March 2016. In a similar vein, the name of the region was changed from Rojava to *Northern Syria* on 28 December 2016, thus confirming the existence of the region as a member state of Syria with an equal multiethnic polity, built on democracy, women's empowerment, and adherence to ecological standards. The region is now administered by the AANES, which was established in 2018 — though the name Rojava is still often used.[187]

The Social Contract of the Democratic Federation of Northern Syria (hereinafter the Contract)[188] governs the seven autonomous regions of Jazeera (encompassing Qamişlo and Hesekê cantons), Euphrates (which contains Kobanê and Girê Spî cantons), Efrîn, Manbîj, Tabqa, Raqqa, and Deir ez-Zor, with Qamişlo as the capital of Rojava.[189] The Contract proposes united Syrian democratic federalism as

186 Adam Baczko, Gilles Dorronsoro and Arthur Quesnay, *Civil War in Syria: Mobilization and Competing Social Orders* (CUP 2018) 38–39, 169–170.

187 Loqman Radpey, 'Self-Determination and Use of Force in Rojava' (2021) 6(1) JHRSW.

188 Social Contract of the Democratic Federation of Northern Syria, RIC, available at https://rojavainformationcenter.com/background/political-system-documents/.

189 RIC, Report: The Political System of North and East Syria.

a model for a future Syria (Preamble of the Contract). The Syrian government has not officially recognised Rojava's self-rule.

Rojava started its confederalist status in 2012 with three Kurdish cantons and the subsequent addition of Girê Spî. It exercises its authority over an estimated 4 to 5 million Kurds (10%–15% of the Syrian population) in Kurdish-majority cantons of Efrîn, Kobanê, and Cizîr and largely Arab sub-regions, the territory of which has recently expanded to over a territory of more than 50,000 square km — a third of Syria's territory.[190] The current territory controlled by AANES meets the criterion of a defined territory being a state. It is noteworthy that Turkey occupied the Kurdish canton of Efrîn (the northwestern border) in January 2018, followed by the cities of Serê Kaniyê, Tel Helef, and Girê Spî in October 2019. The Syrian Democratic Forces (SDF), a multiethnic and multireligious force led by the YPG, had to withdraw from these regions. Therefore, Rojava lost its control of an uninterrupted stretch of 400 km (250 miles) which had been controlled effectively by the Kurds along the Syrian-Turkish border. Should the sufficient consistency of territory be considered, Rojava may not be able to meet the criteria of a defined territory for the purpose of statehood as the Kurdish-majority cantons are non-contiguous. However, that is not a legal hurdle for its statehood, as in the case of Pakistan before the secession of Bangladesh in 1971. The case of Kaliningrad and its hinterland as a territory of the Russian state and Alaska, as a non-contiguous territory of the United States of America are other examples.

Rêveberiya Xweser (the Autonomous Administration), with executive, general, and justice councils and adopting the co-presidency system in all political, social, administrative, and other fields (Article 12 of the Contract), functions effectively as a government in the regions under an autonomous legal framework. Damascus has exercised no power over these regions since 2012. The Kurdish authorities have effectively exercised the governmental power covering internal affairs over the extent of Rojava's territory which they control. In controlling and defending cantons in Rojava and their frontiers, the YPG and YPJ armed forces have played an important role, especially in recapturing Kobanê from ISIS.

September 2014 marked the onset of establishing ties with the international community when ISIS attacked the city of Kobanê. After months of fighting, the YPG and YPJ repelled the invasion with the support of the anti-Daesh global coalition and CJTF-OIR. Since then, Kurdish forces, under the command of the YPG, have been allied with the coalition, indicating the ability of Rojava to conduct international relations.

Rojava is in full control of its external affairs. It is represented by its diplomatic missions in Moscow, Berlin, Stockholm, Prague, Paris, and recently Geneva, thus, making direct connections with foreign states.[191] Foreign representatives visit

190 Sinan Hatahet, *The Political Economy of the Autonomous Administration of North and East Syria* (EUI 2019) 2.

191 Loqman Radpey, 'Kurdish Regional Self-rule Administration in Syria: A New Model of Statehood and its Status in International Law Compared to the Kurdistan Regional Government (KRG) in Iraq' (2016) 17(3) JJPS 468.

Rojava, including members of the US Congress and officials of EU states, notably Sweden and France, as well as UK and Catalonia parliamentarians and delegations. The Department of Foreign Relations for Rojava mandates the external relations of Rojava.[192] As a non-state unit, Rojava has some limited capacity to conduct relations with states. However, such a capacity cannot imply statehood for Rojava. It is worth mentioning that the parliaments of the KRG and Catalonia have recognised Rojava on 15 October 2013 and 21 October 2021, respectively.

The introduction of democratic federalism effectively removed the official presence of the Syrian state.[193] Since then, Syria has not exercised any meaningful public authority there, creating new facts on the ground. Before the emergence of ISIS and in its aftermath, there was no Syrian administrative presence in Rojava, but that was already the case before the international involvement in 2014.[194] The Autonomous Administration in Qamişlo has been capable of exercising the functions of a state and is factually independent in relation to Damascus. However, owing to the continued international involvement in Syria, Rojava may remain a protectorate or a protected autonomous territory, although it has not been administered or subject to administrative control by international actors. The Kurds may not be able to assert the continuance of the full enjoyment of sovereignty absent an international presence. Their *de facto* sovereignty is somewhat conditional or temporary in the sense that the continuance of the title depends on the international presence. This presence is not for the provision of assistance to legislative, executive, and judicial institutions. However, the presence of international actors is of a military and defensive significance as was evident in the face of the major Turkish invasions in 2018, 2019, and 2022 using extremist mercenaries.[195] It should be noted that the international coalition has provided no air defence support for the self-ruled area and this has left Rojava susceptible to Turkey's aerial incursions and on-the-ground use of mercenaries and extremist groups under Turkish control. Also, facing the Syrian use of force, it would most likely witness the possible re-establishment of Syrian sovereignty. The prior problem, thus, remains survival, as its existence is precarious. That said, it could be argued that the effective territorial control of Rojava might be displaced or restored by the Syrian government or be removed by the Turkish state if the title 'Rojava' is discontinued.

Over a decade since its establishment, it could also be argued that Rojava self-rule possesses a sufficient degree of formal, provisional independence, but its long-term political and legal viability remains questionable. The current situation on the ground cannot be expected to be stable in the face of Turkish air aggression and possible Syrian use of force, and the probable vacuum left by any future US withdrawal. To sustain its government and its status, Rojava must be able to defend

192 AANES, available at http://smne-syria.com/gc/.
193 Radpey, 'New Model of Statehood' (n 191).
194 ibid.
195 Radpey, 'Use of Force' (n 187).

its borders militarily and protect its population. This might not be viable without establishing an authorised international protected zone.[196] The international community of states has already set a precedent for this with the success of the KFOR. Under whatever legal framework, Rojava's independence should be maintained with no massive assistance. Unlike Kosovo, Rojava does not need the establishment of functioning institutions, but other states are able to provide its access to international organisations and engagement in international relations that pave the way to its formal recognition. In any case, Rojava's independence from Syria has not been consolidated, and its exercise of state functions over the territory and population is not irreversible. Also, the payment of salaries to public employees and many state bodies still rests on the shoulders of the Syrian state although Rojava' self-rule powers include raising taxes, customs, and duties and the exporting of oil. The Syrian army is nominally present in the central part of Hesekê and controls the Qamişlo airport, encircled by Kurdish forces.

Despite satisfying statehood requirements, the Kurdish Autonomous Administration of Rojava does not espouse the creation of a classic form of the nation-state. In its own words, the classic form of nation-state 'has made Kurdistan, Mesopotamia, and Syria a hub for the disarray happening in the Middle East and has brought problems, serious crises, and agonies' (Preamble of the Contract). Its intention, seemingly, is not to achieve the goal of independent statehood but self-determination, and its implementation has not been off its agenda. Will the Kurds in the West of Kurdistan be able to disassociate themselves from their previous goal which was the independence of all segments of Kurdistan? As is said in Kurdish, plants regrow on their roots (i.e., everything returns to its roots). Statehood is an assertion of right and must be claimed if it is to be acquired. In the absence of such a claim, its status will remain as part of the Syrian state. Otherwise, Rojava cannot meet the criterion of independence and may imply that it refuses to bear the duties of statehood and to be bound by international law. In any event, it requires the support of major sovereign states so that it can sustain its position and continue the formation process of statehood.

As of October 2023, American companies, through a deal with the Rojava self-rule, are in implementation to 'modernize the oil fields in northeastern Syria.'[197] This deal is buttressed by the US administration, which may support effective Rojava control over not only the Kurdish region but also other Syrian territory. The deal creating relations and international subjectivity was entered into with a non-state entity — a state-like non-state that gains rights and duties. Rojava self-rule refers to its treaty-making power in its charter (Articles 59 and 73). Statehood is a pre-condition for a treaty-making authority.

The Rojava self-rule in the West of Kurdistan constitutionally 'guarantees the equality of all peoples in rights and duties, respects the charters of human rights,

196 See Loqman Radpey, 'Assessing International Law on Self-Determination and Extraterritorial Use of Force in Rojava' (*Lawfare Blog*, 13 November 2020).

197 'Syria Says U.S. Oil Firm Signed Deal with Kurdish-Led Rebels' (*Reuters*, 2 August 2020).

and preserves national and international peace' (Preamble of the Contract). It abides by the UDHR and all related charters (Article 17 of the Contract). Although cantons have the right to build and develop their justice system, this must not infringe the Contract and the treaties and charters of the law of international human rights (Article 54(4) of the Contract).

No forms of Kurdish control have been acquired, asserted, or recognised in the Bakûr and Rojhilat, as they are, in effect, non-self-governing territories. However, the Kurdish people there claim self-determination status. As explicated, statehood might be the goal of a self-determination process, whereas the criteria of the former cannot be used to rule out the latter. Should the Kurdish populations there be allowed to implement their right to external self-determination, they might be able to sever their host states' sway over the Kurdish territory and thereby claim statehood by qualifying its criteria. These two Kurdistani segments meet the statehood requirements of permanent population and a defined territory, but there is no Kurdish government ruling over them, and they exercise almost no independence. The Kurds in these segments might contemplate a remedy through secession and the attainment thereby of independent full statehood. But at present, realistic prospects are lacking for a federal sovereign Kurdistan comprising all four units.

8.7 Summary

International law can induce or dissuade the advent of state formation. It, however, does not have the power to create or destroy the existence of the factual status of an entity. Despite this, international legal rules recognise or give effect to the formation of states as a legal fact. Under traditional international law, a state is created once a territorial entity effectively satisfies or integrates the classic checklist of Montevideo Convention. Once these criteria are met, the factual situation of the entity materialises and is validated as a state under the jurisdiction of international law. The legality of its origin is not relevant. Effectiveness is the major factor in the determination of whether the entity can be labelled as a state. The right of external self-determination, for example, in the cases of decolonisation or a justified right to unilateral secession, is a compensatory factor for the absence of effective government or departure from the Montevideo benchmarks. In these situations, the right of external self-determination acts contrary to the strict application of the criterion of effectiveness with respect to 'government.' It also contributes to an exclusive right to exert authority over the respective territory and the people.

Under the modern law of statehood (with new attributes of permanence of ability to comply with international law, recognition, and legal order), the attributes of the international legal personality of an entity are in question. These requirements are elicited from recent developments with respect to the creation of the states. Under these criteria, statehood is verified if a territorial entity is not created in violation of certain international legal norms (e.g., *jus cogens*). Otherwise, its factual situation leads to non-existence or non-recognition. Based on these criteria, the formation of a state is not merely the satisfaction of some factual requirements. In other words, the elements of the 1933 Montevideo Convention and the criterion of recognition do not suffice to clarify the question concerning the legal entitlement of a people to split from a mother state and to create a new sovereign state. Any infringement is an obstacle to the validation of statehood. To put it another way, the role or the principle of legality in the creation of the state is significant. Under modern international law, an entity comes into existence once it meets both the traditional (effectiveness) and the modern attributes (legality) of statehood. In some situations, both effectiveness and recognition are necessary, while, in others, either effectiveness or recognition is sufficient. Indeed, the international law of statehood has been inconsistently, selectively, and contradictorily applied by states and international organisations, as there are entities that would check all boxes of peoplehood, and thereby statehood, but after independence, they might not be able to meet the statehood criteria. The principle that no law arises from unlawfulness is able to explain these cases. There can be entities that fulfil all of the statehood criteria but still do not attain statehood. This can be due to the derogation from territorial integrity of the larger state that the entity secedes. Conversely, there are states that would not pass eligibility for self-determination requirements. Exceptions to the methods for attaining statehood are due to inconsistency in the implementation of the right of self-determination. However, entitlement to a right of external self-determination may help entities acquire statehood. Therefore, state creation is a process which is governed by the law of statehood. This process is taken into account in scaling its advent after its formation.

Recent territorial arrangements in the Southern and Western segments of Kurdistan have established some effective conditions for achieving Kurdish statehood despite its segmented condition — short of statehood. The analysis of the legal status of these units shows that they do not yet entirely fulfil the legal attributes for statehood. This is the result of constrictions in the law of self-determination. The KRG has been working for a long time to establish a Kurdish state. It qualifies in all the classic attributes of statehood. Established in January 2014, the Rojava confederalism, thus far, has been able to comply with the statehood criteria, although it has lost its control over part of its territory following the Turkish invasions. However, these setbacks have not undermined its ability to exercise its power in its internal and external affairs. Its government has a long path ahead of it to arouse interest from the international community.

Self-rule in both the KRG and Rojava has enabled these entities to continue their political existence (permanence criterion). Nonetheless, they have not achieved statehood as they need their host states to give up sovereignty over parts of their territory in order to achieve lawful and definite state creation. These forms of self-determination may create some room for the Kurds, as they can be seen as territorial units under structured constitutional governments possessing a degree of formal and factual independence respectively from Iraq and Syria. Of the two regions, the KRG stands in a better position to assert a plausible claim to fulfil classic statehood criteria. If the effectivity criteria fail, the recognition norm may be able to operate, although prematurely. That would lead to a 'state-in-context' relative to recognising states recognised or treated as a state by some but not all states or for specific purposes but not all purposes of statehood.[198] This is speculative. An effective government which functions independently will have a better standing to be recognised by a considerable number of states, although statehood, while of great importance, cannot depend solely on recognition.

The East and North of Kurdistan have yet to obtain a form of control, rendering them effectively non-self-governing. If the Kurds could move to control more Kurdish areas to wield legitimate authority through earned domestic sovereignty, they would stand a much better chance of successful state creation or external legal sovereignty. They need to retain their hold over Kurdish territory as well. Their main problem concerning the legal criteria for statehood is that they are not fully independent from external control because their formal independence is contested as a result of competing claims of sovereignty from the host states, although they exercise state functions to the exclusion of those states. Iraq and Syria's sovereignty claims do not bar the Kurdish territories from acquiring statehood but threaten Rojava and the KRG's formal independence and their future prospects for statehood. They have to demonstrate substantial and durable independence from their parent states, which would consolidate their effectiveness and their reality as a state. Phased, earned sovereignty that could be achieved through exerting pressure on the host states with the help of the international community or through establishing international territorial administration, will trump the territorial integrity of the host states and act as a precursor to independence. Economic and security concerns and monetary hurdles could be their crucial challenges after the assertion of independence. The KRG and Rojava have managed to keep stability and security and thriving economies in the territories under their control compared to the whole area in the Middle East. This achievement has come at an immense cost, as the Kurds have endured a relentless battle against terrorism and extremism, including ISIS and other jihadist groups. Also, in terms of governability, the Kurdistani regions are functioning much better than their neighbours.

198 Nicholson (n 5) 140.

9 Conclusion

Decolonising Kurdish Self-Determination

A century has elapsed since one of history's most hypocritical, enduring, and consequential betrayals of principle. It is an irony of history: although Kurdistan did not come to be after WWI, Kurdish self-determination then stood a better chance of leading to an independent state than after self-determination became part of international law. By any political theory of self-determination, it at once seems obvious that the Kurdish people should be living in a single sovereign state of their own. Why this result remains unachieved reveals as much about the biases of international law as it does about the merits of the case for Kurdistan.

When contemplating self-determination, one tends to think of either Europe after WWI or Africa and Asia. The contrasts are glaring. In Europe after WWI, a process of plebiscites, minority treaties, and population transfers ensued with traumatic and disruptive effects for some of the people involved. Borders were redrawn according to a set of criteria. In Africa and Asia, the very different Mandate System operated. The right was just never really designed with the Middle East in mind. It was designed, instead, with Africa and Asia in mind. The Middle East does not neatly fit either model because a mix of both the Mandate System and the processes used in Europe was applied. It all came together, inconsistently, in the crucible of the Versailles peace conference. But in the Middle East, there was no tradition of ethnically homogenous nation-states. That was a European idea and criterion for self-determination — although it did not really hold for much of Europe either — whereas multinational states and empires typified the Middle Eastern tradition. The Kurds are poised between the idea of the nation-state and the reality of multinational states. In that regional context, autonomy was not only the better route but the only viable option. For the Kurds, however, this choice did not accommodate aspirations for an independent state of Kurdistan. This is due to 'the qualitatively different manner' by which the system of international law is applied in the Middle East.[1] The situation existing now in the Middle East is a result of the externally imposed Mandate System and of artificially created states with frontiers overdrawn according to the regional tradition of multinational states.

1 See Jean Allain, *International Law in the Middle East: Closer to Power than Justice* (Routledge 2004).

DOI: 10.4324/9781003424314-9

Despite the urge for their own nation-state, the Kurds' status as a nation had no legal consequences during the late imperial episode of dividing up the Middle East. Kurdistan was broken into fragments. This rupture took place without the Kurds' meaningful assent while imposing the hegemony of new nation-states onto them. The relevant credible archival and primary British and Turkish sources, with details covered in Chapter 4, demonstrated how little the Kurdish pleas ultimately meant to the Allies. The British government's failure to implement the Treaty of Sèvres proved decisive for the ultimate partition of Kurdistan with devastating consequences. The principle was sacrificed. The Allies' political and economic interests and the League of Nations accordingly superseded the independence of Kurdistan. The legacy of this policy, prescribed by the British, French, and the Soviet Union, has deprived the Kurds of their own sovereign state up to this date, leaving them at the mercy of the most oppressive, externally created states of the Middle East. Subjected to political vicissitudes, the Kurds were gerrymandered as minority peoples in the Soviet Union, Iran, Iraq, Syria, and Turkey. This is despite the fact that the Kurds were duly acknowledged as a socio-political nation after WWI, when the ideal of self-determination had not yet been codified into a legally defined right. The ideal, nevertheless, failed to become a reality for the Kurdish people. Ultimately, Kurdistan's statehood was sacrificed for the purpose of the reordering of political influence. National sovereignty was deemed suitable for European peoples while some peoples of the Middle East had to settle for alien determination as the Western Allies reconfigured the region. Competing national aspirations, opposing ideologies, and imperialist world policies impeded the self-determination of some nations in the aftermath of WWI. During the interwar period, historical contingencies and a departure from the principle of national self-determination hampered Kurdish statehood despite the existence of Kurdish nationalism before and in the aftermath of WWI.

With a shift from nations to peoples of sovereign states, the concept of self-determination became crystallised as an internal form of self-government rather than internationally recognised statehood. At the same time, the rules giving effect to the principle of self-determination have continued to evolve, particularly after the WWII, albeit not in a manner that is likely to benefit the Kurds as a people. Kurds met the substantive criteria of peoplehood at the end of WWI when they were recognised as a nation eligible for an independent Kurdish state. Nevertheless, their claim to independence does not fit into the current framework of the law of self-determination.

Over the past century, the Kurds have grappled with different policies of assimilation, discrimination, and grave breaches of their human rights. Simply to function in compliance with the law of self-determination, a representative government must uphold the non-discrimination ban. A merely representative government, while necessary, can play only a complementary role and, therefore, does not serve the overall objective. On the local level, effective representation and participation of territorially concentrated national groups should resonate with the territorial arrangements, e.g., autonomy and federalism.

Kurds have been blocked from the meaningful exercise of self-determination internally. Their host states are occupying powers exerting control over security, governance, and resources which has sparked resistance from the Kurds. The states have also put themselves in a position akin to colonial powers. The international community views the issue solely as the states' internal problem, although the states may not rule out references to a right of self-determination for the Kurds. Should their situation be permitted to threaten international peace and security? Human rights violations against the Kurds in Kurdistani territories have, on occasion, escalated to large-scale atrocities and humanitarian catastrophes with the ever-present possibility of recurrence. Despite this, independence through secession for the long-suffering Kurds is not forthcoming or warranted. Their host states have shown that they will not easily relinquish sovereignty over Kurdistani regions. The Kurds' secession should be achieved legally in accordance with the law of the state from which they secede; thus, the procedure of secession should be legitimate. State practice evinces that when the involved state withholds its approval, acquisition of recognition becomes difficult to obtain.

Even if one postulates that the identity of the Kurds in the host states is gravely endangered, their cultural survival is imperilled, their existence is subjected to forms of terror and demonisation, and they have been placed in a subordinate status, the state practice in international law obliges them to find a solution short of forcible secession and independence. They are legally destined to seek political solutions without challenging the territorial integrity of their host states. However, no formal power-sharing institutions or *de jure* mechanisms have been introduced at national levels for the Kurds. Also, measures of inclusive practices are not followed notwithstanding the lack of formal recognition of power-sharing arrangements by their host states. This is not in accord with the United Nations Sustainable Development Goals (SDGs), especially with SDG 16.7, which promotes inclusive institutions. That being said, however, the Kurds have exhausted all efforts toward a peaceful settlement of the dispute as no alternatives for internal self-determination have been proffered by the central governments of Turkey, Syria, and Iran.

They have shown their willingness to meet legitimate claims for internal self-determination within their current boundaries. Indeed, the use of force was not seen by the Kurds as a measure of last resort, but as the only means of safeguarding their rights. The Kurds have not repudiated any proposals, but there has never been a realistic alternative. Developments throughout the twentieth century indicate that any political autonomy as a form of internal self-determination was unacceptable to and encountered opposition from these host states. This stance has not changed in the present century. Since the entrenchment of new borders in the Middle East, the Kurds' host states have unleashed Kurdophobia: antagonism and fascism toward Kurds and Kurdistan. They have employed the terms 'separatist' and 'territorial integrity' as pretexts for eliminating and oppressing the Kurds' quest for their rights. The states have gone so far as to label Kurds as 'terrorists,' despite their loss of over 15,000 lives and more than 25,000 injuries in the ongoing fight against terrorism and extremism. They are still losing lives to recurring Turkish incursions and drone strikes in the West and South of Kurdistan, as well as to ISIS and other terrorist groups in Syria backed and controlled by Turkey. The South is also not immune from the suicide drones and missile attacks by the Iranian regime. The international community must acknowledge and appreciate the contributions and sacrifices made by Kurdistani forces and civilians in this struggle. The presence of oil, water, energy potential, and other natural resources in Kurdistani territorial segments is the practical rationale for opposing any Kurdish autonomy or moves toward secession.[2] Furthermore, the climate of Kurdistan is ideal for farming, and the soils there are fertile.

Although international law recognises self-determination as a legal principle or directive principle of legislation, it is not applicable to any group, entity, or people seeking any variant of it unless its unit determines that it comprises 1) non-self-governing, trust- and mandated territories; 2) states with self-determination units; 3) other territories with distinct political-geographical areas and with inhabitants who are not represented in the government of their mother state, as it is a non-self-governing territory; 4) disputed areas and non-state territories with rights of self-determination desiring freely to choose their own forms of political organisation.

Since identification of sovereign entities — the subjects of the legal principle of sovereignty — has been through 'purely' and 'discretionary' political processes, the virtual purview of self-determination and the identification of the territories capable of wielding it have been nationally or internationally 'as much a matter of politics as law.'[3] In other words, the right has been debated cryptically and, in practice, has only been applied to colonial territories 'either by a form of recognition or by agreement'[4] or at least acquiescence.[5] These include the mandate and trusteeship systems for territories (deemed a sacred trust under Article 22 of the League of Nations Covenant and Chapters IX and XIII of the Charter), for non-self-governing territories (Chapter XI of the Charter), and for particular territorial disputes or situations using plebiscites in settling boundaries.

The present legal regime of self-determination, as a normative right, has defects. First, it ignores the demands of national, cultural, linguistic, and religious minorities under despotic and oppressive states. They are not vested with any type of self-determination, internal or external, and due to the territorial integrity and sovereignty of states, they have no access to reparation. Article 27 of the ICCPR merely protects the members of these groups and their religious, linguistic, and cultural identity, whereas racial groups are only granted equal access to government. Second, it is not universal, i.e., its general principle, free and genuine expression of the will of the peoples, is conferred on the peoples of the State Parties to the two Covenants. Third, it is not perfect. Ethnic groups of colonial territories are not endowed with the external right of self-determination, as

2 For the strategic rationale for territorial power-sharing and secession, see Chapter 9 in Cederman L-E., H. Simon, and J. Wucherpfennig, *Sharing Power, Securing Peace?: Ethnic Inclusion and Civil War* (CUP 2022).

3 James Crawford, *The Creation of States in International Law* (2nd ed, OUP 2006) 115.

4 ibid.

5 ibid 117.

this has to be implemented by the whole people of the colony. In these contexts, withdrawal of the colonial power is not sufficient, and a referendum or plebiscite, e.g., as per Western Sahara, must be held so that people can express their wishes freely. The Human Rights Covenants do not specify the requirements leading to an infringement of self-determination. In other words, the modes of internal self-determination and power-sharing are not specified in the Covenants. Fourth, other principles restrain the implementation of self-determination, including *uti possidetis*. Therefore, the borders must be retained intact and the people living on both sides of the border are not allowed to express their will for choosing their preferred state. Fifth, no reparation is at the disposal of holders of the right in case of violating it, although liberation movements have been given a licence to recourse to force in a case of gross denial of self-determination by the oppressive state.[6] In addition, the people or their representatives cannot submit communications to the UNHRC, but third states can demand the implementation of self-determination as beneficiaries of *erga omnes* obligations, although no precedent has been registered so far. Due to the vulnerability of self-determination to politics, it is perceived as a declaratory right, although its normativity has been endorsed universally by legal instruments. In other words, it is not persuasive when it is needed because it is obscure as to content, meaning, extent, and enforcement; it is obscure in the post-decolonisation era.

The Kurds' host states have pursued divide-and-rule policies, inhibiting Kurdistan's emergence as a contiguous, unitary, self-determining territory and fragmenting the Kurdish people. The withdrawal of self-determination during the 1920s was echoed by the US decision to abandon Rojava in the face of the Turkish incursion on the centenary of the Treaty of Sèvres. Western abandonment of the Kurdish people appears to be a long-ingrained geopolitical habit. This has been the case for many developing nations. To this day, the Kurds remain a peculiar irredentist collectivity spread across the four states and still lack recognised, genuine, legal status within the precise framework of self-determination. Thus, they are still denied a sovereign state of their own. Their aspirations should be recognised normatively in international law and be taken seriously as they advance their reasonable claim to self-determination. Their demand is made by a qualified people and, as such, it should be granted legal force by the international community through positive action to facilitate the right to self-determination.

In practice, the universality of self-determination does not encompass the Kurds. The Kurdish situation exemplifies the weaknesses of the legal principle of self-determination, given the priority on territorial integrity of the four host states. Territorial sovereignty and *uti possidetis juris* or the territorial emphasis on self-determination stand as barriers to implementing the right to sovereign self-determination. The Kurdish attempt to change the contemporary territorial arrangement of the states has entailed certain risks of physical removal, genocide, assault with chemical weapons, and systematic abuse of human rights. Although the exceptional

6 Antonio Cassese, *Self-Determination of Peoples: A Legal Reappraisal* (CUP 1995) 324–328.

circumstances for secession were fulfilled in the 1980s when the Iraqi regime committed genocide against the Kurds of the South of Kurdistan through an *Anfal* campaign, so the opportunity passed, and no outcome was achieved. However, the grounds were not then favourable to the establishment of a new state, as there was no supportive third state. Even if there were any, as in the closely parallel case of Bangladesh, there would be no certainty of a successful state creation, as the dissenting states of Iran, Turkey, and Syria would not tolerate a would-be state of Kurdistan.

The current scope of self-determination fails to capture how the Kurds are treated in reality. That is, the doctrine and its evolution have infringed upon the idea of a people. It is not as if they do not possess the right to self-determination; it is axiomatic that the Kurds have an inalienable right to self-determination and its core elements, the right to a separate identity, and to exist on their territory to determine its fate, but the right of self-determination as currently understood is ill-fitted for a multiterritorial people of four states because the current law is designed for peoples in a single territory. In short, as a whole, they do not satisfy the formal or legal criteria for exerting external self-determination. Dysfunctional at best, the principle of self-determination has a blind spot corresponding to the situation of the Kurds as minorities among four separate states. The way normative self-determination still operates for all peoples is a conundrum and basically is imprecise and problematic at best. Kurds should, ideally, be the paradigmatic example of a distinct people who benefit from self-determination because of their well-defined peoplehood. Nonetheless, neither decolonisation nor internal self-determination has worked for the Kurds — although the latter has not been realised except in the South of Kurdistan to some extent as the outgrowth of the US-led intervention in Iraq. Internal self-determination also limits the Kurds in terms of any political autonomy or even unity as a nation or a people.

The costs of the status quo are massive for the Kurds. How may their grievances be addressed? Although not visible to the global media and international community, their human rights are being visibly threatened. The atrocious treatment of their Kurds by the states of Iran, Syria, and Turkey reduces the salience of their right to territorial integrity. But the emergence of an independent state of Kurdistan remains unlikely, even though the KRG meets all the prerequisites for achieving statehood. It is dependent on international recognition or acceptance, i.e., state power, rather than on meeting the defined attributes of statehood. It can be submitted that the external right of self-determination is obsolescent for Kurds as the currently conceived international law of self-determination continues to be inapplicable under existing conditions. The host states have adopted an intransigent attitude toward hearing Kurdish voices for self-determination, and their policies have stagnated. Kurdistan is an international colony at the mercy of Turkey, Iran, Iraq, and Syria.[7] There is no way to remedy the unfairness, since the host states, for the most part, refuse to acknowledge the Kurds' ethnic singularity. Insomuch

7 See İsmail Beşikçi, *International Colony Kurdistan* (Gomidas Institute 2015).

as the states remain antagonistic to the Kurds' demands and insist on entrenching their sovereignty and territorial borders, the formation of Greater Kurdistan as a recognised sovereign state will continue to be elusive or impossible.

To what extent should a suppressed group be respectful of existing state boundaries? Are they forever destined for subordination and dependence? When does their right to self-determination square with the right of their host states to territorial integrity? Should their situation be considered a serious legal matter to be heeded by the international community of states? Historically, there has been no consistent gauging of the seriousness of oppression for a qualified right to secession that is applicable to every situation. Oppression is something that can be contended because of the specific conditions of groups. Thus, oppression has to be relative to the particular conditions of the minority–state relationship. When it comes to the relations between a state and a seceding people, giving absolute precedence to the territorial integrity of the state is the rejection of the status of self-determination as an underlying right for preserving the individual and collective identity of peoples. It would be unjust to have a law which prohibited secession and left a group vulnerable to regimes prone to abusing their rights. There is no *locus standi* to the Kurds in international law such as before the ICJ. The international community must no longer remain a passive bystander to the Kurds' slaughter but, instead, actively demonstrate pragmatism and grant legal entitlement to the nationalist consciousness of the Kurds, ensuring the protection of their rights as an ethnic victim group suffering from systemic persecution, currently by three states. There should be lawful and legitimate assistance to a people who are struggling for their right to self-determination while the international community continues to look the other way, although, as obligation *erga omnes* and a 'candidate for elusive *jus cogens,*'[8] any state or international body can demand respect for self-determination.

International intervention, in the form of a no-fly zone, a legal regime as the United Nations Mission in East Timor (UNAMET) or the UNMIK deserves recognition and legal justification. Any intervention needs the congruence of competing ideological and geopolitical interests of the states involved in the geopolitics of the Middle East. Yet paradoxically, it should be noted that international law addresses the right of self-determination 'of peoples,' rather than of states, to be able to express their free will in proper conditions. However, self-determination has diligently served the very state system it claims to oppose.[9] Therefore, it is imperative to 'decolonise' self-determination[10] and recognise its inherent structural problems as the historical application, interpretation, or manipulation of the principle has resulted in the perpetuation of colonial legacies, the reinforcement of existing power dynamics, and the production of unequal outcomes.

8 Catriona Drew, 'The East Timor Story: International law on trial' (2001) 12(4) EJIL 651.

9 Gerry Simpson, 'The Diffusion of Sovereignty: Self-Determination in the Post-Colonial Age' (1996) 32 SJIL 255.

10 See Ralph Wilde, 'Using the Master's Tools to Dismantle the Master's House: International Law and Palestinian Liberation?' (2021) 22 PYIL 3.

As long as the international community of states adheres to the sacrosanctity and unassailability of the territorial integrity of non-democratic states, suffocated communities will not be favoured if they assert control over their political and cultural lives, and the principle of self-determination will not serve the ideals for which it was first recognised. There is a people that has historically been recognised but facts on the ground and the division of Kurdistan between four sovereign states make the exertion of self-determination for the Kurds almost impossible. This is a real tension. The denial of the right of the Kurdish people to self-determination has undermined international peace and security in the Middle East, flowing from Kurdistan's partition and leading to a century of human rights violations. Turkey's drones and aircraft have been implicated in the loss of civilian lives and displacement of Kurdish civilians in the West of Kurdistan and in the killing of refugees from the UN registered Mexmûr Camp (Makhmour) in the South of Kurdistan. Over the past decade, Turkey's ongoing invasion has forced hundreds of villages in the South to evacuate, exacerbating the humanitarian crisis. Reports of Turkish forces employing prohibited chemical weapons against Kurdistani forces based in the South have gone unheeded by the international community.[11] The human rights of Kurds in the East of Kurdistan have endured a prolonged history of marginalisation in any interactions between the West and the Iranian regimes. The self-rule in the West of Kurdistan has not yet received official recognition. Western inaction toward the states' systemic persecution against the Kurds provokes numerous questions and criticisms.[12] It is abundantly clear that human rights, even mass atrocities such as those the Kurds have suffered, scarcely enter into the policies of the great powers. The case of Kurdistan demonstrates that we need to re-think the concept of self-determination within international law.

On the centenary of the Treaty of Lausanne and under the current circumstances of a century of partition of Kurdistan, the future political status of Kurds may be within the current boundaries of four states should no more territorial developments occur. Among Kurdistani segments, the North and East of Kurdistan have a better legal standing to potentially invoke a right of remedial secession. That would lead to a situation where only part of the Kurdish people would have achieved self-determination, thereby falling short of what the principle of self-determination promises. Should a Kurdistani segment achieve independence, there will be three Kurdistani *irredentas* ('unredeemed') that might someday, through irredentism, be able to move toward incorporation within the boundaries of their historically or ethnically political unit and create a single sovereign United States of Kurdistan.

11 See Euronews with AP, AFP, 'Doctor Arrested after Calling for Turkish Army Chemical Weapons Probe' (26 October 2022) and Sarah Glynn, 'Kurdish Group Claims Turkey is Using Chemical Weapons. Why is Nobody Investigating?', Open Democracy, 5 November 2021.

12 Noam Chomsky, *The New Military Humanism: Lessons from Kosovo* (Pluto Press 1999).

Appendix

Kurds' Petitions to the League of Nations, the United Nations, Britain, and Their Host States

- Translation of letter signed 'Mahmud' to HE the High Commissioner concerning 'the promises made by Great Britain to the League of Nations regarding the national and legal rights and claims of the Kurds,' 27 January 1927. Anita Burdett, *Records of the Kurds: Territory, Revolt and Nationalism, 1831–1979: British Documentary Sources*, vol 6 (CUP 2015).
- Letter of Appeal from the Deputies of Arbil, Sulaimani, Mosul and Kirkuk to the Prime Minister [of Iraq], 4 April 1929, concerning the League of Nations' recommendations concerning the Kurdish people and putting forward their demands for consideration [AIR 23/414].
- Letter [in form of a petition] from Azmi Beg Baban and others to the Secretary to the League of Nations, Geneva, 26 July 1930, signed by several Kurdish leaders and aghas.
- Wires transmitted from the people of Sulaimania to the Prime Minister, Baghdad, and to the President of the League of Nations, Geneva, and the Colonial Ministry, London, undated, expressing Kurdish dissatisfaction of the exclusion of their rights in the Iraq–British treaty [AIR 23/417].
- Telegrams from people of Sulaimani to the Prime Minister of Iraq, to the President of the League of Nations, Ministry [sic] of Colonies, c. 18 July 1930 [AIR 23/417]. Anita Burdett, *Records of the Kurds: Territory, Revolt and Nationalism, 1831-1979: British Documentary Sources*, vol 7 (CUP 2015) 789.
- Petition, from the Hamawand and Rashawand tribes [listed signatories] to the High Commissioner of Iraq, Baghdad, no date, referring to an earlier petition endorsing the demands of the Sulaimania Kurds [AIR 23/417].
- Letter from the Sulaimani Aghas [of South Kurdistan] and other notables to the High Commissioner for Iraq, 3 August 1930, forwarding copies of previous petitions to the League of Nations for resubmission via HM's Government [CO 730/157/5].
- Kurdish representatives, requesting an independent government either under a British mandate or a form of mandate from the League of Nations [CO 730/157/5].

- Petition from five Kurdish Aghas of Kirkuk to the League of Nations (submitted through the High Commissioner for Iraq), 24 August 1930.
- Petition from various Kurdish tribal chiefs (listed) to the General Secretary of the League of Nations, Geneva, 13 August 1930, demanding an independent administration under the aegis of the British Government [AIR 23/418].
- Kurdish petition signed 'Southern Kurdistan,' to the High Commissioner for Iraq, Baghdad, dated Kirkuk, 25 August 1930, demanding that the recommendations of the League of Nations be enforced [AIR 23/418].
- Petition from the National Central Committee, Sulaimania for the inhabitants of Southern Kurdistan, to the Secretary of Mandates Committee, League of Nations, Geneva, 31 August 1930 [AIR 23/418].
- Petition, received 4 September 1930, for transmission to the Secretary, the Permanent Mandates Commission, Geneva, (via the High Commissioner for Iraq), from Azmi Bey Baban and nine other Kurds [AIR 23/418].
- Petition from several named aghas to the King of Iraq, 28 October 1930 [sent from Special Service Officer, Sulaimani] complaining that Arabs received favourable treatment, specifically requesting that the Arab military evacuate Kurdistan, that civil administration be handed over, and that a Kurdish government under a British mandate be formed as an interim measure [AIR 23/418].
- Letter from Director of the Mandates Section, League of Nations, to Mr Asni Beg Raban, Sulaimani, 7 February 1931, relating the conclusion reached to Kurdish appeals of 26 July and 3 August 1930, essentially rejecting their demand for independence and offering assurance that Britain will oversee legal and administrative measures 'to secure for the Kurds the position to which they are entitled' [CO 730/161/2].
- Petition from representatives of the Kurdish nation in Iraq, Sulamania, to the Chairman, Permanent Mandates Commission, League of Nations, Geneva, 30 October 1930 [CO 730/161/2].
- Statement made to refute the statements by Major Young, the accredited representative of the Mandatory Power in Iraq, at Geneva, made by Taufiq Wahbi in November 1930.
- Letter from Lt-Col Taufiq Wahbi, Ex-Mutasarrif of Sulaimani, and 'Authorised representative of the Kurdish people in Iraq,' Beyrouth, to Secretary of State for Foreign Affairs, London, 19 April 1931, forwarding a series of documents, for transmission to the League of Nations.
- Letter of protest from the Kurds of Erbil Liwa, addressed to the King and the Prime Minister of Iraq, the Colonial Office, the High Commissioner, and others, 11 April 1931, reiterating the causes for their discontent [AIR 23/418].
- Letter of support from D.A. Bedr Khan for the Central Committee of the National Kurdish League (Khoyboun), Damascus, to the Secretary, League of Nations, 17 April 1931, No. 2835 [CO 730/161/2].
- Report (secret), Air Liaison Officer, Sulaimani, to Air Staff Intelligence, Dhibban, 26 March 1937, No. 49, lobbying by Shaikh Jelal, an appeal to the Adviser to the Minister of the Interior for support of Kurdish nationalism [AIR

23/671]; Anita Burdett, *Records of the Kurds: Territory, Revolt and Nationalism, 1831-1979: British Documentary Sources*, vol 8 (CUP 2015).

- Letter, from Délégation Kurde, Paris, to Ernest Bevin, Foreign Secretary and President of the British Delegation to the United Nations, Paris, 29 November 1948, [in French], appealing against general injustices and persecutions experienced by Kurds [FO 371/68438].
- Letter from Shaikh Ahmad al Barzani to the British Consul, Basra, undated [FO 624/160]; Letter, from Emir Dr Kamuran Aaali BedirKhan, Centre d'Etudes Kurdes, Paris, to the British Representative to the European Consultative Assembly at Strasbourg, 18 August 1949, [in French], regarding a memorandum, presented to the United Nations on 29 November 1948, referring to the loss of Kurdish rights both as individuals and as a nation. Anita Burdett, *Records of the Kurds: Territory, Revolt and Nationalism, 1831-1979: British Documentary Sources*, vol 10 (CUP 2015).
- Letter from a delegation headed by Dr Kaimaran Suli, based in Paris, 9 March 1956 [to Foreign Secretary], enclosing a letter, [in French], from the 'Delegation Kurde,' to the United Nations, 3 Mars 1956. A protest over an Iranian massacre of Kurds, refers to previous efforts of this group, continued military action against the Kurds by infantry, augmented with tanks and aircraft, notably the bombardment of villages undertaken in severe cold weather, leaving many homeless [FO 371/120749].
- Letter, [in French], from Emir BedirKhan, Délégation Kurde, Paris, to Son Excellence Lord Home, Ministre des Affaires Etrangères, Foreign Office, Londrès, 16 Juillet 1963, [in French], reminding HM government of their annexation of Southern Kurdistan to Iraq after World War I, then the promise made via the 1922 Treaty with Iraq to allow for Kurdish self-government within the Iraq state, concluding that the British government is directly responsible for the unhappy state of Iraqi Kurdistan today [FO 371/170447]. Anita Burdett, *Records of the Kurds: Territory, Revolt and Nationalism, 1831-1979: British Documentary Sources*, vol 11 (CUP 2015).
- Letter, C.D. Wiggin, British Embassy, Tehran, to J.R. Rich, Eastern Department, Foreign Office, 19 March 1966, No. 1023A/66, enclosing a letter from Mulla Mustafa Al Barzani addressed to the Prime Minister.
- Despatch, J.R. Rich, Foreign Office, to C.D. Wiggin, British Embassy, Tehran, 15 April 1966, No. EQ 1019/22, referring to the letter from Mulla Mustafa Barzani to the Prime Minister and reiterating British policy, especially in terms of supplying arms to Iraq [FO 371/186747].
- Despatch, S.L. Egerton, British Embassy, Baghdad, to D. Montgomery, Eastern Department, Foreign Office, 22 April 1966, No. 10114/44/66, enclosing a list of Kurdish demands addressed to the Iraqi government in early April 1966 by Mustafa al Barzani, which mainly consist of administrative changes to involve or represent Kurds within the government; integration rather than separatist suggestions [FO 371/186747].
- Letter from Mullah Mustafa Barzani to Lord Longford [Leader of the House of Lords and Lord Privy Seal], 22 June 1966, referring to Iraqi government actions

on the Kurds as genocide and appeals for help and support, to which they are entitled as a result of Great Britain's failure to fulfil its mandatory obligations.

- Letter from Mullah Mustafa Barazani, undated, c. early December 1966, to the President of the Iraq Republic, Abdul Rahman Aref, and the Prime Minister, Major General Naji Taleb.
- Foreign Office minute by D. Montgomery, 31 July 1967, 'Visit to London of Kurdish representative — Dr. M. Osman, (17 July),' noting Mulla Mustafa's aspirations to have a British Government representative visit Kurdistan [FCO 17/408].
- Letter from C.C.R. Battiscombe, UK Mission to the United Nations, New York, to G.S. Burton, Middle East Department, Foreign and Commonwealth Office, containing an appeal from Mustafa Barzani to Dr Kurt Waldheim, 28 May 1974, introducing the Kurdish Democratic Party delegation sent abroad to engage the international community; argues that the war being waged by the Iraq government against the Kurds can no longer be considered an 'internal' affair 17 June 1974, and a letter from M.M. Abdul Rahman and M. Dizayee both of the Kurdistan Democratic Party, to various Ambassadors, 7 June 1974, enclosing copy of letter of appeal as sent to the UNO, 6 June 1974 [FCO 8/2307] No. 18/44/8. Anita Burdett, *Records of the Kurds: Territory, Revolt and Nationalism, 1831-1979: British Documentary Sources*, vol 12 (CUP 2015).

Index

Kolibri 360 GmbH
Ferdinand-Jühlke-Straße 7
99095 Erfurt, Deutschland
produktsicherheit@kolibri360.de